THE

INGLENOOK COOK BOOK

New and Revised Edition

CHOICE RECIPES

Contributed by Sisters of the Church
of the Brethren, Subscribers and Friends
of The Inglenook Magazine

ELGIN, ILLINOIS:
BRETHREN PUBLISHING HOUSE
1911

PREFACE

The Inglenook began as a magazine that stood for "material and spiritual progress." Issued weekly by the Brethren Publishing House, Elgin, Illinois, the magazine cost "one dollar per annum, in advance." At one time, however, a single dollar would bring the subscriber not only the magazine but a bonus gift as well, the companion *Inglenook Cook Book*, advertised as worth a whole dollar by itself.

Now several score years later, *The Inglenook Magazine* is all but forgotten, but not its side product. The *Inglenook Cook Book* of 1901 and 1911 sold more than 100,000 copies and is still much in demand. And this even though a sequel, the *Granddaughter's Cook Book*, published by the Brethren in 1941 and imprinted by Harper's, has circulated more than 83,000 copies.

Most popular of the early editions has been the revised and enlarged *Inglenook Cook Book* of 1911, of which this volume is a reprint. It was upon seeing the first printing of that edition that the editors were chagrined to find that after reference was made to burnt sugar cake, no recipe appeared. The omission subsequently was corrected; herein the recipe appears on page 296.

Divulged in the *Inglenook* are the cherished recipes of a segment of rural America, those Church of the Brethren women whose Pennsylvania Dutch tradition placed high value on culinary excellence. What made the book a successful guide to cooking was its appeal to common people, to those whose choice is wholesome, substantial food, simply and tastefully prepared. Commented the editors on the selections published: "As a rule they are dishes one would expect to see on the tables of those who endeavor to practice the principles of the simple life."

Whether "simplicity" still pertains in light of revolutionary change that has come not only to food processing but to life styles is a matter the reader must decide for himself. But at least one assurance holds today as it did in the earliest years of the twentieth century: For those who master the *Inglenook*, some truly delectable eating is in store.

INDEX

Soups hold an important place in our bill of fare and when properly made are appetizing, nutritious, easily digested, and need not be expensive. Soups are served as clear and thickened soup. In the former the stock is served plain with a slight flavoring of some vegetable or combination of vegetables. In the latter the stock is thickened with vegetables, cereals, or some form of paste or dough, such as noodles. The nature of the rest of the meal should determine the kind of soup to be served—clear soup with dishes forming a heavy meal and thickened soup with accompaniments of less substance. The hock or shin of beef, ends of rib roasts and portions of the neck or shoulder are suitable for the making of good stock and are comparatively inexpensive. After the meat and bones are put in a kettle and cold water added, they should be put over a slow fire, so they will not come to a boil for a full hour. Then skim carefully and after boiling a few minutes the fire should be further reduced or the kettle pushed back so that the contents will simply simmer. They should cook here for three or four hours, at least. The seasoning should not be added till after the meat has cooked two hours. When done the stock should be strained to remove small pieces of bone, etc., and if not immediately wanted should be cooled and the cake of fat left on top. It will keep better and longer if left in this way. Of course, where the meat is of more importance than the stock it should be put on in hot water and the cooking hastened at first. Afterward it should also proceed with a slow fire. If soup is oversalted a teaspoonful of vinegar and the same amount of sugar will aid in counteracting the taste. The meat from the soup bones may be used for hashes, croquettes, etc.

Asparagus Soup.—Take a large bunch of asparagus, scrape it nicely, cut off one inch of the tops and lay them in water. Chop the stalks and put them on the fire, with a piece of bacon, a large onion cut up, and pepper and salt. Add two quarts of water and boil till stalks are quite soft, then put through a sieve, strain the water to it and put back into the pot. Put into it a chicken, cut up with the tops of asparagus, boil until done, thicken with flour, add butter and milk and serve.—*Sister Amy V. Furry, Johnsville, Md.*

Beef Soup.—Take 8 tablespoonfuls of flour, enough water to dampen the flour; rivel with the hands and put the rivels into fresh beef broth; add a little salt. Let boil five minutes.—*Sister H. G. Miller, Bridgewater, Va.*

Bean Soup.—Stew 1 pint of beans until tender. Mash through a colander to remove the shells. Add to 1½ quarts of ham broth, and let boil up. Add 1 tablespoonful of flour mixed smooth with 1 cup of cream or rich milk. Add a bit of parsley and season to taste. Serve with inch squares of toasted bread.—*Sister Ira Trostle, Franklin Grove, Ill.*

Buttermilk Soup.—Take 2 quarts of fresh buttermilk; put it in a 3-quart tin pail. Set the pail in a kettle with 1 quart of water. Keep the buttermilk moving to prevent "cheesing." Take a pint of flour, 2 eggs, ½ cup sugar, and smooth with about a pint of cream. Stir this into the hot buttermilk, stirring carefully till well cooked; add sugar to taste. To be eaten hot. If there is any left over try eating it with sweet cream.—*Sister Maggie E. Harrison, Conemaugh, Pa.*

Carrot Soup.—Scrape and slice quite thin 3 medium-sized carrots; boil in clear water 20 minutes, drain carefully. Then add to them 3 nicely sliced Irish potatoes and 1 finely-shredded onion, 2 tablespoonfuls of butter, pepper (red), salt, and enough water to boil all tender; then add a pint and a half of rich milk and a small bunch of minced parsley. Serve very hot.—*Sister John E. Mohler, Warrensburg, Mo.*

Celery Soup.—One cup of diced potato, 1 cup of chopped celery and one small onion. Cook until very tender, almost pulpy and very nearly dry, add a quart of rich milk and a piece of butter. Salt added to the vegetables when they first begin cooking improves the flavor of a soup like this.—*Sister Oma Karn, Covington, Ohio.*

Celery Soup.—Take two bunches celery cut in bits, or chopped fine, cover with water and stew until tender. Drain off water, add 1 quart milk (or more, as desired), salt and pepper to suit taste, and one tablespoonful butter; also add a scant tablespoonful flour mixed into a paste, with a little cold milk or water. Allow to simmer slowly for a minute then serve with crackers or buttered toast.—*Sister Nannie Byer Newcomer, South Bend, Ind.*

Corn Soup.—Put on a little water in pan or skillet (so your milk will not burn so easily), then put in 3 or 4 pints of good sweet milk, pepper and butter. Add one can of corn and when it boils once take off and salt to taste. Eat with crackers.—*Sister L. Clanin, Hicksville, Wash.*

Corn Soup.—Boil a soup bone; when done save enough broth for the soup; put in a pint or more of new sweet corn which has been well cooked; beat 1 egg, add 4 tablespoonfuls of flour and make a thin batter; put it in the broth and corn; season with salt and pepper. Let come to a boil. Serve hot.—*Sister Eliza Miller, Meyersdale, Pa.*

Corn Soup.—Take 1 quart of green corn and put it on the back of the stove with 2 quarts of hot water. Let it cook gently one-half hour, then put it where it will cook more rapidly, and when the corn is tender put in 1 pint of milk. Season to taste. Let it boil up, then add 2 tablespoonfuls of flour, mixed with 3 tablespoonfuls of butter. If you like, after removing the soup from the fire, you may stir in one well beaten egg, beating rapidly to prevent curdling. —*Sister Alice E. Rigler, New Windsor, Md.*

A Good Soup.—As a basis a piece of lean meat should be procured, the larger the better. Put it on in cold water and allow it to simmer with plenty of water till it is done. In the meantime take equal parts of thoroughly well cooked potatoes, beans and rice so that the entire bulk of the vegetables will equal one-half the amount of broth. Mash these vegetables with a potato masher as fine as they can be made. Then strain the broth. In it empty your mashed vegetables and set on the stove where it will simply simmer. You must stir all the time. No cooking is required, as all is already cooked, but there must be a thorough seasoning. The soup may now be colored to suit the fancy, salted to taste, and sufficient catsup or Worcestershire sauce put in to give it a pronounced flavor. The color should be a rich brown, and the flavoring should be such as to make it a very savory and pleasant compound.—*Sister Agnes Mc-Dannel-Fahrney, Elgin, Ill.*

Soup Without Meat.—Take butter the size of a walnut, fry 3 onions in this till soft, then add two tablespoonfuls of flour and let brown. Add next 1 pint of boiling water, salt and pepper, 2 or 3 mashed potatoes and lastly 1 quart of milk. Let come to a boil and pour over toasted squares of bread.—*Sister Mollie Zarger, Franklin Grove, Ill.*

Chicken with Noodles.—Take a nice, fat chicken, cut in pieces, and cook until tender, with plenty of rich broth. About nine o'clock in the morning make a dough with one pint of rich, sweet milk, 2 eggs, a little salt. Roll thin and let dry until dough becomes brittle. Cut up in fine strips and drop into the broth and boil only about 15 minutes.—*Sister Lydia A. Barnhart, Ottawa, Kans.*

Macaroni Soup.—Break into small pieces 2 ounces of macaroni; put in a pan and cover with boiling water; let cook till tender. Take 2 quarts of soup stock and when boiling hot add the macaroni. Cook together about 10 minutes, season with salt and pepper and serve very hot.—*Sister Rose E. Smith, Dunlap, Kans.*

Noodles with Chicken.—Take 2 eggs with enough flour to mix; salt, roll thin and flour both sides; roll up and cut in fine slices, then shake out and sprinkle a little flour over them. They should be made at least an hour or two before cooking. Drop in with chicken, and cook a few minutes.—*Sister Mary Reddick, Sheridan, Mo.*

Noodles Without Meat.—Take 1 tablespoonful of water to each egg. Add salt and enough flour to make a very stiff dough. Use plenty of flour in rolling and cutting. For the broth, brown well a liberal quantity of butter in the kettle,—a piece about the size of an egg for an ordinary dish full. To the browned butter add boiling water, and season well with salt and pepper. Stir in the finely-cut, dried noodles slowly and boil slowly about 20 or 30 minutes. In the winter, especially, it will be found convenient to make a large amount of noodles at one time. Dry thoroughly and put in a cool, dry place to be used as needed.—*Sister Nettie C. Weybright, Syracuse, Ind.*

Noodles.—Break 6 eggs into a tin cup and fill the cup up with water; add a little salt and mix flour in it to make a stiff dough. —*Sister D. W. Inman, Bradford, Ohio.*

Noodles.—Beat up an egg and add about the eggshell full of milk, a little salt, and flour to make a stiff dough; roll out as thin as possible; let it lie an hour or so to dry. Then dust with flour, roll up into a close roll and cut in thin strips. Boil in meat broth for about 20 minutes.—*Sister J. T. Meyers, Oaks, Pa.*

After you have your noodles mixed ready to roll, instead of rolling them, run them through your meat chopper.—*Sister Clara E. Myers, Waddams Grove, Ill.*

Another Way to Make Noodles.—Take 1 egg, ¾ of a cup of sweet cream not too rich, ½ teaspoonful of salt. Make a stiff dough. Cut in several cakes. Roll very thin and cover with flour. Cut in two in the middle. Turn the flour sides together. Rub it again with flour, cutting it through again, making it as small as desired for the length of the noodle. Now cut crosswise ⅛ of an inch wide, shaking them apart, and adding a little more flour to keep them from sticking together. Have some rich broth boiling or broth made from butter, pepper and salt. Drop them in. Boil 20 minutes. —*Sister Mary V. Ebersole, Salem, Oregon.*

Noodles.—Take 3 eggs, 1 tablespoonful of cold water, ½ teaspoonful of good baking powder and flour enough to mix a stiff dough so it will not stick. Roll very thin, cut in long strips about 1½ inches wide. Lay each strip on top of the other, cut down the center, lay ½ on top of the other, the square ends together; with a sharp knife shave very thin from the square end until all used up. Any good fresh meat broth will do. This makes enough for three persons.—*Sister A. E. Bonesteel, Shellsburg, Iowa.*

Okra Soup.—Take ½ dozen tender okra pods, sliced crosswise, 1 onion shredded, 3 good-sized ripe tomatoes; cut into small pieces; a bit of red pepper, salt, and a generous piece of butter. Boil all together until very tender, in fact boil all to pieces, and then add a pint and a half of rich milk. Serve very hot.—*Sister John E. Mohler, Warrensburg, Mo.*

Onion and Potato Soup.—Cut up 1 pint of onions, cover with boiling water, add a teaspoonful of salt and let cook 10 minutes. Then pour off part of the water and add 1 quart of diced raw potatoes. Let cook till well done, then add 1 cup of cream and 2 cups of milk, and salt and pepper to suit the taste. Let boil well and serve. It will need no thickening if it is well cooked. It is wholesome for children and makes a good supper in cold weather.—*Sister Alice R. Mohler, Warrensburg, Mo.*

Grandmother Kline's Potato Soup.—Take 3 quarts of water, 1 quart of potatoes, 1 pint of bread crumbs, the rivels made of two cups of flour and 1 egg, and 4 tablespoonfuls of butter and lard. Cut the potatoes up fine and cook in the 3 quarts of boiling water. Season with salt. At the same time put the lard and butter in a skillet, add the bread crumbs and brown well. When the potatoes are done, stir in the rivels, cook, and lastly stir in the brown bread. Cook up, then take off the fire and let set on the back part of the stove about ten minutes before serving.—*Sister Florence Hays Kline, Broadway, Va.*

Potato Soup.—Take 2 medium-sized potatoes, enough water to cover; boil until tender; do not drain. While cooking, brown 1 large tablespoonful of flour mixed with a bit of milk. When the potatoes are done, add 1 pint of milk, salt, pepper, and a large tablespoonful of butter; add the moistened brown flour and let come to a boil. Serve with bread squares toasted in butter.—*Sister Charles Schubert, Alvada, Ohio.*

Potato Soup.—Put 1 gallon of sweet milk into a double boiler, let come to a boil, then add ½ cup of butter, 1 teaspoonful of salt, 1 teaspoonful of celery seed, ½ teaspoonful of pepper, 1 good-sized onion chopped fine, 12 small potatoes cooked done and mashed fine. Serve while hot.—*Sister Effie I. House, Montserrat, Mo.*

Potato Soup.—Take 2 small teacupfuls of mashed potatoes to 1½ pints of water. While that is heating mix 4 tablespoonfuls of flour in 1 quart of rich milk (the richer the better). When the potatoes have dissolved stir in the mixture. Salt to taste. Pepper if liked. Have a quick fire and stir constantly to keep from scorching until it boils well.—*Sister Fannie Wampler, Cerrogordo, Ill.*

Potato Soup.—Take 1 quart of sliced potatoes, 1 gallon of water, 1 pint of milk or cream—sour cream is preferable—½ teacupful of butter. Brown flour in the butter. When the potatoes have been well cooked in the water, add the cream and the browned flour; season to taste and dip on thin sliced bread.—*Sister Mary Sanger, Bridgewater, Va.*

Potato Soup.—Take 4 large potatoes, pare and cut into small squares; boil in about 2 quarts of water until thoroughly done; season with salt, pepper, and butter the size of an egg. A little parsley added greatly improves it. Serve with crackers.—*Sister John S. Swartz, Goshen, Ind.*

Sour Potato Soup.—Pare and slice potatoes, put in a stew kettle with water enough to boil them quite tender; add butter or meat fryings; pour in a little good vinegar; let come to a boil; add salt and pepper to taste.—*Sister Caroline Nicholson, Hillsdale, Pa.*

Rice Soup.—Boil 2½ pounds of fresh beef and bone for 3 hours; lift meat and skim broth well; add to the broth ½ cup of rice, 1 grated carrot, 1 cup of cabbage, ½ cup of celery, 1 onion. Chop cabbage, celery and onion up fine, cook all together in broth until very tender. Make a batter of 1 egg, ½ cup of sweet milk and 2 tablespoonfuls of flour; stir this slowly into the stock, season with salt and pepper, 1 bay leaf and 2 sprigs of parsely.—*Sister Sadie B. Swank, Johnstown, Pa.*

Rivel Soup or Farmer's Rice.—Put 2 quarts of milk, with a pinch of salt, on the stove over an asbestos mat to boil. Take 2 teacups of flour, break into it 1 egg, mix with the hand and rub into rivels; stir into the boiling milk and let boil a few minutes. Serve with or without sugar.—*Sister Dessa A. Kreps, Independence, Oregon.*—Best in spring when green onions are in use to eat with it and pork.—*Sister David H. Frantz, Bull's Head, Alberta, Canada.*

Salmon Soup.—Put 1 can of salmon into a large dish. Take out all the bones and mince fine. Then take butter the size of an egg, salt and pepper to taste, and 2 quarts of good rich milk. Heat to the boiling point, but do not boil, and pour over the salmon. Serve hot with crackers.—*Sister Mary Gish, Rydal, Kans.*

Sunday Soup.—At night wash a pint of dried beans, place them on the back of the stove in a porcelain vessel, with 2 quarts of cold water and a pinch of soda. In the morning, when they have simmered half an hour or until breakfast, pour off the water through a colander; return beans to cooking vessel; add 2 quarts hot water; let boil until nearly done, then place the vessel where it will keep warm, but not boil. After church, visit or washing (according to the day) add to your beans a teacupful of sweet cream; salt to taste, and serve. They should simmer before serving.—*Sister Nancy Underhill, Collbran, Colo.*

German Tomato Soup.—Chop fine 1 medium-sized onion, 2 medium-sized carrots, 1 small head of celery, and add to 1 quart of tomatoes. Stew gently for one hour. Remove from the fire, and put through a sieve to remove seeds, pressing as much of the pulp through as possible. Return to the fire, adding salt and pepper to taste and a generous amount of butter. When boiling, stir in 2 tablespoonfuls of flour moistened with water, to the consistency of cream. Stir till boiling and serve immediately. This is excellent for those who like highly seasoned soup.—*Sister Grace Holsinger Butterbaugh, Elgin, Ill.*

Grandmother Strayer's Tomato Soup.—Take 1 quart of tomatoes, canned will do, 1 quart of hot water, 1 quart of rich new milk, butter the size of a walnut, salt, pepper, and a pound of oyster crackers. Put tomatoes and water in a kettle together; heat milk in a separate vessel; when all are very hot add the milk, stirring rapidly; add pepper, butter and crackers, and last of all season just right with salt.—*Sister Nannie H. Strayer, Johnstown, Pa.*

Tomato Soup.—Place over the fire 1 quart of peeled tomatoes. Stew them soft, with a pinch of soda. Work through a sieve so no seeds remain. Set over the fire again, and add a little sugar to suit your taste. Then add a pint of good sweet milk with a large teaspoonful of flour mixed in it, stirring it constantly till it boils. Then add salt and pepper, and butter the size of a walnut. Serve hot over crackers. Canned tomatoes may be used.—*Sister S. F. Sanger, South Bend, Ind.*

Tomato Soup.—Take 1 can of tomatoes rubbed through a colander, 1 tablespoonful of butter, a few potatoes cut in small pieces, a piece of celery or a teaspoonful of celery seed, salt and pepper to taste; stew slowly in a crock for 15 minutes, then add 1 pint of boiling water and 1 tablespoonful of flour moistened with ½ cup of cream. Let it boil up, and serve immediately with crackers. If allowed to boil long it will curdle.—*Sister Mary E. Towslee, Colby, Kas.*

Tomato Soup.—Put in a skillet 1 quart of canned tomatoes; in another vessel, 2 or 3 quarts of milk. Place both on stove and bring to a boil. Season the tomatoes with salt, pepper, butter, ½ teaspoonful soda, and pour the mixture into the boiling milk. Eat with crackers.—*Sister Annie Bucher, Astoria, Ill.*

Mock Turtle Soup.—Take 1 calf's head ready cleaned and cracked; put in cold water, season with salt and pepper; let boil till soft, then take the meat off the bones, cut fine, strain the broth; add 1 tablespoonful of sweet marjoram, 1 teaspoonful of whole allspice; let all come to a boil; have about 4 hard-boiled eggs cut up fine in soup tureen, pour soup over the eggs. If there is not enough broth, add boiling water, and it is ready to serve.—*Sister Annie E. Evans, Lancaster, Pa.*

Vegetable Soup.—Boil 3 pounds of beef. When tender, remove from the broth; add to the broth one small head of cabbage cut fine, and a few sprigs of parsley. Let boil three-fourths of an hour, then add 4 or 5 medium-sized potatoes cut in dice, 1 carrot, 2 medium-sized onions, 2 tomatoes, and 1 or 2 ears of corn, according to size. Let cook again until vegetables are tender.—*Sister Mandelia E. Eaton, Baltimore, Md.*

Vegetable Soup.—Boil a beef bone or any kind of beef to make a good soup; when done take it out of the broth and prepare by scraping and paring 2 good-sized carrots, 2 turnips, 2 onions, 2 stalks of celery, 2 potatoes. Put all in a chopping bowl and chop fine, then add it all to the broth together with ½ cup of rice and ½ can of tomatoes.—*Sister Lucy Magie, Tropico, Cal.*

Vegetable Soup.—Boil a piece of beef in plenty of broth until tender; when done, pour off the broth into another kettle; put to soak ½ teacupful of navy beans, ½ cup of rice, or change the amount according to the size of the family. Then take equal parts of cabbage, turnips, and potatoes, cut in small pieces; cook till tender, season with salt and pepper; put all together into the broth and cook. Serve hot.—*Sister Mary Wallace, Mt. Morris, Ill.*

Vegetable Oyster Soup.—Take 6 or 8 good-sized salsify roots, scrape and chip off. To prevent them from turning dark, scrape under water. Cook in just enough water to make them tender, then mash with potato masher, turn ½ gallon of rich sweet milk in. Let come to a boil, season with salt, pepper and butter as for the real oyster. Serve hot with crackers. This is a splendid substitute for oysters.—*Sister Sarah Minick, Lyons, Kans.*

Fish Oysters and Game

In all ages fish has been considered a necessary item in the food supply of the human family. It furnishes nitrogen, mainly in the form of albumen and gelatine, and though not in so large proportion as meat, in sufficient quantity to make a nourishing food. As a rule very large fish are better boiled or steamed; medium-sized ones should be baked or split and broiled and small ones fried. Dark-meated fish, being richer in fat and higher flavored, should not be fried. A fish is in good condition when its gills are a bright, clear red, its eyes full and the body firm and stiff. Soak salt fish in sour milk to freshen them. Pour vinegar over fresh fish to make the scales come off easily.

Wild meat contains a much greater percentage of phosphates than that of domesticated animals, and much more lean than fat and the lean is of greater density. It is therefore a strong food and if well digested is very nutritious. When game is drawn, preparatory to cooking, it should never be washed on the inside, but merely well wiped with a clean cloth. If it is to be kept some time it may be rubbed on the inside with salt and pepper but neither should be allowed to touch the outside till it is cooked.

Creamed Codfish.—Take 1 cup of codfish after it is freshened and picked fine and bones removed. Put in a saucepan, add a little water and a piece of butter half the size of an egg. Let simmer gently for 20 minutes, then add 1 pint of rich milk; let come to a boil; thicken with 3 tablespoonfuls of flour moistened with a little milk. Serve hot.—*Sister L. H. Funk, Kansas City, Mo.*

Codfish Balls.—Take 2 quarts of potatoes mashed and prepared as for the table, ½ pound of codfish boiled and freed from bones; 1 egg, salt and pepper. Form into balls and fry brown in hot lard as you do doughnuts.—*Sister C. E. Eckerle, Chicago, Ill.*

Deviled Crabs.—To the meat of 12 hard-shelled crabs, add 3 tablespoonfuls of stale bread crumbs, ½ wineglass of sweet cream, yolks of 3 hard-boiled eggs, chopped, 1 tablespoonful of butter, pepper and salt to taste. Mix all together and put back into the shells, sprinkle with fine bread crumbs, small bits of butter, and bake in a quick oven.—*Sister Agnes E. Snader, New Windsor, Md.*

Fish Balls.—Take cold fish and pick into small pieces or chop fine; add twice as much mashed potatoes and 1 egg. Mix, shape into balls, and fry in hot lard.—*Sister Jas. F. Thomas, Inglewood, Cal.*

Fish Croquettes.—Take 1 pint of cold flaked fish, 1 pint of hot mashed potatoes, 1 tablespoonful of butter, ½ cup of hot milk, 1 egg well beaten, ⅓ teaspoonful of pepper and salt to taste. Mix the fish with the potatoes and then add all the other ingredients. Mix thoroughly and set away to cool. When cool, make into balls and dip them into beaten egg and roll in cracker crumbs. Just before serving time, fry in deep, hot fat to a delicate brown. Serve at once. All the work but frying can be done the day before.—*Sister Myrtle Holsinger Julius, Modesto, Cal.*

Baked Fish with Tomatoes.—Select large white fish, clean and cut in pieces suitable for serving, season well with salt and pepper. Melt a little butter or lard in a dripping pan, cover with cracker crumbs, then lay the fish in, cover with more cracker crumbs, but not too thick; put a few small pieces of butter on top, then pour over the whole enough canned tomatoes to moisten the cracker crumbs. Bake 1 hour.—*Sister Prudence Miller, New Rockford, N. Dak.*

Fried Fish.—For a 2 or 3 pound fish, split lengthwise, remove backbone and cut in squares of convenient size for serving;

wash thoroughly and dry with a towel; salt and roll in flour; fry briskly in *very hot lard;* have lard at least ½ inch deep in frying pan to prevent burning; when well browned on both sides, serve at once.—*Sister Susie E. Rush, Warrensburg, Mo.*

Boiled Mackerel.—Select good mackerel, one that the brine has not been allowed to get strong on and so taint the fish, soak ½ hour in cold water, then put on the stove in cold water and allow to come to a boil in two waters. Let boil a couple of minutes in the last water, then turn out on a plate and drain off well. Take fresh butter, brown it and pour it over the fish. Serve hot.—*Sister Annie Rupert, Maitland, Pa.*

Breakfast Mackerel.—Soak mackerel in cold water over night. In the morning put on the stove in boiling water and boil until done. Lift from the pan and drain. Make a dressing of ½ cup of sweet cream, or milk and cream, a piece of butter the size of a walnut, salt and pepper to taste, and a little parsley. Boil together and pour over the mackerel and serve hot.—*Sister Susie M. Hout, Sharpsburg, Md.*

Creamed Oysters.—Rinse one pint of oysters in a very little water and drain. Turn them into the oyster liquor, which has been strained and put to heat, and leave till edges curl. Remove and keep hot. Sift together 2 tablespoonfuls of cornstarch and same quantity of flour. Add three tablespoonfuls of butter and brown. Pour in gradually one cup of milk. Cook thoroughly and add oysters, ¼ teaspoonful of salt and a dash of pepper. Cook a moment longer and serve in paste patties.—*Sister W. H. Royer, Dallas Center, Iowa.*

Fried Oysters.—Take 2 eggs, 1 pint of milk, a pinch of salt, beat together, dip the oysters into the batter, roll in rolled crackers, and fry in hot butter until brown. Serve hot.—*Sister Elizabeth Eckerle, Flora, Ind.*

Oyster Pie.—To 1 quart of flour take 2 small teaspoonfuls of baking powder, sift two or three times, add a little salt and 1 small cup of butter, mix as for biscuit, divide into 2 parts and bake on 2 medium-sized pie plates; those somewhat shallow are the best. Be careful not to let bake too brown or they will be too crisp. On 1 of these put the oysters, using the other for a top. Pick over the oysters to rid of any shell that may be found, drain off the liquor, and put oysters into a stewpan with barely enough of the liquor to keep them from burning, season with salt, pepper and butter; add a little sweet cream or milk and 3 crackers rolled fine. Let the oysters simmer, but not boil, or they will shrivel. Fill the dish with the oysters and gravy, put over the cover and serve hot.—*Sister Jas. M. Rowland, Hagerstown, Md.*

Oyster Stew in Milk or Cream.—Drain the liquor from 2 quarts of oysters. Mix it with a small teacupful of hot water; add a little salt and pepper; set it over the fire in a granite saucepan; let it boil up once, then put in the oysters and let them come to a boil. When they ruffle, add 2 tablespoonfuls of butter; when melted and well stirred in, add a pint of boiling milk or part milk and cream. Take from the fire and serve with oyster crackers. If a plain stew is liked, add boiling water instead of the milk and more butter.—*Sister Martha Smith, Johnsville, Md.*

Scalloped Oysters.—Prepare a quart of fine cracker crumbs; butter a deep pan, put first a layer of the crumbs on the bottom; wet this with some of the oyster liquor; next have a layer of oysters sprinkled with salt, pepper, and a few small bits of butter, then another layer of crumbs and more oyster juice, then the oysters, salt, pepper, and butter, and so on till the pan is full, the top layer to be crumbs. Beat an egg in a cup of milk and pour over all, cover the pan and bake for 40 minutes; when done, serve very hot.—*Sister Rose E. Smith, Dunlap, Kans.*

Scalloped Oysters.—Have the bottom of a baking pan well covered with butter, then cover with a layer of cracker crumbs and wet them with cream put on spoonful by spoonful, add pepper and salt, and strew with small bits of butter; next put in the oysters with a little of their liquid, pepper them, stick bits of butter in among them and cover with dry crumbs until the oysters are entirely hidden; add more small pieces of butter very thickly on top, invert a plate over the oysters and set in oven to bake; when the juice bubbles on top remove the plate and leave on upper grate for 2 or 3 minutes to brown on top. Serve in the bake dish.—*Sister Emma Newcomer, Belleville, Kans.*

Oysters on Toast.—Scald and season with pepper and salt 1 pint of sweet milk or cream; add 1 pint of chopped oysters; pour the whole over toasted bread that has been spread on a platter or in a shallow dish.—*Sister Laura Barklow, Lordsburg, Cal.*

Fried Rabbit.—Skin and clean rabbit carefully, cut up and let lie in salt water over night. Drain and add a little salt and pepper to taste; have a skillet with plenty of sweet lard hot, roll the rabbit in flour and fry a nice brown on both sides, then add a teacupful of water; cover and let cook until done.—*Sister Lora Roop, Warrensburg, Mo.*

Fried Rabbit (Free from the strong taste).—Cut the meat from the bones in slices as much as possible, pound, and fry like beef and your friends will think they are eating veal.—*Sister Amanda Witmore, McPherson, Kans.*

Baked Salmon.—Take ½ pound can of best salmon, drain, remove bones and skin, mash fine, and add 4 well-beaten eggs, 12 soda crackers broken in small pieces, 1½ cups of sweet milk, 2 tablespoonfuls of sweet cream, and salt and pepper. Mix all together well and bake in well-greased baking dish ½ hour serve hot with sliced lemon.—*Sister W. H. Neher, Inglewood, Cal.*

Salmon Croquettes.—Take 1 can of salmon, remove all bones and mash fine. Stir into this 2 eggs and five rolled crackers. If it seems dry add some water. Put in also salt and pepper. Then make into small cakes and dip in flour and fry in hot lard or butter.—*Sister Louie Yiengst, Division, Kans.*

Fried Salmon.—Take 1 can of salmon, 2 cups of cracker crumbs, 1 egg, 1 cup of milk. Mix together and fry in a little butter and lard.—*Sister Martha Royer, Dallas Center, Ia.*

Salmon Roll.—Take the bones out of 1 can of salmon, add 1 cup of milk, the yolks of 4 eggs, 1 cup of cracker crumbs, and the juice of 2 lemons. Mix all together and make into two rolls. Roll them in a piece of thin cloth and steam for one hour. When cool, slice and serve with thin slices of lemon. This is very nice for lunches.—*Sister Myrtle Holsinger Julius, Modesto, Cal.*

Salmon Loaf.—Take one can of salmon mashed fine, 1 egg, salt and pepper, 4 tablespoonfuls of sweet cream, and 1 cup of rolled cracker crumbs. Mix all together, form in a loaf and steam. —*Sister Ethel Mishler, South Whitley, Ind.*

Scalloped Salmon.—Take canned salmon from which the bones and other objectionable parts have been removed, separate into small bits; put into a baking dish a layer of dried crushed bread crumbs, then a layer of salmon with a dash of pepper and a little butter; fill the dish with alternate layers of salmon and crumbs, over which turn the liquor of the salmon. Place in oven and bake, browning a little on the top.—*Sister Maggie Bolinger, Redfield, Kans.*

Scalloped Salmon.—Take 1 can of salmon; drain off the liquor and remove all bones. Put a layer of cracker crumbs in a buttered baking dish, then a layer of salmon with bits of butter, salt and pepper; then another layer of cracker crumbs and so on until the salmon is all used, putting a layer of cracker crumbs on top; pour milk over and bake a nice brown.—*Sister C. E. Eckerle, Chicago, Ill.*

Salmon Timbales.—Take 1 can of salmon, remove the small pieces of bone and brown skin from it and mash fine, adding a little salt. Then add the beaten yolks of four eggs and four tablespoonfuls of rich sweet cream, and lastly add the well-beaten whites of the eggs. Place in well-greased cups, filling each about half full, and put the cups in a pan of boiling water and bake until they are a rich brown, in a rather hot oven. When done shake the cups vigorously for a few moments and the timbales will come out quite easily.—*Sister Hattie Sellers Frantz, Beattie, Kans.*

Baked Shad.—Prepare the fish, thoroughly cleansing the inside from as small an opening as convenient; then take sufficient bread crumbs, salt, pepper, parsley, and butter or lard. Mix up with beaten yolk of an egg, and fill the fish with it; now sew it up or fasten a string around it; put it in a dripping pan, pour over it a little water, some butter or lard, and bake same as a fowl. Bake from 1 hour to 1¼ hours. Garnish with parsley or celery.—*Sister Sarah Guyton, Burkittsville, Md.*

Squirrel Croquettes.—Dress squirrel ready to cook, cook until meat will fall off the bones, then let cool; work out the bones with the hands, and chop meat fine; season with a little salt, pepper, and sage; make into cakes; roll in corn meal, and fry in butter.—*Sister Effie I. House, Montserrat, Mo.*

Salt fish are best and quickest freshened by soaking in sour milk.—*Sister Chas. H. Brown, Omaja, Cuba.*

POULTRY

Poultry meat is not as nutritious as beef and mutton, but because of its tenderness and flavor it furnishes an agreeable change in the bill of fare. All kinds of poultry and meat can be cooked quicker by adding a little vinegar or a piece of lemon to the water in which they are boiled; a piece of baking soda the size of a pea will answer the same purpose. By doing this a tainted fowl will lose the bad taste or odor while cooking. One tablespoonful of vinegar will usually be sufficient for desired results. Some of the oily flavor of duck may be removed by parboiling it. An old fowl should be steamed or parboiled before roasting it, the stuffing not being added till it is ready to go into the oven. Giblets of a fowl are the neck, pinions, gizzard, heart and liver; some cooks include also the head and feet.

Broiled Chicken.—Prepare the chickens the same as for boiling, cut in two through the back, flatten them, place on a cold gridiron over a nice red fire; after a little time, when they have become thoroughly hot, set them on a plate or dish, lard them well with a piece of butter, pepper and salt to taste, chiefly on the inside. Then place them on the broiler and continue turning them till done. They will take fully 20 minutes: serve hot with butter and plenty of stewed mushrooms.—*Sister Susie M. Brallier, Johnstown, Pa.*

Creamed Chicken.—Dress and joint the chicken, if it is an old one, boil a little soft and then take out, place in a dripping pan, cover with sweet cream and a little of the broth in which the chicken was cooked; add pepper, salt, and a little butter. Set it in the oven to cook, and by the time the cream is pretty well cooked away the chicken is done. If using young chickens it is not necessary to boil them.—*Sister Sadie E. Sollenberger, Lemasters, Pa.*

Curried Chicken.—Place roasting pan on the stove with ¾ cup of butter and lard mixed; when hot put in the chicken previously rolled in flour, season with salt and pepper, fry to a nice brown quickly, then sprinkle with 2 tablespoonfuls of curry powder; pour in boiling water until the chicken is almost covered. Put on the top of the roasting pan, open the steam escapes, and set in a hot oven until the chicken is browned nicely. It should be turned once. Make gravy and serve immediately.—*Sister Minnie G. Eby, Jacksonville, Oregon.*

Chicken Fricassee.—Cut a nice fat chicken into joints, wash, and put in a pot, cover with cold water, and let come to a boil; skim carefully as long as any scum arises. Boil until well done, season with salt and pepper; cook ⅔ of a cup of flour in ½ cup of butter, stir this into the chicken stock, leaving in the chicken. Toast slices of bread, cut in squares, put on a platter, pour the chicken and sauce over it, and serve.—*Sister Sarah Trimmer, Goshen, Ind.*

Chicken Patties.—Stew a chicken very tender, then remove the bones, picking the meat up fine. Save about half of the broth, having kept the chicken covered with water while cooking. Add the meat to half of the broth, salt and pepper to taste, and a little flour thickening, so it will not be too thin. Then make a gravy with the other half of the broth to put over the patties when served, or they may be a little dry. To make the shells, make a rich pie crust, only add a little baking powder, say, a teaspoonful, mould them over gem tins turned upside down and pick with a fork. Make covers, cutting with a cookie cutter, or anything the size of the pattie. Bake a light brown, fill with the chicken and serve. The patties can be baked any time and set to the stove to warm when desired to use.—*Sister Emma Newcomer, Mount Carroll, Ill.*

Fried Chicken.—Joint the chicken and soak in cold water ½ hour; wash and drain well; salt and immediately roll in flour; be sure to make all the flour stick to it that will. Have the skillet on the fire with plenty of butter and lard (½ of each), having it smoking hot. Put in the chicken, brown it a nice dark brown, turn over each piece and brown well on the other side; when all is well browned pour ½ pint of very cold water in and keep well covered until all the water is boiled out. The steam cooks it through and makes it very tender.—*Sister P. G. Peebler, Jennings, Ia.*

Fried Chicken.—Take young chickens; split them open on the back and roll in flour; put plenty of butter and lard in a pan, let it get hot, put in the chicken, season with salt and pepper. Fry slowly until done.—*Sister Jennie Moore, Duncansville, Pa.*

Pressed Chicken.—Carefully dress as many chickens as desired, cut in pieces and put in kettle with enough cold water to cover nicely. Add salt. Watch closely, and carefully skim off all particles of scum which arise. Boil very tender and until broth has been reduced to about one pint. Remove bones and put meat through food chopper. Put back in liquid, season with pepper, mix well and let simmer fifteen minutes. Pour this into a crock and place weight on top. Set in a cool place and when cold it is ready for use.—*Sister Lucy F. Lohman, Turney, Mo.*

Pressed Chicken.—Stew the chicken quite soft, also let it boil almost dry. When done, pick the meat off the bones in rather small pieces. Put back in liquid; season to taste with salt and pepper. Pour all in a mold, under press, in a cool place. Eat cold.—*Sister Lizzie Warble, Mt. Morris, Ill.*

Cold Pressed Chicken.—Take 2 chickens (medium fat hens), boil till meat is very tender; remove bones, hash fine, salt to taste; hash several hard-boiled eggs with the chicken. Soak about ½ box of gelatine, add it to the broth, which should be reduced to 1 pint. Stir well through the chicken; put in a flat crock and set away to cool. If made right it can be cut with a knife in several hours. It will harden much quicker on ice. The gelatine makes it firm.—*Sister Sarah Witmore Harnly, McPherson, Kans.*

Roasted Chicken with Noodle Soup.—Make a dressing as follows: Take enough stale bread without crust to fill the chicken; grate fine, add ¼ cup of melted butter, salt, pepper, and parsley to taste; beat light 4 eggs, add ½ pint sweet milk, mix well together; fill the chicken; cook until tender, then roast it to a nice brown. Keep out enough of the chicken stock to cook noodles in.—*Sister Kate W. Baughman, York, Pa.*

Roast Chicken.—After dressing your chicken allow it to soak in cold water 30 minutes. Place in a kettle and boil until tender, then fill with a dressing made of bread crumbs moistened with the boiling broth of the chicken, 2 well-beaten eggs, 3 tablespoonfuls of sweet cream, and a little parsley; place in the roasting pan, put in the oven and bake for about an hour.—*Sister John S. Swartz, Goshen, Ind.*

Stewed Chicken.—Take a dressed young chicken, cut up into parts; add salt, then put in a kettle with enough water to cover, boil 20 or 25 minutes (if an older one boil longer or until the wing is tender). Have some flour mixed with water, put in the kettle with chicken, stir and let boil a few minutes, then serve. Season with pepper, parsley or saffron if liked.—*Sister Katie Geib, Mastersonville, Pa.*

Butter Dressing.—Cut stale bread into small pieces and fry in butter. Keep the skillet covered and fry till nicely brown. Add salt and pepper and pour on hot water and steam a few minutes.—*Sister David H. Frantz, Bulls Head, Alberta, Can.*

Oyster and Cracker Dressing for Fowl.—Break the crackers in a bowl, pour over them the oysters, and the liquor from them. If not moist enough, a little broth from the fowl may be used. Stuff the fowl and heap the remainder around it in the roaster, and bake. —*Sister Mamie Sink, Lenox, Iowa.*

Dressing for Turkey or Chicken.—Take enough bread for 10 persons; beat light 4 eggs; brown the bread crumbs in butter, just a light brown, put in eggs, salt, pepper, and sage if liked; moisten with broth from turkey. Have plenty of broth for dressing and gravy. Put dressing in broth and bake ½ hour after turkey is roasted. Make the gravy after the dressing has been taken out.— *Sister Salima Kimmel, Morrill, Kans.*

Dressing for Pair of Ducks.—Take 2 loaves of stale bread, moisten with ½ cup of butter, celery, parsley, or sage as preferred; add salt, pepper to taste; or take 2 loaves of stale bread, ½ cup of butter, 1 small onion, 2 eggs; season with salt and pepper, celery, parsley, or sage; or let a cup of butter get hot, add the stale bread as required; stir until quite brown; season with salt and pepper, and put the dressing in the fowl.—*Sister John T. Gray, Baltimore, Md.*

Recipe for Dressing.—Take 3 pints of sweet milk, salt and pepper to taste; put on the stove and let come to a boil; then put in bread enough to thicken the milk; then break in 6 eggs. Put lard and butter in a frying pan; put in the dressing and bake a light brown.—*Sister Kate Howard, Cambridge City, Ind.*

Roast Duck with Dressing.—Clean and truss a duck in the usual manner. If wild, parboil for about 15 minutes; if a tame duck, this is not necessary. Rub the dressed duck thoroughly inside and out with salt and pepper, then place in a roasting pan. Make a dressing of ½ cup of cold boiled mashed potatoes or some potatoes cut into small pieces, ½ cup of bread crumbs, 1 medium-sized onion shredded, a few sprigs of sage or sweet marjoram, and ½ cup finely-chopped celery; moisten and blend all together with thin cream, adding pepper and salt to taste. Stuff the duck with this, sew up the vent securely and roast, frequently basting, until well done. If 5 minutes before removing from the oven you dredge the duck lightly with flour and baste thoroughly with butter it will look better. Some people like chopped English walnuts added to the dressing; others like the duck filled with sauerkraut that has been soaked over night.—*Sister John E. Mohler, Warrensburg, Mo.*

Roast Goose.—Cut the head off the fowl and slip the body into a narrow vessel to keep it from making the feathers bloody. Next cut off the wings, leaving only one joint on the body. Have a large vessel on the stove in which are at least 5 gallons of water at the boiling point; put the goose in. Hold it down with a piece of wood; turn it over and hold it down a short time. Try the feathers, and if they come out easily, take it out and wrap it in a piece of old carpet or heavy cloth to steam, as the heavy coat of feathers offers strong resistance to water or steam. After awhile try whether the feathers will come off clean from the skin, leaving no down. If so, pick at once. If the scalding is not complete, put it in the water as before. After it is picked, singe and wash it in soda and hot water; draw and lay in salt water over night. Next morning drain, and fill with a dressing, made the same as turkey dressing. Put in a roasting pan half filled with water and roast at least 4 hours, unless the goose is known to be very young.—*Sister N. J. Roop, Warrensburg, Mo.*

Turkey Fricassee.—Dress a fat young turkey and cut in pieces; have ready in a kettle 2 tablespoonfuls of butter, and have it hot, then put in the turkey, and let fry till light brown, stirring occasionally so it does not scorch. When brown enough, pour on boiling water enough nearly to cover; season with salt and pepper and let stew till tender, then have ready a thickening of flour and cream; pour in and let just come to a boil; serve hot.—*Sister Katie Roesch, Quinter, Kans.*

Roast Turkey with Dressing.—For the filling take 2 quarts of fine bread crumbs, butter the size of an egg, 4 eggs; season with pepper and salt and a little parsley; mix all together with 1 pint of milk. Rub 1 small teaspoonful of salt in the turkey and put the filling in, not too tight; sew the turkey shut and place in roaster with plenty of butter and lard. Dressing: Take 1 egg, 1 cup of flour; stir smooth with milk or water. When the turkey is done remove from roaster and put water in the pan; then stir in the thickening and let come to a boil.   Serve in a separate dish.—*Sister Carrie Langham, Newry, Pa.*

Roast Turkey with Dressing.—Dress the turkey; let it stand in salt water ½ hour, then place in a large roaster; pour 4 pints of boiling water in roaster; salt turkey inside and out, and pepper if desired; then grease a clean white cloth with butter and place over the top of the turkey, lay it on its back first having sewed its legs down, and tied its neck shut.   The strings and stitches can all be taken out when ready to put dressing in.   Place in a slow oven, let bake 3 hours if a large turkey; add more water if needed, then take out and fill with the following: Take 5 pints of dry bread crumbs, add 1½ pints of rich milk, 4 eggs, 1 tablespoonful of powdered sage, salt and pepper, and the water off the turkey, saving 1 pint for gravy; add the chopped giblets (heart, liver and gizzard) and stir well; fill the turkey, placing what is left in the end of the pan; return to oven and let stay ½ hour, or until turkey is a nice brown and dressing done.   The buttered cloth should be removed when the stitches are taken out and another spoonful of butter put over the top of the turkey.—*Sister Ida Wampler Mohler, Leeton, Mo.*

Roast Turkey with Oyster Dressing.—Pick and draw the turkey, then wash in 3 waters, adding a little soda to the last water to sweeten; dry it well with a clean cloth; then tie skin over neck, fold the wings over back, tie legs down tightly, put in a baker with water to' cover and bake for 4 hours; sprinkle with flour several times while baking; salt and pepper to suit taste.   Dressing: Take 1 gallon of bread broken in small pieces; first cut the bread in slices and let dry out well, then put it in a crock, pour over boiling water enough to moisten, cover, let steam for 15 minutes; then add 3 well-beaten eggs, 1 quart of fresh oysters, salt and pepper to taste.   One hour before the turkey is ready to be taken from oven, fill turkey with the dressing and let bake 1 hour.—*Sister Mary Rihard, Altoona, Iowa.*

Stuffing for Roast Turkey, or Chicken.—Take 1 pound of veal and 1 pound of lean pork, grind fine, put into a frying pan, and cook, stirring so that it will not burn. Then add 1 quart of bread crumbs. Season with salt, pepper and sage, if desired. Moisten with hot water or milk. Lastly, add 2 or 3 eggs and stuff.—*Sister Elmira Bair, Littleton, Colo.*

Hot Tamales.—Boil a chicken until tender; when done strip the meat from the bones, chop it very fine and add salt and pepper. Have ready made a thick paste of cornmeal mush, make the meat into balls, incase each one of them in the corn meal paste and pack into the inner husks of Indian corn, first washing these in very hot water. Tie the husk securely around each ball, drop into the boiling liquor in which the chicken was boiled and boil fifteen minutes. Serve very hot.—*Sister Lydia Stine, Dallas Center, Iowa.*

MEATS

Flesh foods contain, in condensed form, a number of elements necessary to the sustenance of the human body and are much used by people all over the world, though these same essential elements may be found in other foods outside the line of meats. In order that one may derive only benefit from the use of meat, care should be taken as to its health, freshness, preparation, etc.

Few people, apparently, know that the parts of the animal that are nourished by muscular use secrete the flavor and juices. For example, the neck and forequarters of a sheep or ox, as far as nutritious properties are concerned, far surpass the tenderloin and other more expensive cuts. The following table compiled from the " Diaetetisches Kochbuch " of Dr. Wiel will give the cook some idea of the relative value of certain kinds of meat:

	Water	Albumi-noids.	Fats	Mineral matter.
Lean beef	76.5	21.0	1.5	1.0
Medium fat beef	72.5	21.0	5.5	1.0
Very fat beef	55.5	17.0	26.5	1.0
Medium fat mutton	76.0	17.0	6.0	1.0
Fat mutton	48.0	15.0	36.0	1.0
Lean pork	72.0	20.0	7.0	1.0
Fat pork	47.0	14.5	37.5	1.0

This shows that there is no economy in using underfed meat. Well fattened meats are not only the most economical, but they are generally the best flavored. Much of the value of meat depends on the albumen and fibrine contained in it, and since both of these become hard and indigestible when exposed to a high temperature it follows that meat should be cooked at a low temperature for best results. Apply a high temperature long enough to sear the outside and keep in the juices, then finish with a low temperature, allowing sufficient time to thoroughly soften the connective tissues. In whatever way pork is cooked, it should. be thoroughly done.

Beef Balls.—Take 2 pounds of beef well ground, add 1 cup of sweet cream, 1 cup of cracker dust, 2 eggs well beaten, a lump of butter about the size of a walnut, pepper and salt to taste; mix thoroughly, mold into small cakes and fry slowly in butter.—*Sister Ida C. Shumaker, Meyersdale, Pa.*

American Chop Suey (For one dozen people).—Take 4 pounds pork chops, 15 cents' worth of water chestnuts (Chinese potatoes), 1 can Chinese bamboo; 1 can mushrooms, 5 cents' worth of onions, 10 cents' worth of celery; season with Chinese salt. Chicken lobster or any other kind of meat may be used instead of pork chops. Chop all up into small bits. Brown the bits of pork in hot lard first, then add the rest, stirring constantly for 15 or 20 minutes. —*Brother Moy Wing, Chicago, Ill.*

Beef Croquettes.—Take 1 cup boiled steak, chopped fine, ⅓ cup mashed potatoes, 1 teaspoonful parsley and celery, 1 small onion and 2 eggs. Fry in hot lard in ball.—*Sister Eldora Thomas, Brighton, Ind.*

Meat Croquettes.—Take 2 cups of finely-chopped meat, 1 cup of boiled bread and milk, salt and pepper to taste, butter the size of a walnut. Shape croquettes, dip in egg, roll in cracker crumbs and fry in hot lard.—*Sister S. S. Barklow, Lordsburg, Cal.*

A Breakfast Dish.—Use any bits of cold meat chopped fine, half as much potatoes boiled with the skins on, the same amount of bread, broken fine; moisten the bread with hot water. To 1 pint of the mixture add 2 eggs, salt and pepper; beat all together; fry brown in cakes.—*Sister Mary Mincely, Johnstown, Pa.*

Creamed Dried Beef.—Heat a tablespoonful of butter in a pan and lay thin slices of the beef in it, adding a little water; let it steam and fry until nicely browned; a sprinkle of sugar over the beef helps it to brown better. Then stir in 3 scant tablespoonfuls of flour; add about a pint of rich, creamy milk; season with salt and pepper, and let come to a boil.—*Sister Anna M. Mitchet, Newberg, Pa.*

Creamed Dried Beef.—Take 1 tablespoonful of butter, brown it in a frying pan, put in about ½ pound of chipped beef and let get thoroughly hot, then pour in 1 cup of milk and thicken with 1 teaspoonful of flour. Garnish with scrambled eggs.—*Sister Kate M. Markley, Philadelphia, Pa.*

Curried Beef.—Take 2 or 3 pounds of moderately lean beef, cut into inch-square pieces, boil in clear water until the meat is tender. Cold boiled meat will also do. Put 2 tablespoonfuls of butter into a skillet, cut into this very finely a medium-sized onion and let it gently simmer without browning the butter; then add to it a tablespoonful of flour and enough stock to make a thin gravy, salt to taste and pour over the cubes of meat; then sprinkle from ⅓ of a teaspoonful of curry powder to as much as desired over the whole and let it boil up thoroughly. Serve very hot.—*Sister John E. Mohler, Warrensburg, Mo.*

Frizzled Dried Beef.—Cut into fine shavings as much dried beef as desired, fry in butter, and add as much cream as may be needed to thin sufficiently. Let boil a moment. Best served on toast.—*Sister Maud O. Fahrney, Elgin, Ill.*

Breakfast Hash.—Take scraps of beef or pork, or both together, cut in small pieces; take cold boiled potatoes, cut in small pieces; boil meat and potatoes together in just enough water to boil; when done season with salt, pepper and vinegar.—*Sister Maggie Picking, Buckeye, Kans.*

A Good Dish for Supper.—Take scraps of cooked meat and chop very fine; place in a frying pan with a piece of butter the size of a walnut, a little salt and enough water to moisten. Let this stew on the stove. Then take pieces of stale bread and toast a light brown, placing the pieces on a meat platter and keeping hot. Mix a tablespoonful of flour with milk until quite smooth, and pour in the stewing meat, mixing thoroughly. Drop this mixture on each piece of toast, covering it, and on this lay a second layer of toast, covering the whole with the mixture.—*Sister D. L. Miller, Mt. Morris, Ill.*

Hash Balls.—Grind 2 parts cold beef with 1 part cold potatoes to a hash; season well with salt and pepper, make into balls and fry in hot drippings.—*Sister Alice Garber, North English. Iowa.*

Mock Duck.—Take a round beefsteak; salt and pepper both sides. Make a bread or cracker stuffing as for turkey. Place the stuffing on the meat, roll it up and sew together. Put in a pan and roast for 1 hour.—*Sister Josephine Royer, Mt. Morris, Ill.*

Baked Beef Heart.—Take out the strings from the inside. Some cut the heart open, but I prefer to leave it whole. Wash it well; rub the inside with salt and pepper. Fill it with a stuffing made of bread and butter moistened with a little water. Season with salt and pepper, and if liked a sprig of thyme made fine. Sew up the opening as well as you can by drawing cords across. Rub the outside with salt and pepper, put on some bits of butter, then dredge flour over it, and set on a trivet or muffin rings in a dripping pan. Put a pint of water to baste with, then roast in a hot oven. Turn and baste frequently. The time to roast depends on the size of the heart. When done take it up. Cut a lemon in thick slices, put in the pan with a bit of butter dredged in a teaspoonful of flour. Let it brown, then add a small teacupful of boiling water. Stir it smooth and serve in a gravy tureen.—*Sister Susie M. Brallier, Johnstown, Pa.*

Stewed Kidney.—Take 1 or 2 kidneys (the amount must depend on the size of the family), chip them up into small pieces, being careful to take out all the insides, soak in salt water a few hours or over night if suitable; drain off salt water, wash well, cook until tender, add a lump of butter, pepper and salt if needed, and a little flour dressing made the same as for chicken.—*Sister Susie M. Brallier, Johnstown, Pa.*

Baked Liver.—Take 1½ pounds of liver, do not slice but use in one piece; cut some breakfast bacon in thin slices, and with a clean white thread tie the bacon around the liver, put in a roasting pan, cut an onion over it and sprinkle with flour, add salt and pepper to taste; pour in water and roast the same as other meat, about 1 hour in a moderate oven.—*Sister S. S. Blough, Batavia, Ill.*

Fried Liver.—Scald liver in salt water for about 15 minutes, then slice thin, roll in flour and fry a nice brown.—*Sister H. Beaver, Burlington, Wash.*

Liver with Bacon.—Have ready slices of bacon. Take thin slices of liver, lay on a platter, pour over it boiling water; drain off immediately, season with salt and pepper and roll in flour. Put the bacon in a hot frying pan and fry until sufficient fat is fried out in which to fry the liver; then add liver and fry both together until well done and a dark brown. Serve immediately.—*Sister Mary L. Miller, Cando, N. Dak.*

Liver with Onions.—Boil a dozen medium-sized onions till done. Fry the liver till done, and then put in the pan with the liver the boiled onions, and fry together till completely cooked.—*Sister Grace Hileman Miller, Lordsburg, Cal.*

Baked Beef Loaf.—To 2 pounds of chopped beef add ½ cup of bread crumbs, 2 eggs well beaten, ½ cup of milk, pepper and salt, also cayenne pepper and celery salt. Mix well, and shape into a loaf. Then put a cup of fresh sliced tomatoes in the baking pan— place the beef loaf on this and add another cup of tomatoes on the top and small bits butter and bake ¾ of an hour.—*Sister Jos. H. Johnson, Royersford, Pa.*

Beef Loaf.—Take 3 pounds of Hamburg steak and 1 onion chopped fine; add 1 large cup of bread crumbs, 1 cup of milk, 1 egg; season with salt and pepper and a little thyme (or whatever flavor is desired); make up into a loaf and bake 1 hour; baste frequently.—*Sister Mary S. Geiger, Philadelphia, Pa.*

Beef Loaf.—Take 2 pounds of finely-ground beefsteak, 1 or 2 beaten eggs, 3 soda or 6 small crackers rolled fine, salt and pepper. Mix thoroughly, form into a loaf, put into pan with a little hot water and small bits of butter, cover and bake 1 hour. Before quite done remove cover and let brown.—*Sister G. N. Falkenstein, Elizabethtown, Pa.*

Beef Loaf.—Take 2 pounds of raw beef and ½ pound of pork chopped fine and thoroughly mixed, 1 cup of cracker crumbs (rolled), 2 well-beaten eggs, 1 cup of sweet milk, piece of butter the size of a walnut, add salt and pepper. Mix and bake 2 hours.—*Sister Naomi Shaw, Des Moines, Iowa.*

Beef or Veal Loaf.—Take 2 pounds of chopped beef or veal, 1 cup of cracker crumbs, 2 eggs, ½ teaspoonful of salt, 1 cup of sweet milk. Mix in ¾ of the milk and pour over the ¼ cup when it is in the pan ready to bake. Bake 1½ hours.—*Sister P. R. Keltner, Rockford, Ill.*

Beef Roll.—Take 5 pounds round steak, ground fine. Add 3 cups of sweet milk, 2 cups of cracker crumbs rolled very fine, salt and pepper to taste. Mix with your hand (as you would sausage). When well mixed put in a roaster with a top cover. Put bits of butter over the top, and bake 2½ hours.—*Sister Lucinda Stutzman, Virginia, Nebr.*

Roast Beef.—Cut beef in medium-sized pieces, put in roasting pan, cover with cold water; add a little salt and pepper; cover meat with flour; when brown, turn; baste often. When it is soft it is ready for the table.—*Sister Mary Rowland, Astoria, Ill.*

Swedish Roast.—Take about 2 or 3 pounds of round steak 1½ to 2 inches thick, pound as much flour into it as it will take, place in a roaster with 2 tablespoonfuls of lard and brown on both sides, on top of the stove. Chop 1 onion fine and add to it 1 pint of tomatoes seasoned to suit the taste and pour this evenly over the top of the meat. Pour 1 pint of water in the bottom of the roaster, place in the oven, adding more water as needed, and roast 2½ hours.—*Sister Susie McLellan, Litchfield, Nebr.*

Bread Balls with Roast Beef.—Take scraps of bread, crumb them fine, add pepper, salt, butter, and 1 egg; moisten the whole with sweet milk, then make up into balls and lay in pan with beef roast, with rich gravy.—*Sister Joseph Amick, Elgin, Ill.*

Scrapple.—Boil a good-sized soup bone until the meat falls off the bone. Remove the meat, chop fine and return it to the liquor; season it with 1 teaspoonful of powdered sage, salt and pepper. Let boil again and sift in corn meal, stirring constantly until it is the consistency of soft mush. Cook slowly for 1 hour, watching carefully, as it scorches easily. When cooked, pour into a greased oblong tin, and put in a cool place. Cut in thin slices and fry brown, or it can be served warm without frying.—*Sister Ida Wagner Hoff, Maywood, Ill.*

Meat Souffle.—Make a sauce of 3 tablespoonfuls of butter, 2 tablespoonfuls of flour, ¾ cup of milk, 1½ teaspoons salt and a sprinkle of pepper. Add ¾ cup of cold cooked meat (ham, beef or chicken), chopped finely and the yolks of 3 eggs. Lastly fold in whites of 3 eggs beaten stiff and dry. Turn into a buttered dish and bake in slow oven until firm and nicely browned.—*Sister Myrtle Blocher, Greenville, Ohio.*

Broiled Steak.—Into a slightly-greased, smoking-hot pan put the steak, which has been pounded and trimmed of bone and tough tissue. Salt and turn from side to side as it browns. When done butter well and serve very hot.—*Sister Lulu N. Miller, Firth, Nebr.*

Beefsteak.—Take either round or loin steak, having it at least an inch thick. Remove the bone, and cut off the skin on the edge. Remove everything that cannot be eaten. Then if thought necessary give it a good beating with the rear edge of a flat-iron. Turn and beat and cut again at right angles till the entire steak is broken in fibre. Cut into as many pieces as there are portions to be served. Take half and half of water and rich milk in a bowl. Salt this to taste, and if you like it a dash of catsup or Worcestershire sauce, or paprika, to taste. Have this prepared and at hand. Some put a spoonful of flour in the bowl and beat it in. Now put the pan on the stove, in it put some of the fat of the steak, or butter will do, and let this pan get hot, not warm, but seething hot. Put the plate on which the steak is to be served in the oven of the stove to warm. The rest of the meal must be ready and all other things prepared. Now with a plate of butter near by drop the pieces of steak in the smoking hot pan. Turn them immediately, and keep on turning them throughout the whole process. After turning 3 or 4 times put thin slices of butter on the cooking steak as you turn it over. The meat must be so cooked that it is a crinkly crusted brown on the outside, and juicy within. Then, when done, whip up the material in the bowl with a fork, and pour all in the sizzling hot pan. The moment it boils, pour into a clean bowl or gravy float and serve all immediately. Garnish with Saratoga chips. Each guest to salt the portion served.—*Sister Agnes McDannel Fahrney, Elgin, Ill.*

Breakfast Steak.—Select choice steak. Roll cracker crumbs to dust, beat 1 egg; dip steak first in the egg, then in cracker dust; fry in hot suet.—*Sister L. A. Eshelman, Los Angeles, Cal.*

Hamburg Steak.—Take 1 pound of steak from the round, or 1 pound or more of good boiling beef, 1 teaspoonful of salt, 1 tablespoonful of chopped parsley, or finely-chopped onion may be added if desired. Chop the meat fine, mix well with the seasonings. Melt a tablespoonful of butter in the frying pan; cook the meat until a nice brown, then pour over it ½ cupful of water and let steam for a short time. This is more healthful than when simply fried in round cakes. —*Sister Ida Wagner Hoff, Maywood, Ill.*

Stewed Beefsteak.—For stewing the steak should weigh about 3 pounds and be cut 1½ inches thick; sprinkle with salt and pepper and lay in saucepan with 2 ounces of butter and brown on both sides over a brisk fire; then cover with brown stock or water and stew with 2 tablespoonfuls of minced onion and 4 large tomatoes cut in halves. Cover the pan closely and stew gently for 1½ hours. Serve on a hot platter.—*Sister Minnie C. Christopher, Warrensburg, Mo.*

Swiss Steak (Delicious.)—Ask your butcher for 2½ pounds of round steak cut 1 inch thick. Place the steak on your meat board, season one side with salt and pepper to your liking and cover thickly with flour. Then, with the chopping knife, chop lightly all over this side of the steak, not cutting deeply. When chopped sufficiently, turn the steak over and treat this side as you did the first. Take part butter and part lard and place in frying pan and make very hot. Into this place your beefsteak, turning it once a minute until each side is a golden brown. Then cover with boiling water and let simmer one hour and a half. Remove to a platter and take one tablespoonful of flour, mix with milk or water, and pour into the pan, stirring briskly. When thick enough, place in a gravy bowl and serve. This is enough for a family of five or six persons.—*Sister D. L. Miller, Mount Morris, Ill.*

Brown Beef Stew.—Put on the stove a rather thick piece of beef with little fat (I usually use a piece of the neck, preferring the second cut) 4 hours before needed; add about a quart of boiling water, cover with close-fitting lid and boil gently, adding boiling water as needed to keep from burning, so that when the meat is tender the water may be all boiled away; the fat will allow the meat to brown without burning; turn and brown on both sides; take up and make a gravy by adding flour to drippings and using water to make it the consistency of thick cream; season with salt and pepper. Salt should be added to the meat about an hour before it is done.—*Sister Minnie C. Christopher, Warrensburg, Mo.*

Tender Beefsteak.—Take any good steak and chop with a knife or pound it, then salt and pepper and roll in flour and fry in smoking hot lard as quickly as possible without burning. That is the secret of tender beefsteak. When fried extra well so no water is in it it can be put down in lard and kept for summer use.—*Sister L. Clanin, Hicksville, Wash.*

Spanish Stew.—Cut 1 pound of steak into small pieces, roll in flour, salt, and fry in hot lard with 1 chopped onion. When done add 1 pint of water, 5 mashed tomatoes, 2 Irish potatoes cut fine and 3 seeded green peppers finely chopped. Cook slowly until done; salt and thicken with a little brown flour.—*Sister Mabel Brenaman, Lordsburg, Cal.*

Tripe.—Take the warm beef paunch, cut crosswise, turn inside out, wash thoroughly, place in hot water, not boiling, and peel out the inside skin. Then cut into pieces of suitable size, soak in salt water over night and boil eight hours, or until tender. It is then ready to pickle or fry. To pickle: Take ½ gallon of vinegar, 1 cup of brown sugar, 1 tablespoonful of salt, ½ teaspoonful of pepper, and 1 teaspoonful of celery seed. To fry: Roll the pieces in cornmeal and fry in 2 tablespoonfuls of hot lard until nicely brown. Then cover with sweet milk and let boil until a nice gravy is made.—*Sister Nora E. Petry, Westminster, Md.*

Boiled Veal Cutlets.—Take six even veal cutlets from a good piece of the lean of white veal, pare and flatten slightly, lay on a dish, season with 1 tablespoonful of salt, 1 tablespoonful of pepper, 1 tablespoonful of sweet oil; turn the cutlets over several times, then put them on broilers and broil 8 minutes on each side; remove from fire, arrange on a hot dish, pour melted butter over them, garnish with parsley and serve very hot.—*Sister Kate Smith, Charleston, W. Va.*

Veal Loaf.—Take 3½ pounds of minced veal (the leg is best for this purpose), 3 eggs well beaten, 1 tablespoonful of pepper, 1 tablespoonful of salt, 1 grated nutmeg, 4 rolled crackers, 1 tablespoonful of cream, butter the size of an egg; mix these together and make into a loaf, roast and baste like other meats.—*Sister G. D. Zollers, South Bend, Ind.*

Veal Loaf.—Chop very fine 4 pounds of raw veal with ¼ of a pound of ham; add 2 cups of cracker crumbs, 4 eggs, salt and pepper, and enough water to moisten. Press in a buttered bread pan and butter the top; bake 1 hour.—*Sister Sarah A. France, Huntington, Ind.*

Lamb Chops.—To fry lamb chops or veal steak, beat 1 egg and drop meat in, then roll in cracker dust and fry in hot lard.—*Sister W. G. Lint, Meyersdale, Pa.*

Baked Mutton.—Parboil the mutton until tender, then remove from kettle, put in a roasting pan, season well with salt and pepper, put in the oven and bake until brown. Serve on a hot platter.—*Sister Annie B. Gaunt, Crowson, Tenn.*

Broiled Mutton Chops.—Trim off all superfluous fat and broil on a gridiron or frying pan over a clear fire; add a very little pepper and salt while cooking; butter them after placing them on a hot dish.—*Sister Alice Musselman, Falls City, Nebr.*

Mutton Stew.—To 1 pound of odds and ends or flanky portions of mutton, chop 1 onion very fine, add salt and pepper, and water enough to boil 3 hours. If desired, a little cream and flour may be added when ready to serve.—*Sister J. D. Teeter, Rex, Fla.*

Pot Roast Mutton.—To a medium-sized roast of 5 or 6 pounds put a pint of boiling water in a large dinner pot and drop in the mutton early in the morning and cook slowly without cover; when almost done, remove pot to back of stove or lower the heat and brown the roast in its own juices; turn over as it browns so as to get a nut-brown all over; add salt 20 minutes before removing from the pot. When carefully done, remove from pot, drain off all grease, place in a refrigerator or cool place and serve sliced cold.—*Sister Howard H. Keim, Newburg, Oregon.*

Bacon and Eggs.—Take bits of either boiled or fried bacon, cut fine and put in a skillet; take 4 or 6 well-beaten eggs, pour over bacon; when heated through, season well with salt and pepper; stir together, cook till done, then turn without stirring.—*Sister Lizzie Deardorff, Kansas City, Mo.*

Fried Bacon and Potatoes.—Cut bacon into slices ¼ of an inch thick and 3 inches long; line a pan with the slices. Put pared potatoes, whole, on top of bacon, pour over a little water, set on stove and fry slowly; then when fried soft and brown, pour off all the fat, and add ½ cup of sweet milk. The bacon usually salts the potatoes enough; add a little pepper.—*Sister Barbara Becker, Mastersonville, Pa.*

Head-Cheese.—Wash as many hogs' heads as you wish, scrape clean, take out eyes, put in kettle with sufficient water to cover and keep water over the top till the meat begins to drop from the bones; set off the fire and let cool. When cold enough to put bare hands in put in a pan, then with your hands take out all the bones; to each gallon of meat allow 1 tablespoonful of pepper, 2 teaspoonfuls of ground sage, 1 teaspoonful of salt; with the hands squeeze all up together, taking out all the lumps that will not mash up, then mold in dish or granite pan and set in a cool place; when cold slice in thin slices and serve.—*Sister Sarah Hayes, Rural, Oregon.*

Baked Ham.—Cover a ham with cold water and simmer gently just long enough to loosen the skin so that it can be pulled off; this will probably be from 2 to 3 hours, according to the size of the ham; when skinned put it in a dripping pan in the oven; pour over it 2 teacupfuls of hot water, in which has been dissolved a teaspoonful of English mustard; bake slowly, basting with the liquid for 2 hours; then cover the ham all over to the depth of 1 inch with brown sugar, press it down firmly, and do not baste again until the sugar has formed a thick crust, which it will soon do in a very slow oven. Let it remain in the oven a full hour after covering with the sugar, until it becomes a rich golden brown. When done, drain from the liquor in the pan and put on a dish to cool; when it is cool, but not cold, press by turning another flat dish over it and a weight on that. The pressing makes it cut firmly for sandwiches or slicing. *Sister C. N. Tombaugh, Rodney, Mich.*

Fresh Boiled Ham.—Soak the ham in very salty water over night; in the morning put ham on to boil with sufficient cold water to cover; boil it until tender, remove the skin, sprinkle it with pepper and sugar; place in slow oven till a nice light brown.—Sister *Kittie Forrer, Stuarts Draft, Va.*

Fried Ham.—Cut ham about ½ inch thick, sawing bone if a nice large slice is desired; remove the rind and niche the edges of fat so that it will lie flat in the skillet; if the ham is very lean add a little butter or lard when frying and fry quickly but thoroughly, turning it frequently until it is a nice brown; remove to a hot platter, pour out the grease, put in a little butter, add ½ teaspoonful of flour, 1 cupful of rich sweet milk; stir, let come to a boil and pour over ham. Some prefer parboiling ham a few minutes before frying.—*Sister Emma Spickler, Polo, Ill.*

Ham and Eggs.—Cut ham in thin slices; put 2 or 3 tablespoonfuls of lard in a frying pan, have very hot before putting in ham; fry a delicate brown. Remove ham and drop in eggs while drippings are very hot, sprinkle with salt, turn quickly or shake frying pan so as to cook whites only; remove quickly.—*Sister Mary E. Needles, Wayside, Kans.*

Pork and Beans.—Remove the strings of ¼ of a peck of beans, cut into pieces about 1 inch long, put them into a saucepan of boiling water; add 2 ounces of ham and boil gently 1 hour; drain, remove the ham, return the beans to the saucepan; add 1 ounce of butter, 1 gill of cream, and a palatable seasoning of salt and pepper. —*Sister Ellie M. Zug, Mastersonville, Pa.*

Potted Ham.—Take two parts of boiled lean ham to one part of fat, chop very fine, then season as you desire. Dissolve a heaping teaspoonful of gelatin in a small amount of water, add to the meat, put into a pan and bake in an oven for 30 minutes. Then press and set away to cool.—*Sister J. P. Holsinger, Mount Morris, Ill.*

Fried Pork Steak.—To 1 pound of steak take 1 large tablespoonful of butter, and half as much lard; put it in the frying pan and heat; score the steak until perfectly tender; have 2 eggs beaten well, into which drop the steak, then roll it in cracker crumbs and then put it into the hot butter which has been slightly browned; fry about 20 minutes, or until it is a crispy brown on both sides; keep the pan covered, season with salt, pepper, and a pinch or two of finely-ground sage. Take the steak out before making the gravy. For the gravy put about 3 tablespoonfuls of flour into the pan, stirring until it is slightly brown, then add 2 cups of boiling water, and 1 cup of rich sweet cream; season to taste.—*Sister E. D. Kendig, Stuarts Draft, Va.*

Pigs' Feet Souse.—Clean the feet, put on to boil, season with salt, boil until tender; remove all the bones and leave the meat in as large pieces as possible; place in a mold and pour the broth, which should be boiled down so that it just covers the meat; add good sour vinegar enough to give it a sour taste, season with black pepper and allspice; set away until perfectly cold.—*Sister C. J. Miller, Somerset, Pa.*

Sausage and Dumplings.—Take a piece of sausage and 1 quart of thickly-sliced potatoes, put in a kettle with about 3 pints of water, season with salt and pepper; put over the fire and when it comes to a boil drop in the dumplings which are made as follows: Take 1 pint of buttermilk, 1 egg, a piece of lard the size of an egg, a little salt, 1 teaspoonful of soda sifted in enough flour to make the batter as stiff as it can be stirred with a big spoon; drop in small spoonfuls into the kettle, sprinkle parsley all through them and over it all; cover the kettle and let boil slowly for 20 minutes. Have a skillet on the stove with some browned butter in it; dip the dumplings out in the butter and fry to a light brown.—*Sister Sarah Miller, Sabetha, Kans.*

Roast Spareribs.—Have spareribs washed nicely, lay them on a steak plate, cover with filling, then lap them over and fasten with wooden pins; put in a pan to roast; season with pepper and salt, dredge a little flour or cracker dust over them and 1 large tablespoonful of flour in the pan with a lump of butter the size of a walnut, and a pint of boiling water. Place in the oven, baste frequently, and when a nice brown turn them over that they may be an equal color all around. Make the filling with 2 ounces of onions (about 4 medium sized), and 1 ounce of green sage chopped very fine; then add 2 large cupfuls of stale bread crumbs rubbed up fine, a little pepper and salt, a bit of butter and 2 eggs; mix well together. —*Sister Ida C. Shumaker, Meyersdale, Pa.*

Yetcamein (A Chinese dish).—Stew a chicken until a soup can be made; add noodles, a little onion cut in small pieces and a little shrimp. Season with salt.—*Brother Moy Wing, Chicago, Ill.*

Fresh Meat beginning to sour, will become sweet again if placed out of doors over night.—*Sister Chas. H. Brown, Omaja, Cuba.*

Because of their palatableness, wholesomeness and abundance, eggs form a most acceptable and considerable item in our list of foods. An important consideration in the selection of eggs is their freshness. Various methods are used to determine this. In appearance a fresh egg is rough or "gritty" looking; if shaken it will give no sound. The "candling" test consists in looking through the egg at a light, or holding it between you and the sun. If it shows up clear and spotless so that the yolk can be perceived, it is good; otherwise not. It is claimed also that "when 4 ounces of salt are dissolved in 40 ounces of water, an egg a day old will sink to the bottom; one two days old will nearly reach the bottom; three days old will float near the top, and five or more days old will project above the surface more and more as it becomes older."

Baked Eggs.—Take a dish or pan in which you serve eggs on table. Put butter in the pan the size of a walnut, and melt it. Then break in the pan 6 eggs, and pour over the eggs 3 tablespoonfuls of rich sweet cream. Season with pepper and salt. Bake about 5 minutes; longer if the eggs are desired harder, and less if softer. —*Sister H. I. Buechley, Carlisle, Ark.*

Battered Eggs.—Beat 7 eggs till light; take 8 tablespoonfuls of flour, 1 teaspoonful of salt; make into a batter with sweet milk; beat both together, then add 1 pint of sweet milk; put in pans and fry; put 1 tablespoonful of grease in each pan; put enough of the batter in a pan so as to be ½ inch thick when fried.—*Sister H. G. Miller, Bridgewater, Va.*

Beauregard Eggs.—Put 5 eggs into boiling water and boil 15 minutes. While these are boiling make a sauce of 1 tablespoonful of flour, 1 tablespoonful of butter and ½ pint of milk. Mix flour and butter then add milk, ½ teaspoonful of salt and some pepper. Take eggs from fire, peel, and add the whites, pressed fine through a sieve or fruit press, to the sauce. Then put sauce over toasted bread on a plate; but yellow through press and put over the top. Sprinkle a little parsely over all and it is ready to serve.—*Sister Mary Hoerner, Auburn, Ill.*

Soft Boiled Eggs.—Take clean, fresh eggs; place them in a wire egg basket, if one is to be had; set them in boiling water and allow to boil about 4 minutes, no longer. Serve while hot, with buttered toast.—*Sister E. C. Miller, South Bend, Ind.*

Creamed Eggs.—Put 3 cups of morning milk in a bright vessel, bring to boiling point; have ready and add broken scraps of light bread, crusts preferred, enough to absorb about half of the milk. Then break 6 fresh eggs into the mixture, adding a small lump of butter. Salt and pepper to taste. Stir all together and don't cook too long.—*Sister Mary H. Ellenberger, Turney, Mo.*

Creamed Eggs.—Take one-half dozen hard-boiled eggs and cut in halves. Make a white sauce as follows: Two tablespoonfuls of butter, and 2 level tablespoonfuls of flour. Melt the butter and stir in the flour, then add slowly ½ pint of milk. Season with salt and pepper and a little celery and vinegar, if desired. Pour over the eggs and serve.—*Sister Clara E. Myers, Waddams Grove, Ill.*

Fried Eggs.—Break eggs separately into a saucer, and put all in one bowl. In a hot skillet place a tablespoonful of butter; when it is slightly brown, pour the eggs into it. Shift the yolks if necessary so they are about equally distributed in the skillet. Sprinkle with salt and cover closely. When the whites are firm as jelly add a spoonful of hot water. This causes the steam to cook all white over the top.—*Sister Barbara Culley, Elgin, Ill.*

Omelet.—Take 2 rounded tablespoonfuls of flour, 2 eggs, 1 small cup of sweet milk, salt; beat together the flour, milk and yolks of the eggs; whip the whites and fold into the mixture just before turning it into a hot frying pan containing enough butter or lard to cook nicely. When ready to turn, cut with a knife in quarters, turn carefully and cover, allowing room to rise. Serve immediately.—*Sister S. Z. Sharp, Fruita, Colo.*

Omelet.—Take 6 eggs, 1 tablespoonful of flour, 1 cup of milk, a pinch of salt; beat the whites and yolks separately; mix the flour with the milk and salt, add the yolks, then the beaten whites; bake in a quick oven.—*Sister Annie M. Whitmore, Quincy, Pa.*

Omelet.—Take 6 well-beaten eggs, ½ pint of milk, salt and pepper, and turn into a well-buttered frying pan; lift edges gently from the pan while cooking; cut like a pie after it has thickened; turn and fry a minute longer, and serve.—*Sister Mary E. Towslee, Colby, Kans.*

Omelet.—Take 8 eggs, reserve whites of 5, beat light; for each egg add 3 tablespoonfuls of rich milk or cream, salt to taste; pour all into a hot, well-buttered skillet; fry slowly while beating whites of reserved eggs very light; pour the latter over the contents of skillet and set it in the oven; bake to a delicate brown; then turn one-half over the other half and serve immediately.—*Sister Fannie Hershberger, Waterloo, Iowa.*

Omelet.—Take 2 eggs, 4 tablespoonfuls of flour, ½ teaspoonful of salt, a pinch of soda, stir well with a pint of sweet milk; put into a skillet 2 tablespoonfuls of butter and when hot pour in the batter; as it browns lift from bottom with knife; continue this process till thoroughly cooked.—*Sister Grandma Johnson, Redfield, Kans.*

Omelet.—Beat 6 eggs together until very light, pour half the beaten eggs into a teacup and to the remainder add 2 large tablespoonfuls of flour; mix until a smooth batter, then return the eggs from the teacup; mix again and add 2 cups of sweet milk and a little salt; fry half at a time in a skillet with a little butter and meat drippings until a delicate brown on the underside.—*Sister Mary Snowberger, Leeton, Mo.*

Baked Omelet.—Take 4 eggs; beat the yolks and add ⅔ of a cup of hot milk, a small piece of butter, 1 tablespoonful of flour, and salt and pepper to suit taste. Beat the whites to a stiff froth and add them last. Bake in a buttered dish a few minutes till a nice brown.—*Sister Annie R. Stoner, Union Bridge, Md.*

Pickled or Creamed Eggs.—Boil 12 eggs about 8 minutes, peel and cut lengthwise; lay on the platter, yolks up. Then boil ½ cup of sour cream with 1 tablespoonful of butter, ½ teaspoonful of ground mustard, pepper and salt; pour this over the eggs. Good hot or cold, the butter may be omitted.—*Sister L. Clanin, Hicksville, Wash.*

Pickled Eggs.—Boil eggs ½ hour, then place them in cold water so that the shells may be easily removed. Put them into a jar and cover with vinegar in which red beets have been previously pickled; add 1 tablespoonful of sugar. After allowing them to remain in this liquid for 24 hours, they will be ready for use.—*Sister J. E. Keeny, Natchitoches, La.*

Poached Eggs with Cheese.—Put 1 tablespoonful of butter in a frying pan and when melted add 1 cupful of rich milk; when hot, break in 4 eggs, sprinkle generously with grated cheese; lift on buttered toast, pour milk over them and serve immediately.—*Sister Minnie G. Eby, Jacksonville, Oregon.*

Egg Pudding.—Take 5 tablespoonfuls of flour, 1 teaspoonful of salt 1½ pints of sweet milk, 5 eggs. Put flour and salt in a large bowl, add about half of the milk, and stir it into a batter, then add the eggs and beat well; put in the balance of the milk, mix well. Have a skillet hot with butter and lard melted in it, pour in the batter; as it bakes, lift the edges with a knife until all of it is set; then place it in a hot oven to finish baking.—*Sister Susie Forney Puterbaugh, Kidder, Mo.*

Scrambled Eggs.—Take 6 eggs, beat well, add 2 tablespoonfuls of flour, 4 tablespoonfuls of sweet milk. Stir all together well, fry in hot lard.—*Sister Sarah A. Crowl, Nappanee, Ind.*

Shirred Eggs.—Put butter in a pan as for frying eggs, but not quite as much; when warm, break in the eggs, and to each egg take 1 tablespoonful of sweet cream; season with salt and pepper, then put in the oven and bake.—*Sister Emma Newcomer, Lanark, Ill.*

Steamed Eggs.—Heat a pan not hot enough to brown butter; grease the pan with a small piece of butter, put in the eggs, pour a little boiling water around the edge and cover with a hot lid for a few minutes. Season to taste when served.—*Sister D. F. Kelley, North Georgetown, Ohio.*

Stuffed Eggs.—Boil the eggs hard; when cold, take off the shell and cut the eggs in halves; remove the yolks, then put in a bowl and mix very fine, adding salt, pepper, butter, and vinegar, a little mustard may be added if desired; when all are well mixed, fill up the hollows with this mixture, and stand on a platter, and serve. —*Sister John E. Gnagey, West Milton, Ohio.*

Eggs on Toast.—Toast as many pieces of bread as there are guests. See that the toasting is a light brown, and thoroughly well 'done. Then butter on one side. Take these pieces of toast and put on a plate with hot milk in it and allow them to absorb what they will without turning, while the eggs are being poached. Salt the toast slightly. Take twice as many fresh eggs as there are pieces of toast, and poach them in water that is boiling hot, but not boiling when the eggs are dropped in. If the water boils it will break up the eggs, and if only kept near the boiling point will jelly the eggs. When done put on the toast, 2 to each piece, and serve hot. Garnish if desired.—*Sister Agnes McDannel Fahrney, Elgin, Ill.*

Potpies Dumplings and Fritters ♣ ♣ ♣

These are all rich dishes and judgment should be used as to when and to whom the dishes are served. In each case one runs more or less risk of having her efforts result in a mess of indigestible dough and great care and skill are therefore needed to insure success. Steamed or baked dumplings and baked potpies are as a rule more wholesome than boiled. Never allow the water or broth to stop boiling while dumplings or potpies are in the kettle. In making fritters do not have the batter too thick or they will be too brown on the outside before the inside is done. The lard should be kept at boiling heat. While frying, handle the fritters with a skimmer or split spoon, as a fork stuck into them would cause them to absorb grease. Serve immediately; they become heavy after standing awhile. Some kinds of fritters may be served as dessert with a suitable pudding sauce, or they may be served with powdered sugar or syrup.

Baked Noodles.—When the noodles are made, cut fine as for soup; stew and drain. Put in a bake dish, one in which they may be served; add milk and butter, and season to taste. Bake until nicely browned on top. Serve hot. Some think noodles must be dried before using, but that is not necessary.—*Sister Grace Gnagey, Pasadena, Cal.*

Potpie.—Make a short pie crust, roll in sheets and bake a crisp brown, break in pieces, and pour chicken or beef gravy over it and serve. The beef gravy is improved by adding an egg to the flour, milk or water.—*Sister Alice Garber, North English, Iowa.*

Potpie Dough.—Take 1 pint of sweet milk, ½ cup of sour cream, a pinch of soda and salt to taste. Do not mix too stiff with flour.—*Sister Eveline Skiles, Rossville, Ind.*

Baked Potpie.—Take 1½ pints of sour milk, ½ teaspoonful of soda, ½ teaspoonful of salt, 1 teacupful of lard, make a stiff dough and roll ½ inch thick, put in a pie pan; have fresh beef or pork cooked, cut it in small pieces; put one layer of meat on the dough, a little pepper and broth; cover with dough ½ inch thick; bake to a light brown; serve with broth.—*Sister H. G. Miller, Bridgewater, Va.*

Beef Pie.—Take 2 pounds of choice beef, cut in pieces about as large as an egg, 1 pound of liver cut into pieces half as large. Soak liver well, then parboil the beef and liver together, drain the liquor off, parboil some potatoes in it. Then make a rich biscuit dough, line a medium-sized bread pan, put in the beef, liver, potatoes and 6 hard-boiled eggs " cut half in two." Then drop in a few dumplings of the crust, pour on the liquor, and put on upper crust. Pierce the crust in a few places to let out the steam, and bake.— *Sister Lillie G. Yearout, Warrensburg, Mo.*

Baked Chicken Potpie.—Cut up and stew slightly a couple of young and tender chickens, but don't cook them soft. Make a crust with flour, lard, sweet milk and baking powder, same as for pie crust, but not quite so short. Roll out the crust and line a baking pan, put in the chicken and a layer of sliced potatoes, salt, pepper and butter (the more butter the better). A handful of thyme or parsley cut fine and sprinkled over helps it. Cover with crust and then pour the chicken broth over the top so that it will not get too dry while baking. Bake in a moderately hot oven.—*Sister Anna M. Mitchel, Newburg, Pa.*

Chicken Potpie.—Boil 1 large chicken until tender, turn it out, have a few potatoes sliced, and put in the bottom for boiling, lay the chicken over these. Make a crust as follows: Take 1 quart of flour, a piece of lard half the size of an egg, 3 teaspoonfuls of baking powder, both rubbed well into the flour; beat 1 egg well, add milk to egg to make a soft dough and stir into the flour with a knife, roll out ½ inch thick and cut in squares or rounds, lay these on top of the chicken, pour the gravy over boiling hot; cover tight and do not disturb until well done; keep boiling fast about ½ hour.—*Sister Agnes E. Snader, New Windsor, Md.*

Chicken Potpie.—Boil a good fat chicken quite tender. Then take 1 egg, 1 cup of sweet milk (the richer the better) and ½ cup of butter. Make a stiff dough, roll very thin, cut in small squares. Drop in the broth and let boil 10 minutes. You may think this would be a " sad " mess, but try it and you will be surprised.—*Sister Nannie Neher, Hudson, Ill.*

Chicken Pie.—Dress and cut in pieces a young chicken and pare 8 or 10 potatoes, slice ½ an inch thick, add butter, salt, parsley, and pepper to suit taste; put in a deep dish lined with a dough made same as pie dough, only adding some baking powder; bake 1 hour.—*Sister Mahala Stoner, Aultman, Ohio.*

Chicken Pie.—Sauce: Three tablespoonfuls of butter, and 3 tablespoonfuls of flour rubbed together, 1 cup of milk and 3 cups of warm broth. Crust: Two cups of flour, 2 teaspoonfuls of baking powder, 2 teaspoonfuls shortening, 1 egg beaten light and 1 cup of milk. Put all together and beat with a spoon. Cook the chicken until it falls off the bones, then put it in a pan, pour the sauce over it and spread the crust on top with a spoon. Bake in a quick oven. —*Sister Effie Coffman, South English, Ohio.*

Chicken Potato Pie.—Pare potatoes, cook soft, mash, put salt, pepper, butter, cream, parsley, 1 egg; stir well. Take flour, 1 egg, salt, lard, baking powder, sweet milk. Make dough, like pie dough, not so short; roll, cut in pieces 7 inches square; put 2 spoonfuls of the potatoes on one half of the dough; turn the other half of the dough over and make moon pies. Take the broth of the cooked chicken, put your pies in and boil 20 minutes. This is one of our harvest dinners.—*Sister Sarah A. Sell, Newry, Pa.*

Dressing Potpie.—Cook a nice fat chicken till tender in plenty of broth. For the dressing, take 1½ pints of bread crumbs, put in a pan and fry till brown with plenty of butter; beat 2 eggs well, pour ½ pint of milk over the eggs, pour this over the crumbs, and stir well, add pepper and salt to taste, parsley also if you have it. For the dough take ½ pint of water, 1 large tablespoonful of lard, 1 teaspoonful of baking powder, make stiff enough to roll; make it into 4 cakes and roll out thin; fill 1 side of the cake with the dressing, cover the other side over and press edges together firmly. Remove chicken from pan; drop the half moon pies in and let boil 20 minutes.—*Sister Anna Wampler, Harrisonburg, Va.*

Fruit Potpie.—This can be made of canned or fresh fruit of any kind; if apples, pare as for pies; cherries should be pitted. For the dough sift together 1 quart of flour and 2 teaspoonfuls of baking powder, add lard size of a hulled walnut, pinch of salt, 1 pint of lukewarm water. Roll, cut in squares; butter the bottom of your cook kettle, put in some fruit, sprinkle sugar and a little flour over it, put in a bit of butter, then your dough, and so on until all is in; then put on stove and pour enough boiling water on it to cover nicely and not burn it. Boil 20 minutes or till done. Serve with sweetened milk and a little cream mixed.—*Sister Sarah A. Crowl, Nappanee, Ind.*

A Good Potpie.—Boil any kind of meat, and when done lift out, then take 1 quart of flour in a dish, dip boiling broth on the flour, just enough to make a soft dough, then roll thin and cut in squares; have 1 pint of thinly-sliced potatoes, some finely-chopped parsley, and pepper to suit the taste; put potatoes and paste in layers in the remaining broth and boil about 15 minutes.—*Sister Ida M. Benner, Duncansville, Pa.*

Ham or Irish Potpie.—Take a ham bone after the meat is pretty well used, then boil till tender; slice 2 or 3 good-sized potatoes; take out the ham bone and put in the potatoes, let cook while making dumplings. Take about 3 pints of flour, a pinch of salt, and a rounding tablespoonful of shortening, mix together with water, roll out as thin as pie crust; cut in any desired shape and drop into the broth with a sprinkle of black pepper.—*Sister M. C. Whitesel, Wayside, Wash.*

Healthful Potpie.—Take 3 pints of flour, 1 teaspoonful of salt, have 1 quart of milk boiling hot; pour the milk over the flour and stir it to a smooth batter; let stand until cool, then use plenty of flour to roll out the dough; roll just a little thicker than pie crust, cut in squares; have some good meat broth boiling hot, drop the squares into the boiling broth, boil a few minutes.—*Sister S. D. Royer, Bradford, Ohio.*

Meat Pie.—Use any left-over meat; turkey, steak, roast meat, or even some pork would be good. Cut the meat into small pieces and make a rich, plentiful gravy over it. The pie is best made in the dish it is to be served in. Fill the dish half full of meat and gravy and cover with a dough made with flour, salt, baking powder and sweet cream, using 1 teaspoonful baking powder to 1 pint of flour, or if sour cream is used, use about ¼ teaspoonful of soda also. Have the paste ½ inch thick when rolled out.—*Sister Allie Mohler, Cando, N. Dak.*

Fresh Pork Pie.—Boil fresh pork and potatoes until quite tender. Bone the pork; make crust not as short as usual pie dough. Put in large pan or earthen dish, fill in with meat and potatoes, pepper and salt to taste; cover with pie dough. Bake in quick oven. A little baking powder and sweet milk added to shortening and flour make the crust crisp and brown.—*Sister J. G. Royer, Mt. Morris, Ill.*

Shepherd's Pie.—For using left-over mutton this is excellent. Mince cold mutton, season with chopped parsley or onions if preferred, add pepper and salt to taste, moisten with gravy, put in a pie dish and cover with a thick layer of mashed potatoes. Smooth the top over with a knife and brush with milk. Bake one-half hour and serve hot.—*Sister Amy V. Furry, Johnsville, Md.*

Meat Pie.—Thoroughly boil 3 pounds of meat. Lift the meat from the broth, of which there should be a pint or more. Slice an onion, brown in butter a golden tint, add to broth. Throw 5 medium-sized potatoes, sliced, in boiling water, when nearly done drain and set aside. Take a quart of flour, a teaspoonful of baking powder, lard size of unhulled walnut, and water. Make a dough and line small dripping pan. Take half the meat, cut in slices, place in pan with potatoes and bits of dough. Add the broth; see all is properly seasoned and cover with top crust. Bake an hour. Bits of cold meat may be used if you have the broth.—*Sister Galen B. Royer, Elgin, Ill.*

Rouzer Potpie.—Dress a nice fat chicken and cook till nearly done in plenty of water to which has been added a quart of sliced potatoes. They will cook enough in 20 minutes. Have ready a nice short paste, like good pie crust, about as much as would make 5 pies. Lift the chicken and potatoes out in a dish. Line a pan or skillet with the dough, or part of it. Lay in a few pieces of chicken and some of the potatoes, then some strips of dough, and so on, alternately, until full, sprinkling in a little salt and pepper, and butter ½ as large as an egg. Pour in some of the broth and cover with top crust, cutting a few places to let out steam. Put in the heated baker to cook, still filling in more broth to keep it juicy. Bake ½ hour.—*Sister Susan Rouzer, New Paris, Pa.*

Virginia Potpie.—Take 1 pint of sweet milk, 1 large teaspoonful of baking powder, lard the size of a walnut, a little salt, and flour enough to make a soft dough. Roll out about ¼ of an inch thick and cut in strips about an inch wide and 3 inches long. Bake in hot lard the same as doughnuts. Have a fat chicken boiled till tender, remove and roast with dressing. Make a thin gravy as with stewed chicken. Place the cakes in a deep dish and pour the gravy over them, and they are ready for the table.—*Sister Effie Wiggs, Pyrmont, Ind.*

Yankee Potpie.—Stew a good, fat chicken until tender.

Make plenty of gravy with milk thickened with enough flour. Season to taste. Bake a good shortcake, rolled thin, break in pieces and drop in the gravy just before serving.—*Sister Eliza J. Englar, New Windsor, Md.*

Snitz and Knep.—Cook 1 pound of smoked breakfast bacon, in 1 piece, 2½ hours. Put a quart of dried *sweet* apples, with plenty of water, on the back of the stove where they will simmer gently. Sweet apples are usually dried with the skin left on. When the meat has cooked 1 hour, put the apples in with it and let them cook together another hour. For the knep: Take 3 cups of flour, 2 heaping teaspoonfuls of baking powder, a pinch of salt; break into this 2 eggs, and use enough sweet milk to make a stiff batter. Drop the batter by spoonfuls upon the apples; when apples are covered, replace the lid and let cook a few minutes; then drop in more batter, and so on until all the batter is used. Boil for 20 or 30 minutes, and be sure there is sufficient water in the boiler to keep from burning.—*Sister R. E. Arnold, Elgin, Ill.*

Snitz and Knep.—For a small family take ½ pound smoked bacon, or 1 pound smoked ham, wash, put on the fire at 9 o'clock. Soak ½ pint dried sweet apple snitz with or without paring. At 10 o'clock put the snitz in with the meat, when soft, take 1½ pints of flour, 1 heaping teaspoonful baking powder. Stir well together, using enough water or sweet milk to make a stiff batter. Drop on top of snitz and meat and boil 15 minutes without uncovering.—*Sister Chloe Goughnour, Middlebranch, Ohio.*

Snitz and Knep.—Put on a piece of bacon to cook about 9 o'clock, also put some dried sweet apple snitz, with the paring on, in water to soak. About 10 o'clock put the snitz in with the bacon. Then take some flour, 2 eggs, a teaspoonful of baking powder and a pinch of salt; mix with sweet milk, stir to a batter. Take out the bacon, put a small handful of sugar on the snitz and drop the batter in by the spoonful. When done take out and serve while hot.—*Sister Fannie Bucher, Astoria, Ill.*

Snitz and Knep.—Take 3 handfuls of dried sweet apples and soak in water 3 hours. Then add a lump of butter the size of a hen's egg. For the knep: Take a large teacupful of buttermilk, 2 eggs, 1 teaspoonful of soda, pinch of salt; thicken with flour until a little stiffer than cake batter. Boil in a porcelain kettle until thoroughly done.—*Sister Joannah Mason, Clarksville, Iowa.*

Snitz and Knep.—This is to be made only on bread-baking day. Soak 1 pint of dried apples for 2 hours, then place in a kettle with a pound of smoked ham, or shoulder, not too old, and boil for 1½ hours. Take from your raised bread dough a sufficient quantity to make at least 1 fair-sized bun for each of your family. Work into this 1 egg; leave it rise awhile, then work out in tiny cakes; leave them rise until quite light, then gently drop them, 1 at a time into the kettle with the meat and " snitz." Let them boil for 20 minutes, when all will be ready to serve. Do not lift the lid before the 20 minutes, unless you want heavy and soggy biscuits. In eating them they are good when covered over with the broth they have been boiled in, or spread with jelly, preserves, or apple butter. —*Sister Jennie Kinsey, Boyd, Ohio.*

Snitz and Knep.—Take 1 quart of dried apples and soak them 2 hours. Then take meat broth and boil the snitz till soft; then make the batter as given here: 2 eggs, 1 cup sweet milk, 1 teaspoonful of baking powder, a pinch of salt, 1 tablespoonful of melted butter, flour enough to make a stiff batter. Put this in when the broth is boiling. Boil 15 minutes.—*Sister Eldora Thomas, Warrensburg, Mo.*

Apple Dumplings.—Pare and quarter apples, place in vessel with plenty of water, when boiling make a biscuit dough, roll out the size of kettle or vessel, lay on top of apples and let boil rapidly for 15 minutes; keep covered tightly and do not remove cover till done; when done, cut the dumplings in quarters and remove; serve immediately with rich milk, sweetened.—*Sister Ella Stutsman, Clayton, Ohio.*

Apple Dumplings.—Take 1 pint of sour milk, ½ teaspoonful of soda, a pinch of salt, flour to make a stiff dough, roll out, cut in squares; into each square put 1 small-sized quartered apple, pinch dough all around it tight, drop into a pot of boiling water, let boil ½ hour, take out, serve hot with sugar and cream.—*Sister Elizabeth Eckerle, Flora, Ind.*

Apple Dumplings.—Take 1 quart of flour, 1 teaspoonful of salt, 2 tablespoonfuls of butter and lard, 2 teaspoonfuls of baking powder, sweet milk to make a soft dough; roll out thin, cut in pieces large enough to cover each apple; bake in a hot oven.—*Sister Lottie Taylor, Spring City, Pa.*

Apple Dumplings.—Make a dough same as for biscuit, only a little shorter; roll out the dough and cut in pieces large enough to hold 1 pared and cored tart apple; wrap the apple in these pieces and fasten the edges securely, bake 1 hour or boil ¾ of an hour. If baked, place in the oven and after baking 5 or 10 minutes make a syrup of 1 pint of water and 1 teacupful of sugar; pour this over them and baste while baking. Serve with sugar and cream.—*Sister Katie Moore Strickler, Ivester, Iowa.*

Baked Apple Dumplings.—Pare and halve a dozen good tart apples of medium size. For the crust, take 3 pints of flour, ¾ of a cup of lard, 1 teaspoonful baking powder, and 1 teaspoonful of salt. When these ingredients are thoroughly mixed, add sweet milk to make it the consistency of pie crust. Roll out rather thin, cut in squares, place the apples thereon and make the dumplings. Grease a pan well with butter and place the dumplings in. A few bits of butter scattered over the dumplings will improve them. Bake in a moderately hot oven. Serve with sugar and milk.—*Sister Anna M. Mitchel, Newburg, Pa.*

Baked Apple Dumplings.—Pare, halve, and core 8 medium-sized apples; make enough pie crust for 2 pies, divide into 8 parts, roll out thin, set 1 apple on each crust, fill center full of sugar with a small pinch of cinamon, roll crust up over each apple, then set dumplings in a dripping pan; fill the pan with water to half cover dumplings, set in oven and bake slowly to avoid burning till apples are soft when pierced with a fork. Serve with sweetened cream.—*Sister Sarah Hayes, Rural, Oregon.*

Rolled Apple Dumplings.—Make a rich baking powder biscuit dough, roll out in a thin sheet, cover thickly with chopped apples, roll up compactly, then cut in slices about two inches thick. Place in a well greased pan, not too close together, and pour over the following: Mix 1 tablespoonful of flour with 1 cupful of sugar, add 1 cupful of boiling water, stirring until it boils and thickens smoothly. Flavor with nutmeg or cinnamon. Bake and serve with cream and sugar.—*Sister C. D. Bonsack, Union Bridge, Md.*

Steamed Apple Dumplings.—Make a nice short dough as for baking powder biscuit. Roll out in small round pieces and lay upon each piece 6 slices of apple, or halve the apples, take out the cores and lay a half upon each piece of dough, fill the hollow with sugar; fold over the dough, pinching the edges tightly together to retain the juice. Put them into a steamer, cover tightly and steam for 1 hour. To be eaten with cream and sugar.—*Sister Ada Beeghly, Johnstown, Pa.*

Bread Dumplings.—Take bread dough, work in a piece of butter the size of an egg, ½ cup of sugar, 1 egg, work thoroughly into the dough, then make it into little balls; let rise till light; have enough boiling water in a kettle to cook them; drop the dumplings into the boiling water, cover kettle tight, let boil ½ hour; do not remove cover till dumplings are done. A little salt added to the water before putting in the dumplings improves them. Serve with sweetened milk.—*Sister Mary Wallace, Mt. Morris, Ill.*

Bread Dumplings.—Take 1 cup of bread sponge, 2 cups of water, 2 eggs, 1 teaspoonful of salt; mix same as for bread; let rise until light, then make into balls as large as a teacup; when very light drop into boiling water and cook until done. Serve with sweetened cream.—*Sister Josie Sloniker, Burroak, Kans.*

Cherry Dumplings.—Take 1 pint of sour milk, 2 eggs, a pinch of salt, ½ teaspoonful of soda sifted in 1 quart of flour; this makes a stiff batter; drop small spoonfuls into greased cups, then a layer of cherries, alternately, until the cups are ¾ full; place cups in steamer over a pot of boiling water and steam 20 minutes. Cover steamer closely to keep in steam and do not uncover until done; serve immediately with rich milk sweetened. This requires about 1½ pints of seeded cherries.—*Sister Ella Stutsman, Clayton, Ohio.*

Dumplings for Chicken.—Take 2 eggs, a pinch of salt, lard the size of an egg, 1 pint of water, thicken with flour to make a dough stiff enough to roll; roll thin, cut in squares, drop in the chicken broth, cook quickly.—*Sister Ida B. Hamilton, Springport, Ind.*

Drop Dumplings.—Tage 2 eggs, 2 teaspoonfuls of baking powder, 1 pint of sweet milk, flour enough to make the batter stiffer than cake batter, a good pinch of salt. Beat all together very hard and drop into broth which has been previously strained and is boiling fast. Cover them after all the batter has been used and do not uncover until sure they have cooked long enough. Allow 15 minutes for their cooking. Dish out with the broth into a large vegetable dish.—*Sister D. L. Miller, Mt. Morris, Ill.*

Drop Dumplings with Chicken.—Take 3 eggs well beaten, a pinch of salt, ½ cup of sweet milk, ½ cup of sour milk or cream, ½ teaspoonful of soda, flour enough to make a thick batter. Drop with a spoon into the broth after the chicken is done; cook a few minutes.—*Sister Mary Reddick, Sheridan, Mo.*

Drop Dumplings with Fruit.—Boil tender 1 quart of dried fruit,—apples, peaches or any kind that is not too mushy. At mealtime add 1 quart boiling water and make dumplings as follows: 1 quart sifted flour, 1 scant teaspoonful baking powder, a pinch of salt, 4 eggs, and sufficient sweet milk to make a stiff dough, to drop with a spoon. Boil about 15 minutes, serve at once with rich, sweetened milk-dip. These dumplings are also good dropped in chicken broth.—*Sister Ida Puterbaugh, Cando, N. Dak.*

Dumplings and Snitz.—For the dumplings take 1 pint of bread sponge, 1 pint of fresh milk, ½ teacup of lard and mix well, then let rise well and work in cakes and lay on dough board, well floured. Let rise again. Now have a piece of ham well boiled and take ½ gallon of the broth and a quart of dried apples stewed, 2 teacupfuls of sugar and stir together and put in a baking pan. Then put in the dumplings and bake in a quick oven. This will make 15 dumplings.—*Sister Katie Replogle, Osceola, Mo.*

French Dumplings.—Take 1 quart of flour, 1 heaping teaspoonful of baking powder, salt, and lard to make as short as pie crust, buttermilk or water to wet flour; roll ½ inch thick and bake; break in pieces and pour chicken gravy over it.—*Sister Mahala Stoner, Aultman, Ohio.*

Hot Water Dumplings.—Stir quickly 1 cup of boiling water into flour, add a pinch of salt. Have plenty of flour on board, roll and cut into inch squares, drop into boiling broth as quickly as possible and cook about 15 minutes.—*Sister Alice S. Wallick, Cerro Gordo, Ill.*

Irish Dumplings.—Cook 1 pint of sour dried apples in 1 quart of water; add a little salt, and butter the size of a walnut; take 10 tablespoonfuls of flour, stir to a stiff batter with part sweet and part sour milk, add a little salt; drop into the apples with a spoon; cook 10 minutes; serve with sweetened cream.—*Sister H. G. Miller, Bridgewater, Va.*

Lemon Dumplings.—Into a granite-lined pan put half the grated rind and all the juice of 1 lemon. Add a large tablespoonful of butter, 1 cupful of sugar, and 1 tablespoonful of flour. Into this place rich baking-powder biscuits, not touching, pour in boiling water until level with the top of the biscuits and bake in a quick oven. The lemon mixture is sufficient for twelve dumplings.—*Sister Orvilla C. Ogle, Adams, Nebr.*

Light Dumplings.—When you bake bread and your dough is ready to put into pans, take as much of it as you wish to make into dumplings and make it into cakes the size of biscuits. Set them aside to rise until quite light. Have ready a kettle with 1½ or 2 pints of boiling water in which you have put about a teacupful of sugar (brown is best), a pinch of salt, and a little butter or lard. When boiling briskly, put in your dumplings and cover up tightly. Boil rapidly for 15 or 20 minutes, being careful to stick them with a fork every time you remove the lid to see whether they are done. This prevents them from " dodging down." Let them boil until the water is nearly all evaporated and then *remove from the stove.* Eat while warm, with sweetened milk.—*Sister Susan Ikenberry, Mt. Morris, Ill.*

Light Drop Dumplings.—Take 1 cup of flour, 1 egg, 1 heaping teaspoonful of baking powder, a little salt; mix with sweet milk not too stiff; drop in with potatoes and meat or sauerkraut, cover and let steam for 10 or 15 minutes.—*Sister Esther H. Sell, Roaring Spring, Pa.*—These dumplings may also be dropped in soup beans that are cooked with pork, or in chicken or beef broth.—*Sister C. S. Colony, York, N. Dak.*

Delicious Meat Dumplings.—Take 1 well-beaten egg, a pinch of salt, a pinch of sugar, a small cup of sweet milk, 1 teaspoonful of soft butter and 2 large teaspoonfuls best baking powder, sifted with a pint of flour, adding enough more flour to make a stiff batter. Then drop in small tablespoonfuls into a kettle of boiling meats eight minutes before ready to serve. Do not allow steam to escape while cooking.—*Sister Emma E. Kindig, Inglewood, Cal.*

Baked Peach Dumplings.—Take 1 quart of flour, 2 tea-spoonfuls of salt, mix well together, add 2 tablespoonfuls of butter and lard mixed and enough sweet milk or water to make a soft dough; roll out into half-inch sheets; peel peaches and halve, removing seeds; put 2 halves on a square of dough, sprinkle over with sugar and press edges together firmly; put in a pan, sprinkle sugar and bits of butter over each dumpling and bake in a moderate oven. —*Sister Agnes E. Snader, New Windsor, Md.*

Boiled Peach Dumplings.—Take a sufficient quantity of raised bread dough, roll thin, and cut in 4-inch squares; enclose the fruit with a small quantity of sugar in the squares. Have enough water boiling to swim them, drop in the dumplings and boil briskly for 25 minutes, lift in wire basket and serve at once with sugar and cream.—*Sister W. H. Shank, Waynesboro, Pa.*

Potato Dumplings.—Boil potatoes in plenty of water as for mashing. When done, pour the water into another kettle and save. Season this water with salt and butter. Now proceed to mash the potatoes, and season as for mashed potatoes. Then add 2 tablespoon-fuls of flour and 2 eggs, and beat until light. Carefully drop this batter with a spoon into the boiling water already seasoned. Let boil 15 minutes without removing the lid. If properly seasoned they will be excellent. Serve at once. This makes enough for a family of three.—*Sister Hettie C. Hardman, Polo, Mo.*

Prune Dumplings.—Take 1 pint of good sweet prunes, stew very tender in a granite dish, then put into a kettle, add water until the whole makes ½ gallon; season the broth with butter, salt and sugar to taste; or better still, omit the butter and add ham drippings; then drop in batter made as follows: Take 1 pint of flour, 1 egg, salt to taste, sweet milk and cream; make a thick batter; drop in the boiling broth and cook until it begins to settle. It is then ready to serve.—*Sister Mary V. Ebersole, Salem, Oregon.*

Rice Dumplings.—Boil the rice until done, then season with a little salt and butter. Have 9-inch squares of cheese cloth; spread the rice on those until about the size of an ordinary saucer and about ⅓ of an inch thick. Take good cooking apples, pare, cut in halves and core. If very large, use only half of one for each dumpling. Place on the rice, and take cloth together, forming a ball, tie with strong thread. Then steam them for ½ hour to be well done; or you can put them into boiling water just enough to cover them and boil for 20 minutes. When done remove the cloth and eat with sugar and cream. They are better steamed. Other tartish fruits can be used if preferred.—*Sister J. P. Holsinger, Mt. Morris, Ill.*

Sauerkraut and Dumplings.—Put the kraut on to boil and let cook at least 10 minutes, while you make a batter of 1 cup of flour, 1 teaspoonful of baking powder, a pinch of salt (unless the kraut is too salty), and water enough to make a very stiff batter, so that you can cut it off by teaspoonfuls and drop it on the boiling kraut. Let all boil fifteen minutes. Then cover and let boil five or ten minutes more. Take up, pour melted butter, lard or meat fryings over all (about three tablespoonfuls) and serve.—*Sister W. J. Haynes, Moorefield, Nebr.*

Apple Fritters.—Take 1 pint of sweet milk, 3 eggs, a little salt, 2 cups of flour. Beat well. Take 4 tart apples, pare, core, cut in slices, dip in batter and fry in hot lard.—*Sister Sarah A. Sell, Newry, Pa.*

Apple Fritters.—Take 1 quart buttermilk, 2 eggs, 1 teaspoonful soda, and flour enough to make quite stiff. Pare the apples, cut slices around the apple ¼ of an inch thick. Put the apples in the batter and fry in hot lard till brown, then turn and brown the other side.—*Sister Eldora Thomas, Warrensburg, Mo.*

Apple Fritters.—Beat well the yolks of 2 eggs, add ½ pint of sweet milk, a pinch of salt, and 2 cups of sifted flour; beat until smooth and light; stir in 1 pint of pared and sliced apples and the whites of the eggs beaten to a stiff froth. Drop into boiling lard, a spoonful at a time, and take out with a skimmer; serve at once with syrup.—*Sister Annie Sell, McKee Gap, Pa.*

Apple Cakes.—Take 10 to 12 sour apples, according to size. Pare, cut out core, and then cut around the apple, in slices ½ inch in thickness. Now take 1 quart of flour, 2 teaspoonfuls of baking powder, a pinch of salt, 3 eggs and sweet milk to make this amount into a batter as for pancakes, but not so thin. Then take lard and fry as doughnuts, dipping the apples in the batter, covering them with it. Then fry in hot lard, eating maple syrup with them. Serve hot or cold; best hot.—*Sister Sarah A. Crowl, Nappanee, Ind.*

Asparagus Fritters.—Take 1 teaspoonful of butter, 1 level teaspoonful of baking powder, 2 eggs, a pinch of salt, ¼ cup of sweet milk and enough flour to make drop batter. Add cold cooked asparagus and fry in deep, hot lard.—*Sister Phoebe Foft, Kingsley, Iowa.*

Banana Fritters.—Sift 1 cup of flour and 1 teaspoonful of baking powder into a bowl, add 1 tablespoonful of butter; rub the butter and flour together, add ½ cup of milk, 1 tablespoonful of sugar and the yolks of 2 eggs; beat the whites of the 2 eggs to a stiff froth, add the batter gradually to the whites. Peel 6 bananas, cut each one into 4 pieces, dip separately into the batter and fry in deep hot lard to a golden color; remove and lay them on paper; serve on a hot dish with sauce.—*Sister Annie Sell, McKee Gap, Pa.*

Banana Fritters.—Sift together 1 cup of flour and 2 teaspoonfuls of baking powder. Add 1 tablespoonful of sugar, ½ teaspoonful of salt, 1 egg well beaten, and ½ cup sweet milk. Mix and add 3 bananas, mashed fine, and the juice of 1 lemon. Drop tablespoonfuls in deep fat, fry golden brown; drain and serve with syrup or clear sauce.—*Sister L. U. Kreider, Omaja, Cuba.*

Cherry Fritters.—Take 2 quarts of flour, 2 eggs, 2 teaspoonfuls of baking powder, a pinch of salt, and sweet milk enough to make a batter to drop from a spoon nicely. Add a pint of seeded cheeries and fry in hot lard.—*Sister Fannie Lichtenberger, Carlisle, Pa.*

Frogs.—Take 2 eggs, 1 cup of milk, a little salt, and flour enough to make a stiff batter, drop into boiling lard. Serve hot with syrup or sweetened cream.—*Sister E. M. Cobb, Elgin, Ill.*

Orange Fritters.—Peel and quarter the oranges, remove the seeds and all the extra outside skin. Make a batter of 2 eggs, 1 teaspoonful of olive oil, 1 teaspoonful of sugar, 1 cup of flour, ½ cup of cold water, or sufficient to make a thin batter. Roll the quartered oranges in powdered sugar, dip them immediately into the batter and fry in hot lard.—*Sister Annie Sell, McKee Gap, Pa.*

Peach Fritters.—Beat 2 eggs light, then add 1 pint of buttermilk, in which a small teaspoonful of soda has been dissolved, a pinch of salt and enough flour to make a rather thick batter. Have ready peaches, peeled and sliced thin; stir these into the batter, then drop this by spoonfuls into hot lard and fry until a nice golden brown. Serve hot with maple or other syrup.—*Sister Evelyn T. Keiser, Lordsburg, Cal.*

Macaroni and Cheese Dishes

Macaroni combined with other foods, such as milk and cheese, makes a very palatable and wholesome dish and may be made to take the place of meat in some of our meals. The digestibility of cheese depends much on its physical properties and degree of ripeness, fat cheeses or well-ripened cheeses being more easily digested than others. The percentage of water in a cheese, or whether it is hard or soft, does not appear to affect its digestibility. An authority on cooking says that " in cooking cheese in any form it is well to add bicarbonate of potash in the proportion of one-fourth saltspoon to four ounces of cheese. This restores the potash salts lost from the milk in the process of cheese making and renders it more digestible." Another authority states that cheese may be kept from moulding by being wrapped in a cloth wet with good cider vinegar.

Macaroni.—Boil ½ pound of macaroni 15 minutes; have ½ pound of cheese grated or chipped fine; place in a baking dish a layer of macaroni and then one of cheese alternately, with a little salt and pepper and bits of butter; then pour over all a teacupful of milk or cream; put in the oven and bake 30 minutes.—*Sister Bernice Ashmore, Mansfield, Ill.*

Macaroni.—Take about ½ pound of macaroni, cook until tender in salted water and drain. Fry a medium-sized onion until a nice brown in plenty of drippings. Have a pint of tomatoes or more cooking, add your onion to the tomatoes, also about ⅛ teaspoonful of cayenne pepper or paprika, or a little green pepper (hot). Cook a long time. Put a layer of the tomatoes into a pudding dish, then a layer of macaroni and a layer of grated cheese, having the tomatoes as a top layer. Bake.—*Sister J. F. Thomas, Inglewood, Cal.*

Macaroni.—Boil about ¼ pound of macaroni in slightly-salted water until tender. Drain and put into a pan with alternate layers of cracker crumbs and bits of cheese until all the macaroni is used, add a pinch of salt with butter. Cover with sweet milk and bake twenty minutes. Serve hot in the dish in which it is baked.—*Sister Luverna Sheets, Mt. Solon, Va.*

Baked Macaroni.—Stew macaroni in slightly salted water till tender, then make alternate layers of the macaroni and cooked hominy in a deep bake dish, season with salt, pepper, and bits of butter; nearly cover with rich milk, sprinkle cracker crumbs on top, and bake.—*Sister Annie R. Stoner, Union Bridge, Md.*

Creamed Macaroni.—Drop one pint of broken macaroni into boiling water. Boil for twenty minutes, then drain off most of the water. Add to the macaroni ⅓ pint of condensed milk, butter the size of an egg, ½ cup of sugar, and a liberal grating of nutmeg. It is then ready to serve. If fresh milk is used, drain the macaroni dry, as it is not so rich as the condensed milk.—*Bro. H. D. Michael, Myrtle Point, Oreg.*

Macaroni with Cheese.—Take 1 package of macaroni, break up in small pieces. Cover with boiling water, salt to taste, and let boil until soft. Then butter a pudding or bread pan well, cover bottom with macaroni, then sprinkle thickly with grated or chopped cheese, pepper well and put small bits of butter over top, then another layer of macaroni, then cheese, and so on until the macaroni is all used, having cheese on top. Pour over this a cup of cream or milk and bake until nicely browned. Can be prepared the same with oysters, using oysters same as the cheese.—*Sister Pearl Weimert, Heizer, Kans.*

Egg Macaroni.—Take 4 cups of raw macaroni, 4 eggs, 1½ cups of cream, 1½ cups of milk and salt. Put macaroni in four quarts of boiling water which has been salted a little. Cook until just tender, drain, rinse off thoroughly with hot water and put in a well buttered baking dish. Beat the eggs thoroughly, stir in the cream and milk, add a little salt, pour over the macaroni and bake until set.—*Sister Bertha Dutcher, Sterling, Ill.*

Macaroni and Oysters.—Break 3 ounces (about a teacupful) of macaroni into 2-inch pieces; throw it into boiling water, and boil rapidly for 2 minutes. Drain and throw into cold water for a few moments to blanch. Use 25 oysters. Put a layer of macaroni in the baking dish, then a layer of oysters with a dusting of salt and pepper and a few bits of butter, then another layer of macaroni and oysters, and so on until you have the dish full. Pour over the top ½ pint of cream or milk. Cover with bread crumbs and bake in a moderately quick oven for ½ hour.—*Sister J. T. Meyers, Oaks, Pa.*

Macaroni and Tomatoes.—Take 1 can of tomatoes, put in a pinch of soda and cook a few minutes. Have prepared one cup of macaroni broken in small pieces and cooked until tender. Stir this into the tomatoes, then add a little thickening made of flour and milk, season with salt, pepper and sugar and it is ready for the table.—*Sister Louie Yiengst, Division, Kans.*

Macaroni with Tomato Sauce.—Break half a pound of macaroni in pieces, put into a saucepan with plenty of boiling, salted water, and cook until tender. Melt a tablespoonful of butter in a saucepan, chop a slice of onion and a small bunch of parsley and stir in the butter; let simmer until the onion is brown; add a pint of chopped tomatoes and boil half an hour; then take up, strain through a wire sieve, put in a clean saucepan and set over the fire to boil till thick, season with salt and pepper. Drain the macaroni, put a layer of it in the bottom of a buttered baking dish, cover with the tomato sauce and then more macaroni and sauce till all is used, putting butter on top. Set in oven to brown, and serve hot.—*Sister Esther M. H. Brown, Omaja, Cuba.*

Crackers with Cheese.—Spread water or soda crackers with butter, then grate cheese over them, arrange in a dripping pan and place in the oven until the cheese is melted.—*Sister Catharine Yundt, Lordsburg, Cal.*

Cheese Entree.—Place over the fire in a saucepan 2 table-spoonfuls of butter; when it is hot add a heaping tablespoonful of flour and stir until smooth, then add ½ cup of cream or milk, salt and pepper to taste. Beat light the yolks of 3 eggs, add them with a cupful of grated cheese, remove from the fire, put in a cool place; when cold, add the whites of the eggs beaten to a stiff froth, pour into a buttered dish and bake 20 minutes, taking immediately from the stove to the table.—*Sister Jas. F. Thomas, Inglewood, Cal.*

Escalloped Cheese.—(A good way to use the bits of cheese.) Line a common-size pudding dish with cracker crumbs; cut over this bits of cheese in the thinnest possible slices, then another thin layer of the cracker crumbs and another layer of cheese, and so on until the dish is full. Take butter the size of a hickory nut and cut in bits over the top. Pour over this milk enough to almost cover crackers and bake in a moderate oven until a light brown. Serve while hot.—*Sister Minnie Replogle, Mt. Morris, Ill.*

Cheese Fondue.—Soak 1 cup of bread crumbs in 2 cups of milk, add 3 eggs beaten lightly, 1 tablespoonful of melted butter, pepper and salt to taste, and lastly 2 cups of grated cheese. Mix all together and bake brown.—*Sister Ella Eckerle, Chicago, Ill.*

French Rarebit.—In a well-buttered earthen dish, place a layer of bread buttered, next a layer of cheese cut thin, then another layer of the bread and butter, then cheese till the dish is full, leaving a layer of cheese on top; turn over this 2 cups of milk, to which 2 eggs beaten have been added. Bake 20 minutes.—*Sister Perry Broadwater, Lonaconing, Md.*

Welsh Rarebit.—Cut into small pieces ½ pound of good cream cheese, together with a piece of butter the size of a small walnut, a pinch of salt, pepper, and cayenne pepper if you wish it right hot. Put on the stove and let the above melt well together. Just before ready to use it, add 2 tablespoonfuls of good morning milk. Have a large meat dish with large square crackers (water crackers will do) placed side by side on it. Just before you are ready to serve supper, dip a spoonful of the above mixture over each cracker. They are to be served hot.—*Sister Ora Beachley, Hagerstown, Md.*

To Make Croquettes.—The sauce is the most important item in making croquettes. It should be made in the proportion of 1 cup of milk to 1 tablespoonful of flour and 1 tablespoonful of butter. This amount is sufficient for 2 cups of minced meat. For other fillings the amount would depend on the nature of the filling. Rub the flour and butter to a paste and stir it into the scalded milk. Continue stirring until smooth and thick. On removing from the fire a well-beaten egg may be stirred in, but this is not really necessary. Season with salt and pepper; onion juice—a teaspoonful for this amount—a dash of cayenne pepper and a little nutmeg may also be added. Stir the minced meat into this sauce, pour into a rather flat pan and set away for two or more hours. It will then be stiff enough to mold easily. The softer the mixture the better will be the croquettes; simply aim to have it stiff enough to handle. To mold take a tablespoonful of the mixture and roll it lightly between the hands into a ball. Have a plentiful supply of breadcrumbs spread evenly on a board and roll the ball lightly on the crumbs into the shape of a cylinder. Have ready a bowl containing a well-beaten egg. (If the egg is small more than one will be needed.) Add to the egg water in the proportion of one tablespoonful to each egg. Immerse the cylinders in the egg, being careful that every bit of the surface is covered so the grease may not penetrate. Then lift out on a knife blade and roll again in the crumbs. If a light yellow color is desired, use fresh white breadcrumbs on the outside of the croquettes and do not use the yolk of the egg. Coarse, fresh crumbs are used for fish croquettes which are usually made in the form of chops or half-heart shaped. Cracker crumbs are used where a smooth surface is wanted. Have all the croquettes of perfectly uniform size and shape and lay them aside on a dish so that they will not touch one another for an hour or more before frying. This will make the crust firm. The white of an egg alone may be used for egging them, but not the yolk alone. Whip the egg with the water, just enough to break it, as air bubbles in the egg will break in frying and let the grease penetrate. To fry let the fat become smoking hot, then test it with a piece of bread. If the bread colors while you count 40 it is right. After dipping the frying basket in the fat to grease it, lay in it four croquettes so that they do not touch one another and immerse them in the fat. Cook only long enough to give them a delicate color. Let them drain a moment over the hot fat, then lift them from the basket with the hand, very quickly, so as not to burn the hand, and place on a brown paper on the hot shelf or in the open oven until all are ready. Do not fry more than four at one time, as more would reduce the heat of the fat too much. Let the fat become smoking hot before each immersion of croquettes. Hang the basket on a long iron spoon so the hand will not be burned by the spattering fat. Croquettes may be made of any sort of meat, though chicken, veal and sweetbread croquettes are the most delicate and popular of the meat croquettes. They may be made of oysters, lobsters, fish of any sort, meat and boiled hominy in equal proportions, meat and rice, macaroni and of many other things.

BREAKFAST DISHES

Breakfast foods that require cooking should be thoroughly cooked over a slow fire. Thirty minutes is none too long for the cooking of such cereals as graham, wheat meals, oatmeal, etc. A double boiler should be used for cooking these foods, as none of the food is wasted by sticking to the vessel and less attention is necessary. Oatmeal is improved by soaking over night in half the water required for cooking it, the other half being added in the morning boiling hot, when it is put on to cook. Let the inner vessel of the boiler sit on the stove until the meal begins to boil briskly, then set in outer vessel of boiling water. Griddle cakes and the like should be served as soon as taken from the stove. If they are not served immediately, they should be placed in a warmed dish and closely covered. A little shortening added to pancake batter makes them more tender. A soapstone griddle does not need to be greased. As a substitute for the bacon rind the griddle may be rubbed with the cut side of a white turnip. If a griddle has become rough from any cause smooth it by rubbing thoroughly with salt. Always have grease hot before putting potatoes or mush to fry and fry briskly but not too fast.

Bread Griddlecakes.—Soak dry bread in milk until soft, add flour, soda, and eggs; fry the same as other griddle cakes.—*Sister M. C. Whitesel, Wayside, Wash.*

Bread Pancakes.—Take bread that has become dry and cut it in small pieces in a dish and cover with sour milk or buttermilk. Let stand over night, and mash up fine in the morning. Put in 1 egg and add 1 teaspoonful of soda, 1 cup of flour, and salt. Don't have too thin, and bake as pancakes.—*Sister Libbie Hall, Batdorf, Ohio.*

Buckwheat Cakes.—Take ½ of a yeast cake, 1 quart of warm water, and enough buckwheat flour to make a thin batter. Let set over night in a warm place and in the morning add ½ teaspoonful of soda and salt. Bake on a hot griddle. Some add to the buckwheat flour a small quantity of wheat flour.—*Sister Galen B. Royer, Elgin, Ill.*

Corn Cakes.—Take 1 pint of buttermilk, 1 egg, butter the size of a hulled walnut, ½ teaspoonful of soda, a pinch of salt, corn meal enough to make a soft batter. Bake on a griddle well greased with lard. This can be baked in one pan, and makes a nice pone.—*Sister Eleanor Booth, Lancaster, Pa.*

Corn Cakes and Puddings.—Take 2 cups of buttermilk, 1 teaspoonful of salt, 1 large teaspoonful of soda, ½ cup of flour, 1½ cups of corn meal. Mix thoroughly and bake on a hot griddle as served. Puddings to be eaten on the cakes: Put the required amount of puddings in a frying pan on the back of the stove to melt. When soft break in an egg and stir well. Cook for 5 minutes. stirring often. Take from the stove, heap the puddings in one side of the pan and hold so that the grease will run to the other side. Dip out the grease with a spoon. Return to the stove, add enough water to make rather thin and cook for a few minutes. Puddings prepared in this way are much more healthful than when the grease is left in.—*Sister M. Jane Stauffer, Polo, Ill.*

Corn Cakes.—Put 1 cupful of bolted corn meal into a large bowl, pour over it enough boiling water thoroughly to moisten the meal, thin with cold water to an ordinary thin batter; add ½ teaspoonful of salt, 2 tablespoonfuls of flour, the yolks of 2 eggs, and last the whites of the eggs beaten very stiff, and lightly beaten into the batter. Bake on a hot griddle.—*Sister Annie Saylor, Myersdale, Pa.*

Corn Cakes.—Scald 1 pint of corn meal with enough boiling sweet milk to stir, let it cool, add 2 well-beaten eggs, 1 teaspoonful of baking powder and ½ cup of flour. Stir all together; if not thin enough for the batter, thin with sweet milk. Bake on a hot griddle.—*Sister Bernice Ashmore, Mansfield, Ill.*

Flannel Cakes.—Take 2 cups of flour, 3 eggs, buttermilk to make a good batter; put butter the size of a hulled walnut in a tin cup on the stove to get hot, then add 1 teaspoonful of soda and a little boiling water; add this to the batter, and bake on a hot, well-greased griddle; heap the cakes up in a deep dish to keep warm and serve.—*Sister Salina Kimmel, Morrill, Kans.*

Graham Pancakes.—For a family of four or five persons take 2 cups of sour buttermilk, into which is dissolved a small teaspoonful of soda, 2 eggs well beaten, and a little salt; then stir in sifted graham flour until the batter is a little thicker than usual for cake batter. Bake on a hot greased griddle and keep warm in a tureen or other covered dish. This makes a good breakfast dish with a little butter and hot syrup. The syrup may be made of ½ cup of sugar and 1 cup of water boiled to the thickness desired. I prefer thin syrup.—*Sister Lillie M. Price, Polo, Ill.*

Hominy Cakes.—Take 2 cups of cold, boiled hominy, 1 egg, 1 teaspoonful of salt, ⅓ cup each of sweet milk and flour. Mix well, and form into cakes, ½ inch thick. Fry in a hot frying pan, with a spoon, using just enough grease to prevent the cakes from sticking to the pan. Cover while frying so that they will cook through.—*Sister M. Jane Stauffer, Polo, Ill.*

Pancakes.—Take 2 pints of buttermilk, 2 well-beaten eggs, 1 teaspoonful of soda, a little salt, then add enough flour (graham, buckwheat or wheat flour) to make a batter.—*Sister Katie Moore Strickler, Eldora, Iowa.*

Pancakes.—Take 2 eggs, 2 cups of sour milk, 1 tablespoonful of sugar, 5 teacupfuls of flour, and 1 teaspoonful of soda. Beat the eggs, and add them to the milk, sugar, and butter, which should be melted; stir the mixture into the flour; dissolve the soda in 3 tablespoonfuls of hot water and add, last thing, to the batter. Have a deep pan of boiling fat and drop the batter into it in small spoonfuls, having first dipped the spoon in water or milk. Cook about 5 minutes.—*Sister Nannie H. Strayer, Johnstown, Pa.*

Sour Dough Pancakes.—Take 1 pint of flour and 2 table-spoonfuls of graham flour and stir in water to make a batter. Set in a warm place to sour. Then add 1 egg, 1 teaspoonful of soda and a pinch of salt to half of the mixture and fry on a hot griddle, add more flour and water to the rest of dough for the next morning. Always stir soda and other things in of evenings.—*Sister Chas. H. Brown, Omaja, Cuba.*

Rice Cakes.—To 2 cups of seasoned left-over rice, add two eggs, 1 cup of flour, with a teaspoon of baking powder, a little more salt and sweet milk enough to thin like batter cakes. Fry in hot lard. Eat with syrup.—*Sister Florence Hays Kline, Broadway, Va.*

Rice Pancakes.—Take 2 cups of cooked rice, 1 cup of graham flour, 1 cup of white flour, 1 cup of sour cream with 1 cup of sour milk, or 2 cups of sour milk with a small piece of butter added, 1 teaspoonful of soda, 1 teaspoonful of sugar, 1 teaspoonful of salt, and 3 eggs beaten separately. Bake on a griddle.—*Sister Amanda Brown, Whitewater, Ind.*

Waffles.—Take 1½ pints of wheat flour, ½ pint of graham flour, 1 pint of sour cream, 1 pint of buttermilk, 2 eggs, 2 teaspoonfuls of baking powder, 1 teaspoonful of soda, a pinch of salt, and 1 teaspoonful of sugar. Bake on waffle irons.—*Sister Belle Rihard, Altoona, Iowa.*

Waffles.—Take 3 eggs, 1 quart of sour milk, 1 teaspoonful of soda, a pinch of salt, and 2 tablespoonfuls of melted butter; beat the yolks of the eggs thoroughly, stir in the milk, add the butter and soda, and last the whites of the eggs beaten stiff. Use enough flour to make it drop nicely from a spoon; have the waffle iron well greased (grease it every time you remove a waffle). Serve the waffles in layers with butter and sugar between them. This proportion will be sufficient for 6 persons.—*Sister Mary Griffith, Mastersonville, Pa.*

A Teaspoonful of sugar added to pancake batter, will make the cakes a golden brown.—*Sister Chas. H. Brown, Omaja, Cuba.*

Toast.—Take 4 slices of bread, spread lightly with butter, place on pie pans and put into the oven till nearly brown. Have ready 3 pints of sweet milk; let it come to a boil and put over the bread, adding a pinch of salt. This is a very healthful dish.—*Sister Anna Zimmerman, Mt. Solon, Va.*

Breakfast Toast.—Mix 1 tablespoonful of sugar, a little salt, 1 tablespoonful of flour and 2 well-beaten eggs in ½ pint of sweet milk. In this mixture dip slices of bread and fry them on a buttered griddle until they are a light brown on each side.—*Sister Emma A. Miller, Sharpsburg, Md.*

Milk Toast.—For 1 large dish of toast, take 2 slices of bread, toast brown, sprinkle with sugar; let 1 quart of milk come to a boil, then pour it over the bread and serve.—*Sister Barbara Johnson, Roaring Spring, Pa.*

Milk Toast.—Take 3 slices of bread, toast to a light brown; take 3 pints of fresh milk, heat it till it comes to a boil, add a pinch of salt and a tablespoonful of sugar; put the bread in a dish, pour over it the hot milk. Let it stand a few minutes before serving.—*Sister Ida M. Nelson, Kearney, Nebr.*

Wholesome Toast.—Save all your bread crumbs, broken bits of bread and dry crusts. Put them on pie tins in a very moderate oven until thoroughly dried and a golden brown. Put all in a pan and crush fine with a wooden potato masher. Put 4 heaping teaspoonfuls in a dessert dish, cover with hot milk in which a little salt has been sprinkled. It may be eaten with sugar, but is more wholesome without. If you do not wish to use at once, put in a bag in a dry place until wanted. As it contains no moisture, it will keep indefinitely. This makes a pleasant change from oatmeal and other cereals.—*Sister Adaline H. Beery, Elgin, Ill.*

Fried Bread.—Slice stale bread. Take 1 egg, beat it well, add a pinch of salt and ¼ cup of cold water; dip the slices in the batter and fry in hot lard or butter.—*Sister Kate Royer, Celina, Ohio.*

Fried Bread.—Beat 1 egg to a froth. Pour into this 1 teacupful of sour cream or milk into which a pinch of soda has been stirred; then add a little salt and stir all well together. Put a lump of butter, suet or drippings in the frying pan, and let it get real hot. Take bread scraps or slices of bread, not less than three or four days old, and dip in the batter. Fry a nice brown on both sides and serve with hot sugar syrup.—*Sister Martha E. Lear, Cerro Gordo, Ill.*

Fried Bread.—Put a large tablespoonful of butter or lard in a skillet. Crumb up a large dish of bread (scraps can be used), put into the skillet, salt and pepper the same as for potatoes, and fry nice and brown. Stir to keep from burning. Then take ½ cup of sugar and 2 tablespoonfuls of flour and stir together, adding enough milk to fill the dish. Stir up and pour over the fried bread. Rinse the dish with another cup of milk and pour in. Let boil up and serve.—*Sister Almeda Caskey, Corning, Iowa.*

Fried Bread.—Slice the bread about 1 inch thick. Take 1 quart of hot water, 1 tablespoonful of sugar; dip the bread in the hot water, put in a hot pan with melted butter and fry a light brown on both sides. —*Sister Laura Anglemyer, Huntington, Ind.*

Fried Bread Using Eggs.—Slice the bread about 1 inch thick. Take 6 eggs, 1 cup of sweet cream 1 teaspoonful of salt; beat to a batter; then dip the slices of bread in the batter, and fry a light brown in hot butter.—*Sister Laura Anglemyer, Huntington, Ind.*

Breakfast Mush.—Put 1½ cups of water, 1½ cups of sweet milk, a piece of butter the size of an egg, and salt to taste, in a pan. Let come to a boil, then stir in corn meal to make a soft mush easily dropped with a spoon; cook a few minutes, then add 2 eggs, beat well, cook a minute or two longer. Have the pancake griddle hot, with a liberal supply of butter and meat fryings melted. Drop the mush in by the spoonful and fry brown on both sides. Serve hot.—*Sister Susie Forney Puterbaugh, Kidder, Mo.*

Good Fried Mush.—Put lard or suet in a pot kept for this purpose, enough to cover the mush. Have a wire bucket or kettle.

Slice your mush, place it in your wire kettle, not too much at a time. Now have the lard very hot; then put mush in. When brown enough lift it and let it drip a moment. Repeat until you have enough for your meal. Be sure to keep your lard hot enough. This is quicker done and much better than to fry in a pan.—*Sister Daniel Vaniman, McPherson, Kans.*

Good Fried Mush.—In the morning when you want to fry mush, take as much boiling water as you think you will need, salt and stir in corn meal till the mush will not run when put in the pan. Have the pan hot with enough grease to fry. When brown, turn and brown again. Do not make too stiff, or it will break in the pan and will not be good. Put it into the pan by spoonfuls.—*Sister M. Catherine Strickler, Lanark, Ill.*

Granula (A Hygienic Dish).—Get good graham flour, take pure spring or soft water, nothing else, and knead to a stiff dough. Roll and mould as for biscuit (not as thick). Bake thoroughly in a hot oven. When well done, or *over* done, remove and cool, then cut each piece in halves and put back in a warm baker and dry to a crisp, not brown or burnt. A yellow brown will not hurt. Now crush or break in small bits and grind them as you would coffee. You now have one of the best health foods known. It can be served in various ways. Soaked in good, rich milk is the best way to eat it. Some like to add a little sugar, some a little salt (but don't add salt when you bake it, it spoils the flavor). Some eat it with fruit. It makes a nice cold Sunday dish and is always ready. It can be used in puddings and mixed with bread for dressings. We have made and used this hygienic food for 23 years, and know its merits. The biscuits, or graham crackers, warm from the oven, well baked, with crispy crust, make a delightful bread. We have a small hand mill to grind them. If you cannot get good graham flour, if it is too rough with bran, add a little white flour, or sift the coarsest bran out. Graham made of white wheat is best.—*Sister Amanda Witmore, McPherson, Kans.*

Breakfast Food.—Brown stale light bread (scraps will do) in the oven till golden-brown and crisp. Pulverize with the rolling-pin on a cloth. Serve with sugar and cream or fruit juice, if desired.—*Sister L. V. Forehand, Gerster, Mo.*

Graham Gruel.—Take 1 quart of boiling water, 1 cup of graham flour, ½ cup of sweet cream or rich milk, salt; stir the flour smooth with a little cold water. Stir into the boiling water and cook rapidly about 30 minutes; add the milk or cream just before taking from the fire. Serve with sugar.—*Sister S. Z. Sharp, Fruita, Colo.*

Graham Mush.—Sift graham meal into boiling salted water, stirring briskly until quite stiff. Serve with sugar and cream or with butter and syrup. This mush is much improved by removing from kettle and steaming from 1 to 3 hours; eat cold or slice and fry like corn meal mush.—*Sister Minnie C. Christopher, Warrensburg, Mo.*

Graham Mush.—Take 2 quarts of water, 1 pint of graham flour, 1 teaspoonful of salt. Have the water boiling and stir in the meal briskly with an egg beater, boil 15 minutes, and serve with rich milk and sugar either hot or cold.—*Sister Catharine Wampler, Dayton, Va.*

Graham Mush.—Take boiling water, salt to taste, make a mush by stirring in good graham flour, boil 5 minutes, stirring constantly to keep from sticking. Serve warm or cold with sugar and cream.—*Sister Lizzie Bagwell, Bremen, Ohio.*

Potato and Celery Hash.—Take 3 cups of cold boiled potatoes, minced, 1 cup cooked celery, minced, and salt. Mix thoroughly, put in baking pan which has been oiled, sprinkle butter over hash and let brown. Stir occasionally.—*Sister Bertha Dutcher, Sterling, Ill.*

Bread Warm and Cold

Bread may truthfully be considered the " staff of life." Quoting from a chemist and authority on the subject, " White bread is more nearly a perfect ration, and will maintain life longer than any other single food; because its tissue-forming constituents, the proteids (gluten, and its energy-yielding portion, the carbohydrates (starch), are nearly in the proportions demanded by the system. The human body demands from the food daily about a hundred grains of protein, 50 grains of fat, and 450 grains carbohydrate. In 100 grains of bread there are 7.8 grains of assimilable protein, 1.3 grains of fat, and 53.1 grains of carbohydrate, so that to get the necessary amount of protein from bread a man would have to eat about 1,300 grains—about three pounds—a day. This would give 35 grains too little fat, and 240 grains too much carbohydrate, but since fat and carbohydrate are both energy formers, and to a certain extent interchangeable, the variation from a standard diet is not great. We have instinctively recognized these facts by eating our bread with butter—a fat—or taking it with milk, which contains a large amount of proteid and fat." To make good bread one should have good flour—always sifted before using—fresh yeast, pure water or scalded milk, sweet butter or lard where shortening is used, and a good oven. The flour and milk or water should all be of the same temperature, 70°, when mixed. While rising the bread should be kept at an even temperature of not less than 60° and not more than 80°. One cup of yeast means wet yeast, and is equal to 1 cake of compressed yeast. In making bread an earthen vessel is better than wood, tin or granite. If the bread does not rise fast enough set the crock in warm water kept warm by the addition at intervals of warmer water. After bread is moulded into loaves it should double its bulk before being baked. Test the oven by sprinkling a little flour on a paper and placing in it. The flour should take on a good color in five minutes to be just right for loaf bread, and should become quite brown in three minutes to be hot enough for rolls. To prevent bread from hardening on top after it is moulded into loaves cover with a thin cloth wrung out of water; or if it has been moulded into round pans, turn crocks over the pans. If the dough is too cold and is slow in rising, warm these crocks a little before turning them over the pans and they will hasten the rising. Biscuits made with baking powder and sweet milk, or part milk and part water, need not be hurried into the oven; in fact after they are cut out and placed in the baking pan they are nicer if allowed to rise awhile before baking. They may even be made in the evening and allowed to stand till morning before being baked.

Biscuit.—Take 1 cup sweet cream, 2 cups sweet milk, 3 teaspoonfuls of baking powder and a pinch of salt. Mix baking powder and salt first in flour. Then add cream and milk and as much flour as will make a dough stiff enough to roll out on board. Mix as little as possible. Cut out and bake at once, in hot oven, to a light brown.—*Sister Mate W. Krieghbaum, South Bend, Ind.*

Biscuits without Shortening.—Take 1 quart of sifted flour, 1 teaspoonful of salt, 1½ pints of sour cream, in which stir 1 teaspoonful of soda; bake in a hot oven.—*Sister E. Hodgden, Huntington, Ind.*

Cream Biscuits.—Sift 1 quart of flour with 1 heaping teaspoonful of baking powder, add 1 teaspoonful of salt, and cream to make a soft dough; mix well, roll thin, cut in biscuits, bake in a very hot oven.—*Sister Mamie Viney, Bath, Ind.*

Drop Biscuits.—Take 1 pint sour milk, lard the size of an egg, 1 scant teaspoonful of soda, ½ teaspoonful baking powder, ½ teaspoonful salt, and flour enough to stir as thick as you can with a spoon. Grease your pan or muffin rings and drop 1 tablespoonful at a place.—*Sister Ida Wampler Mohler, Leeton, Mo.*

Good Biscuits.—To 1 quart of flour add a level teaspoonful of soda, the same of salt; about ¼ teaspoonful of baking powder. Sift together and add one large tablespoonful of lard. Mix thoroughly with the hand. Into this stir, with a spoon, about 2 cups of sour milk or enough to make a soft dough. Roll to less than ½ inch and bake in a quick oven. In case the milk is very sour, use a little more soda.—*Sister Mattie Mohler, Warrensburg, Mo.*

Graham Biscuits.—Dissolve 1 heaping teaspoonful of soda in a pint of thick milk, stir into this with a spoon enough sifted graham flour to make a rather stiff batter, just so that the biscuits can be easily dropped by spoonfuls on the tin a few inches apart; bake about 15 minutes in a hot oven.—*Sister Sallie G. Kline, Richland Station, Pa.*

Graham Biscuit.—Take 2 cups of graham flour, 1 cup of white flour, 1 cup of sweet milk, 2 tablespoonfuls of sugar, 4 tablespoonfuls of yeast, ½ teaspoonful of salt. Let rise very light, then work in 1 tablespoonful of butter, ½ teaspoonful of soda; cut out as for other biscuits, and bake.—*Sister J. E. Price, Dallas Center, Iowa.*

Maryland Biscuits.—Take 5 pints flour, 1 teacupful of lard, a reasonable amount of salt, 3 teaspoonfuls of baking powder, ½ pint milk, 1 pint water, and beat hard with a rolling pin ½ hour. Make out by hand in small biscuits, and stick with a fork several times. Bake in hot oven.—*Sister Mary A. Weybright, Double Pipe Creek, Md.*

One, Two, Three, Four Biscuit.—Take 4 cups of flour, 3 teaspoonfuls of baking powder, 2 tablespoonfuls of shortening and 1 teaspoonful of salt. Mix to a soft dough with sweet milk. This makes fine biscuit, shortcake or potpie.—*Sister Lulu N. Miller, Firth, Nebr.*

Sweet Biscuit.—Take 3 eggs, 1 cup of sweet milk, 1½ cups of sugar, 1 cup of lard or butter, and 4 teaspoonfuls of baking powder. Bake in a quick oven.—*Sister Jennie Nicholson, Hillsdale, Pa.*

Tea Biscuits.—Sift together 1 quart of flour, 2 teaspoonfuls of baking powder and ½ teaspoonful of salt. Beat with 1 pint of sweet cream and bake in a hot oven.—*Sister Sue Sisler, Dallas Center, Iowa.*

Breakfast Gems.—Take 1 cup of sweet milk, 1 egg, 1 teaspoonful of salt, 1½ cups of flour, 1 teaspoonful of baking powder, beat together 5 minutes. Bake in gem pans 15 minutes.—*Sister Josie Sloniker, Burroak, Kans.*

Corn Gems.—Take 1 cup of corn meal, 1 cup of flour, 1 cup of sweet milk, ½ cup of lard or butter, ½ cup sugar, 2 eggs, 2 teaspoonfuls of baking powder, ½ teaspoonful of salt. Stir eggs, sugar and butter together.—*Sister W. J. Swigart, Huntingdon, Pa.*

Graham Gems.—Take 1 egg beaten lightly, 1 tablespoonful of shortening, 2 tablespoonfuls of sugar, a little salt, 1 tablespoonful of soda dissolved in boiling water in a pint cup; then fill the cup with sweet milk, stir all together, then add 2 cups of graham and ½ cup of white flour; bake in gem pans.—*Sister Sadie S. Young, Beatrice, Nebr.*

Graham Gems.—Take 1 pint of graham flour, 1 pint of white flour, 2 teaspoonfuls of baking powder, a little salt (about what you can hold between thumb and first finger); sift all these together; add 1 egg well beaten, 1 teaspoonful of shortening, and 2 cups of sweet milk; heat the gem pans and keep them where they will remain very hot while putting the batter in them. Bake in a quick oven.—*Sister Hattie Yoder Gilbert, Los Angles, Cal.*

Graham Gems.—Take 1½ cups of sour milk, ½ teaspoonful of salt, 1 teaspoonful of cream of tartar, 1 teaspoonful of lard, 2 tablespoonfuls of sugar, ½ cup of wheat flour, 3 cups of graham flour sifted, or if sweet milk is used instead of sour, take 1 teaspoonful of baking powder instead of the cream of tartar and soda. Bake in gem pans in a hot oven.—*Sister Annie R. Stoner, Union Bridge, Md.*

Graham Gems.—Mix 2 tablespoonfuls of butter to a cup of cream, add 1 tablespoonful of sugar and 2 eggs, stir well; add 1 cup each of graham and white flour, a pinch of salt, and 2 teaspoonfuls of baking powder; stir this into a smooth batter with sweet milk. Bake in well greased gem pans in a hot oven.—*Sister Laura Smucker, Timberville, Va.*

Graham Gems.—Take 1 cup of white flour, 1 cup of graham flour, 1 teaspoonful of baking powder, 1 cup of milk, a piece of butter the size of a walnut, melted, a little salt, ½ cup of sugar, 1 egg. Bake.—*Sister Mary E. Shafer, Trotwood, Ohio.*

Graham Gems.—Take 1 pint of buttermilk, 1 egg, ½ cup of sugar, 1 teaspoonful of soda, 3 tablespoonfuls of butter, a pinch of salt, graham flour enough to make a stiff dough. Bake in a hot oven.—*Sister Esther H. Sell, Roaring Springs, Pa.*

Oatmeal Gems.—Take 1 pint of oatmeal soaked over night in sweet milk, add the yolks of 2 well-beaten eggs, 2 tablespoonfuls of sugar, a little salt; add the whites beaten to a stiff froth. Bake in hot gem pans 20 minutes.—*Sister Margaret Bricker, Downsville, Md.*

Whole Wheat Gems.—Mix 1 heaping teaspoonful of baking powder in 1 pint of whole wheat flour; add the yolks of 2 eggs, 1 tablespoonful of butter or fresh lard, 1 teacupful of sweet milk, a pinch of salt; then add last the beaten whites of the 2 eggs. Bake at once in a hot oven about 20 minutes.—*Sister S. Cassie Hoover, Bradford, Ohio.*

Whole Wheat Gems.—Take 1 pint of buttermilk, ½ pint of sweet milk, 1 egg, 1 teaspoonful of salt, 1 teaspoonful of soda, 2 tablespoonfuls of sugar, 1 tablespoonful of shortening, and 1 cup of white flour. Then add enough whole wheat flour to make a rather soft batter. Have gem pans greased and hot, when the batter is put in. Bake in a rather hot oven until nicely brown.—*Sister Jennie Neher, Mountain Grove, Mo.*

Muffins.—Take 2 cups of buttermilk, 1 teaspoonful of soda, 2 eggs, 1 teaspoonful of salt, flour enough to make a smooth batter. Pour through a funnel into hot lard and fry in rings. Serve with maple syrup.—*Sister May Hoover, Webster, Ohio.*

Muffins.—Take 1 cup of flour, a pinch of salt, 1 cup of sweet milk, 1 egg, 1 level teaspoonful of baking powder. Bake in gem or muffin tins and serve with maple or sugar molasses.—*Sister Mary E. Towslee, Colby, Kans.*

Muffins or Turnovers.—Take 1 tin of flour, 1 tin of boiling water poured on flour and mixed; stir in 4 or 5 eggs according to size, salt. The batter will not be smooth. Drop by spoonfuls in boiling hot lard, eat while warm with molasses.—*Sister Mattie O. Weaver, Hinkletown, Pa.*

Breakfast Muffins.—Beat 1 egg, add to it 1 cup sweet milk, 2 tablespoonfuls sugar (granulated is best), and a large pinch of salt. Stir well, then sift into it 2 heaping teaspoonfuls of baking powder mixed with 2 cups of flour. Mix, and if batter is not stiff, add a little more flour. Lastly, stir into it a lump of butter size of an egg, which has been previously melted. Bake in hot oven 15 minutes. This quantity will make 12 muffins.—*Sister Lillie B. Cassell, Washington, D. C.*

Buttermilk Muffins.—Take 2 eggs, 1 quart of buttermilk, 1 teaspoonful of soda dissolved in 1 tablespoonful of hot water, 1 teaspoonful of salt, flour enough to make a good batter. Beat the eggs well, add them to the buttermilk, then add the flour, salt, and soda. Pour in muffin pans and bake in quick oven.—*Sister Fannie Michael, Greenland, W. Va.*

Corn Muffins.—Take 1 egg, 1 tablespoonful of sugar, 1 pint of sour cream, 1 cup of corn meal, ½ cup of wheat flour and 1 scant teaspoonful of soda. Drop into hot muffin rings and bake in a quick oven.—*Sister Emma G. Reitz, Friedens, Pa.*

Dyspeptic Muffins.—Take 1 egg, 1 cup of sweet milk, 1

tablespoonful of sugar, 1 scant teaspoonful of baking powder, 1 pint of flour. Drop in gem pans and bake 20 minutes in a hot oven.— *Sister Grace M. Hileman Miller, Lordsburg, Cal.*

Gondaliers.—Put 2 ounces of butter into a pan, add a half pint of hot water, then add hastily a half pint of flour. Stir until smooth, take from fire; and when cool, add 4 eggs, one at a time. Then turn into a pastry bag. Bake in moderate oven thirty minutes in gem pans. If dough is left standing for some time it will be much lighter. While these are baking, boil together 2 ounces of chocolate, 2 cups sugar and a half cup of milk. Boil until it forms soft balls when dropped into cold water. Then spread on the gondaliers.—*Sister Mary H. Hoerner, Auburn, Ill.*

Pop Overs.—Take 1 scant pint of milk, 2 eggs, 1 teaspoonful of soda, a pinch of salt, flour to make stiff enough to fry in hot lard.—*Sister Malinda S. Geib, Mastersonville, Pa.*

Raised Biscuit.—Take 1 pint of new milk scalded, let cool, add a piece of lard and butter together the size of an egg, 2 teaspoonfuls of sugar, 1 teaspoonful of salt, 1 yeast cake dissolved in ½ cup of tepid water, white of 1 egg beaten to stiff froth; mix into a hard loaf in the evening, let stand over night; in the morning, or when light, mould into biscuit; let rise, and bake.—*Sister Amanda Brown, Whitewater, Ind.*

Buns.—Take 2 cups of bread sponge, 1½ cups of sugar, 1 cup of sweet milk, 2 eggs, butter the size of an egg; mix well together, adding enough flour to make a stiff batter. Let it rise until very light. Mix stiff. Let it rise again. Make into biscuits. Let rise again, and bake.—*Sister Ida M. Saylor, Meyersdale, Pa.*

Buns.—At noon soak 1 yeast cake, then add 1 quart warm water, 1 egg, 1 small cup sugar, ½ cup butter. Mix to a stiff batter, and let it rise till bedtime. Then mix not quite as stiff as bread dough. In the morning mould out in tins and let rise 3 or 4 hours. Bake in quick oven.—*Sister Eliza Slifer Cakerice, Conrad, Iowa.*

Buns.—Take 2 cups of bread raising, 1 cup of warm water, ¾ cup of white sugar, ½ cup of lard, flour enough to make it stiff. Let rise, then work it down and let rise again; make it into buns and let rise until very light. Bake in a moderately hot oven.—*Sister J. E. Price, Dallas Center, Iowa.*

Breakfast Buns.—Take 1 cup of bread sponge, 2 cups of luke-warm water, 1 cup of sugar and ½ cup lard. Mix flour in and make stiff as for bread, let rise till night in a cool place, and before going to bed make into little cakes and place on greased pans. Put them far enough from each other to have plenty of room to rise; let rise till morning and bake in a quick oven before breakfast. —*Sister Susie M. Blocher, Greenville, Ohio.*

Cellar Buns.—Take 1 pint of potato beer, the same as you use for baking bread, ½ cup of granulated sugar, 3 tablespoonfuls of lard, ½ teaspoonful of salt. Put all together, mix the same as for bread, put in the cellar to rise and then work out into small cakes. Set them again in the cellar to rise and when very light bake in a moderate oven until nice and brown.—*Sister Emma Fisher, Baltic, Ohio.*

Cinnamon Buns.—Set aside 2 cups of dough after it has had the second rising on baking day. Cream ½ cup of butter and ½ cup of sugar; to this add 1 well-beaten egg and work these into the dough. Add ½ teaspoonful of cinnamon, 1 teaspoonful (scant) of soda dissolved in hot water and ½ cup of currants dredged with flour. Knead diligently for five minutes, make out into buns and let them rise for half an hour, or until they have doubled the original bulk, before baking. Cover for the first half hour they are in the oven; then brown.—*Sister Emma T. Boone, Pasadena, Cal.*

Currant Buns.—Take 3 cups of flour, 1 cup of sugar, 1 tablespoonful of lard, 2 teaspoonfuls of baking powder, 1 cup of currents and a little salt. Use milk enough to make a dough as soft as for biscuits. Bake about twenty minutes in a hot oven.—*Sister Sadie Shank, Downsville, Md.*

Potato Buns.—Take 1 cup of mashed potatoes, 1 cup of

sugar, ¼ cup of lard, 2 eggs, 1 cup of yeast and a little salt.   Mix the above ingredients and add flour enough to make batter as for cake.   Set this sponge after dinner and about bedtime mix as stiff as bread dough.   Grease thoroughly and let rise over night.   Early in the morning mould and let rise again; when very light, bake.— *Sister Anna Brown, Winchester, Va.*

Rice Rolls, or Buns.—Take 2 eggs, 1 cup of sugar, 1 cup of cooked rice, 1 pint of sweet milk, butter the size of an egg, and 4 large tablespoonfuls of yeast.   Make up stiff in the evening.   Next morning knead and let rise again.   Then make out in rolls and put in pans.   When ready for the oven, beat the yolk of 1 egg, mix with a little sugar, and spread on top.   These are fine for afternoon lunch, and if directions are followed, they are sure to be good.— *Sister Alice L. Powell, Polo, Ill.*

Rowland Buns.—Take 1 pint of lukewarm water, ½ cup of lard, 1 cup of sugar, 1 cup of yeast, a little salt.   In warm weather make up about 10 A. M., work until smooth, set away to rise, cover closely to avoid heavy crust.   In the evening late work into tiny rolls and place in pans not too close together, set away until morning; then as soon as you can heat your oven, bake 20 minutes.— *Sister Jas. M. Rowland, Hagerstown, Md.*

Sweet Buns.—Take 2 cups of bread sponge, 1 cup of warm milk and a little flour.   Stir up like pancakes and set to rise.   When light stir in ¾ cup of sugar, ½ cup of lard and a little salt.   Add flour enough to make stiff like bread dough and let get very light before making out in buns.   After made into buns let get very light before putting in oven.   Bake 20 minutes in a moderate oven. —*Sister Viola Sheeler, Kingsley, Iowa.*

Cinnamon Rolls.—Take a portion of your raised dough, roll out to the thickness of half an inch, spread thickly with butter, sprinkle over this a generous amount of sugar and cinnamon, roll up and cut crosswise into slices ½ or ¾ of an inch in thickness. Place in a well-greased pan; let rise again, and bake.—*Sister Mamie Sink, Lenox, Iowa.*

Cinnamon Rolls.—When baking bread, and it is ready to mould in the pans, take out dough the size of a medium-sized loaf; mix into it 1 cup of sugar, butter the size of an egg; add more flour and knead smooth; then roll down to about 1 inch thick, spread over with butter, sugar and cinnamon; then make into a roll, slice in cakes about one inch thick, and place them in a baking pan close together; let rise very light; again spread over with butter, sugar and cinnamon. Bake quickly as light buns.—*Sister M. Lizzie Demmy, Astoria, Ill.*

Cinnamon Rolls.—Sift together 1 pint of flour, 1 tablespoon sugar, ½ teaspoon salt, 1 heaping teaspoon baking powder. Rub in 2 tablespoons butter, mix with milk to soft dough. Roll out ½ inch thick, spread with soft butter, granulated sugar and powdered cinnamon. Roll up like jelly roll, cut in inch slices, lay close together in greased pan, and bake in quick oven.—*Sister Anna W. Frantz, Raisin, Cal.*

Astor House Rolls.—Take 1 pint of sweet milk boiled and while warm put in a lump of butter the size of an egg, 2 tablespoonfuls of sugar, a little salt and ½ cake of yeast dissolved in a little warm water; stir in flour enough to make a stiff batter. When light, put in a little more salt and knead 15 minutes; let rise again, roll out and cut into round cakes, spread each with butter and fold one half over the other half. Put into pans and when light bake in a quick oven.—*Sister Kate Moore Strickler, Eldora, Iowa.*

Graham Rolls.—Scald graham flour with boiling salted water, making a rather soft dough, that can be handled after it is turned onto the moulding board. While pouring the water, stir the dough briskly with a pot stick. Have the moulding board well sprinkled with bolted flour. Knead quickly until smooth, putting on more flour as needed. Roll convenient portions of the dough to the thickness of 1½ inches, flatten slightly with the hands, prick and cut into lengths of three or four inches. Be sure the oven is hot when put in. After they rise, let the heat be a *little* less. We usually bake them on the grate and turn them as soon as well raised. Bake from twenty to thirty minutes. The better the *quality* of the flour, the less stiff the dough will need to be.—*Sister Phoebe Zook, Mattawana, Pa.*

Parker House Rolls.—Take 1 cup of yeast, 1 tablespoonful of sugar, butter the size of an egg, salt, 1 pint of sweet milk and flour enough for a stiff batter. Put the milk on the stove to scald and put the butter in it. Mix the salt, sugar and yeast into the flour and add the milk, being careful not to put it in too hot. Mix up at night and knead thoroughly then. Knead only lightly in the morning, roll to an inch in thickness, cut out with large cookie cutter, spread with butter and fold one half over the other. Let rise again and bake in a quick oven. These are very fine.—*Sister Rachel Armey, Big Timber, Mont.*

Rice Rolls.—Take 1 pint of sweet milk, 1 pint of fresh yeast, 1 teacupful of sugar, 1 teacupful of boiled rice, 2 eggs, shortening the size of an egg, a little salt and flour as for other rolls. Let rise several times before moulding, then let rise light before baking. Bake in slow oven.—*Sister Emma Newcomer, Lanark, Ill.*

Sweet Potato Rolls.—Take 2 pounds of boiled sweet potatoes, mashed very fine, 2 tablespoonfuls of butter, ½ cup of yeast, 1 pint of sweet milk and pinch of salt. Use enough flour to make a soft dough. Let rise till light, then cut into any shape desired, put into pan and let rise one hour and bake. Irish potatoes can be used in same way.—*Sister Cassie Martin, Bloom, Kans.*

Tea Rolls.—Take a piece of bread dough, roll out an inch thick, brush over with melted butter and cover thick with sugar and cinnamon; commence at one side and roll up; then cut in pieces an inch thick, lay in a well-buttered pan as biscuits and bake 20 minutes. —*Sister Annie G. Falls, Dayton, Va.*

Bread Dough Cinnamon Cake.—When bread is ready to put into the pans, take a small piece of the dough, roll it a little thicker than for pie; lay it on a greased pie plate, spread over it a little butter, sprinkle a little cinnamon and sugar over it, let it rise a little, then bake till a light brown color. This is best when eaten fresh.— *Sister G. R. Goughnour, Middlebranch, Ohio.*

Coffee Cake.—Take 1 pint of bread sponge, ⅔ cup of A sugar, 1 egg, 1 cup of raisins and butter the size of an egg, mix in flour to make stiff enough so as not to stick to the hands. Let rise till very light, mould out on pans, and put melted butter, sugar and cinnamon on top. Let rise again till light and then bake slowly about 30 minutes, or according to size of your cake.—*Sister Susie M. Blocher, Greenville, Ohio.*

Coffee Cake (Hygienic).—On bake day take 1 cup of the sponge, add ½ cup of milk, ½ cup of sugar and butter size of an egg. Stir with a strong spoon, adding flour until a stiff dough or batter is obtained. (Do not mix with your hands.) When light, stir down, and when light again, put in two cake pans. (You will find it a little difficult to spread, as it is rubber-like, but moisten the spoon, and your fingers, to prevent sticking then you can readily spread it over the tins.) When light, prepare a top dressing with flour, sugar and butter, as for crumb pie, and put on top with a liberal sprinkling of cinnamon. Have the oven medium hot and bake quickly but not overdone. This delicacy can be attended to when you attend to the bread and will not make much extra trouble. —*Sister Amanda Witmore, McPherson, Kans.*

A Dakota Delicacy.—Take light bread dough, after it is ready for light cakes, a piece as large as a pint cup. Work into the dough ¾ teacup sugar, 3 tablespoonfuls of butter. Roll the size of pie pan. Cover the top neatly with butter. Add to butter 1 teaspoonful of ground cinnamon and 2 teaspoonfuls of sugar. Then let rise till perfectly light. Bake in a moderate oven.—*Sister Caroline Culp, Carrington, N. Dak.*

Cream Rusks.—Take 1 pint of warm water, 1 cup of sugar, 1 cup of rich cream, 1 pint of yeast, or 1 yeast cake previously dissolved in warm water, flour enough for a stiff batter. If wanted for dinner, set to rise the evening before; if desired for tea, for which no bread is better, set early in the morning. After it has risen sufficiently, or over night, work it down several times. This gives the dough a very light and fluffy feeling and makes the rusks perfect in sponginess. When ready to bake, roll about 1 inch in thickness, cut with a cake cutter like biscuits, put in a buttered pan, let rise and bake in an oven heated about the same as for biscuits. If desired, sprinkle with sugar when taken from the oven.—*Sister Flora Teague, Lordsburg, Cal.*

Potato Rusks.—Take 1 pint of mashed potatoes, 1 cup of yeast, 1 pound of sugar, 1 cup of butter, 2 eggs. Mix potatoes, yeast and ½ of the sugar in the evening and let rise over night. In the morning add the remainder of the sugar, butter and eggs; work up same as bread dough; let rise till light, then roll out; cut with a biscuit cutter, put on tins and let rise again. Bake in a moderate oven.—*Sister Sallie E. Keifer, Palmyra, Pa.*

Sweet Rusks.—Take 1 quart of warm milk (new is best), 1 cup of butter. 1 cup of sugar, 2 eggs, 1 teaspoonful of salt, ½ cake of yeast foam; dissolve the yeast in a very little warm water and stir to a paste; make a sponge with the milk, yeast, and flour enough to make a thin batter; let rise over night in a warm place; in the morning add the sugar, butter, eggs, and salt, well beaten together, with flour enough to make a soft dough; let it rise again, then make into round balls and let rise a third time; bake in a moderate oven.—*Sister Mary Wallace, Mt. Morris, Ill.*

Brown Bread.—Take 2 eggs, 1 cup of sour milk, 1 cup of molasses, 1 teaspoonful of soda, 1 cup of corn meal, 2 cups of graham flour, 1 tablespoonful of melted butter, and ½ cup of hot water. Mix and steam 2 hours.—*Sister Lucy Magie, Tropico, Cal.*

Brown Bread.—Take 1 quart of corn meal after it is sifted, 1 pint of flour, 1 quart of sour milk, 1½ pints of molasses, 1 teaspoonful of soda, 1 teaspoonful of salt. Steam 3 hours and then bake just enough to brown the top.—*Sister Nancy Babcock, Nora Springs, Iowa.*

Brown Bread.—Take 3 cups of corn meal, 1 cup of flour, 1 cup of Orleans molasses, 4 cups of milk, 1 teaspoonful of salt, and 1 teaspoonful of soda. Steam 4 or 5 hours.—*Sister Kate Royer, Celina, Ohio.*

Brown Bread.—Take 2½ cups of sour milk and ½ cup of molasses; into these put 1 heaping teaspoonful of soda, 2 cups of corn meal, 1 cup of graham flour and 1 teaspoonful of salt. Pour into a covered mold and steam for 3 hours.—*Sister Laura E. Goetze, Saratoga, Wyo.*

Brown Bread.—Take 2 cups of flour, 2 cups of corn meal, ½ cup of molasses, and 1 teaspoonful of soda. Mix with sour milk so it can be stirred with a spoon. Steam 3 hours.—*Sister Lizzie Mineely, Johnstown, Pa.*

A Good Brown Bread.—Take 2 cups of sifted graham flour, 1 cup of white flour, 2 cups of corn meal, ⅔ of a cup of sorghum or New Orleans molasses, 1 teaspoonful of salt, 1 teaspoonful of soda, sour milk enough to mix rather stiff. Place in a well-greased pan, filling not more than ⅔ full, place over pan a cover also greased—I use an inverted pie plate—and set in a steamer; place cover on steamer and set it over a kettle filled with boiling water, and steam not less than 3 hours. Boiling water, greased pan, steamer, etc., should all be in readiness before mixing is done, as standing after mixing allows the meal to swell and spoils the loaf more or less. Do not allow the water to stop boiling till bread is done; set in an oven to dry off a few minutes; serve hot. Any that is left over may be made as palatable as the fresh by returning to the steamer till heated through.—*Sister Gallop, Redfield, Kans.*

Corn Bread.—Take 1 pint sour cream, 1 pint sweet milk, 4 eggs, ½ cup of lard or melted suet, ½ pint of flour, 1½ teaspoonfuls of soda, 1 tablespoonful salt, and corn meal to make a not too stiff batter. Bake in gem irons or in a cake dish with tube in the center.—*Sister Maggie E. Harrison, Conemaugh, Pa.*

Corn Bread.—Take 1 cup of corn meal, 1 cup of wheat flour, 1 egg, 2 tablespoonfuls of sugar, 2 of melted butter or 3 of sweet cream, and a little salt. Mix with sweet milk, not too stiff, and bake.—*Sister Lizzie Lichty, Morrill, Kans.*

Corn Bread.—Take 1 pint of bolted corn meal, 1 pint wheat flour, 1 pint thick sour milk, 2 eggs, ½ cup sugar, butter the size of an egg. Stir all together, then add 1 teaspoonful soda stirred in a little milk. Bake in a moderate oven.—*Sister Mell E. Wenger, South Bend, Ind.*

Corn Bread.—Take 2 cups of corn meal, 1 cup of flour, 1 cup of sour milk, 1 cup of sweet milk, ½ cup of sugar, ½ cup of molasses, 1 egg, 1 teaspoonful of salt, and 1 teaspoonful of soda; shortening the size of an egg.—*Sister Ida M. Eshelman, Elgin, Ill.*

Corn Bread.—Take 3 eggs, 1 pint of buttermilk, ½ cup of sugar, ¾ cup of lard, 1 teaspoonful of soda, and a pinch of salt; beat sugar and eggs well together and stir in the lard; thoroughly dissolve the soda in the milk. Make a batter about the thickness of soft gingerbread with ½ flour and ½ corn meal; bake in a moderate oven ½ hour.—*Sister Rachel Myers, Ore Hill, Pa.*

Corn Bread.—Take ½ pint of corn meal, ½ pint of wheat flour, 1 pint of sour milk, 1 egg, a piece of butter the size of an egg, ½ teacupful of sugar, salt, and 1 teaspoonful of soda; beat egg, sugar and butter together light; add all the flour, salt and soda, dry. Beat thoroughly and bake in a hot oven.—*Sister Annie R. Stoner, Union Bridge, Md.*

Corn Bread.—Take 2 cups of buttermilk, 2 tablespoonfuls of sorghum molasses, ⅔ of a cup of sifted graham flour, ½ teaspoonful of salt, 2 teaspoonfuls of soda, and 1½ cups of corn meal. Bake in a moderate oven.—*Sister Rachel C. Merchant, Laporte, Ind.*

Fine Corn Bread.—Take 3 heaping teacupfuls of corn meal, 1 teacupful of wheat flour, 4 eggs well beaten, 1 teaspoonful of salt, ¾ teacupful of sugar, 1 teaspoonful of soda, 1 teaspoonful of cream of tartar, and 1½ pints of sour milk. Dissolve the soda in the milk. The cream of tartar should be mixed with the flour while dry. Pour the batter into pans to the depth of 1½ inches. Bake in a hot oven; serve while warm.—*Sister W. P. Englar, Uniontown, Md.*

A Nice Corn Bread.—Take 3 eggs, 1 cup of sugar, 1 cup of sweet milk, ½ cup of butter, 1½ cups of corn meal, ½ cup of wheat flour, and 2 teaspoonfuls of baking powder. Mix the sugar and butter into a cream, then add eggs, mixing well. Mix the baking powder in the flour, put all together, adding a pinch of salt, and stir well. Bake in a moderate oven.—*Sister Anna Bolender, Dayton, Ohio.*

Steamed Corn Bread.—Take 2 cups of corn meal, 1 cup of flour, 2 cups of sweet milk, 1 cup of sour milk, ½ cup of sugar, 1 teaspoonful of soda and a pinch of salt. Steam 2½ hours and dry in the oven for half an hour.—*Sister Mary E. Towslee, Colby, Kans.*

Johnny Cake.—Sift a quart of corn meal into a pan, make a hole in the middle and add 1 teaspoonful of salt and 3 of sugar; stir about in some of the meal and then add 1 tablespoonful of butter or lard. Then pour in hot or scalding water (not lukewarm), make very stiff and pat out smoothly with hands. Bake in hot oven, or in spider on top of stove, or upright on the hearth before a clear fire. When well done split open and butter the halves while hot. Most excellent with honey and milk.—*Sister Mary Gibson, Des Moines, Iowa.*

Mush Bread.—Put 1 pint of milk into a pan; when it is hot put in ¾ cup of corn meal, just as if you were making mush. Add ½ teaspoon of salt, and cook it well. Take from fire and add yolks of four eggs well beaten, stir carefully. Beat whites and add to mixture. Turn into a baking dish and bake in moderate oven twenty minutes. Serve hot and do not remove from pan.—*Sister Mary H. Hoerner, Auburn, Ill.*

Corn Pone.—Take 1 pint of sour milk, 1 pint of sweet milk, 3 eggs, ¼ cup of butter, 1 teaspoonful of soda, 1 teaspoonful of salt, ⅓ of wheat flour and ⅔ of corn meal to make a soft batter. Bake in a moderate oven.—*Sister Lizzie Warble, Mt. Morris, Ill.*

Corn Pone.—Take 2 cups of corn meal, 1 cup of wheat flour, 1 pint of sour milk, 2 eggs, 1 tablespoonful of sugar, 2 tablespoonfuls of butter, a pinch of salt, and 1 teaspoonful of soda. If buttermilk or part cream is used, not much butter is needed.—*Sister Ida A. Bonsack, Westminster, Md.*

Corn Pone.—Take 1 cup of white flour, 1 cup of corn meal, ½ cup of sugar, 2 teaspoonfuls of baking powder. lard size of a walnut, a pinch of salt. Mix the flour, baking powder, meal and sugar together; rub in the lard cold, add salt and mix with a cup of cold water. Bake in a moderate oven.—*Sister Sallie E. Kiefer, Palmyra, Pa.*

Corn Pone.—Take 2 cups of corn meal, 1 cup of flour, ½ cup of sugar, ½ cup of melted lard, 1 egg, 1 even teaspoonful of soda, and a pinch of salt. Take sweet milk enough to make a thin batter. Then bake till done.—*Sister Ida E. Gibble, Lykens, Pa.*

Corn Pone.—Take 1 pint of buttermilk, butter the size of an egg, 1 heaping teaspoonful of soda, ½ cup of sugar, 1 pint of wheat flour, and 1 pint of corn meal. Stir well together and bake in a moderately hot oven about 20 minutes.—*Sister Anna G. Reitz, Friedens, Pa.*

Corn Pone.—Take 2 cupfuls of corn meal, 2 cupfuls of wheat flour, 1 cup of sugar, ½ cup of melted butter. Add 1 beaten egg, 1 scant teaspoonful of salt, 1 teaspoonful of soda; mix with enough fresh buttermilk to make a moderately stiff batter. Bake in a hot oven. Serve with cream or butter.—*Sister Alice Smith, Rockton, Pa.*

Corn Pone.—Take 1 cup of sweet milk, 1 cup of sour, or buttermilk, ¼ cup of lard, 2 eggs, a little sugar, and corn meal enough to make a batter, not too stiff, and a little salt and 1 teaspoonful of soda. Mix and bake brown.—*Sister Lizzie G. Arnold, Albert City, Iowa.*

Corn Pone.—Take 2 cups of corn meal, 1 cup of wheat flour, ½ cup of granulated sugar, and 1 teaspoonful of salt. Mix well together, then add 2 eggs and 1½ cups of good sour cream with a heaping teaspoonful of soda. Have the batter about the thickness of loaf cake and bake 20 or 30 minutes.—*Sister Daniel Hoover, Washburn, Iowa.*

Corn Pone.—Take 2 cups of corn meal, 1 cup of flour, 1 cup each of sweet and sour milk, ½ cup of sorghum molasses, 1 tablespoonful of melted butter, 1 egg, salt to taste, and ½ teaspoonful of soda. Bake in a moderate oven in not too shallow pan for about 40 minutes.—*Sister Lydia Bucher, Astoria, Ill.*

Corn Pone.—Take 1 pint of sour cream, 1½ pints of sweet milk, 2 pints of corn meal, ½ pint of wheat flour, 3 eggs, and 1 tablespoonful each of salt and sugar, or season to suit taste, ½ teaspoonful of soda.—*Sister E. S. Moore, Eldora, Iowa.*

Old-Fashioned Corn Pone.—Make 3 pints of corn meal mush. Cool this with ½ gallon of water; thicken this with meal until it is as stiff as dough. Put in a pint of flour, and salt to taste. Make this up in the morning, and let rise until the afternoon. Thicken a little more with corn meal and put in a greased pan. Place in a hot oven and bake a little longer than common corn bread.—*Sister Eliza Weaver, Sinking Spring, Ohio.*

Soft Corn Bread.—Take ¾ of a quart of corn meal, ¼ quart of wheat flour, 1 cup of sugar, and 1 level tablespoonful of salt. Pour over this enough boiling water to make into a stiff paste, add 2 eggs and thin with sweet milk to make a thick batter. Lastly, add 1 teaspoonful of baking powder. Bake about forty minutes. This will be of fine grain and will stay soft. Eat with butter or syrup. If any is left over, it can be sliced out and fried.—*Sister W. E. Prigel, Gittings, Md.*

Graham Bread.—Make a beer and sponge it with white flour as you would for white bread. When it is light add graham flour till it is as stiff as you can stir with a spoon. Let this rise. When light mix stiff with white flour or graham flour whichever you prefer. Let rise again and mold into loaves. Make small loaves and put them into round pans; let rise again and bake one hour.—*Sister Maggie Waggoner, Celina, Ohio.*

Nut Bread.—Take 1 cup of nuts, either rolled or ground, 2 cups of sour milk, ½ cup of sugar, ½ cup of molasses, 1 cup of raisins, 2 cups of graham flour, 1 cup of white flour, 1 tablespoonful of melted shortening, 1 teaspoonful of baking powder, and 1 tea-spoonful of soda. Dissolve soda in a little boiling water.—*Sister Emma T. Boone, Pasadena, Cal.*

Nut Bread.—Sift 3 cups of flour, 1 teaspoonful of salt and 5 teaspoonfuls of baking powder together, then add ½ cup of sugar. 1 scant cup of milk, 1 egg well beaten, and lastly 1 cup of floured nuts.—*Sister Edna Crowe, Des Moines, Iowa.*

Economical Way to Use Dry Bread.—Soak dry bread in water for several hours, or until it becomes soft, then with the hands work it into a pulpy mass; stir in more flour and water with a cup of yeast; let rise, and it will be a good bread sponge for light bread. —*Sister M. C. Whitesel, Wayside, Wash.*

Bread.—Take 6 potatoes, boil and mash fine, add 1 teaspoonful of salt, ½ cup of sugar, boiling water enough to make 3 quarts of sponge; stir in flour until thick; when cold add yeast; let it rise till morning, then add flour to stiffen, work smooth, let rise, work down, then mold into pans, and when light bake in a moderate oven.—*Sister Perry Broadwater, Lonaconing, Md.*

Bread.—For the yeast take 1 handful of good rivels, 1 table-spoonful of sugar, 1 tablespoonful of salt, 1 handful of flour, stir in about 1 pint of lukewarm water. Leave it a day or so in a cool place; then in the evening before you want to bake, take 3 medium-sized potatoes, pare and boil till soft; take out the potatoes, put a small handful of hops in the potato water. Let the hops boil a short time; mash the potatoes, add 1 big spoonful of flour, salt, and sugar; strain the hops and pour the boiling water over the flour and potatoes; then put in water until the whole is lukewarm (it will take about a quart of water), then pour it in your yeast can, stir well together. Let it sit over night. In the morning take out about 1 pint of potato beer for the next baking; take the rest of the beer, strain, stir in flour till it stirs nicely; let it stand till it is light, then put in flour, knead it stiff; let it rise, then put it in pans; let rise till light, then bake in a moderate oven about 1 hour.—*Sister G. R. Goughnour, Middlebranch, Ohio.*

Bread.—Put the flour in a warm, dry place in an open pan to dry thoroughly before using. Take 1 quart of warm water, 1 small teacupful of yeast, flour enough to make a stiff batter; let rise over night in a warm place. In the warmest weather let rise about 3 hours; then add flour enough to knead without sticking to the pan, knead ½ hour; set to rise again, when risen sufficiently, knead 10 minutes without using more flour; mold into loaves; set to rise, and bake 1 hour.—*Sister Amy Roop Shaw, Westminster, Md.*

Good Bread.—At night take 1 pint of potato water, sometimes the potatoes, 3 tablespoonfuls of sugar and 1 of yeast dissolved in lukewarm water. Pour into a crock potato water, yeast, sugar and one sifter of flour. Next morning take three sifters of flour (warm flour always), and 1 tablespoonful of salt. Pour in the yeast and 1 pint of water. Mix stiff, let rise, knead and let rise again and make into loaves. Then let rise until when dented it stays dented. It is then ready to bake.—*Sister Edna Shearer, Girard, Ill.*

Good Light Bread.—To make a good light bread, boil 6 good-sized potatoes till tender, pour all into a vessel containing 2 large spoonfuls of flour, mash all together until smooth, then add cold water till milk warm. Add about 1½ pints of good fresh hop yeast; set it to rise over night; in the morning warm it slightly and strain through a colander into the flour in the tray, making a thin sponge; let it rise till light; then salt to taste and put in a large handful of sugar, knead moderately stiff, and when light, mold into loaves.—*Sister L. Schock, Huntington, Ind.*

Good Light Bread.—Take 1 egg well beaten, 1 heaping tablespoonful of lard, 1 tablespoonful of sugar, 1 tablespoonful of salt, 1 yeast cake that has been previously soaked in warm water, 1 quart of lukewarm whey; stir in 1½ pints of sifted flour; let rise over night. In the morning add 1 quart more of whey, stir in flour until it is the consistency of pancake batter; let rise till very light, then knead to a stiff dough; after standing an hour, work down, then when it is nicely risen knead into loaves; let rise and bake in a moderately hot oven for 40 minutes. After removing from the oven, rub a little lard over each loaf.—*Sister Jennie Neher, Mountain Grove, Mo.*

Good Light Bread.—Soak 1 cake of yeast in a cup of luke-warm water for 2 hours in summer; then stir in flour to make a thin batter and let stand until light, say about 2 hours. In the evening when getting supper peel and cook 2 or 3 medium-sized potatoes in plenty of water. When done mash in the water they were cooked in; if too thick put some more water in to make thin. Before going to bed stir the yeast in this. In the morning put what flour you need in the bake pan, then pour this potato and yeast in and stir a batter tolerably thick. Let this rise until very light, make up stiff, let rise again, work down and let rise again. Then mould out in pans, let rise again and when light bake.—*Sister Della Smith, Eldora, Iowa.*

Light Bread.—Use good home-made rivels. To two parts water use one part whey and 1 tablespoonful each of salt, sugar and lard to each half gallon of liquid. Mix to a stiff batter in the even-ing. In the morning work stiff and knead well. Let rise, then work in loaves, let rise light, and bake ¾ to 1 hour, according to the size of the loaves. In cold weather leave part of the water until morning to stir in hot. Stir briskly so you won't scald the sponge.—*Sister Florence Hays Kline, Broadway, Va.*

Perfect White Bread.—Take 1 cake of compressed yeast,—if this cannot be had, use dry yeast,—break up fine and dissolve in a cup of lukewarm water. Take 3 pints of milk and water (half of each) and put into a large pan, add a large tablespoonful of salt and same amount of sugar. Now stir in the dissolved yeast and add flour till stiff enough to knead. Knead until it will not stick to bread board. Set to rise. As soon as light knead again for about ½ hour, then make into loaves and put into pans and let rise. After it is light bake in a moderate oven. This makes a small baking and requires no work in the evening previous to baking.—*Sister Minnie Mae Cripe, Delphi, Ind.*

Light Bread without Potatoes.—Soak ½ cup of yeast in a little warm water at supper time. Then before bedtime take 3 pints of lukewarm water, 1 tablespoonful of sugar, and two pounds of flour; stir all together. It should be a little thicker than pancake dough. When the yeast is soaked and light add to above batter and let it rise until morning, or until it is light. Then add 1 pint of warm water and 1 tablespoonful each of sugar, salt and lard. Sift about 3 pounds of flour into a pan or dough tray, pour the sponge into the flour and knead it stiff, or about 15 minutes kneading. Set in a warm place, let rise until it is light, then knead down. Let rise again, mold into loaves and put into pans. Let rise until light, then bake about one hour in a moderately hot oven. Then take out of pans and put on a table or board and grease the loaves slightly while hot, with butter or lard.—*Sister Mary E. Ritter, Crescent, Okla.*

Quickly Made Salt-Rising Bread.—Pour boiling sweet milk on a heaping tablespoonful of corn meal and stir to a smooth paste. Then set this snugly covered in a real warm place over night. The next morning this should be swelled up light. Heat half a cupful of sweet milk and cool to a good warm temperature, not scalding, with a cupful of water. Into this stir a pinch of salt, a pinch of soda, a level tablespoonful of sugar, the light corn meal and flour for a smooth batter. Set this in a vessel of warm water snugly covered till it foams up twice the size of first quantity. Next take a deep pan or bowl and a cupful of sweet milk, a pint of warm water, the light sponge and flour to make a smooth, stiff batter. Sift over this one inch of flour, set contents in warm water snugly covered, and when the sponge breaks through all over and at the edges, sift a pile of flour on the moulding-board and pour out on it the light sponge, catching it up and kneading it up into a soft mass. Pinch into three loaves and put into greased pan, allowing an inch for rising; grease top of loaves with butter. When risen to top of pan bake forty minutes in a quick oven.—*Sister M. M. Cooney, Nebr.*

To Make Light Bread.—Take 4 good-sized potatoes, boil until done and mash in another dish; pour potato water over potatoes and set away to cool. When still slightly warm add 1 yeast cake, ½ cup of sugar and 1 tablespoonful of salt. Set in a warm place and let foam, it should foam within twenty-four hours. Take potato water and a few potatoes the evening before you want to bake and add above to it. Let sit over night. The first thing in the morning stir mixture and take out a pint and a half of liquid and place in quart fruit jar, adding ½ yeast cake and place in cool cellar to use next baking day. Now add sufficient water to remaining liquid to make baking as large as desired and mix stiff. Let rise till light and make into loaves. Let rise again and bake.—*Sister Zelma Bosserman, Burkey, N. Dak.*

To Make Bread with Spook Yeast.—Spook yeast is a liquid, and what we like about it is that it takes less time and trouble than other kinds of bread. After the yeast is started some should be saved from one baking, to bake with the next time, by sealing it up in a fruit jar. To make it, take 1 cake of yeast foam and soak in 1 cup of warm, unsalted potato beer; add 1 tablespoonful of sugar, and set in a very warm place, just warm enough that it does not scald. Stir now and then, and if it does not foam inside of 5 hours, it is very likely no good, and should be started again with new yeast. In about 24 hours it will be ready to use. Strain out the corn meal, and at noon add 3 cups of potato beer, and 1 teaspoonful of sugar to each cup of beer that is added. Stir off and on, and see that it foams. Let it stand till evening, and just before going to bed, mix up the bread. Take 3 cups of water, or less if less bread is wanted and more for more bread, 1 tablespoonful each of lard and salt, 3 cups of the yeast (seal up the remaining cup and set in the cellar, or some other cool place) and flour enough to make stiff, but not quite as stiff as other bread dough. Put all together and knead well. Let it rise over night. Make into loaves the first thing in the morning the earlier the better. Let it rise 3 or 4 hours, or until very light, and bake 1 hour. This makes 5 loaves of bread. This kind of bread will stand more rising than other bread. The second time you bake, open the jar of yeast, and put in potato beer as before.—*Sister Olive M. Heckman, Polo, Ill.*

White Bread.—Pare and cook 3 medium-sized potatoes in 1 quart of water; when soft scald 1 tablespoonful of flour with the potato water; mash the potatoes fine and mix with the scalded flour; when cool, add 1 quart of warm water and 1 cup of home-made yeast (which has been soaked) or ¼ cake of yeast foam, let stand over night and add 1 quart of sifted flour; let rise and stir down 2 or 3 times; add 2 tablespoonfuls of salt and mix with flour enough to make a stiff dough; let stand in a warm place ½ hour, mix down and let rise again; shape into loaves and bake 1 hour in a moderate oven. Graham bread: Make same as for white bread except use ¼ graham flour and add 1 cup of sugar.—*Sister Minnie M. Whisler, Udell, Iowa.*

When mixing bread try standing on a footstool instead of setting pan on a chair.—*Sister L. Clanin, Hicksville, Wash.*

Yeast.—Take 12 good-sized potatoes, boil and mash fine; save the water they were boiled in, and have a small handful of hops, boiled in a separate pan; strain the hop water; add 1 teacupful of sugar and the same of salt; put all together to make 1 gallon. Always save a pint of the yeast to start with when you make again. Keep corked in a jug in a cool place.—*Sister Amy Roop Shaw, Westminster, Md.*

Yeast.—Grate 2 large potatoes, add 3 pints of boiling water, 1 tablespoonful of sugar, and 1 tablespoonful of salt. Stir all together; when cold add 1 cup of baker's yeast. Let it rise, then set away.—*Sister Perry Broadwater, Lonaconing, Md.*

Beer Yeast.—Take 4 large potatoes, 1 double handful of hops, put in a sack and boil with the potatoes; dip the potatoes out of the water when done into a gallon crock and mash them fine, then pour the water over gradually; mix well, then fill the crock with cold water and stir in ½ cup of salt, 1 cup of sugar, 1 pint of good yeast; then set in a warm place to ferment. Eight hours will suffice, and then tie up and keep in a cool place.—*Sister Eliza A. Wenger, Long Glade, Va.*

Good Dry Yeast.—Take 3 tablespoonfuls of corn meal and 1 tablespoonful of wheat flour, 1 tablespoonful of salt; then pour over boiling water until well mixed; when cold, add a cupful of good yeast, then set in another vessel containing warm water; when it rises, stir down; let it rise again, then stir in corn meal to make it just stiff enough to handle; break in small pieces and dry in the air.—*Sister Eliza A. Wenger, Long Glade, Va.*

Homemade Yeast.—First make a hop tea, using 1 handful of hops; scald 1 quart of water thoroughly, using the hop tea and sufficient boiling water thoroughly to scald the flour; when this is cool, add 1 cup of dry yeast previously soaked in lukewarm water, place in a warm place to rise, stirring often lightly; when perfectly light, add 1 tablespoonful of ginger, 1 tablespoonful of sugar, 1 teaspoonful of salt, 1 teaspoonful of powdered alum dissolved in warm water; make into a loaf with corn meal. Let rise over night, then pinch off and spread to dry in a cool, airy place.—*Sister Catharine Snyder, Robins, Iowa.*

Jug Yeast.—Take 6 large potatoes, 1 handful of hops, ½ cup of sugar, 1 cup of flour, 1 quart of water. Boil the potatoes and hops together (hops in a bag). When done, mash the potatoes, squeeze out the hops, pour over the sugar and flour. When cool, add 1 cup of yeast or 3 yeast cakes. Keep warm 24 hours, then put in a jug, but do not seal until it has risen.—*Sister J. E. Price, Dallas Center, Iowa.*

Sponge for Light Yeast.—Take 12 good-sized potatoes and boil in 1 gallon of water; have 1 cup of sugar and 1 cup of flour mixed in a 2-gallon jar; pour over this the potato water boiling hot, then whip the potatoes and put them in when lukewarm, put in 1 cup of yeast and let it rise till next day. For bread: To 3 pints of flour, add 1 tablespoonful of sugar, 2 tablespoonfuls of lard or butter, 1 teaspoonful of salt, 1 egg, enough of the sponge to make a soft dough, work 20 minutes and make into rolls or loaves. Let rise 1½ hours, and bake.—*Sister D. S. Thomas, Bridgewater, Va.*

Light Bread Yeast.—In the morning when you make light bread save a cupful of the sponge, add a teaspoonful of sugar and cornmeal to make it stiff enough to pinch off into small pieces, or to press into a roll and cut into slices, and dry in the air.—*Sister Mary E. Ritter, Crescent, Okla.*

Potato Yeast.—Take 2 medium-sized potatoes and grate them; take a small pinch of hops—peachtree leaves will do—and boil in a quart of water; strain, and add 1 tablespoonful each of salt and sugar. Let it come to a boil, then stir in the grated potatoes. When cool, add a little good yeast; set it away until it rises, then it is ready for use. Keep in a cool place. One teacupful of the yeast is enough to make 10 or 12 loaves of bread.—*Sister Rachel E. Gillett, Camp Verde, Ariz.*

Communion Bread.—Take 1½ pints of sweet cream, butter the size of two eggs, ½ cup of white sugar, and flour enough to make about like pie dough. Bake in sheets, marking each sheet into strips and piercing the strips with a fork before baking. Flat sheets of tin kept for the purpose are nice for baking it on.—*Sister E. S. Moore, Eldora, Iowa.*

Communion Bread.—Take 3 pints of milk and 1 pound of butter, and as much flour as to give it a body similar to pie dough. Divide it into 4 parts and work each part until it blisters; then roll out till about the thickness of pie dough. Lay it off with a ruler an inch broad into inch strips, at the same time cutting the creases or divisions about half the thickness of the cake. Perforate each strip with 2 rows of holes from end to end and then bake. This will make enough for 250 members.—*Sister Sadie K. Imler, Ridgely, Md.*

Unleavened Bread or Communion Bread.—Sift for 2 or 3 times 3 parts of graham flour and 1 part of bolted flour; stir into it with a spoon 1 pint of sweet cream. When as stiff as can be stirred, remove to kneading board and knead well; bake in a moderate oven. This is sufficient for 50 communicants.—*Sister Emma Click, Tekoa, Wash.*

Vegetables

We should cultivate the habit of eating plenty of vegetables, and to do this easily we must know what particular food elements the various vegetables afford and then learn to prepare each vegetable in the most appetizing and wholesome ways. Much of the value of vegetables depends on the cooKing; their nutritive elements may be wasted by soaking, burning, cooking too long or not long enough. Since all vegetables are compounds of cells surrounded by a woody fiber, rapid boiling tends to toughen this fibre and break up the cells, allowing many of their principles to be lost that should be retained as food. When vegetables are put on to cook the water should be kept steadily boiling until they are done. No arbitrary rules can be laid down as to the length of time vegetables should be cooked, since the time varies with the age of vegetables, their manner of growth, degree of freshness, nature of water used for cooking and degree of heat applied. The skillful cook will consider these influences and soon control them successfully. Green vegetables should be cooked with cover partly withdrawn, as this method gives them a better color and more delicious flavor. All delicately flavored vegetables, such as asparagus, peas and potatoes, should be cooked in only enough water to cover them, while those with strong flavor, as dandelions, cabbage, carrots, onions and turnips, should be cooked in a generous quantity of water. Vegetables specially lacking in fatty substances, as peas and beans, should have butter or some substitute in their dressing. In fact almost all vegetables are improved by a seasoning of this kind. Beets, turnips, squash, peas and generally beans require some sugar as seasoning to make up for the sweetness lost in boiling. Cabbage and lettuce contain alkalies and should therefore be served with an acid condiment or seasoning. Onions are not only a wholesome food in themselves, being almost the best nervine known, but they are excellent used as seasoning for many other dishes.

Baked Apples.—Take 18 apples, pare and quarter; put 1 layer of apples in a pan, sprinkle 1 teaspoonful of sugar, 1 teaspoonful of butter, and 1 tablespoonful of flour over them. Put in 5 layers of the apples, then pour over them ¾ teacupful of water. Flavor with lemon to suit the taste; bake in a quick oven; serve while warm.—*Sister H. G. Miller, Bridgewater, Va.*

Baked Apples.—Select as many good baking apples of same size as wanted for use, halve them, but do not pare; take out the core and in each half put a large teaspoonful of sugar and a piece of butter the size of a hickory nut, and bake. Serve with cream or not, as desired.—*Sister Jennie B. Miller, Robins, Iowa.*

Baked Apples.—Peel and cut in halves five or six good tart apples. Soak three tablespoonfuls of tapioca several hours. Then put two tablespoonfuls of butter, one cup of sugar and one tablespoonful of flour in a dish; pour one pint of boiling water over it and stir until all is dissolved. Put your tapioca in this and pour it over the apples; put in hot oven and bake until apples are done.—*Sister Tuda Haines, North Manchester, Ind.*

Baked Apples.—Cut apples into halves (do not peel), put in a bread pan, sprinkle over them sugar, nutmeg and flour, pour over them 1 cup of cream or milk and lay bits of butter on top and bake.—*Sister Elizabeth Piper, Ossian, Ind.*

Fried Apples.—Pare the apples and slice them a little thicker than potatoes for frying, put them into a pan in which there is melted butter, sprinkle sugar over them to season to taste, put in a pinch of salt, and sprinkle cinnamon over them. Fry slowly until brown.—*Sister Lizzie Harnish, Mt. Carroll, Ill.*

Fried Apples.—Use rather tart apples. Do not pare but cut them in halves and core. Place in a frying pan open side up; then season with sugar to taste, a little salt, butter, flour, ground cinnamon, and a dash of pepper. Then pour on a little water, cover the pan and let them cook soft and dry after which remove the lid and brown nicely.—*Sister Katie Moore Strickler, Eldora, Iowa.*

Riced Apples.—Boil ⅔ of a cup of rice in sweet milk, put in a little salt and some butter. Have ready some good cooking apples; that is, have them pared and cored; put in a pan and pour the cooked rice over them. Bake till the apples are thoroughly done. Serve with cream and sugar.—*Sister Hattie Yoder Gilbert, Los Angeles, Cal.*

Roasted Apples.—Pare and core 12 large apples, put them in a pan and then in a hot oven to roast. When roasted, put 2 tablespoonfuls of sugar and 1 teacupful of cream over them. Serve while warm.—*Sister H. G. Miller, Bridgewater, Va.*

Asparagus with White Sauce.—Cook 1 bunch of asparagus 1 hour or less, according to age, then drain off all the water, season with pepper and salt. Add a spoonful of butter and a dressing made of 1 tablespoonful of flour and 1 cup of sweet cream. Serve on buttered toast.—*Sister Katie E. Keller, Enterprise, Mont.*

To Cook Asparagus.—Cut the asparagus into small pieces, boil until tender; add butter the size of a walnut, season with salt and pepper, then add 1 teacupful of cream into which has been mixed 1 scant tablespoonful of flour. Stir until it boils. Toast brown pieces of bread, put in a dish, then pour the asparagus over them and serve while hot.—*Sister Bernice Ashmore, Mansfield, Ill.*

Baked Bananas.—Allow 1 level tablespoonful of sugar, 1 teaspoonful of melted butter, a few grains of salt, 1 teaspoonful of lemon juice, and 2 tablespoonfuls of water to each banana. Bake till the fruit is red and the syrup thick.—*Sister Pearl Weimer, St. Elmo, Va.*

Baked Beans.—Cook dried beans until soft, then put in a pan, season with salt and ½ cup of sugar or molasses; put in oven and bake until brown.—*Sister Mary Rowland, Astoria, Ill.*

Baked Beans.—Take 3 pints dry Lima beans soaked in plenty of fresh water over night. In the morning drain the water off and put the beans on to cook in cold water. Boil until tender, then drain again, and set aside. In the meantime boil a 3 or 4 pound piece of beef until done, then remove the beef from the broth and add to the broth 1 teaspoonful of prepared mustard, 4 tablespoonfuls of tomato catsup or Chili sauce, 1 tablespoonful of salt, ⅓ teaspoonful of pepper. Strain this mixture over the beans in a baking pan and then lay 6 thin strips of bacon over the top, and then place the pan with contents in a hot oven. Bake until thoroughly done and the top nicely browned over.—*Sister Viola Mohler, Warrensburg, Mo.*

Baked Beans.—Take 1½ pints of navy beans, soaked in clear water over night. Put on to boil in cold water, boil till thoroughly done. About 8 o'clock put in the oven a 2 or 3 pound pork roast. When done remove from pan, make a thickened gravy in the pan where the meat has been roasted, then put in the beans. Salt and pepper and mix well. Bake in a moderate oven.—*Sister Winnie E. Duncan, Denbigh, N. Dak.*

Baked Beans.—Look over and wash 3 cupfuls of beans and put to soak over night, in plenty of water. As soon as fire is kindled in the morning put them in a pan, pot, or closely-sealed kettle, add 1 pound of salt pork or bacon (salt pork is best), 1 teaspoonful of ground mustard, 1 teaspoonful of black pepper, 1 teaspoonful of soda, 1 teaspoonful of salt, 2 tablespoonfuls of cooking molasses, 1 tablespoonful of sugar and 1 pint of water. Bake from four to six hours, adding more water if necessary. They should be a rich brown and moist when done.—*Sister M. M. Cooney, Enders, Nebr.*

Baked Beans.—Take 1 quart of small white beans, 1 onion, ½ cup of white sugar, 1 tablespoonful of salt, and a slice of salt pork. Boil all together on top of the stove for a half hour. Cover the kettle tightly and set in the oven with water not quite covering, stir two or three times, when brown enough cover with water again and bake until tender. Serve cold or warm.—*Sister Sadie Hays, Le Grand, Cal.*

Boston Baked Beans.—Boil soup beans until soft. Put in a pan a layer of beans, then a layer of tomatoes cut in pieces. Sprinkle with salt, pepper, sugar and syrup. Continue until you have the pan full, ending with beans on top. Slice breakfast bacon in thin slices, cut into small pieces, fry and stick these pieces down into the beans. Pour the grease that fried out of the meat over all. Bake until brown.—*Sister W. E. Prigel, Gittings, Md.*

Boston Baked Beans.—Take 1 quart of white navy beans, wash and let soak in water over night. In the morning boil with plenty of water till beans begin to break, then pour off water and put into baking jar, adding bits of salt pork, as the beans are put in, using as much pork as you wish for seasoning. When the beans are all in put on top 2 tablespoonfuls of baking molasses, pepper, and salt and cover with fresh water. Bake from 6 to 8 hours, adding water to keep beans covered.—*Sister Chas. H. Brown, Omaja, Cuba.*

Creamed Beans.—String and break green beans in small pieces, cook in salted water until tender; pour off the water in which they were cooked. To ½ gallon of beans add 1 teacupful of sweet cream or rich milk, butter the size of a hulled walnut. Canned beans are as nice cooked in this way as green beans.—*Sister Lula O. Trout, Hollins, Va.*

Fried Beans.—Put butter, meat fryings, or any grease preferred into a flat-bottomed kettle, let get smoking hot, then drop in string beans that have been washed and prepared for cooking. Add salt and pepper and cover. Stir often, and as they begin to dry, add a little hot water each time. Cook one hour and they will be fine.—*Sister Sadie. Finch, Portersville, Cal.*

Green Beans.—For 2 quarts of green beans, put ½ cup of butter and lard into a kettle; when very hot, add 1 tablespoonful of flour. Brown well, then add 1 cup of water, and then the beans. Stir well, cover with water, and when tender, cook dry.—*Sister H. P. Albaugh, Chicago, Ill.*

Green Beans.—Prepare the beans for cooking, scald them in boiling water, let them remain in the water until it becomes luke-warm; then put them on to cook with meat. Add salt and a little sugar.—*Sister Margaret A. Cawly, Sidney, Nebr.*

Lima Beans.—Remove the unripe ones from Lima beans, cook the beans in water until they are tender, then when about dry, season with salt, pepper, and a small piece of butter, and pour over them about ⅔ of a cup of cream, and let them come to a boil. Dried Lima beans are cooked in the same way.—*Sister Grace Gaffin Price, Oregon, Ill.*

String Beans.—Cook the beans until tender in salted water and drain. Have some onions and chillies sliced, mix with the beans and fry. A few tomatoes added before removing from the fire, makes a good dish.—*Sister J. F. Thomas, Inglewood, Cal.*

Boiled String Beans.—Slice a half pound of bacon as for frying, place it in the kettle and fry it slowly until done. Add a spoonful of flour, a spoonful of sugar and water, the amount depending on quantity of beans; let come to a boil, then add the string beans and cook about three hours.—*Sister Jos. H. Johnson, Royersford, Pa.*

Baked Red Beets.—After you have washed the beets, place them in a baking pan with a little water. Cover them and as soon as soft pickle them the usual way. They are delicious.—*Sister Jos. H. Johnson, Royersford, Pa.*

Fried Young beets.—Take young and tender red beets, boil until quite tender, then peel, hash fine, then fry in butter, add salt to taste, fry lightly until seasoned through. In taste this is a substitute for green corn.—*Sister Amanda Witmore, McPherson, Kans.*

Beet Hash.—Take ⅔ cold boiled potatoes and ⅓ cold boiled beets; chop these together until fine as mince meat; have your skillet hot with a large spoonful of butter in it browned, scrape your hash into it, salt and pepper it, and pour over it a cupful of sweet cream, that is, that much cream for a skillet full of hash, if you have less hash use less cream; stir it slightly and serve hot or cold.—*Sister Bessie Miller, North English, Iowa.*

Italian Beets.—Take ½ dozen beets, ½ cup butter, 6 table-spoons of flour, ⅔ cup of lemon juice, 3 cups of water and 3 tea-spoons of salt. Method.—Cream two-thirds of butter and flour, add water and salt and stir constantly. Just before serving add re-mainder of butter and the lemon juice. Pour over the cooked beets which have been sliced, and serve.—*Sister Bertha Dutcher, Sterling, Ill.*

Beet Sauce.—Take 1 cup of vinegar and water mixed, 1 tablespoonful of sugar, then salt, and pepper, add butter the size of a walnut; thicken with 1 tablespoonful of cornstarch; let come to a boil, then pour over beets which have been cooked soft and cut into small pieces. Serve hot.—*Sister Joseph Amick, Elgin, Ill.*

Boiled Cabbage.—Boil a piece of salt pork, and when almost done add cabbage which has been washed and cut in large pieces; boil with the meat until tender; salt to taste and add 1 large table-spoonful of sugar. At the table add vinegar and pepper.—*Sister Ella V. Roller, Carrington, N. Dak.*

Cabbage with Celery.—Cut 1 gallon of cabbage, add 4 bunches of celery cut fine, 1 tablespoonful of mustard seed; mix all together, put in a porcelain or granite kettle with ½ pint of water, 1 pint of vinegar, and ½ pint of sugar; boil till tender, not too done. It can be canned if sealed while hot.—*Sister D. F. Kelley, North Georgetown, Ohio.*

Creamed Cabbage.—Cut fine a head of cabbage that is tender and crisp; put 1 tablespoonful of lard and 1 tablespoonful of butter in a pan and brown it, put in the cabbage, season with 1 teaspoonful of salt and a dash of pepper; fry it 5 minutes, then pour ½ cup of cream over it and serve.—*Sister Fannie Zug Hostetler, Mt. Joy, Pa.*

Creamed Cabbage.—Beat together the yolks of 2 eggs, ½ cup each of sugar and vinegar, and a piece of butter the size of an egg, salt and pepper to taste, 1 cup of cream. Add all together in a saucepan, and stir till it boils. Pour over finely-cut cabbage.—*Sister Amanda Nicholson, Hillsdale, Pa.*

Creamed Cabbage.—Cut cabbage into 4 or more pieces, according to size of head, and boil in salt water until tender; remove carefully with a fork and place in a colander to drain for a few minutes. Put into a large pan enough butter to oil well; when slightly brown, dust each piece of cabbage with seasoned flour and put in the pan, but do not allow them to overlap each other; place the pan in a slow oven and turn carefully until each piece is light brown, then pour over it ½ cup of rich sweet cream and remove from fire when cream is heated. The secret of having this dish just right is in being careful that no portion of the tender cabbage is allowed to become too brown. If some parts are too brown, remove the brown portion before adding cream.—*Sister Emma Click, Tekoa, Wash.*

Creamed Cabbage Slaw.—Take 1 head of solid cabbage, chopped very fine or cut on the slaw cutter, a small pinch of salt, ½ cup of vinegar, ½ cup of granulated sugar, and ½ pint of thick sweet cream; put sugar in cream and whip stiff; put vinegar over cabbage first then the whipped cream, and serve.—*Sister R. L. Powers, Grant City, Mo.*

Fried Cabbage.—Cut the cabbage fine, salt and pepper to taste, work until juicy, then put into hot grease to fry; stir often to prevent browning, and when done add a little sweet cream. Put no water about the cabbage, as it destroys the sweetness.—*Sister Charity White, Ari, Ind.*

Fried Cabbage.—To 1 medium-sized cabbage head, cut with a slaw cutter, take a scant ½ pint of water. Fry with 1 large tablespoonful of butter, with salt and pepper to taste.—*Sister M. L. Fellers, Roanoke, Va.*

Cabbage Slaw.—Take the yolks of 2 eggs, 1 teaspoonful of sugar, ½ teaspoonful of salt, and 2 tablespoonfuls of vinegar; cook in a double boiler; thin with water if too thick; when cold pour over chopped cabbage.—*Sister Flora Doughty, Eldora, Iowa.*

Cold Slaw.—Take 1 quart of sliced cabbage, ½ pint of sour cream, ½ teaspoonful of salt, 2 tablespoonfuls of sugar, 1 tablespoonful of good vinegar, mix well together. If you can get it cold enough to froth, froth it, which is much nicer than when left plain.—*Sister Mary Wampler, Dayton, Va.*

Cold Slaw.—Cut cabbage very fine; to 1 quart of cabbage take 1 cup of rich sour cream, and ½ cup of sugar; mix well. If you do not have the cream, use 1 cup of sweet milk, 2 tablespoonfuls of sugar, and a little vinegar.—*Sister Mary E. Whitney, Kearney, Nebr.*

Cold Slaw.—Sprinkle with salt 1 quart of finely-cut cabbage. Mix together 1 cup of sour cream, ¼ cup of good sour vinegar, and ½ cup of sugar and add pepper. Pour over the cabbage and mix well.—*Sister Lura Flickinger, Morrill, Kans.*

Cold Slaw.—Cut cabbage very fine, salt, and let sit a few minutes, then press with your hands. Take ½ cup of thick sweet cream, 4 tablespoonfuls of sugar, and vinegar to suit the taste. Pour over cabbage and mix thoroughly.—*Sister Cassie Bowser, Lineboro, Md.*

Hot Slaw.—Boil the slaw tender, with just enough salted water to keep from burning. For dressing take 2 tablespoonfuls of sour cream, 2 teaspoonfuls of sugar, pepper, and 3 tablespoonfuls of vinegar. Pour over cabbage, bring to boiling point, and serve at once.—*Sister Sarah Hohf, Mt. Morris, Ill.*

Pickled Cabbages.—Slice 1 head of cabbage fine, then salt and pepper it and press it down firmly with the hands or a potato masher. Then pour over it sufficient vinegar to cover, adding a little sugar and mustard seed if liked, and it is ready to serve.—*Sister Mary McDannel, Elgin, Ill.*

Scalloped Cabbage.—Take ½ head of cabbage, 2 tablespoonfuls of flour, 4 eggs, 2 ounces of butter, 1 pint of milk, 1 teaspoonful of salt, and a dash of pepper. Wash and chop the cabbage coarsely, throw it into boiling salted water, boil 20 minutes, drain. Have ready 4 hard-boiled eggs chopped fine, and put the butter into a saucepan; when melted add the flour and milk, stirring it constantly until it boils, add the eggs, salt and pepper. Put the cabbage in a dish, pour over it the sauce, sprinkle with bread crumbs and bake in a hot oven for 15 minutes.—*Sister Sarah Reese Eby, West Elkton, Ohio.*

Stewed Cabbage.—Take tender fresh cabbage, about 1 pound, cut pretty coarsely, put on to boil in boiling water and cook 15 minutes. Then drain, put on sweet milk to cover and then stew until tender. Take 1 heaping tablespoonful of butter, mixed to a paste with 1 teaspoonful of flour, pepper and salt to taste. Boil up and serve.—*Sister Nancy Bahr, Damascus, Oregon.*

Warm Slaw.—Take the yolks of 2 eggs, 2 tablespoonfuls of sugar, 2 tablespoonfuls of sour cream, 1 cup of vinegar, butter the size of a walnut. Boil all together and pour over finely cut cabbage. *Sister Myra Troyer, Baltic, Ohio.*

Warm Slaw.—Cut 1 head of cabbage up fine. Take butter the size of an egg, the same amount of lard (meat fryings are nice), put in a kettle, let get hot, then put in the cabbage; season with salt and pepper, add enough water to boil cabbage tender. When cooked tender and dry, make a dressing of 1 tablespoonful of flour, ½ cup of sweet milk, and 1 egg. Just before lifting the cabbage, put over it 4 tablespoonfuls of vinegar, then add the dressing, stirring it through the cabbage. Let it come to a boil, take up and serve hot.—*Sister Sarah C. Myers, Syracuse, Ind.*

Warm Slaw.—Put into a well-heated skillet one tablespoonful of lard, add 1 quart of finely-chopped cabbage, 1 teaspoonful of salt, 1 of sugar, and 1 small cup of vinegar. Stir until heated through, then serve immediately.—*Sister C. H. Diehl, Jonesboro, Tenn.*

Dressing for Warm Slaw.—Prepare cabbage in the usual way, make a dressing as follows: Take 1 egg well beaten, 3 table-spoonfuls of sugar, ½ cup of sweet cream, ½ cup of vinegar. Pour over slaw, boil a few minutes, serve hot.—*Sister Cassie Bowser, Lineboro, Md.*

Mustard Dressing for Cold Slaw.—Chop cabbage fine in chopping bowl, then salt and let stand while you fix dressing as follows: 1 cup vinegar, 1 cup sugar, 1 egg well beaten, butter size of an egg, 1 teaspoonful of mustard, 1 tablespoonful of flour. Cook all together. Then squeeze cabbage out, put in a dish and add dressing. This is excellent.—*Sister J. N. Brumbaugh, Sabetha, Kans.*

For Cooking Cabbage.—Have the water at the boiling point. Put the cabbage in and then cook rapidly for ¾ to 1 hour, adding a little sugar.—*Sister I. C. Myers, Greenmount, Va.*

Boiled Sauerkraut.—Wash fresh spare ribs or backbone and add kraut with sufficient water to prevent boiling dry. Boil until done.—*Sister Catharine Snyder, Robins, Iowa.*

Fried Sauerkraut.—Place in frying pan butter and lard in equal parts, when hot add kraut and fry until done; not too brown. *Sister Catharine Snyder, Robins, Iowa.*

Sauerkraut and Knep.—Boil 1 quart of kraut for 20 or 30 minutes, after which add a batter made as follows: Take 1 well-beaten egg, 3 tablespoonfuls of flour, ½ teaspoonful of baking powder, a pinch of salt, add milk sufficient to make a batter just stiff enough to drop from the spoon. Add this to the boiling kraut, by spoonfuls, and boil all together for 20 minutes.—*Sister Catharine Snyder, Robins, Iowa.*

Fried Carrots.—Scrape and slice carrots ¼ inch thick, cover with salted water, and boil until tender. Drain, roll each slice in flour and fry in 2 tablespoonfuls of lard in a hot skillet, browning on both sides. Place in a hot dish and sprinkle each layer well with sugar.—*Sister Nora E. Petry, Westminster, Md.*

Carrots.—Scrape 6 nice-sized carrots and cut crosswise into thin slices. Put on in cold water and boil 20 minutes. Drain carefully, then sprinkle a tablespoonful of sugar over them, also a dash of pepper and salt, 2 tablespoonfuls of butter and 1 very finely minced onion. Add a pint or a little more of thin meat broth, and boil slowly nearly an hour. About 5 minutes before serving, add a small bunch of finely-minced parsley.—*Sister John E. Mohler, Warrensburg, Mo.*

Stewed Carrots.—Pare and slice carrots, put them on the stove with enough water to cook them tender, drain, and cover with milk sweetened to suit taste, and cook 5 or 10 minutes longer.—*Sister M. C. Whitesel, Wayside, Wash.*

Corn on Cob.—Select ears of corn not too far advanced in milk stage, thoroughly clean off all silk. Then place in a porcelain or agate cooking vessel previously filled with boiling water to which enough salt has been added to season well. Cook 30 minutes or until done. Serve hot with salt and plenty of fresh butter.—*Sister Jane Thomas, Carrington, N. Dak.*

Fried Corn.—Take 6 juicy ears of corn and shave it off the cob; heat a lump of butter the size of a small egg; when hot put the corn in and fry not too hard; when done, add salt and pepper. break 3 eggs over the corn, and scramble.—*Sister Mary Taylor, Spring City, Pa.*

Corn Fritters.—Take 12 ears of sweet corn, score through the center of each row, press out the pulp with a fork, add 3 well-beaten eggs, 1 cup of milk, 1 teaspoonful of salt, a little pepper, 1 teaspoonful of baking powder, and flour to make a batter not too stiff; fry in deep, hot, lard; serve hot.—*Sister Margaret Bricker, Downsville, Md.*

Stewed Green Corn.—To 1 quart of corn add 1 teaspoonful of salt and enough water to cook well done; then add 1 tablespoonful of sugar and a piece of butter the size of an egg. If butter is plenty, more butter will improve the corn.—*Sister Sadie Boyer, Lena, Ill.*

Corn Oysters.—Mix into one pint of corn, 3 tablespoonfuls of milk, 1 cup of flour and a piece of butter the size of an egg, Drop by dessertspoonfuls into a little hot grease and fry on both sides.—*Sister Edna Crowe, Des Moines, Iowa.*

Corn or Sham Oysters.—Take 8 large ears of field corn, well filled, score and scrape or press out the pulp, leaving all hulls on cob. To this pulp add 2 eggs, 2 tablespoonfuls of thick cream, and beat thoroughly. Put 2 tablespoonfuls of lard or butter in a frying pan and when hot drop the mixture by spoonfuls into it. When brown on one side, turn and brown the other. Serve very hot.—*Sister Gertrude F. Finnell Seese, Uniontown, Pa.*

Scalloped Corn.—Take 1 can of corn or the same amount of fresh sweet corn, put a layer of the corn in a pudding dish, pepper and salt to taste, then a layer of rolled cracker crumbs; continue in this order till the corn is all used, finishing with a layer of cracker crumbs and butter; pour over milk until it appears above the top layer, put in oven and bake ½ hour or until a nice brown. —*Sister Addie Blocher, Pearl City, Ill.*

Corn Souffle.—Heat one pint of milk with ½ teaspoonful of salt. Stir into the milk ¾ cup of cornmeal. Cook until smooth and thick. Add 4 eggs, beaten separately, the whites last. Bake in a pan of hot water about twenty-five or thirty minutes. Serve at once.—*Sister Myrtle Blocher, Greenville, Ohio.*

Baked Hominy.—Take 1 quart of sweet milk, 1 cup of cold cooked hominy flakes, 3 eggs, 2 tablespoonfuls of sugar and a little salt; bring the milk to a boil and stir in the hominy and salt. Let cool and then stir in the beaten eggs and the sugar · bake 30 or 40 minutes. The top may be *meringued* with the beaten whites of a couple of eggs and 2 tablespoonfuls of sugar, or not, as preferred Serve with any pudding sauce or with cream and sugar.—*Sister D H. Ikenberry, Quinter, Kans.*

Hominy Croquettes.—To each cupful of cold boiled hominy, necessary for the family, put 1 teaspoonful of melted butter or drippings, stirring well together; add sufficient milk to make a paste; beat 1 egg with 1 teaspoonful of sugar to each cup of hominy used; mix in, and with floured hands roll into balls (croquettes) and fry in butter or drippings. If made rather stiff, they may be dipped in beaten egg and then in cracker crumbs before frying.—*Sister D. H. Ikenberry, Quinter, Kans.*

Flake Hominy.—Place the required amount of hominy flakes in a thick vessel, porcelain or crockery, with sufficient salt to season, and pour on boiling water. Stir frequently and add more water as needed; cook about 20 minutes and serve with butter or cream and sugar, as desired.—*Sister D. H. Ikenberry, Quinter Kans.*

Fried Hominy.—Boil hominy until done, season with butter and salt; put some meat fryings into a skillet, put in hominy, stirring often; fry till a good brown.—*Sister Elizabeth Rogers, Hanging Rock, W. Va.*

Succotash.—Cook the beans with a piece of bacon for two hours. Then add to each half gallon of beans, one quart of green corn cut from the cob. They should be boiled dry.—*Sister Florence Hays Kline, Broadway, Va.*

Succotash.—Use double the quantity of corn to that of string beans. Cook the beans until very tender, then add the corn (if new corn, cut very fine) and cook 15 minutes.—*Sister L. N. Moomaw, Roanoke, Va.*

Succotash.—Take a piece of boiling beef and cook with it about an equal quantity of beans and sweet corn; then make rivels of 1 egg and enough flour to work it into small crumbs or pieces; put these rivels into the soup and boil 15 or 20 minutes; serve while hot. Fresh green beans (no pods) and fresh sweet corn are best, but soup beans and salted, canned, or even dried corn is very nice. The amount of beans, corn, and rivels may be proportioned to suit. —*Sister Katie Moore Strickler, Eldora, Iowa.*

Cucumbers Fried in Batter.—Pare 2 or 3 large cucumbers, cut them in slices ¼ inch thick, sprinkle with pepper and salt, press with a light weight for an hour or two, drain on a napkin; dip each slice in beaten egg, then in cracker dust, and fry in butter until a light brown.—*Sister S. E. Neff, Huntington, Ind.*

Fried Cucumbers.—Slice nice, large cucumbers, salt and let stand for about ½ hour, press as for salad; have ready 2 beaten eggs and bread crumbs or rolled crackers, dip cucumbers into eggs and crumbs and fry in cottosuet or lard and a little butter.—*Sister D. Buckwalter, Los Angeles, Cal.*

Stewed Cucumbers.—Pare 6 cucumbers, cut into quarters, remove the seeds; put 1 tablespoonful of butter into a frying pan with 1 small onion sliced, fry until brown, then add the cucumbers, shake them carefully until they are a light brown, then lift them out carefully with an egg-slice; add 1 tablespoonful of flour to the butter remaining in the pan, mix until smooth, then add ½ pint of stock. Stir constantly until it boils, season with salt and pepper, return the cucumbers, cover and stew gently 20 minutes. Serve on squares of buttered toast.—*Sister F. Mae Zug, Mastersonville, Pa.*

Dandelion Dressing.—To ½ pint of sweet cream and milk take 1 egg, 1 teaspoonful of flour, 2 teaspoonfuls of sugar, salt, vinegar to taste; mix all together; put lard in pan, heat, then pour in the dressing; let come to a boil, then stir in the dandelion; heat just enough to scald it. Let stand about 10 or 15 minutes and serve.—*Sister Esther H. Sell, Roaring Spring, Pa.*

Fried Eggplant.—Pare the eggplant and cut in slices ¼ inch thick; place slices in a vessel and cover with water, adding 2 tablespoonfuls of salt; let it stand 2 hours. When ready, prepare a batter of 2 eggs, ½ cup of milk, and 2 tablespoonfuls of flour; dip each slice into this batter and roll in cracker dust on both sides; fry in hot butter a golden brown on both sides.—*Sister Lizzie Hackman, Mastersonville, Pa.*

Baked Eggplant.—Take 2 medium-sized eggplants, 1 pound of ham, 2 or 3 onions, and 3 medium-sized slices of bread. Grind these, add salt and pepper, and mix well. Bake 1 hour.—*Sister Esther M. H. Brown, Omaja, Cuba.*

Kohl Rabi.—Take 1 quart of pared and sliced kohl rabi; boil in salt water until tender, drain, and dress with 1 cup of sour cream, 1 tablespoonful of sugar, 1 tablespoonful of butter, ½ cup of vinegar, a little salt and 1 tablespoonful of flour. Let boil up once and serve.—*Sister Nora E. Petry, Westminster, Md.*

Baked Onions.—Onions are delicate and delicious cooked thus: Cover 6 large ones with boiling water; boil 10 minutes, drain and cover again with boiling water; add ½ teaspoonful of salt and boil till tender but firm. Drain, put in a baking dish, sprinkle with salt, put a lump of butter on each and cover with rich milk; give a heavy sprinkling with bread crumbs and bake till a light brown. The milk can be heated before put in the baker, requiring less heat in the baker than if put in cold.—*Sister Mary Wampler, Dayton, Va.*

Creamed Onions.—Prepare as many onions as are wanted, slice them, cook in boiling salted water until tender and drain. Then make a white sauce of 1 cup of milk, 2 tablespoonfuls of butter, 2 tablespoonfuls of flour, and a pinch of salt. Mix butter and flour together, stir into the milk and cook till thick; then add onions. —*Sister Pearl Weimer, St. Elmo, Va.*

Fried Onions.—Heat 1 rounding tablespoonful of lard; pour into it ½ gallon of sliced onions and a scant ½ cup of hot water; add salt and a pinch of sugar; cover and let cook until tender. Remove the cover and let fry a rich brown, taking care that they do not burn.—*Sister Lula Goshorn, Ladoga, Ind.*

Delicious Fried Onions.—Put 2 tablespoonfuls of lard into a pan and let it become hot. Then put in 1 quart of sliced onions, stir frequently until tender and add a heaping tablespoonful of flour and 1 tablespoonful of vinegar. Stir and cook until done. Season with pepper and salt and serve hot.—*Sister Susie M. Hout, Sharpsburg, Md.*

Escalloped Onions.—Take 2 quarts steamed onions, ¾ quart cream sauce, ½ quart bread crumbs, 2 tablespoonfuls butter and ⅔ tablespoonful salt. Place one quart of the onions in the bottom of a well-oiled baking dish, then one-half the salt and 1 tablespoon of butter, then one-half the bread crumbs, then one-half the cream sauce, now add the remainder of the onions and other ingredients accordingly. Finish with three-fourths cup of finely-rolled cracker crumbs. Bake until a nice brown.—*Sister Bertha Dutcher, Sterling, Ill.*

Hygienic Way of Preparing Onions.—Take onions of about equal size, peel, leave whole, parboil once, pouring the water off, then boil until very tender, which will take two to three hours. Boil dry or drain well, put in a vegetable dish, and sprinkle over with salt. Have ready rich, sweet milk, brought to a boiling heat, and pour over the onions. A little butter added to the milk will improve them but is not as hygienic. Cooking the onions without salt will render them very sweet and palatable. Try it.—*Sister Amanda Witmore, McPherson, Kans.*

Scalloped Onions.—Parboil 12 sliced onions. Prepare cracker or bread crumbs enough to make a layer of crumbs and of onions, putting crumbs first, and on the top adding butter, salt, and pepper to season. And last pour over 1 pint of milk and bake.—*Sister W. J. Swigart, Huntingdon, Pa.*

Stewed Onions (Excellent).—For a small family, prepare about one dozen small onions (mature ones), parboil them a few minutes, drain and add boiling water enough to cover them, also add ½ teaspoonful of salt, a sprinkling of red pepper and a lump of butter the size of a hickory nut. Boil until tender. Then add half a cup of cream and let boil a minute or two longer. Serve hot. —*Sister N. D. Underhill, Collbran, Colo.*

Stewed Onions.—Take about 12 large onions, slice, and cook in salt water until done; then put in butter the size of a walnut, and about a cup of cream, and pepper to taste. Be careful not to let it boil, as it will curdle, only let it get good and hot.—*Sister Nettie Smith, Red Cloud, Nebr.*

Parsnip Balls.—Take about 1 quart of parsnips cooked well done and mash fine, season with butter, salt and a little good cream; add 3 well-beaten eggs, 2 small tablespoonfuls of flour; mix well, form into balls, and fry in plenty of butter.—*Sister Clara Alstadt, Carrington, N. Dak.*

Fried Parsnips.—Pare parsnips and cut lengthwise; boil in salt water until tender, take out, and drain; roll in flour and fry in hot butter until nicely browned.—*Sister Mary E. Shafer, Trotwood, Ohio.*

Fried Parsnips.—Pare and slice parsnips and fry in lard just the same as raw potatoes.—*Sister M. C. Whitesel, Wayside, Wash.*

Stewed Parsnips.—Prepare and put the parsnips to cook in a porcelain kettle in 1 quart of water, stew for 15 minutes, drain, pour over them 1 quart of boiling water, cook from 45 to 60 minutes, drain again, season with pepper, salt, and butter, or fresh beef stock if you have it.—*Sister E. E. Scroggs, Centerview, Mo.*

Baked Pears.—Halve and core your pears and make the following mixture: To one cup of sugar add 1 cup of flour and a heaping tablespoonful butter. Mix well and fill each half with this mixture and put enough water in pan so as not to burn. Bake until well done. Apples can be baked in the same way.—*Sister Grace Moats, Polo, Mo.*

Dried Peas.—Wash well in warm water a good-sized cup of peas, then put them into the kettle in which they are to be boiled with plenty of cold water, and let them soak for twelve or fourteen hours. When they are swelled up nicely, season with salt to suit taste and put in butter the size of a walnut and boil slowly until done, being careful to add water, if necessary, to prevent them from burning. When cooked, mix to a cream a small teaspoonful of flour and add to ½ cup of cream (not milk), then pour it into the kettle and stir a few minutes while boiling. The water should not be drained off the peas before adding the dressing, neither should there be too much water, or they will lack flavor.—*Sister Lovena S. Andes, Elgin, Ill.*

Green Peas.—Shell peas and put in cold water for 10 minutes; take out and put in boiling salt water and cook till tender; add a tablespoonful of sugar; take up, drain, put in a hot dish and pour melted butter over them. Season to taste with pepper and salt. Serve at once.—*Sister Perry Broadwater, Lonaconing, Md.*

Green Peas.—To 1 quart of green peas shelled, put ½ cup of butter in a stew pan; when very hot, turn in the peas, stir quickly, add boiling water to cook, salt to taste; when ready to serve, add ½ cup of sweet cream.—*Sister J. D. Teeter, Rex, Fla.*

Garden Peppers Stuffed With Meat.—The sweet peppers form one of the nicest receptacles for the use of cold meats—beef, mutton, chicken, or turkey. Chop the meat fine, mix with an equal quantity of cold boiled rice or bread crumbs, add a few tomatoes (with the seeds removed) chopped fine, and also 1 chopped onion and a little salt. Remove the tops and seeds from the peppers, scald and wash them, fill with the meat mixture, stand in a baking dish, add ½ cup of stock, or water and a little butter, and bake in a slow oven one hour, basting frequently.—*Sister J. F. Thomas, Inglewood, Cal.*

Baked Potatoes.—Wash nice and clean, cut in thick slices, lengthwise, a common-sized potato. Cut in about 4 slices, lay them in the oven. Bake until well done, nice and brown, when they will be crisp and palatable and good enough for a guest. To pare them makes them nicer, but it is not considered as healthful.—*Sister Amanda Witmore, McPherson, Kans.*

Baked Potatoes.—Pare medium-sized potatoes, roll in flour and put in dripping pan, with a generous quantity of butter and lard; season well with salt and pepper, bake till done. Serve with cream gravy made by adding flour to the grease that is left in the pan. After the potatoes have been taken up, brown slightly, add milk or cream, and let boil up.—*Sister Alice Garber, North English, Iowa.*

Baked Potatoes.—Scoop out the inside of a well-baked potato, add salt, butter and hot cream. Beat until white and light. Put this back into the shell and return to the oven until the exposed filling is a golden brown. This is an attractive, appetizing dish for an invalid's tray.—*Sister Oma Karn, Covington, Ohio.*

Browned Potatoes.—Pare the potatoes, cut them in halves, put in the dripping pan, season with salt, pepper, and butter the size of an egg, add ½ pint of water. Let them bake until done; then take a spoonful of flour and ½ pint of cream and make a dressing and put over the potatoes. Let them come to a boil, then dish and serve hot.—*Sister Lizzie E. Smith, Morrill, Kans.*

Potato Cakes.—Take any cold pork that may be left over, chop fine, add 3 times as much cold mashed potatoes as you have meat, enough eggs to make a thin batter, season with salt and pepper; beat well and fry the same as griddle cakes.—*Sister S. E. Renner, Payette, Idaho.*

Potato Chips.—Have potatoes clean, pare them, wipe dry with clean cloth. Slice thin on slaw cutter, only slicing several potatoes at a time, as they color if sliced long before frying. Have 1½ pints of lard real hot. Drop the sliced potatoes into this. Stir carefully once or twice while frying, only allow them to become a light-brown. Lift into a sieve or colander to drain, afterward putting them into an earthen or porcelain vessel, sprinkling a little salt over them as you put them into this. When cold, cover and keep in a dry place, where they can be kept for a few weeks. The lard can be used a number of times if covered and kept in a cool place. Use a wire spoon or wide fork for stirring and lifting the potatoes.

They are to be kept dry in order to retain the crispness, which makes them more palatable.—*Sister J. P. Holsinger, Mt. Morris, Ill.*

Potato Chowder.—Pare 6 good-sized potatoes, dice them and put on to boil in clear water with a medium-sized finely-shredded onion. Dice about ⅓ of a pound of nice bacon and put it into a skillet and fry a nice brown, then add the bacon to the potatoes, first pouring off most of the grease. Put 2 tablespoonfuls of butter into the skillet, add a tablespoonful of flour and about ½ pint of rich milk, more if you like it thin; after this boils up, pour it into the potatoes and bacon, add salt, red pepper, and a small bunch of minced parsley; let it boil up well and serve hot.—*Sister John E. Mohler, Warrensburg, Mo.*

Creamed Potatoes.—Pare and cut potatoes into dice-shaped pieces; season with salt, pepper, and butter; add water to cook them. Cook until soft, but not mushy. Then make a thickening of flour and milk and stir it into the potatoes. Let boil up and serve.—*Sister L. H. Funk, Kansas City, Mo.*

Dewey Potato Cakes.—Take 2 cups of cold mashed potatoes, the well-beaten yolks of 2 eggs, season with salt, pepper, and a very little nutmeg. Mix well together, make into round cakes, roll in flour, fry in butter, turning carefully; beat the whites of the eggs to a stiff froth and spread on top of each cake. Bake a delicate brown.—*Sister Mary E. Whitney, Kearney, Nebr.*

Potatoes With Dressing.—Pare as many potatoes as you wish and put into a kettle to cook with plenty of water to prevent burning. Boil a few minutes while you prepare a dressing, the same as for chicken. Make in balls and drop into the kettle with the potatoes and cook briskly for one-half hour. Prepare a cream gravy and pour over all when done. Let come to a boil and serve. —*Anna Zimmerman, Mt. Solon, Va.*

Fried Potatoes.—Chop potatoes very fine, put them into a frying pan with a little hot fat; when they have slightly browned on the bottom, turn and fry until thoroughly cooked.—*Sister Mary E. Whitney, Kearney, Nebr.*

French Fried Potatoes.—Pare potatoes and slice lengthwise about ¼ inch thick, cutting the slices in strips the same thickness, lay on a dry cloth. Have a skillet half full of hot lard, drop the potatoes in this, stirring once or twice while frying. Let them fry until a light brown, lift into a colander with a wire spoon to drain, salt and turn them in a dish; serve hot.—*Sister Lillie Wagner, Virden, Ill.*—If the fat is too hot they will not be cooked well on the inside when they are brown enough on the outside.—*Sister Pearl Weimer, St. Elmo, Va.*

Fried Potatoes and Onions.—Pare ½ gallon of potatoes, cook in salt water, slice 6 large onions and fry in grease till soft; slice the potatoes with the onions and let fry 10 minutes. Salt to suit the taste.—*Sister H. G. Miller, Bridgewater, Va.*

Potato Fritters.—Take 4 small potatoes, mash till smooth, add 1 quart of sweet milk, 4 eggs, 1 teaspoonful of baking powder, a little salt, flour enough to thicken. Drop in hot lard and fry in small cakes. Serve hot.—*Sister Ella Miller, Darlow, Kans.*

Potato Hash.—Peel 1 quart of onions and 1 of potatoes. Slice them together and boil them tender in ½ gallon of water. Then add 1 pint sweet cream, a lump of butter the size of an egg. A good supper dish.—*Sister Charlotte Roberts, Artemas, Pa.*

Mashed Potatoes.—Pare the potatoes, wash and put on to cook in enough water to keep them from burning, put some salt in while cooking, stick with a fork and see when done. Mash fine, add butter and cream to make as thin as you want them.—*Sister Sadie A. Good, New Market, Va.*—When the potatoes are ready to mash put the cream on the stove in a vessel and when hot add to the mashed potatoes.—*Sister Florence Hays Cline, Broadway, Va.*

Mashed Potatoes.—Mash and beat your potatoes until quite light and white. Season with salt, butter, and rich milk. Then make a division through the center of the potatoes, have 2 well-beaten eggs, whites and yolks separate. Stir the whites in one half, yolks in the other. Now take a large spoonful alternate, stack on a pie pan, smooth a little, set in hot oven for 15 minutes to brown.

With a broad knife blade place on potato tureen.—*Sister Mary B. Peck, Manvel, Texas.*

Baked Mashed Potatoes.—Boil, cook and mash potatoes, add milk and cream with 2 well-beaten eggs, stir until light and drop in well-buttered pan by spoonfuls, bake in oven till nicely brown.—*Sister Anna Zimmerman, Mt. Solon, Va.*

New Potatoes.—Select potatoes of the same size, about the size of a large egg, boil until just tender in salt water and drain. Have a frying pan with a generous amount of hot lard and a lump of butter in it, and carefully lift the potatoes with a fork or spoon into the hot grease. Fry a nice brown on both sides. They should not break but remain whole. They are a nice dish for company or any one.—*Sister L. Clanin, Hicksville, Wash.*

To Cook New Potatoes.—Cook potatoes in salt water until tender, cut in halves, then dip in flour and fry in butter until a nice brown, the same as you would fry chicken.—*Sister Clara Ringer, Oregon, Ill.*

Potato Puffs.—Take 2 cups of cold mashed potatoes, 1 cup of sweet milk, 2 eggs well beaten, and 1 tablespoonful of melted butter. Stir well together, bake in gem pans, and serve while hot. —*Sister Laura Barklow, Lordsburg, Cal.*

To Roast Potatoes.—Half boil large potatoes, drain, put them into a small pan under meat that is roasting, baste them with some of the drippings; when they are browned on one side then turn and brown the other. Serve with the meat.—*Sister Amy V. Furry, Johnsville, Md.*

Scalloped Potatoes.—Take 3 pints of thinly-sliced potatoes, lump of butter the size of an egg; put in a deep dish, salt and pepper to taste, add sweet milk to cover the potatoes, then put in the oven and bake.—*Sister Charity White, Ari, Ind.*

Scalloped Potatoes.—Take about 1 quart of bread crumbs, put in oven and brown a light brown; then pare and slice potatoes; take a pan 3 inches deep or any size that will suit the family; first put in a layer of potatoes, then bread crumbs, a little salt, pepper, and butter till the amount is all used; then cover with milk and set in a hot oven and bake ½ hour.—*Sister M. C. Whitesel, Wayside, Wash*

Scalloped Potatoes.—Pare as many potatoes as you wish. Slice them. Then take a bread pan and put in enough potatoes to cover the bottom. Sprinkle salt and bits of butter over them, and then another layer of potatoes, salt and butter, and so on until the potatoes are all in the pan. Then pour in rich milk, enough to cover the potatoes. Set in oven to bake. Bake until the potatoes are soft and a little brown on top. Serve while warm.—*Sister Ella Heckman, Cerro Gordo, Ill.*

Scalloped Potatoes.—Pare and slice the potatoes the same as for frying, place half of them in a baking pan, season with pepper, salt, and bits of butter; then add the other half of the potatoes and season again the same as before. Pour in enough sweet milk to cover the potatoes. Bake in the oven about 1 hour, or until the potatoes are soft. Cold boiled potatoes may be used the same way and do not require more than ½ hour for baking.—*Sister Mary Snowberger, Leeton, Mo.*

Cold Scalloped Potatoes.—Hash fine cold boiled potatoes, put in a pudding dish or skillet, pour over boiling milk with a little butter and salt to season. Bake 1 hour or more, until the milk is all taken up by the potatoes. Quite palatable if just right. Raw potatoes can be scalloped the same, only slice instead of hash the potatoes.—*Sister Amanda Witmore, McPherson, Kans.*

Sour Potatoes.—Take about 1 quart of pared potatoes, cut them in thick slices, put in a stew kettle with 1 pint of water and cook until done. Let 2 tablespoonfuls of lard get hot in a frying pan, then stir in a tablespoonful of flour; have ready ½ teacupful of vinegar and 1 teacupful of good sour cream; pour it into the lard and flour, stir, then season with salt and pepper; when it boils, pour it over the potatoes and serve.—*Sister Sarah Miller, Sabetha, Kans.*

For Cooking Potatoes.—Have the water boiling hot when the potatoes are put into the pot, either pared or with the skins on. —*Sister I. C. Myers, Greenmount, Va.*

In frying sliced potatoes, especially the last old ones or the first new ones, just sprinkle a teaspoonful of flour over them and salt and pepper to taste and mix thoroughly when first put on and see how much quicker and better they brown, do not use any water on fried potatoes, but have the lard smoking hot before they are put in. A cast iron skillet is best for good results.—*Sister L. Clanin, Hicksville, Wash.*

To Cook Sweet Potatoes.—Pare potatoes and cut lengthwise, put in a vessel, cover with beef or chicken broth, cook quickly.—*Sister Ida B. Hamilton, Springport, Ind.*

To Cook Sweet Potatoes.—For ½ gallon of potatoes, take 1 cup of sugar, butter the size of a walnut, 1 tablespoonful of flour, and a little salt. Put all in a kettle and let brown just a little, then add about a quart of water and boil until almost dry, and there will be a good, rich syrup over the potatoes.—*Sister Lizzie Warble, Mt. Morris, Ill.*

Sweet Potatoes Baked with Apples.—Take 4 large sweet potatoes or 6 medium-sized ones, the same number of apples, 1 cup of sugar, ½ cup of butter and ½ pint of hot water. Scrub potatoes clean; boil until tender, slice, after having peeled them, in slices ¼ of an inch thick. Pare the apples, slice them in the same way and put in baking dish in alternate layers. Sprinkle the sugar on top and scatter the butter over the top; pour over the water and bake one hour slowly. Serve hot, as a vegetable.—*Sister Pearl Weimer, St. Elmo, Va.*

Creamed Sweet Potatoes.—Pare the potatoes, cut in pieces, and boil in salt water till nearly done, then season with butter and a little sugar, and add 1 cup of sweet cream. Put the seasoned potatoes into a pudding dish and bake slowly until done.—*Sister John E. Metzger, Rossville, Ind.*

Baked Sweet Potatoes.—Pare and cut lengthwise in rather thin slices. Roll in flour. Lay in a large pan, in which are lard and butter melted. Sprinkle with salt and sugar. Add some water. When baked on the underside, turn. Bake slowly.—*Sister Nettie C. Weybright, Syracuse, Ind.*—We add the sugar and salt to the flour in which the potatoes are rolled, but do not use any water in baking them. This is an excellent way to prepare sweet potatoes.—*Sister Blanche Lentz, Elgin, Ill.*

Baked Sweet Potatoes.—Take ½ gallon of sweet potatoes, wash and pare; put them into a stew pan with enough water to cook them half done; then take a dripping pan and melt in it a piece of butter the size of an egg; put the potatoes in the melted butter and turn them so they will be buttered all over; sprinkle a little sugar over them, and bake in a moderately hot oven until they are brown. They are then ready to serve.—*Sister Sarah Shirk, Plattsburg, Mo.*

Boiled Fried Sweet Potatoes.—Pare and cut potatoes lengthwise in rather thin slices; place them in a skillet with water enough to cook them tender. Add a little salt, a tablespoonful of sugar, and enough butter or lard to fry them a nice brown when boiled dry.—*Sister Susie Peters, Emporia, Kans.*

Pumpkin Fritters.—Take 1 quart of pie pumpkin, mash, add 1 to 3 eggs, 1 teaspoonful of salt and enough flour stirred in to make them into a batter. Fry like pancakes in hot lard.—*Sister Daisy Evans, Los Angeles, Cal.*

Radish Slaw.—When radishes get too strong for table use, pare and slice thin, sprinkle salt over them and let stand about 20 or 30 minutes; pour off the water and dress with cream and vinegar.—*Sister Maggie Picking, Buckeye, Kans.*

To Cook Rice.—Boil 1 cup of rice till done, then drain and add sugar, a little milk and the yolk of one egg. Beat the white of the egg to a stiff froth and stir into it the rice while boiling hot. Flavor with nutmeg or cinnamon.—*Sister J. T. Myers, Lena, Ill.*

Baked Rice.—Take 1 pint of rice, cook it, then add 1 cup of currants, 1 cup of raisins, 1 cup of sugar and 3 eggs well beaten; put all together in a baking dish, then pour over it rich sweet milk till the rice is covered. Bake in a hot oven.—*Sister Lydia Hoover, Bevansville, Md.*

To Prepare Rice.—Take ½ cup of rice to about 1 quart of cold water, and let boil a few minutes; then pour off the hot water and add cold water which should again come to a boil, and boil a short time, pouring off the hot water a second time; then add cold water a third time. Let boil 5 minutes, then put on the back of the stove and cook slowly; season and stir only sufficiently to keep from sticking, until it is soft. To bake it, remove the rice before it is cooked soft, put in a pudding dish, season with salt and butter and 1 pint of rich milk, after which bake for 20 minutes or ½ hour.—*Sister J. J. Keim, Elklick, Pa.*

Baked Rice.—Take ½ cup of rice to 1 quart of milk, 2 tablespoonfuls of sugar, flavor with nutmeg or lemon to suit taste; put in the oven and bake until the rice is done. Serve with cream.—*Sister Sarah Gates, Beattie, Kans.*

Baked Rice.—Wash 1 cup of rice and 1 cup of raisins. Pour over them 3 pints of rich sweet milk and add ½ teaspoonful of salt. Pour in a baking pan, and bake till the rice is tender. Stir occasionally while baking. Serve with cream and sugar.—*Sister Minna Robinson, Ellison, N. Dak.*

Rice Balls.—Take 1 teacup of rice, cook until well done, then add 1 teaspoonful of salt, and 1 well-beaten egg. Make in balls the size of an egg. Roll in cracker dust and drop in hot lard until a nice brown. Serve warm. -*Sister Annie Keim, Elklick, Pa.*

Cold Creamed Rice.—Take cold cream, whip, sweeten, and flavor with vanilla, mix with cold cooked rice. This is an excellent way to use left-over rice.—*Sister Martha Reiff Tobias, Camden, Ind.*

Rice and Cheese.—Cook 1 cup of washed rice in plain boiling water, to which salt has been added. When done put in a pan enough rice to cover the bottom, then a layer of grated cheese, with a sprinkle of salt and some butter. Then put in more rice, and so on till the pan is filled or the rice is all used. Moisten with good milk or cream, put in the oven and bake slowly until brown.—*Sister Pearl Plum, Polo, Ill.*

Rice Croquettes.—Take 1 quart of cold cooked rice, 1 egg and 2 tablespoonfuls cream. Mix thoroughly, mold into croquettes, put into well-oiled pan, sprinkle finely rolled or sifted cracker crumbs on top, then a little butter, and put in oven to brown. Serve a tomato sauce with them. Tomato sauce: Mix together 1½ cups· condensed tomato, ½ cup water and 1 tablespoon melted butter. Thicken with a little flour.—*Sister Bertha Dutcher, Sterling, Ill.*

Rice and Curry.—Cut in inch pieces 1 pound of mutton or beef, place in a kettle with 2 cups of water, let stew till tender, then thicken with flour and milk. While the meat is stewing, wash thoroughly 1 pound of good rice, place in a kettle with 2 inches or more of water to cover it, cook till done. Take a grain of the rice between the thumb and finger, when soft enough to mash, it is done; then throw into the rice 1 quart of cold water, turn into a colander to drain. When well drained, return to the kettle and keep in a hot place on the stove till needed. If properly cooked, there will be no gluey substance in the rice and every grain will be separate. Into a hot frying pan put 1 tablespoonful of butter, let it brown but not burn, throw into the hot butter a finely-cut onion, stirring briskly; when done, add 1 tablespoonful of curry powder, stirring all briskly as when browning flour. Into this mixture put the meat stew; let cook a few minutes, season to taste, and it is now ready to serve. Serve your guests with rice, dipping over it a spoonful of the curry dressing, mixing it thoroughly with the rice. This is enough for 8 persons.—*Sister D. L. Miller, Mt. Morris, Ill.*

French Rice.—Put 1 cup of rice in boiling water and boil until tender. Take off and add 1 quart of tomatoes, which have previously been put through a colander to get rid of the seeds and lumps. Slice in ¼ of a pound of cheese, and add salt and 1 table-spoonful of sugar. Stir well. Then bake twenty minutes. Do not have this too dry. To be extra good it must not be thick enough to stand when a spoonful is dipped out.—*Sister W. J. Haynes, Moorefield, Nebr.*

Fried Rice.—Cook 1 cup rice till soft, add 2 eggs, 1 table-spoonful of flour, and a little salt and pepper. Stir all together thoroughly. Have a spider ready with a tablespoonful of butter or lard melted, drop the rice in, a spoonful at a time. When a nice brown turn and fry on the other side. This makes a fine breakfast dish.—*Sister Ella Pratt, Payette, Idaho.*

Spanish Rice.—Take a slice of bacon cut into small bits, a small onion chopped fine, 4 medium-sized tomatoes, 1 cup of cold boiled rice; put the bacon and onion in a frying pan and brown, add the tomatoes, then the rice. Season to taste with salt and pepper. —*Sister Mary E. Whitney, Kearney, Nebr.*

Rice Stew.—For a small family take a 1-pound veal stew, wash, cover with boiling water and allow to boil rapidly for a few minutes. Then skim, turn fire low and allow to simmer slowly un-til tender. Remove from liquid and add ½ cup of rice which has been previously soaked, 1 or 2 onions cut fine, some celery chopped fine and 1 pint of tomatoes run through a colander. Add salt and pepper to suit taste. Cook until rice is done. Rice stew made with fresh pork is also very wholesome, omitting onions, celery and toma-toes.—*Sister Nannie Byer Newcomer, South Bend, Ind.*

Spinach.—Wash the spinach thoroughly and cook in salted water till it is tender. Then drain the water off and season with butter, a little salt and one cup of sweet cream. Vinegar may also be added, if desired.—*Sister Mary C. Hoke, Goshen, Ind.*

Spinach.—Wash spinach carefully, then cook in salted water until soft, which may require 10 or 20 minutes; drain, and pour over it melted butter or fry slightly in ham drippings. Serve with vinegar if liked.—*Sister Leah Sell, Sharpsburg, Md.*

To Cook Summer Squash.—Pare squash, remove the seeds, cook till dry and soft; mash and season with butter, salt, pepper, and sugar. A little cream added will improve it, but it is very good without.—*Sister Hannah Kreitzer, Sabetha, Kans.*

Baked Tomatoes.—Prepare tomatoes as to cook; put in a saucepan, dredge with flour, add butter and sugar to taste; put in the oven and bake.—*Sister Sarah C. Gates, Beattie, Kans.*

Baked Tomatoes.—Slice 1 layer of ripe tomatoes in a dish, put over it one layer of bread, a pinch of salt, a little pepper, 1 tablespoonful of sugar, 1 teaspoonful of butter; continue until the dish is full. Bake to a light brown. Serve while warm.—*Sister H. G. Miller, Bridgewater, Va.*

French Fried Tomatoes.—Cut firm ripe tomatoes in thick slices, dip each slice in beaten egg, then in cracker crumbs and fry brown in butter.—*Sister Effie Eugenia Reese, Warrensburg, Mo.*

Fried Tomatoes.—Take tomatoes not too ripe, cut into slices ½ inch thick, roll in flour, and fry in plenty of hot butter; after they are nicely browned on both sides, pour in cream for dressing and season with pepper and salt.—*Sister J. G. Royer, Mt. Morris, Ill.*

Fried Tomatoes.—Peel some ripe tomatoes and cut them in slices ½ inch thick; put 2 ounces of butter into a frying pan; when hot, put a layer of the slices of tomato into the pan and fry brown on both sides. Remove to a warm vegetable dish; put ½ cupful of hot water into the frying pan, season with salt and pepper and a little sugar, thicken with browned flour; pour the gravy over the fried tomatoes and serve.—*Sister S. E. Neff, Huntington, Ind.*

Fried Tomatoes.—Peel solid tomatoes, cut in halves, dip in flour and fry in butter on a very hot stove; when fried on one side, slice onion into them, add salt, pepper, and sugar; after being fried brown add sweet cream and bake in oven until well done.—*Sister J. D. Buckwalter, Los Angeles, Cal.*

Fried Green Tomatoes.—Take nice, firm, green tomatoes; slice very thin, roll in flour and fry in butter and lard until nicely browned on both sides. Sprinkle with salt and pepper while frying. Serve while hot.—*Sister Luverna Sheets, Mt. Solon, Va.*

Tomato Mush.—Take as many tomatoes as you desire for a meal, peel and slice them in a dish, then crumb up as much bread as you have tomatoes; put in a skillet a large piece of butter, put it on the stove and let brown; then stir the crumbed bread into it, then the tomatoes; stir until the tomatoes are done; season with salt, pepper and sugar; when done, pour over them ½ cupful of sweet cream; take up and serve.—*Sister Sarah Miller, Sabetha, Kans.*

Stewed Tomatoes.—Take a piece of butter the size of an egg, put it in the frying pan; cut 1 onion in small pieces and let stew in the butter with 1 tablespoonful of flour until a light brown; pour in 1 can of tomatoes or 1 quart of fresh ones, with a pinch of salt and a dash of pepper. Cook until as thick as desired.—*Sister Luanna Smith, South Bend, Ind.*

Stewed Tomatoes.—Stew your tomatoes, add a pinch of soda, stir and let boil up, then add butter, sugar and pepper. To this add a thickening made of sweet milk and flour. Let come to a boil and then add salt. Pour into a dish of broken bread crusts or crackers.—*Sister F. E. Miller, Chanute, Kans.*—Toasting the bread before using it with the tomatoes in this way improves the dish.—*Sister Blanche Lentz, Elgin, Ill.*

Stuffed Tomatoes.—Select smooth, medium-sized tomatoes. Cut out the smooth end carefully, remove the seeds and fill with the following dressing: 1 cup of bread crumbs, 1 cup of ground meat, 1 teaspoonful of salt and milk to soften. Add the tomato seeds and fill each tomato. Then replace the ends and bake in a buttered pan. Onions may be added to the dressing if liked. Serve whole.—*Sister Martha E. Lear, Cerro Gordo, Ill.*

Stuffed Tomatoes.—Take 12 large, smooth tomatoes, 1 teaspoonful of salt, a little pepper, 1 tablespoonful of butter, 1 tablespoonful of sugar, 1 cupful of bread crumbs, and 1 teaspoonful of onion juice. Arrange the tomatoes in a baking pan, cut a thin slice from the smooth end of each; with a small spoon, scoop out as much of the pulp and juice as possible without injuring their shape. When all have been treated in this way, mix the pulp with the other ingredients, and fill the tomatoes with this mixture. Put on the tops, and bake slowly ¾ of an hour. Slide the cake turner under the tomatoes and lift gently on a flat dish. Garnish with parsley, and serve.—*Sister Kate C. Hershberger, Vinton, Va.*

Turkish Poulette.—Cook ½ cup of rice as usual. When done add ½ pint of tomatoes, either canned or fresh cooked, and 3 large onions, which have been previously cooked in salt water and drained. Season with salt, pepper and butter.—*Sister Pearl Plum, Polo, Ill.*

Boiled Turnips.—Peel and slice the turnips. Have water boiling hot, put the turnips in and boil about five minutes. Then drain the water off. Put the turnips back over to cook done with a third the amount of potatoes as turnips. Season with salt, butter and lard, or beef broth.—*Sister Florence Hays Kline, Broadway, Va.*

Mashed Turnips.—Boil the turnips quite tender, drain them as dry as possible, put them into a saucepan and mash with a spoon.

Add a little butter and keep stirring them till the butter is melted. Season also with salt and pepper and serve.—*Sister Amy V. Furry, Johnsville, Md.*

Turnip Sauce.—Take of turnips ⅔ and potatoes ⅓; pare, and cook until done. Then mash or put through a potato ricer. Season with salt, pepper, and butter, and serve. Unlike mashed potatoes alone, this is good cold or can be reheated.—*Sister Joseph Amick, Elgin, Ill.*

Turnip Slaw.—Slice the turnips on a slaw cutter. Cook in salt water until very tender; then pour off water and make a dressing of vinegar, sugar, sour cream and a little flour. Serve hot.—*Sister Guy E. Foresman, Lafayette, Ind.*

Turnip Slaw.—Pare the turnips and slice thin. Put a little lard, about a teaspoonful, in a skillet, put the turnips in, and when wilted pour water on and cook until done and dry. Season with salt. Then make a dressing with sugar, sweet cream, 1 egg, and a little vinegar, if desired, pour this over the turnips and let come to a boil.—*Sister R. F. Brubaker, San Dimas, Cal.*

A Substitute for Meat.—When boiling beans, cabbage or turnips, brown some flour in lard and put in with the vegetables instead of meat, and it will taste just as good.—*Sister Cora Sell Brubaker, Hollidaysburg, Pa.*

When Corn or Rice Is Left Over, add ½ cup of sweet milk, a pinch of salt, a scant ½ teaspoonful of soda, and enough flour to thicken like pancake batter. Eat with warm or cold syrup.—*Sister Lillus E. Mahan, Omaja, Cuba.*

Salt will Curd New Milk; hence in preparing dishes containing milk, the salt should not be added until they are cooked.—*Sister Chas. H. Brown, Omaja, Cuba.*

RECIPES FOR FIRELESS COOKER.

CEREALS.

It is supposed that most cereals can be cooked sufficiently within a few minutes, but they really require considerably more time in the cooking to make them thoroughly digestible. These can be cooked in the fireless cooker for several hours with the least amount of gas or other fuel, to say nothing of the need of watching to prevent burning or boiling over. If your cereal is for breakfast it can be prepared at night and allowed to stand in the cooker until morning, when it will be found perfectly cooked.

Corn Meal Mush.—To 4 cups of boiling water add 1 teaspoon of salt, and sift slowly in between the fingers 1 cup of corn meal, stirring all the time. Leave in the cooker 5 hours or longer.

Rolled Oats.—One part oatmeal, two and one-quarter parts of water. Salt the water and have it boiling. Stir in oatmeal slowly, and cook for 5 minutes, in upper part of double cooker. Fill lower with boiling water and put both in the fireless cooker. The oatmeal will cook in 2 hours, or may be allowed to stand over night. Rolled wheat, Vitos, Wheatena, etc., may be cooked in the same manner.

Rice.—One cup of rice, three cups of water, a little salt. Boil rice in water 5 minutes, then put in the cooker for an hour or two.

Hulled Wheat.—Hulled wheat for breakfast can be prepared the same as rice, boiling perhaps 10 minutes instead of 5, and placed in cooker the night before wanted.

—Sister Barbara Mohler Culley, Elgin, Ill.

Asparagus.—Wash, and boil 5 minutes; then put in cooker for 1 hour. Serve with cream sauce, mayonnaise dressing or pour melted butter over it.—*Sister Barbara Mohler Culley, Elgin, Ill.*

Baked Beans.—Wash 1 quart of beans and soak over night, In the morning drain and cover with more cold water. When this comes to a boil, drain and cover with boiling water, adding small pieces of salt pork, salt and about 3 tablespoonfuls of molasses. Cook for 15 minutes on the stove, then put in cooker for 3 hours; then reheat and put in cooker for 3 hours longer. Brown in oven.— *Sister Barbara Mohler Culley, Elgin, Ill.*

To Boil Green Snap Beans.—Break and wash beans, place on fire and boil fifteen minutes. Make dressing with 1 tablepoonful of flour, 1 cup of sweet cream, a small piece of butter and salt to taste. Let all come to a boil and place in fireless cooker 3 hours.— *Sister A. C. Thompson, Adena, Ohio.*

Dried Lima Beans.—Wash a pint of beans, soak for a few hours in warm water and place on fire and boil 10 or 15 minutes. Drain and season with ½ cup of sweet cream and piece of butter. Let come to boil and place in cooker 3 hours.—*Sister A. C. Thompson, Adena, Ohio.*

String Beans.—Break the beans into small pieces of about one-half inch, add salt, and pour boiling water over them. Boil 5 minutes, then put in cooker for 3 hours. If they are to be creamed, use milk instead of water, and thicken before serving. Season well. Serve in warm dish.—*Sister Barbara Mohler Culley, Elgin, Ill.*

Carrots and Peas.—Are delicious served together. Cut carrot into *very* tiny dice. To a cup of these add 1½ cups of green peas. Boil in salted water for 5 minutes and place in cooker for 3 hours. Serve with cream sauce.—*Sister Barbara Mohler Culley, Elgin, Ill.*

Celery Soup.—Three cups of celery cut in inch pieces, 4 cups of boiling water, 1 sliced onion, 2 tablespoonfuls of butter, 3 tablespoonfuls of flour, 2 cups of milk, and seasoning. Boil celery 5 minutes, then put in cooker for 2 hours. Scald onion in milk, remove onion, put celery through sieve, add to milk, put butter and flour together, add to soup, season and serve hot.—*Sister Barbara Mohler Culley, Elgin, Ill.*

Codfish Croquettes.—Shred one pint of codfish, pare and quarter one quart of potatoes. Put fish and potatoes in kettle, cover with boiling water, cook 5 minutes; then place in cooker for 3 hours. Drain well, mash and beat until light. Add 2 teaspoonfuls of butter and, when slightly cool, 2 eggs well beaten. Drop by tablespoonfuls in hot fat.—*Sister Barbara Mohler Culley, Elgin, Ill.*

Macaroni.—Pour boiling salted water over broken macaroni, and cook for 5 minutes. Place in cooker for 3 to 4 hours. Serve with cream sauce and grated cheese.—*Sister Barbara Mohler Culley, Elgin, Ill.*

Dried Peaches.—Wash peaches in cold water, drain and cover with fresh water, soak over night and boil slowly for ten minutes in water in which they soaked. Add sugar to taste and place in cooker for 4 hours.—*Sister Harry Fahrney, Elgin, Ill.*

Peas.—Shell peas and cover with cold water, bring to boiling point and allow to boil slowly for 5 minutes. Place in cooker 2 hours if peas are small and very tender, but allow the larger peas to remain 3 hours. Add salt, pepper, butter and cream and reheat when ready to serve.—*Sister Harry Fahrney, Elgin, Ill.*

Rice.—Wash 1 pint of rice through six waters, drain, add 1 teaspoonful of salt and 3 pints of boiling water. Set on the stove and boil ten minutes. Add ½ pint of sweet cream and sugar to suit the taste, let come to a boil and place in fireless cooker 3 hours or until ready to serve next meal. When dished sprinkle with grated nutmeg.—*Sister A. C. Thompson, Adena, Ohio.*

Rice Croquettes.—Mix 3 cups of rice, cooked in fireless cooker, with beaten yolks of 2 eggs. Mould into croquettes, dip into the beaten whites of the eggs, roll in fine bread or cracker crumbs and fry like doughnuts, in deep fat. Arrange on a platter, and when ready to serve pour over all the peanut sauce which follows. This dish easily fills the place of meat. Served with stewed tomatoes, followed by a pie or pudding, or simply by fruit sauce, it makes a satisfying vegetarian meal. Peanut Sauce.—In a shallow stewpan heat 1 tablespoonful of butter, or oil and butter, or olive oil. Grate into it 1 small onion and fry until well browned. Add a *heaping* tablespoonful of peanut butter rubbed smooth in a cup and a half of warm water (added a little at a time until the peanut butter is smooth). Cook all together gently, for 15 minutes or so, stirring frequently. See that more water is added if necessary to give proper consistency. Pour very hot over rice or other croquettes and serve instantly.—*Sister Barbara Mohler Culley, Elgin, Ill.*

SALADS AND SAUCES

It is possible that many do not value the salad as they should and recognize its importance in the bill of fare. Mrs. Rorer, a well-known authority on cookery, says that salad is "nature's lubricant for the animal machine." Nearly all vegetables, as well as meats, may be used in salads. The "making" of a salad is the dressing. High-class cooks and chefs almost invariably make use of mayonnaise or French dressing in the preparation of their salads, using the former for all meat salads and with asparagus, cauliflower and tomatoes, and the latter with cabbage, cucumbers, dandelions, lettuce and cooked green beans. Boiled dressings and cream dressings, however, combine well with most salad material and are in favor with many people, especially those who do not relish the salad oil which is the main ingredient in the mayonnaise and French dressings. Noting that no one has contributed directions for making these two salad dressings we give them here. Mayonnaise: The yolks of 2 eggs, 1 cup of salad oil, ½ teaspoonful of salt and about 2 tablespoonfuls of lemon juice or vinegar. Use a soup plate or flat-bottomed dish in making the mayonnaise and stir it with a silver fork. Have all the ingredients and also the plate and fork as cold as possible. Put the egg yolks in the soup plate, add salt and several drops of oil, and stir slowly with the fork, always stirring in the one direction throughout the process. Continue adding the oil, a little at a time, alternating with several drops of the vinegar or lemon juice when the mixture becomes too thick. As the process continues, a greater amount of oil or lemon juice may be added each time. The dressing when done—when all ingredients have been incorporated—should have the appearance of custard and be jelly-like in nature. If not wanted for immediate use the dressing may be put in a jar and will keep for several days on ice or in a cool, dark place. Other seasoning, as mustard or a dash of cayenne, may be added when the salad is to be made at which time the dressing may also be thinned, if thought necessary, by the addition of a little vinegar. French dressing is made of vinegar and oil seasoned with pepper and salt, the proportions being two-thirds oil to one of vinegar. For 2 tablespoonfuls of oil and 1 of vinegar take 1 saltspoonful of salt and ½ saltspoonful of pepper. Dissolve the salt and pepper in 1 tablespoonful of the oil and pour over salad material in bowl. Then add remainder of oil and toss up thoroughly. Lastly pour the vinegar over all and toss together again. The salad is then ready to serve.

Apple Salad.—Take 1 bunch of celery cut fine, 3 large apples cut fine with the celery; pour over them the following dressing: Take 2 eggs, ½ cup of sugar, ½ teaspoonful of salt, a little butter and pepper, 1 cup of vinegar, and 1 teaspoonful of mustard, if liked; boil a few minutes and pour over hot.—*Sister James J. Thomas, Inglewood, Cal.*

Apple Salad.—Take 4 medium-sized apples, pare, core, and chop not too fine; of chopped celery ½ the bulk of the apples; 1 cupful of fresh English walnut kernels, broken in pieces, not cut. Mix all together. For dressing take 2 tablespoonfuls of sugar, 1 tablespoonful of butter, and a teaspoonful each of flour, mustard and salt. Mix this with 1 well-beaten egg. Turn on this a cup of boiling milk. Stir briskly and add ½ cup of vinegar. Make the dressing several hours ahead of using, so that it will be cool, and do not chop the apples long before using, or they will discolor.—*Sister W. R. Miller, Chicago, Ill.*

Apple Salad.—Prepare apples enough to make a quart when chopped. Add 1 cup of chopped English walnuts. Then prepare the following dressing: One egg, ½ teaspoonful of salt, 1 teaspoonful of prepared mustard, 2 teaspoonfuls of flour, 6 teaspoonfuls of butter, 4 tablespoonfuls of sugar and ⅔ cup of sour milk.

Cook these thoroughly, then add 4 tablespoonfuls of vinegar. When this is cold pour over the nuts and apples.—*Sister Martha E. Lear, Cerro Gordo, Ill.*

Bean Salad.—Cook the beans (string) tender, slice a small onion with them after removing from the stove and cover with the following dressing: Two eggs, ½ cup of sugar, ½ teaspoonful of salt, a little butter and pepper, and 1 cup of vinegar. (A little mustard may be added, if liked.) Cook until it thickens. It may be used cold or hot.—*Sister J. F. Thomas, Inglewood, Cal.*

Cold Bean Salad.—Take 1 can of kidney beans, 4 hard boiled eggs, 1 large sour pickle, 1 large onion, 2 tablespoonfuls of vinegar, and salt and pepper to taste. Chop eggs (reserve one to garnish), pickle and onions separately, and add to the beans. Place in salad bowl and garnish. Eggs to be used in salads are much nicer if put on to boil in cold water, boiled twenty minutes and allowed to cool in the same water.—*Sister Grace Holsinger Butterbaugh, Elgin, Ill.*

Beet Salad.—Boil 6 medium-sized beets till quite tender, peel and chop fine. Put 1 large tablespoonful of butter in a saucepan and brown nicely. Beat 1 tablespoonful of flour and 1 tablespoonful of sugar with ¼ cup of vinegar and ¼ cup of water. Add this to the browned butter. When boiling, add to the chopped beets. If the vinegar is not very sour, do not use so much water.—*Sister C. S. Colony, York, N. Dak.*

Red Beet Salad.—Wash and cook 3 or 4 red beets tender, pierce with a fork; peel and hash not too fine; have some nice ham gravy in a hot skillet, turn the hashed beets into it and fry slightly, stirring all the time. Have a dressing ready made of ½ cup of cream, 1 egg, with good sour vinegar enough to suit the taste, add salt and pepper; pour over the beets, cook a few minutes, stirring briskly; turn out in a dish at once.—*Sister Sarah Minick, Lyons, Kans.*

Cabbage Salad.—Take 1 large red pepper, 12 ears of sweet corn, 1 head of cabbage, 3 onions, 4 tablespoonfuls of ground mustard, 2 tablespoonfuls of salt, ½ cup of sugar and enough vinegar to season. Cook fifteen minutes, or until corn is tender. Be sure not to have corn too old. This makes three quarts. Can while hot. This is excellent.—*Sister Cora H. Root, Sabetha, Kans.*

Cabbage Salad.—Take a good-sized head of cabbage cut in slaw and three medium-sized onions cut fine; mix together. Then mix together the yolks of three eggs, ½ cup sugar, salt and pepper to taste and ½ teaspoonful of mustard and stir into ½ cup of vinegar previously brought to boiling point. (If vinegar is too strong weaken with a little water.) Stir in also 1 tablespoonful cornstarch dissolved in a little water. Let boil up, then cool and pour over cabbage and onions. It is very fine.—*Sister Jennie Sheeler, Kingsley, Iowa.*

Cabbage Salad.—Take 4 eggs, ½ cup of sugar, 1 small cup of vinegar, 1 teaspoonful of ground mustard, ½ teaspoonful of celery seeds, a lump of butter. Salt to taste, stir briskly until thoroughly cooked. When cool, stir together with 1 small head of cabbage, 2 cucumber pickles, 2 apples, and 1 stalk of celery, all chopped fine.—*Sister Lida A. Duncan, Denbigh, N. Dak.*

Cabbage Slaw.—Chop fine 1 medium-sized head of cabbage, and salt. Put into a hot skillet 1 cup of good vinegar, and 1 heaping tablespoonful of butter. Break 1 egg into a dish, then pour in ½ cup of sugar. Beat this well, then pour it into the hot vinegar. Stir until all comes to the boiling point, then add your chopped cabbage and some black pepper. Stir until all comes to a boil again. This is excellent either cold or hot.—*Sister Effie E. Miller, Jonesboro, Tenn.*

Cold Slaw.—To ½ gallon of cabbage cut fine add salt, pepper, ½ cup of vinegar and 3 tablespoonfuls of sugar dissolved in the vinegar; mix well. A few bleached celery leaves cut fine and added, give a good flavor, if desired.—*Sister Martha Ross, Sidney, Ind.*

Celery Salad.—Take 3 bunches of celery, cut into bits ½ inch long, boil in water until tender, drain, and dress with ½ cup of sour cream, vinegar to suit the taste, and butter the size of a walnut; season with salt and pepper.—*Sister Annie Mineely, Johnstown, Pa.*

Chicken Salad.—Boil the chicken tender, cut the meat up into small pieces, or put it through a food grinder. Take one-half as much celery as chicken, 2 cups of hickory or walnut kernels and 4 hard boiled eggs. Then make the following dressing: Take the yolks of 6 eggs, 2 teaspoonfuls of prepared mustard, 4 teaspoonfuls of salt, pepper to taste, 8 tablespoonfuls of sugar, 4 tablespoonfuls of melted butter, 2 cups of sweet cream and 1 cup of vinegar (hot). Boil all together, and when cold pour over the chicken, celery, nuts, and eggs, mixing thoroughly. Set in a cool place until ready to serve.—*Sister Bertha L. Yoder, Bellefontaine, Ohio.*

Chicken Salad.—Boil the fowls tender, remove all fat, gristle and skin, mince the meat in small pieces, but do not hash it. To 1 chicken put twice its weight in celery, cut in pieces ¼ inch in length, mix thoroughly and set in a cool place. In the meantime prepare a mayonnaise dressing and when ready for the table pour this dressing over the chicken and celery, tossing and mixing thoroughly. Set in a cool place until ready to serve. Garnish with celery tips, hard-boiled eggs, cut fine, and a little green parsley.—*Sister Rose E. Smith, Dunlap, Kans.*

Chicken Salad.—Boil 1 chicken until tender, chop moderately fine, add the chopped whites of 12 hard-boiled eggs, add equal quantities of chopped celery and cabbage; mix all together. Make a dressing as follows and pour over the mixture: Mash the yolks of the 12 hard-boiled eggs fine, add 2 tablespoonfuls of butter, 2 tablespoonfuls of sugar, 1 teaspoonful of mustard, pepper and salt to taste, ½ cup of good cider vinegar; mix all thoroughly. If celery cannot be obtained. cucumbers and celery seed may be used. —*Sister Mattie A. Lear, Hudson, Ill.*

Chicken Salad.—Boil the chicken until it is tender and chop it in small pieces, chop also the whites of 12 hard-boiled eggs; add chopped celery and cabbage in equal quantities. Pound the yolks of the eggs fine and add 2 tablespoonfuls of sugar and butter, 1 tablespoonful of mustard, and pepper and salt to taste, last add a teacupful of cider vinegar; mix thoroughly.—*Sister Lizzie Harnish Mt. Carroll, Ill.*

Chicken Salad.—Take 3 boiled chickens chopped fine, 10 eggs boiled hard, the whites chopped and added to the chicken. Mash the yolks and moisten with 6 teaspoonfuls of melted butter and olive oil, to which add 1 tablespoonful each of mustard, pepper, salt, sugar, 3 tablespoonfuls of cream, and last add 6 bunches of celery chopped fine, with sufficient vinegar to moisten the whole.—*Sister Lona Cripe, Battle Creek, Iowa.*

Corn Salad.—Take 1 can of corn, 1 pound of ground cabbage, ½ teaspoonful of mustard, and ½ cup of vinegar. Add salt and pepper to suit the taste.—*Sister Ella B. Price, Lanark, Ill.*

Dandelion Salad.—After dandelion is cleaned, cut it in shreds, wash it, drain, and boil about ten minutes. This removes the bitterness. Drain again. For the dressing: Add salt to an egg, beat, add pepper, mustard, and a teaspoonful of sugar. Thicken ½ cup of milk with 1 teaspoonful of flour, pour into the egg, add vinegar till sour enough, then set on the stove and stir till it boils. Mix with the dandelion and serve. Prepared in this way it can be used late in the season.—*Sister Adaline H. Beery, Elgin, Ill.*

Egg Salad.—Chop 6 hard-boiled eggs and add to 1 cup of chopped almonds or English walnuts. Mix with salad dressing.—*Sister Stella A. Parret, Lordsburg, Cal.*

Fruit Salad.—(For fourteen people). Take the yolks of 4 eggs and 1 tablespoonful of vinegar to each yolk. Stir this together in a double boiler and add ½ cup of granulated sugar and a lump of butter the size of an egg. When cold add grated rind and juice of 1 lemon and ½ cup of cream. Then add ½ dozen oranges, cut up 2 apples cut in dice, ½ pound malaga grapes cut in half and seeded, 4 bananas, and ½ pound English walnuts blanched. Serve on lettuce leaves.—*Sister Myrtle Branson, Nappanee, Ind.*

Fruit Salad.—Take 4 oranges, 4 bananas, and ½ pound of English walnuts. Peel the oranges and bananas and crack the nuts. Slice the fruit and put in a dish in layers with nut meats sprinkled over it. Take a ten-cent package of Advo Jell (or any kind of jell preparation) and dissolve in 1 pint of boiling water. Pour this over the fruit and let stand until cold. Then serve.—*Sister Martha Priebe, Kearney, Nebr.*

Fruit Salad.—Take 1 package of gelatine dissolved in 1 pint of cold water for ½ hour, then pour 1 pint of boiling water over it, add 1 can of pineapple, 6 oranges in small pieces, 6 bananas in thin slices, ⅔ cup of grated cocoanut. Stir all together and set in a cool place to harden; or if it is warm, put on ice and stir occasionally until it begins to set, so that the fruit will be all through the gelatine.—*Sister Sue Sisler, Dallas Center, Iowa.*

Fruit Salad.—Soak ½ box of good gelatine in 1 pint of cold water for 1 hour, and prepare the fruit as follows: 2 oranges and 2 bananas, cut fine, 1 can of pineapple, the *sliced* pineapple preferred, juice and grated rind of 3 lemons, and 1½ cups of granulated sugar. Mix fruit and sugar together. Add 1½ cups of boiling water to gelatine. Pour over fruit and mix well. Set in a cold place until it hardens. If allowed to stand over night the most satisfactory results will be obtained.—*Sister Della Kessler, Red Cloud, Nebr.*

Lettuce Salad.—Make a dressing of 2 eggs, 1 tablespoonful of flour, sugar, salt and vinegar to taste, and enough water so as not to be too thick. Boil, add the lettuce, stir well until lettuce is wilted. Slice 1 hard-boiled egg and stir into the lettuce. Then put into dish and slice 1 hard-boiled egg over the top. Serve warm.—*Sister Ettie Holler, Hagerstown, Ind.*

Lettuce Salad. (With Cold Dressing).—Over a good-sized dish of lettuce washed and well drained sprinkle a good pinch of salt and a cooking spoonful of granulated sugar. Melt a lump of butter the size of an egg and pour it over the lettuce and mix well. Then add ½ cup of sweet cream and vinegar enough to give it a good taste.—*Sister Esther Horner Baker, Baltic, Ohio.*

Lettuce Salad.—Take ½ pint of sour cream, 6 tablespoonfuls of vinegar, 1 egg well beaten; put on the stove and let come to a boil; then make a thin batter of 1 tablespoonful of flour and water, add this to the cream; when this boils, remove from the fire, add enough sugar to suit the taste and a pinch of salt; let this dressing partly cool, then pour it over the lettuce. Slice a hard-boiled egg over the top, and serve.—*Sister Anna M. Lichty, Meyersdale, Pa.*

Onion Salad.—Peel and slice 6 good-sized onions and fry to a nice light brown in equal parts of butter and lard, then beat 1 egg well and add ¾ pint of rich milk; stir and pour over the onions; let boil up, then add salt and pepper and about 2 tablespoonfuls of vinegar, and serve hot.—*Sister Hannah M. Neher, Hollywood, Ala.*

Onion Salad.—Take six or eight good-sized onions, peel, slice thin and cook tender in salt water to season. Then put over them a dressing of 1 tablespoonful of flour, 1 teacupful of cream, 1 tablespoonful sugar and vinegar to suit the taste.—*Sister Florence Hays Kline, Broadway, Va.*

Onion Salad.—Take 6 large onions chopped fine (do not use fruit chopper, as it bruises them too much); let stand in cold water ten minutes and drain off. Then take ¾ of a cup of vinegar, 3 tablespoonfuls of sugar, ½ teaspoonful each of salt, cinnamon and allspice. Mix and pour over the onions. Let stand thirty minutes before serving. Stir them several times, so that the spices will be evenly distributed.—*Sister W. J. Haynes, Moorefield, Nebr.*

Oyster Salad.—Take 1 can of cove oysters, 3 hard-boiled eggs, 3 or 4 stalks of celery, same quantity of broken crackers as oysters, butter size of an egg. Chop the whites of the eggs, oysters, and celery separately, season and toss together lightly with a fork.

Mash yolks very fine with the butter, add ⅔ pint of vinegar, ½ teaspoonful of prepared mustard. Let come to a boil, stirring constantly, and pour over the mixture.—*Sister Sara Reese Eby, West Elkton, Ohio.*

Peanut and Cabbage Salad.—Take 1 quart of chopped cabbage, ½ teaspoonful of salt and 1 cup of ground peanuts. Dressing: Two eggs beaten, ½ cup of vinegar and butter size of a walnut. Cook and when cold add four tablespoonfuls of cream and ½ cup of sugar.—*Sister Phoebe Foft, Kingsley, Iowa.*

Pimento Salad.—Take ½ package of gelatine, 1 cup of boiling water, 1 cup of chopped cabbage or celery, ¼ can of pimentoes (chopped), ½ cup of vinegar, 1 cup of sugar and 1 teaspoonful of salt. Mix gelatine and water then salt, vinegar and sugar. When solid, add pimentoes and cabbage or celery. Serve with mayonnaise dressing.—*Sister Mary Christner, Cerro Gordo, Ill.*

Potato Salad.—Take 6 boiled potatoes, butter size of a hickory nut, 1 good-sized onion chipped up fine, pepper and salt to suit taste. Add 4 boiled eggs, 2 sliced in the salad and 2 on top. Garnish with celery, parsley, or lettuce, also add vinegar to suit the taste.—*Sister Carrie L. Arnold, North Manchester, Ind.*

Potato Salad.—Take 6 large boiled potatoes, 3 good-sized onions, 4 hard-boiled eggs. Chop fine, with the exception of the yolks of 2 eggs, which save for the dressing. Dressing: A lump of butter the size of an egg, melt in a frying pan, then add 1 teaspoonful of flour, 1 teaspoonful of sugar, the yolks of 2 eggs pulverized, ½ cup of boiling water, ⅓ cup of strong vinegar, salt to taste. Boil up as for gravy and pour over salad, with 1 teaspoonful of prepared mustard. When cool it is ready to serve.—*Sister Lavina Brower, North Manchester, Ind.*

Potato Salad.—Slice boiled potatoes and hard-boiled eggs alternately in a dish, season with salt and pepper; make a dressing with 1 cup of good sour cream, 2 tablespoonfuls of sugar, vinegar to suit the taste; pour over the potatoes and eggs, and serve cold.—*Sister Hannah Kreitzer, Sabetha, Kans.*

Potato Salad.—Take 7 eggs, boil hard and cut up into squares, boil 7 potatoes size of eggs, let cool, then cut in squares, 1 onion cut fine. Mix all together, salt, make a dressing of 1 cup of sour cream, 1 egg, ½ cup of vinegar, 1 tablespoonful of sugar, pepper and salt to taste.—*Sister Jinia Stark, Centerview, Mo.*

Potato Salad.—Boil 12 medium-sized potatoes, and 3 or 4 eggs, when cool cut into dice, then make the following dressing: Take 1 egg, pinch of salt, 1 tablespoonful of flour, 1 tablespoonful of sugar, ½ cup of sour cream, 1 cup of vinegar and water; boil al! together; let cool, then mix with the potatoes and eggs.—*Sister Minnie M. Uhl, Brooklyn, Iowa.*

Potato Salad.—Take 1 medium-sized dish of left-over mashed potatoes, 7 hard-boiled eggs, 1 medium-sized onion, 1 heaping teaspoonful of sugar; chop the onion and 5 eggs fine, add the sugar, salt, pepper, and vinegar to taste. Slice the 2 remaining eggs on top of salad.—*Sister Anna Sniteman, Keota, Iowa.*

Potato Salad.—Take 8 large boiled potatoes, 3 good-sized onions, 3 hard-boiled eggs; chop all together. Dressing: Take 1 egg, 3 spoonfuls of sour cream, 1 spoonful of sugar, 1 spoonful of salt; beat this together, add vinegar to suit the taste.—*Sister Myra Troyer, Baltic, Ohio.*

Potato Salad.—Take 1 quart of potatoes chopped fine, put in stew pan with enough water to cover, salt and pepper to taste, let boil until tender, then put in ¾ teacupful of good vinegar, ½ cup of sour cream, 2 tablespoonfuls of butter or meat gravy. Boil 2 or more eggs hard and slice over when taken up.—*Sister C. N. Huff, Amsterdam, Va.*

Potato Salad.—Boil eggs hard, mash or grate the yolks and cut the whites fine; take boiled potatoes, cut in blocks not too fine; put in a dish first a layer of potatoes then yolks and whites of eggs and pour over the following dressing: Put butter into a pan, brown flour in it, pour in sweet milk, boil until it thickens, put in vinegar to season, and if liked cut a few onions quite fine and mix with the dressing.—*Sister Eliza Miller, Meyersdale, Pa.*

Potato Salad.—Take 10 medium-sized potatoes and cook them with the peeling on. Be careful not to let them cook too soft; peel and cut in small squares; take 1 or 2 medium-sized onions, 1 stalk of celery, 2 hard-boiled eggs, cut and mix with the potatoes; then season with salt, pepper, celery and mustard seeds. Dressing: Take butter the size of a walnut, 1 tablespoonful of yellow mustard, a pinch of salt and ¼ cup of vinegar diluted with water (1 egg can be used if liked); boil together until it thickens, pour over the potatoes, and serve cold.—*Sister Ora Beachley, Hagerstown, Md.*

Potato Salad.—Pare and boil in salt water as many potatoes as desired, when done, take out, let cool, then slice in a dish to serve from, and slice 3 hard-boiled eggs over the potatoes. Brown 1 tablespoonful of butter and ½ tablespoonful of flour; beat 1 egg with 2 tablespoonfuls of vinegar; pour this to the flour and butter, add 1 cup of water and stir until it thickens; pour over the potatoes and serve cold.—*Sister Pinkie E. Vetter, Pyrmont, Ind.*

Potato Salad.—Take 6 medium-sized potatoes, boil tender, and as many hard-boiled eggs, 1 onion, a lump of butter the size of a walnut, chop together, salt and pepper to taste, a little celery seed (mustard seed will do), then add some vinegar. Mix together, then slice 2 hard-boiled eggs on top.—*Sister Hannah F. Dunning, Denbigh, N. Dak.*

Potato Salad.—Cut in fine pieces 6 cold boiled potatoes, 2 onions, and 3 hard-boiled eggs; make a mustard dressing for same as follows: The yolks of 3 eggs, 3 tablespoonfuls of prepared mustard, 3 tablespoonfuls of white sugar, 2 teaspoonfuls of salt, 1 dessertspoonful of flour, 1 teacupful of very sour vinegar. Let boil, stirring it until it is thick.—*Sister Sue Sisler, Dallas Center, Iowa.*

Potato Salad.—Slice cold boiled potatoes in a dish, add a couple of hard-boiled eggs chopped. Mayonnaise dressing is best, but a dressing may be made cold which is made much quicker. Take cream, sugar, vinegar, salt, pepper, and a small amount of mustard. Use your judgment as to amount of each. Onions, if liked, are a nice addition; celery, too, is good in it.—*Sister Eliza J. Englar, New Windsor, Md.*

Potato Salad.—Take cold boiled potatoes sufficient to make about 1 quart when chopped fine; slice 1 small onion with the potatoes, enough to flavor. Make a dressing of 1 large cup of sour cream, ½ cup of sugar, and nearly ½ cup of vinegar; pour over the potatoes and set over the fire until it comes to a boil; then take off and mix in 4 hard-boiled eggs chopped fine, same as potatoes; put in a salad dish and garnish the top with slices of hard-boiled eggs; sprinkle with pepper.—*Sister Lillie Calvert, Redfield, Kans.*

Potato Salad.—Boil 5 or 6 good-sized potatoes, mash, add 1 onion chopped fine, 4 hard-boiled eggs, and mix well together. Dressing: Take 1 egg, 2 tablespoonfuls of sour cream, 2 tablespoonfuls of sugar, 1 teaspoonful of salt and pepper, ½ cup of vinegar; beat the egg and cream together, then add the rest; put on the stove, let come to a boil; pour over the potatoes and mix well, then slice 1 egg and lay on top.—*Sister Theodosia Harris, Ladoga, Ind.*

Potato Salad.—Take several cold boiled potatoes, chop, then mince 3 good-sized onions; slice 2 hard-boiled eggs; mix all together, season with salt, pepper, and celery seed, then add vinegar to suit the taste. Or mix the potatoes and onions, then make a dressing of ⅔ cup of vinegar, salt, pepper, butter the size of a walnut; beat 2 eggs lightly, then turn into the vinegar, and stir while pouring. Boil in double boiler until thick, and then pour it over the potatoes.—*Sister Mary Reddick, Sheridan, Mo.*

Potato Salad.—Take 12 good-sized potatoes boiled and salted, 4 hard-boiled eggs, 2 small onions, 1 bunch of celery, chop all together. Then take ½ cup of sour cream, ½ cup of vinegar, 2 eggs, and ½ cup of sugar. Beat together, then let come to a boil;

pour over the potatoes, stir well and serve cold.—*Sister Elizabeth Eckerle, Flora, Ind.*

Salmon Salad.—Cut fine a head of cabbage that is tender and crisp. To this add ½ that amount of salmon, and a pinch of salt and pepper. Mix well, and pour over it a dressing made as follows: One cup of thick cream (sweet or sour), ½ cup of vinegar, and sugar to taste; beat well and pour over the above.—*Sister Della Kessler, Red Cloud, Nebr.*

Salmon Salad.—Remove the bones from 1 can of salmon; season with salt and pepper. Boil 2 eggs 20 minutes so that the yolks will be dry, plunge them into cold water immediately after taking them from the boiling water to prevent the whites turning blue. Cut the whites into small pieces and either mix with the salmon or use as a garnish for the top. Mash the yolks with a lump of butter, size of 1 yolk, to a smooth paste. Add a little mustard if liked; then vinegar, a little at a time, until the dressing is like cream. If the butter and vinegar separate, warm the dressing before mixing with the salmon.—*Sister R. E. Arnold, Elgin, Ill.*

Salmon Salad.—Take 1 can of salmon, 1½ dozen crackers broken into small bits, and 1 good-sized cucumber pickle chopped into small pieces. Mix all well together. Dressing: Three tablespoonfuls of sugar, 1 tablespoonful of flour, 3 eggs well beaten, 1 cup of sour cream, 1 cup of vinegar, and 1 teaspoonful of salt. Put in a sauce pan and boil till thick. When cool, stir well through the salad and serve.—*Sister Fannie Hollar, Hardin, Mo.*

Sweetbread Salad.—Dash the sweetbreads into boiling salted water, let stand for a few minutes, then lay in ice water to whiten them. When cold cook fifteen minutes in boiling salted water: Let cool then break into bits, add as much celery as sweetbreads, a few English walnuts and olives cut fine. Pour on mayonnaise dressing and serve in tomato cups.—*Sister Edna Crowe, Des Moines, Iowa.*

Tomato Salad.—Select as many solid tomatoes as you wish to serve people. Scald, peel, remove the core and seeds; fill the tomatoes with finely-chopped celery and cabbage, seasoned with salt and pepper; dress the whole with mayonnaise dressing and serve on lettuce leaves.—*Sister Cora A. Keim, Elklick, Pa.*

Continent Mustard (French).—Beat 2 eggs, add 1 cup of thick sweet cream, 1 teaspoonful each of salt, butter and sugar, and ½ cup of ground mustard. Set the dish into a pan of boiling water. Stir until thick, then add slowly one cup of strong vinegar.—*Sister Lydia Deal, Brumbaugh, N. Dak.*

Salad Dressing.—Take 4 eggs beaten separately, ½ teaspoonful of salt, 2 tablespoonfuls of sugar, 1 tablespoonful of mustard, ½ cup of vinegar, lump of butter; put all into beaten yolks, add whites last. Cook until thick and smooth, stirring all the time. If too thick, add cream or vinegar. If there are yolks left from a cake, they can be used alone by adding cream to the mixture and boiling with it. If mustard is not liked, it can be omitted. This makes a good dressing for either potatoes or cabbage.—*Sister Katie R. Trostle, Stratford, Ill.*

Salad Dressing (Will Keep for Months).—To the beaten yolks of 6 eggs, add 1 teaspoonful each of pepper, salt and mustard, and 1 cup of sugar. Beat till very light and add ½ cup of butter. Pour gradually into the above mixture 1 pint of boiling vinegar. Add the juice of 1 lemon, if desired. Let cool before using.—*Sister Katie E. Keller, Enterprise, Mont.*

Salad Dressing.—Take ¾ of a cup of water, 1 tablespoonful of butter, 1 tablespoonful of flour, 1 tablespoonful of vinegar, 1 teaspoonful of mustard and 1 egg well beaten. Mix the mustard, flour, butter and yolk of the egg together. Then add the vinegar and water. Boil until it is a smooth dressing. Stir in the well-beaten white lightly, and when cold pour over the salad.—*Sister Esther Horner Baker, Baltic, Ohio.*

Salad Dressing.—Take the yolks of 4 raw eggs, 4 mustard spoonfuls of mustard, 1 teaspoonful of flour, 4 tablespoonfuls of sugar, 1 tablespoonful of butter, ½ cup of sweet milk, ½ cup of vinegar, a little salt, a pinch of red pepper; mix all together and stir while heating in a double boiler; do not let it boil.—*Sister Mary S. Geiger, Philadelphia, Pa.*

Salad Dressing.—Break 1 egg into a glass; add 1 tablespoonful of flour, ½ teaspoonful of salt and 1 teaspoonful of mustard. Mix until smooth; then fill up the glass with sweet cream (milk will do). Let come to a boil 1 cup of sugar and 1 cup of vinegar; pour in the above ingredients and let all come to the boil. Let it cool and it is ready for use. This may be used on lettuce, cold slaw, sliced tomatoes, potato salad or any vegetable that can be eaten with a salad dressing.—*Sister Grace C. Beam, Elgin, Ill.*

Salad Dressing.—Take 1 tablespoonful sugar, not quite 1 tablespoonful of flour, butter size of a shellbark, 1 egg, milk, ½ teaspoonful mustard mixed with the vinegar, boil, and let cool if you do not wish the salad wilted.—*Sister J. T. Myers, Philadelphia, Pa.*

Dressing for Chicken Salad.—Beat together 1 egg, 1 tablespoonful of sugar, ½ teaspoonful of mustard, 1 teaspoonful of flour, 1 teaspoonful of butter, a pinch of salt, a dash of pepper, 4 teaspoonfuls of vinegar, 2 teaspoonfuls of hot water; boil, stirring until thick, then pour over prepared chicken.—*Sister Mary Rihard, Altoona, Iowa.*

Mustard Dressing.—Take 1 tablespoonful of mustard, 1½ tablespoonfuls of sugar, ½ teaspoonful of salt, 1 tablespoonful of flour, a pinch of cayenne pepper, 1 egg well beaten, ¾ cup of vinegar not too sour; mix all the ingredients together and let come to a boil, stirring all the time; then put in a lump of butter the size of a hulled walnut; beat well, then thin with sweet cream.—*Sister Mary Taylor, Spring City, Pa.*

Cranberry Sauce.—Take 1 quart of cranberries, wash, and pour over them 1 pint of water, put in a double boiler or granite kettle; boil until the berries break, then press through a colander. Now put back in the kettle with 1 pint of granulated sugar, boil until it forms a jelly, then pour in molds or dishes and set away in the cold and serve with cream and sugar.—*Sister Susan M. Gibble, Manheim, Pa.*

Cranberry Sauce.—Take 1 quart of cranberries and 1 pint of water; simmer slowly until berries burst; strain through a colander, then measure liquid; to every pint of strained juice add 1 pound of sugar; cook 5 minutes and turn into wet moulds.—*Sister Mary Taylor, Spring City, Pa.*

Cranberry Sauce.—Pick and wash 1 quart of cranberries; put in the preserving kettle with ½ pint of water; add a pint of sugar on top of berries; set on the fire and stew about ½ hour, stirring frequently. They will need no straining and will preserve their rich color cooked in this way.—*Sister Nannie H. Strayer, Johnstown, Pa.*

Cranberry Sauce.—Put 2 cupfuls of sugar and 2 of water in a kettle, and when boiling add 1 quart of cranberries, and 3 apples. Boil until tender. This is the best recipe for cooking cranberries I have found.—*Sister W. J. Swigart, Huntingdon, Pa.*

Dainty Rhubarb Sauce.—Prepare a quart of rhubarb sauce. Soak ½ box of gelatine in a little cold water, till it all dissolves, then add the red coloring that comes in each box of gelatine, and stir it in the sauce. Sweeten the whole to taste. Set away several hours. When ready for use, slice oranges on top.—*Sister Sarah Witmore Harnly, McPherson, Kans.*

Shortcake Custards and Puddings

It may be that puddings and the like have come into their present disfavor with hygienists not so much because they are bad in themselves, but because they have often been badly made and badly handled. Too often a pudding is offered toward the end .of a meal to tempt an appetite that has already satisfied the needs of the body. Sometimes, too, a pudding is offered that naturally wars with the dishes that have preceded it and consequently the eater suffers. The cook should watch this point. Also be careful not to have the first part of the meal so ample that the dessert cannot be considered a necessary part. Be careful, too, to have meals well balanced, serving the lighter desserts at meals where the preceding dishes are somewhat heavy and vice versa. The art of using flavorings in custards, etc., is one worthy of cultivation. Nothing so quickly marks the amateur or careless cook as " loud " or unsuitable flavorings. For boiling a pudding one should have a bag made of firm white goods with felled seams and rounded corners. When preparing to use turn the bag with seams out, dip into hot water, squeeze out lightly and rub the inside plentifully with flour. When tying the bag be careful to allow for the pudding to swell. Place a saucer upside down in the kettle to prevent the pudding sticking, lay in the pudding and cover with boiling water. Cover the kettle and keep the water boiling constantly, adding boiling water from the teakettle to keep the pudding covered. When done dip the bag hastily into cold water, turn out the pudding and serve immediately. Puddings may also be boiled in a tin mold or earthen dish. These should be well greased and after the pudding is in, a well-floured cloth should be tied over the top if the receptacle has no well-fitted

187

cover. Steamed or baked puddings are to be preferred to boiled ones, as they are lighter and more digestible. Boiled or steamed puddings take about twice as long to cook as baked ones.

Shortcake.—Take 1 pint of flour, 1 heaping teaspoonful of baking powder sifted together, a little salt, soften with rich sweet cream to the consistency of biscuit dough; roll out and fit in a pie pan; bake in a quick oven. When baked, split in two with a sharp knife and spread the inside with butter, then put in fruit and lay together. Serve warm with cream over it.—*Sister Sadie S. Young, Beatrice, Nebr.*

Prune Shortcake.—Take the pits out of stewed prunes, mash smooth, sweeten and flavor with allspice. Bake three sheets of large shortcake; when cool, spread the prunes between the sheets, and on top dot with frosting. Do not spread the prunes on till ready to serve.—*Sister Sadie Hays, Le Grand, Cal.*

Strawberry Cake.—Work ½ cup of butter and 2 of sugar to a cream. Add 4 eggs, well beaten, 1 cup of milk, 3 cups of flour, and 1 heaping teaspoonful of baking powder. Bake in flat pans, thicker than for jelly cake. Mash strawberries and sweeten them. Spread them thickly between the layers. Sift sugar over the top, and serve with or without cream.—*Sister Jennie Stouffer, Benevola, Md.*

Strawberry Roll.—Take a full quart of strawberries, chop or mash as for shortcake, and add sugar to suit the taste. Make a dough of 1 quart of flour, 2 teaspoonfuls of baking powder, butter or lard and sweet milk to make up the flour. Divide the dough into two parts. Roll out round, spread butter on them and also the berries and roll up. Butter a bread pan, lay in the layers, put some sugar and a little butter between, and pour a little water on the sugar. Then bake in a moderately hot oven. This is fine made with dried apples. Instead of strawberries, substitute the apples; stew and mash as for pies and spread the same as the berries.—*Sister Eliza Replogle Ulery, Savage, Mont.*

Strawberry Shortcake.—Take ⅓ cup of sugar, 1 egg, ¼ cup of butter or lard, ½ cup of sweet milk, ½ pint of flour, 1 teaspoonful of baking powder; do not roll; bake in a round cake tin. This makes enough for a family of 2 or 3.—*Sister L. A. Pollock, Batavia, Ill.*

Strawberry Shortcake.—For a shortcake, 2 hours before wanted, crush a large quart of berries with 2 cups of granulated sugar, and set away in a cool place. For the crust, take 2 cups of flour and 1 heaping teaspoonful of baking powder sifted together, add ⅓ cup of butter and mix like meal. Add 1 cup of sweet milk, mix as little as possible and have the dough as soft as it can be handled; roll and halve the dough; put in a tin and butter to prevent the layers from sticking together; cover with the other half of the dough and bake; lift off top layer and put half the berries on; cover with top and put on the remaining berries. Serve with cream. Peaches or apricots can be used if desired instead of berries.—*Sister Emma S. Andes Zobler, Lancaster, Pa.*

Strawberry Shortcake.—Make a short pie crust, roll out same as for pies; make enough for 4 pie plates; bake; when done take 1 quart of strawberries, put a quart of water on them with sugar to taste, boil down to a syrup; divide into the 3 crusts and set one into the other when all is cold.—*Sister Lucy Magie, Tropico, Cal.*

Strawberry Shortcake.—Take 1 quart of flour, 3 teaspoonfuls of baking powder, 1 teaspoonful of salt, 2 tablespoonfuls of butter, 1 pint of sweet milk, 1 cup of sugar, 2 quarts of berries. Sift flour in a bowl; add salt and baking powder, mix well; add melted butter and milk; mix thoroughly. Have ready 4 greased pie plates, put dough in and bake in a quick oven. Have berries crushed and sugared. When cakes are done, put on a plate, butter and put the berries between the layers; serve immediately.—*Sister Alice Garman, Lancaster, Pa.*

Strawberry Shortcake.—Sift together 1 quart of flour, 2 teaspoonfuls of baking powder, 2 tablespoonfuls of sugar, and a pinch of salt; add enough sweet cream to make a soft dough, the same as for biscuit. Bake in two layers on cake pans; when done, with a sharp knife divide each layer. Then take a layer of cake and cover with sweetened berries, and so on until you have your cake completed. Serve with sweetened milk.—*Sister Ira G. Blocher, Union City, Ind.*

Ambrosia.—Take 6 oranges, 6 bananas, peel and slice, then put in a dish a layer of oranges, sprinkle with sugar, then a layer of bananas, sprinkle with cocoanut, and so on till the dish is full. Serve with cream or a sauce.—*Sister Mary Netzley, Batavia, Ill.*

Apple Custard.—Take the yolks of 3 eggs, 1 pint of milk, 1 cup of apple sauce sweetened to suit the taste, and 1 tablespoonful of cornstarch. Bake with bottom crust only. Beat the whites of the eggs stiff, add 3 tablespoonfuls of sugar, and when pies are done, spread the whites over the tops and return to the oven to brown. This makes 2 pies.—*Sister Jennie S. Brengle, Frederick, Md.*

Apple Pudding.—Take 1 egg, 1 cup of sugar, 1 cup of sweet milk, and flour enough to make a batter as stiff as for cake, 2 teaspoonfuls of baking powder; grease a pudding dish with butter and cover the bottom with apples, pared and cut in quarters; pour over them the batter and bake until done. Serve with rich milk sweetened.—*Sister Clara Ringer, Oregon, Ill.*

Apple Pudding.—Take tart apples, pare, and punch out the cores, put in an earthen pudding dish, fill the holes with sugar and grate over them some nutmeg; mix in ½ pint of water 1 tablespoonful of cornstarch; pour over the apples and bake until the apples are soft. Serve hot.—*Sister Josiah Clapper, Salemville, Pa.*

Apple Pudding.—Fill a baking dish half full of sliced apples, pour over them a batter made of 1 tablespoonful of butter, ½ cup of sugar, 2 eggs, 1 cup of sweet milk, 2 cups of flour in which have been sifted 2 teaspoonfuls of baking powder. Serve with cream.—*Sister Annie G. Falls, Dayton, Va.*

Apple Pudding.—Slice pudding dish half full of apples and pour over them the following mixture: 1 cup of sugar, 1 egg, a little salt, 2 tablespoonfuls of butter, 1 cup of sour cream, 1 teaspoonful of soda or 1 cup of sweet cream, ½ teaspoonful of soda, and 1 teaspoonful of cream of tartar, nutmeg to taste, 1 pint of flour. Sauce: 2 teaspoonfuls of flour mixed with a little cold water, 1 cup of hot water, butter size of an egg, ½ cup of sugar, a little nutmeg; boil about 15 minutes, then add 2 tablespoonfuls of sweet cream.—*Sister J. E. Price, Dallas Center, Iowa.*

Apple Pudding.—Pare, core, and slice 6 or 8 large apples; good cooking apples are the best. Grease your pan and put your apples in. Then make a dough of 1 cup sugar, 1 cup cream, 1 cup milk and 2½ cups flour, with 2 heaping teaspoonfuls baking powder well sifted into the flour, and pour over the apples. Then bake in a moderate oven about 1 hour. Serve with sugar and cream while warm.—*Sister Lottie E. Shick Perry, Dodge City, Kans.*

Apple Pudding.—Fill a buttered baking dish half full of sliced apples, sweeten, add a few drops of water and pour over them a batter made of 1 tablespoonful of butter, ½ cup of sugar, ½ cup of water, 1 cup of flour, and 1 teaspoonful of baking powder. Bake in a moderate oven till brown. Serve with cream and sugar. —*Sister Eva Miller, Sidney, Ind.*

Apple Pudding.—Fill a pudding dish ½ full of apples, add 1 pint of hot water and set on the stove. Take ½ cup of sugar and butter the size of a small egg and 2 tablespoonfuls of flour; mix together and put in apples. Let that cook while you prepare a dough by taking 1 pint of flour, 2 tablespoonfuls of butter and 2 teaspoonfuls of baking powder; wet with enough sweet milk to make a soft dough. Roll out; put over apples, then put in the oven and bake.— *Sister Lillie M. Blickenstaff, Cerro Gordo, Ill.*

Apple Pudding.—Take 1 pint of sour cream, ½ teaspoonful of soda, and flour enough to make a stiff batter. Then take stewed apples, sweeten them, mix ⅓ of the batter in the apples, and put in a pudding dish and spread the remainder of the batter over the apples. Bake in a moderate oven until brown. Eat with sugar and cream.—*Sister Vera Rodabaugh, Stet, Mo.*

Apple Pudding.—Almost fill 2 pie plates or deep pans with sliced apples or peaches and pour over them a custard made of 3 cups of milk, 3 eggs, ½ cup of sugar, 2 tablespoonfuls of flour, a little salt and 2 cups of bread crumbs. Bake all together.—*Sister Lizzie Shirk, Mt. Morris, Ill.*

Apple Pudding.—Take 2 cups of flour, ½ teaspoonful of salt, 3 teaspoonfuls of baking powder, 2 tablespoonfuls of butter and 1 cup of milk. Roll ½ inch thick and spread on this one cup of chopped apples, and ½ cup of butter. Roll, and then pour over this 1 cup of sugar, and ¾ quart of boiling water. Bake 45 minutes.—*Sister Lena M. Long, Elgin, Ill.*

Apple Butter Roll.—Take 1 pint of bread dough, roll it out ½ inch thick, spread with apple butter, roll up, lay it on a plate; let rise a little, then place plate and roll in a steamer and steam until done. Serve with milk and sugar.—*Sister Belle Jordan, Melbern, Ohio.*

Apple Rolls.—Take bread dough, a little shortening, 1 egg, and flour to stiffen. Take a lump of dough size of a walnut, roll out flat and roll stewed apples in the dough. Let them rise in the bake pan and bake in a moderately hot oven. Eat with sweet dip, same as dumplings.—*Sister Amanda Maust, Meyersdale, Pa.*

Apple Tapioca.—Take 1 cup of tapioca, soaked, 6 apples, 1 quart of water and 1 cup of sugar. Bake, and serve cold with ice cold cream.—*Sister Amy Roop Straw, Westminster, Md.*

Apple Tapioca Pudding.—Soak ½ cup of tapioca 3 hours. Halve, core, but do not peel 6 red medium or small apples. (Jonathan or Winesap preferred.) Put in a bake dish with 1 pint of water, 1 cup of sugar and butter the size of a walnut. Pour the tapioca over with a little grated nutmeg. Bake in a slow oven 1 hour. To be eaten warm.—*Sister Jennie Wampler, Falks Store, Idaho.*

Baked Custard.—Take 1 quart of sweet milk, 1¼ cups of sugar, 5 eggs, well beaten with good egg beater, and nutmeg to taste. Bake in pudding pan, or custard cups, which is better, in pan of hot water in moderate oven until firm and light brown. This is a fine change of diet for a convalescent.—*Sister Myrtle Blocher, Greenville, Ohio.*

Berry Pudding.—Take 2 eggs well beaten, 1 cup of sweet milk, 2 teaspoonfuls of baking powder mixed with flour enough to make a stiff batter and as many berries (raspberries, blackberries, or cherries) as can be stirred into the batter. Bake half an hour and serve with sugar and milk.—*Sister Emma G. Reitz, Friedens, Pa.*

Biscuit Pudding.—Heat to the boiling point 1 quart of water, add a piece of butter the size of a hulled walnut, stir 1 heaping teaspoonful of flour with 2 tablespoonfuls of sugar, and half a grated nutmeg together with a pinch of salt; add to the water to make it smooth; cut cold soda biscuits in two or three slices, drop in, let boil up, and serve.—*Sister Jessie J. Thomas, Butler, Ind.*

Blackberry Flummery.—To 1 pint of blackberries add 1 pint of water, boil until tender, then add 1 cup of sugar, 4 tablespoonfuls of cornstarch, a pinch of salt; stir until it boils, flavor to taste; serve with cream and sugar.—*Sister Laura Smucker, Timberville, Va.*

Black Pudding.—One-half cup sweet milk, ½ cup molasses, ½ cup of sugar, 1 cup of flour, 3 eggs, ½ teaspoonful of soda, 1 teaspoonful each of cinnamon and cloves. Steam 1 hour. Sauce: 1 pint of boiling water, 1 cup of sugar, 1 tablespoonful of butter, a pinch of salt, 1 tablespoonful of cornstarch dissolved in cold water. Stir all together. Let come to a boil. Season with nutmeg. —*Sister Sarah A. Crowl, Nappanee, Ind.*

Blanc Mange.—Place over the fire in a kettle or sauce pan, 2 quarts of sweet milk, which must be stirred frequently to prevent scorching. Into a bowl beat 2 eggs, and add a small teacupful of sugar. Into another bowl place 4 heaping tablespoonfuls corn-starch, which moisten with cold milk until it is about the consistency of cream. Add this to the beaten eggs and sugar, and stir the whole into the milk as soon as it comes to a boil. Continue stirring a few minutes, until the starch is well cooked. Remove from stove, add a teaspoonful of extract, lemon or vanilla; pour into cups which have previously been rinsed with cold water. Serve cold, with stewed or canned fruit. Cherries are suitable.—*Sister Nannie B. Underhill, Collbran, Colo.*

Bread Dough Pudding.—Take enough bread dough for a small loaf; work in it 1 egg; lay it in a thin cloth, fold over the dough; let rise until light; then have boiling water in a pot, drop it in and boil half an hour. Serve with sweetened cream and any kind of fruit desired.—*Sister J. M. Kagey, Dayton, Va.*

Bread Pudding.—Take 2 quarts of sweet milk, 1 quart of bread crumbs, butter the size of a walnut, 5 eggs. Put in the oven and let brown on top; then take the whites of 2 eggs, beat to a froth, add jelly and spread over top of pudding; let get brown. Serve with sweet cream.—*Sister Elsie Huff, Ft. Definace, Va.*

Bread Pudding.—Take 2 eggs, 2 tablespoonfuls of sugar, 1 quart of bread crumbs, 1 quart of sweet milk, 1 tablespoonful of butter, flavor to suit the taste. Bake in a quick oven. When baked, remove from oven; cover with the well-beaten white of an egg mixed with 2 tablespoonfuls of sugar; put back in the oven to brown. Serve warm with cream.—*Sister Caleb Long, Boonsboro, Md.*

Bread Pudding.—Take bread broken fine and covered with milk; set it on the stove, where it is not too hot, to soften; remove and stir in 1 beaten egg, ½ cup of sugar, ½ cup of raisins, a pinch of salt, ⅓ cup of butter, 1 teaspoonful of ground cinnamon; bake 1 hour. Serve with sugar and cream.—*Sister Lizzie Culp, Leeton,*

A Hasty Bread Pudding.—Take 5 or 6 slices of light bread; lay in a deep pan; take 4 eggs, 1 teacupful of sugar; beat well together, then add 1 quart of sweet milk; pour over the bread; flavor with any flavoring to suit taste—a teaspoonful of ground cinnamon sprinkled over the top is good. Bake in a hot oven.—*Sister Rachel E. Gillett, Camp Verde, Ariz.*—Butter both sides of the slices of bread. A few well-washed currants may be sprinkled between the slices of bread, if desired.—*Sister Susie Smith, Conway Springs, Kans.*

Steamed Bread Pudding.—Take 1 quart of bread crumbs soaked in sweet milk; when soft mash with a spoon; add a little salt, 3 tablespoonfuls of flour, 3 eggs beaten well; mix and steam 1½ hours. Slice and serve with butter and sugar.—*Sister Catharine Yundt, Pomona, Cal.*

Brown Betty.—Roll crackers real fine, put a layer in a buttered pan, then a layer of apple sauce and a little butter, alternately a layer of crackers, then apple sauce and butter; have the last a thick layer of cracker crumbs; pour on enough to bake and put in a moderately hot oven till brown. Serve with cream and sugar.—*Sister Louisa Plum, Maryland, Ill.*

Brown Betty.—Put a layer of bread crumbs into a pudding dish, then a layer of sliced apples with sugar sprinkled over them, and a little butter. Continue until your dish is full. Then add a little water and bake. To be eaten with sugar and cream.—*Sister John H. Rinehart, Union, Ohio.*

Charlotte Russe.—Take ½ pint of milk, yolks of 2 eggs, 3 tablespoonfuls of sugar, 1 heaping tablespoonful of gelatine; beat the milk, sugar and yolks together, then add the gelatine dissolved in cold water; let boil until creamy, using the double boiler; let cool until it begins to get stiff, then add 1 pint of whipped cream, 2 teaspoonfuls of vanilla, and ½ cup of chopped and blanched almonds; pour in molds lined with sponge cake or lady fingers and set on ice until stiff.—*Sister Josie Lohmiller, Pueblo, Colo.*

Cherry Cobbler.—Take 1 quart of flour, a pinch of salt, lard the size of an egg, 1½ teaspoonfuls of baking powder, mix into a stiff batter; spread a layer of the batter in a pan, then a layer of fruit; sprinkle fruit with sugar and lay over it bits of butter, then another layer of dough, and so on until the pan is almost full; then bake in a slow oven. Serve while hot with sugar and cream.—*Sister Elizabeth Eckerle, Flora, Ind.*

Cherry Pudding.—Take 1 cup thick milk, 1 egg, ½ teaspoonful baking soda, 1 teaspoonful salt, 1 large cup seeded sour·cherries (fresh are best, but the canned will do), flour to make a rather stiff batter. Mix in earthen dish, take a large kettle, put cold water in it and set the earthen dish in, cover each, let steam for about 2 hours or until dry when picked with broom splint. Eat while warm with good milk sweetened. What is left over can be steamed again and is good.—*Sister Mattie O. Weaver, Hinkletown, Pa.*

Corn Pudding.—Take 1½ cups of corn meal, 1½ cups of flour, 1¼ cups of sweet milk, ½ cup of lard, ½ cup of sugar, 2 eggs, 3 teaspoonfuls of baking powder.—*Sister Kate Zug, Mastersonville, Pa.*

Green Corn Pudding.—Take 1 quart of corn, 1 pint of new milk, 1 egg, butter the size of a walnut, 1 tablespoonful of flour, 1 tablespoonful of sugar, salt and pepper. Beat the egg and mix all together in a pudding dish; bake in the oven about 30 minutes. The corn should be fresh plucked and carefully taken from the cob, either by running a sharp knife through the center of the rows or by shaving the tips off and then pressing the pulp out with a blunt knife. —*Sister Nannie H. Strayer, Johnstown, Pa.*

Cornstarch Custard.—Take 1 pint of milk, 2 eggs, 2 tablespoonfuls of cornstarch, and 3 tablespoonfuls of sugar. Heat the milk to boiling point, mix the cornstarch dissolved in a little water with the sugar and yolks of eggs; stir in the milk and let thicken, stirring constantly. Pour this over the stiffly-beaten whites of the eggs; flavor to suit the taste, and stir very lightly, so that the whites of eggs can be distinctly seen. Serve cold.—*Sister Ida M. Ellenberger, Polo, Mo.*

Cornstarch Pudding.—Take 1 pint of milk, whites of 3 eggs, 2 tablespoonfuls of cornstarch, 3 tablespoonfuls of sugar, and a little salt. Put milk in double cooker, and when about the boiling point add the sugar and cornstarch wet with a little of the milk, lastly the eggs whipped to a stiff froth; beat and cook a few minutes; put in moulds and cool; serve the following sauce: Bring to the boiling point 1 pint of milk, 3 tablespoonfuls of sugar; add the beaten yolks of the 3 eggs thinned with 1 tablespoonful of milk; stir until it thickens; flavor sauce and pudding to suit taste.—*Sister Martha L. Fitz, Panora, Iowa.*

Cornstarch Pudding.—Take 1 quart of milk, let come to a boil, 3 large tablespoonfuls of cornstarch wet with some cold milk, sugar to taste; when boiled remove from the stove and stir in the whites of 3 eggs well beaten; turn into a large bowl to cool. Sauce: Take 1 pint of milk, let come to a boil, 1 tablespoonful of cornstarch wet with a little cold milk, yolks of 3 eggs, sugar to taste; when boiled flavor with vanilla. When cold, turn the white part into a large glass dish and pour the sauce around it.—*Sister Kate Renneker, Baltic, Ohio.*

Cottage Pudding.—Take 1 egg, 1 cup of sugar, ½ cup of milk and cream, butter the size of a walnut, 2 teaspoonfuls of baking powder, and flour enough to stiffen. Bake in a loaf. Serve with the following sauce: Take 1½ tin cups of water, ½ cup of sugar; let boil, add a small lump of butter, 1 tablespoonful of cornstarch; flavor to taste.—*Sister Anna Showalter, Lattasburg, Ohio.*

Cottage Pudding.—Take 2 eggs, 1 cup of sugar, ½ cup of butter or lard, 1 cup of sour cream, 2½ cups of flour, 1 teaspoonful of soda, 1 teaspoonful of cream of tartar. Mix thoroughly; bake in a long pan 20 minutes. Serve with cream or lemon sauce.—*Sister Alice Garman, Lancaster, Pa.*

Cottage Pudding.—Take 3 cups of flour, ½ cup lard, 1 cup of sugar, 1 cup of buttermilk, 1 teaspoonful of soda. Stir well, pour into a pan and bake. Serve warm with sweet milk.—*Sister Sarah A. Sell, Newry, Pa.*

Cottage Pudding.—Take 1 cup of sugar, ½ cup of butter, 1 cup of sweet milk and 1 teaspoonful of soda. Dissolve in milk 2 teaspoonfuls of cream of tartar and add 1 teaspoonful of lemon extract. Sprinkle a little sugar over the top of the batter just before putting it into the oven. Bake in a bread pan and serve with sauce made of 2 tablespoonfuls of butter, 1 cup of sugar and 1 tablespoonful of flour. Mix with a little cold water and stir till like cream; then add 1 pint of boiling water and boil a few minutes, stirring all the time. After it is taken off the fire, add ½ teaspoonful of lemon extract.—*Sister Martha Royer, Dallas Center, Ia.*

Crow Nest Pudding.—Put 1 pint of raspberries into a pan, sweeten and sprinkle a little flour over the top, and cover with a batter made of 1 cup of sugar, butter the size of a walnut, 1 egg, ½ cup of milk, 1 teaspoon of baking powder, 1 teaspoon of vanilla, and flour to mix a little stiffer than cake batter. Bake and serve with the following sauce: Butter the size of a walnut browned in a pan; to this add 1 pint of milk and water, ½ cup of sugar, and 1 tablespoonful of cornstarch. Let come to a boil and flavor with vanilla.—*Sister Eva Miller, Sidney, Ind.*

Currant Roll.—Make a rich pie crust, using a small amount of baking powder; roll out about the same thickness as for pies, only much larger, then sprinkle with currants, then sugar, grate nutmeg over it, drop bits of butter here and there; roll up and put in a bread pan, sprinkle sugar, grated nutmeg and a pinch of salt over it; then cover with boiling water, and bake. A few raisins used with the currants improve it.—*Sister Pearl Weimert, Larned, Kans.*

Duchess Cream.—Take ½ cup of tapioca, cover with water and soak over night. Drain off in the morning and cover with boiling water. Simmer until clear, stirring frequently. Then add 1 cup of sugar, ½ can of pineapple, the juice of 1 lemon and the white of 1 egg well beaten. Serve with whipped cream.—*Sister Edna Eisenbise, Lanark, Ill.*

Date Pudding.—Take 1 cup of seeded dates and cook in 1½ cups of boiling water, to which a pinch of salt has been added. Thicken with graham or whole wheat flour, not too thick. Cook well and mould. To be eaten with whipped cream or cold cream and sugar. Enough for four persons.—*Sister J. F. Thomas, Inglewood, Cal.*

Delicious Pudding.—Take a piece of light bread dough the size of a small bowl, cut it up fine in a pan; add 1 cup of brown sugar, 1 tablespoonful of cinnamon, 1 cup of currants or raisins, ½ cup of sour milk, 1 teaspoonful of soda, 2 or 3 eggs well beaten; mix into a smooth batter and steam 4 hours in a buttered dish.—*Sister Minnie Rexroad, Darlow, Kans.*

Duff Pudding.—Take 4 cups of flour, 2 pounds of suet chopped fine; add 1 cup of sugar, 1 cup of molasses, ½ pound of raisins, 1 tablespoonful of baking powder; mix together well, then put in a vessel; put some water in a kettle; let it boil, then set the vessel in the water, cover a cloth over it and put a lid on the kettle so it will be tight. Keep the duff covered with water; let water boil 30 minutes, then take out and serve with cream. Duff can be put in a cloth in the kettle instead of the vessel.—*Sister Mary Rowland, Astoria, Ill.*

Economy Pudding.—Save bread scraps or biscuit until you have a good dish full; have a skillet hot with several spoonfuls of lard and a bit of butter in it; pour in the bread well chipped up; let fry a few minutes; pour over milk with which has been mixed 1 egg, salt and pepper to taste, and flavored with small celery tops chipped very fine; stir all together into a mass; place in the oven and bake 15 or 20 minutes.—*Sister Mary B. Ebersole, Salem, Oregon.*

English Pudding.—Take 1 coffee cup each of English currants, seeded raisins, suet chopped fine, sugar, sour milk, ½ teaspoonful of soda, a little cinnamon, cloves, nutmeg, and allspice, 2 well-beaten eggs; add enough flour to make a stiff batter; pour the batter in a thin muslin sack, first dipping the sack in boiling water to prevent the pudding from sticking to the sack; have the sack large enough so the batter will not fill it full, or it will not get light; drop into a kettle of boiling water, boil or steam 2 hours. Serve hot with cherry juice or any desired dressing.—*Sister Sue Sisler, Dallas Center, Iowa.*

Float.—Take 1 quart of sweet milk sweetened to taste, yolks of 3 eggs beaten light; let milk come to a boil then stir in yolks with enough milk to stir easily; cook, and as you take it off stir in the whites of the eggs beaten to a froth. Flavor to taste.—*Sister Mary Reddick, Sheridan, Mo.*

Float.—Beat stiff the whites of 6 eggs; have ready on the fire a pint of milk sweetened and flavored with vanilla; as soon as it boils drop the beaten eggs into it by tablespoonfuls, and as soon as they become set, dip them out with a thin slice and arrange them according to fancy upon a broad dish; allow the milk to cool a little, then stir in the yolks of the eggs very gradually; when thick pour around the snowed eggs, and serve cold.—*Sister Sue Wire, Acton, Okla.*

Flummery.—Boil together 1 pint of juice of any kind of fruit and water; add 1 cup of sugar and 2 heaping tablespoonfuls of cornstarch; when done, stir in 1 pint of the fruit. Serve with whipped cream.—*Sister Martha L. Fitz, Panora, Iowa.*

Fruit Pudding.—Make a batter of 1 egg, 1 cup of sugar, 1 cup of sweet milk, 1 tablespoonful of cold lard, 2 teaspoonfuls of baking powder and 3½ cups of flour. Put a layer of batter into a deep pan, then one of berries or cherries, and sprinkle with sugar.

Then put in another layer of batter. Bake one hour and serve with cream or milk.—*Sister Irene Stoner Weybright, Detour, Md.*

Fruit Pudding.—Take 2 cups of flour, 1 cup of sweet milk, ½ cup of sugar, 1 egg, 2 tablespoonfuls of baking powder; add 1 pint fruit last. Any kind of fruit or berries that may suit the taste can be used.—*Sister Kate H. Zug, Mastersonville, Pa.*

Galaway Cream Custard.—First make a soft custard, using nearly a pint of milk; 1 egg, a scant tablespoonful of cornstarch and flavoring to taste. Cake part: 1½ cups of flour, 2 teaspoonfuls of baking powder, 1 cup of sugar, 3 eggs and 2 tablespoonfuls of water. Sift the baking powder through the flour, then add sugar, eggs (do not beat the eggs) and water, and with a strong spoon stir until well mixed. If the eggs are small it will require a little more water. It should be just a little stiff so as to spread in the tins with a knife. Make four layers, bake in a quick oven a golden yellow, not overdone or it will get too dry, remove from the tins and spread the custard between the layers. If just right it will be light and moist, and almost melt in the mouth. It makes a nice wedding cake.—*Sister Amanda Witmore, McPherson, Kans.*

Gooseberry Cobbler.—For the crust take 1 pint of sour milk, 1 teaspoonful of soda, ½ teaspoonful of salt, 2 tablespoonfuls of lard, flour enough to make a soft dough; roll out until a little thicker than pie crust. Spread over the dough 1 quart of gooseberries; sweeten to taste. Roll the berries and crust together, place in a bread pan, pour over 1 pint of water; bake in a moderate oven ¾ of an hour.—*Sister Etta Archer, Lenox, Iowa.*

Graham Pudding.—Take 2 cups of graham flour, 1 cup of molasses, 1 cup of raisins, 1 cup of sweet milk, 1 teaspoonful of soda, spice to taste. Steam 3 hours; eat with sugar and cream or sauce.—*Sister A. W. Hawbaker, Kenmare, N. Dak.*

Graham Pudding.—Take 1 cup of sugar, 1 cup of molasses, 1 cup of sweet milk, 1 cup of raisins ½ (scant) cup of butter, 1 cup of wheat flour, 2 cups of graham flour, 1 egg, 2 teaspoonfuls of soda, 1 teaspoonful of cream of tartar, 2 teaspoonfuls of ground cinnamon. Mix thoroughly in a pan that holds at least ¾ of a gallon; place in a steamer and steam for 2 hours. This pudding can be kept for weeks in winter, can be resteamed at any time and be just as good as when first made. Serve warm with cream of the following dressing: 2 tablespoonfuls of sugar mixed with 1 table-spoonful of flour; pour over it slowly ½ pint of boiling water, stirring constantly; let boil till clear; add butter size of a walnut, 1 teaspoonful of vanilla; pour upon slices of the pudding.—*Sister Felicia E. Shaffer, Morrill, Kans.*

Hard Times Charlotte.—Take 1½ pints of sweet milk, set on the fire to boil. Mix together the following: ½ large cup of sugar, 1 beaten egg, 1 heaping tablespoonful of cornstarch, ½ cup of milk, 2 tablespoonfuls of grated chocolate, a pinch of salt, blend smooth and pour gradually into the boiling milk; let simmer a few minutes, stirring all the time. Fill a large fruit dish with any kind of stale cake cut in small pieces; when the cream is nearly cold, flavor with lemon or vanilla and pour over the cake. Serve cold.—*Sister Jas. F. Thomas, Inglewood, Cal.*

Huckleberry Pudding.—Take 2 eggs, beat the whites separate, 1 cup of sugar, ½ cup of sweet milk, 1 tablespoonful of butter, 2 tablespoonfuls of baking powder, 2 cups of flour, 1 pint of berries put in a dish and floured well, mixing up with the hands. Do not have berries wet when using the flour. Serve with sweetened milk. —*Sister Sadie K. Imler, Lancaster, Pa.*

Huckleberry Pudding.—Take 1 cup of white sugar, 1 egg, ½ cup of sweet milk, 2 tablespoonfuls of melted butter, 2 cups of flour, and 1 teaspoonful of baking powder. Mix and add the huckleberries or strawberries. Bake in a moderate oven and serve while hot with sweet milk.—*Sister Susan Danner, Abbottstown, Pa.*

Baked Huckleberry Pudding.—Mix 2 cups of light brown sugar, ¾ of a cup of butter, 1 cup of sour milk, 4 eggs, 1 teaspoonful of soda, 1 quart of huckleberries; make a dough as thick as for jelly cake; bake ¾ of an hour in moderate oven. Serve with hard sauce or milk.—*Sister Mahala Stoner, Aultman, Ohio.*

Indian Pudding.—Take ½ cup of corn meal sifted in 1 quart of boiling milk; then mix together ½ cup of molasses, ½ cup of sugar, 3 or 4 eggs, 1 pint of cold milk, 1 teaspoonful of butter; mix thoroughly and add to the boiling milk and meal, then bake 2 or 3 hours in a moderate oven.—*Sister Mary E. Towslee, Colby, Kans.*

Kiss Pudding.—Put 1 quart of sweet milk to boil, adding about 4 tablespoonfuls of cornstarch just before it begins to boil. Beat the yolks of 4 eggs with ½ cup of sugar and add when the starch is done. After adding the yolks stir constantly and remove from fire; after about 2 minutes flavor. Pour into a pan and cover with whites beaten very stiff with enough sugar to sweeten just a little and a little flavoring. Put in the stove to brown lightly. Eat cold with cream.—*Sister Mary E. Clapper, Larned, Kans.*

La Fiesta Pudding.—Take 1 heaping pint of flour, ½ cup of sugar, ½ cup of milk, 1 teaspoonful of baking powder, 1 tablespoonful of butter; flavor with vanilla; bake in a moderate oven.—*Sister Lucy Magie, Tropico, Cal.*

Lemon Jelly.—Moisten 2 tablespoonfuls of corn starch, stir into one pint of boiling water, add the juice of 2 lemons and ⅓ cup of sugar. Grate in a little of the rind. Put in molds to cool.—*Sister Martha V. Flory, Sterling, Ill.*

Lemon Pudding.—Scald 1 pint of milk, into which put 1 cup of fine bread crumbs, and 1 tablespoonful of butter; let boil once, then set aside to cool a little, then add the yolks of 3 eggs beaten with ½ cup of sugar, and grated rind of 1 lemon; pour in pudding dish and bake 15 to 20 minutes; remove from the oven, spread over the top the whites of the 3 eggs beaten with ½ cup of sugar and the juice of the lemon; set in oven to brown slightly. Serve warm.—*Sister Laura Smucker, Timberville, Va.*

Excellent Lemon Pudding.—Take 1 quart of sweet milk, 1 pint of bread crumbs, 2 tablespoonfuls of sugar, yolks of 2 eggs, 1 lemon—grated rind and extract to taste. Frosting: Take the whites of 2 eggs beaten stiff, pulp and juice of 1 lemon, 1 tablespoonful of sugar. Set in oven till light brown. Serve cold.—*Sister Gertrude Stoner, Hutsonville, Ill.*

Marshmallow Fluff.—Take 1 pound of marshmallows, cut each in four dice, one pint of cream whipped stiff, the beaten white of one egg and pulverized sugar to taste. Add marshmallows and ¼ pound of English walnuts broken in small pieces to cream and mix all together. Will serve six persons.—*Sister Edna Crowe, Des Moines, Iowa.*

Marshmallow Pudding.—Dissolve 1 rounding tablespoonful of granulated gelatine in ½ cup of cold water. Place over the fire and stir until thoroughly dissolved. Add ½ cup of cold water and let stand to cool. Take the whites of 4 eggs beaten very light and stiff, and pour over the gelatine slowly, beating all the time while pouring in. Sprinkle in 1 cup of granulated sugar and beat while adding. Add 1 teaspoonful of almond extract and beat again. Take ⅓ of the mixture and color pink. Then spread one layer of the white in the pan and sprinkle with chopped nuts; then the pink layer and chopped nuts, and the rest of the white for the top layer. Let get cool and serve with whipped cream.—*Sister Anna B. Wales, North English, Iowa.*

Molasses Pudding.—Take 2 eggs, ½ cup of butter, 1 cup of molasses, ½ cup of sugar, 1 cup of buttermilk, 2 scant teaspoonfuls of soda, and flour enough to make a thick batter. Bake and serve with any kind of sauce desired.—*Sister Minnie B. Smith, Berthoud, Colo.*

Mountain Dew Pudding.—Take 1 pint of milk, yolks of 2 eggs, 2 tablespoonfuls cocoanut, ½ cup rolled crackers, 1 teaspoonful lemon extract, and a little sugar. Bake half hour. Make a frosting of whites of 2 eggs and ¼ cup granulated sugar. Brown in oven.—*Sister Etta Eckerle; Lanark, Ill.*

Minute Pudding.—Have a vessel of boiling water into which stir enough flour to make it thick like mush. Let it cook thoroughly done, stirring all the time to prevent lumps. Serve while hot with cream and sugar.—*Sister Maggie Moomaw, Versailles, Mo.*

Orange Custard.—Take the juice of 8 oranges, 6 eggs, 2 cups of sugar, 1 cup of water, and ½ cup of flour. Mix together all except the whites of the eggs and boil until thick. Beat the whites stiff and stir into the custard as soon as you take it off the stove.— *Sister R. F. Brubaker, San Dimas, Cal.*

Orange Float.—Take 1 quart of water, the juice and pulp of 2 lemons, 1 coffeecup of sugar; boil all together; add 4 tablespoonfuls of cornstarch dissolved in a little cold water; let boil 15 minutes, stirring all the time. When cold, pour over it 4 or 5 seeded and sliced oranges. Beat the whites of 3 eggs with a little sugar, flavor with vanilla; spread over the top of the float.—*Sister Mina Colclesser, Huntington, Ind.*

Orange Pudding.—Pare and slice 3 large oranges, cut very fine, lay in a pudding dish and sprinkle with 1 cup of sugar. Let stand ½ hour. Then take the yolks of 3 eggs, ½ cup of sugar, 3 tablespoonfuls of cornstarch or flour and 1 quart of new milk. When the milk boils, stir in eggs, sugar and flour or cornstarch, and boil till it thickens. Let cool a little and pour over the oranges. Beat the whites of the eggs to a stiff froth, add ½ cup of sugar and spread over the pudding and brown. The addition of 2 bananas, sliced thin, improves this delicious pudding.—*Sister Hazel Brown, Winchester, Va.*

Orange Pudding.—Peel and cut in bits 4 oranges, rejecting the seeds. Sprinkle a cup of sugar over them. Boil a pint of milk, to which add the yolks of 3 eggs, well beaten, with 1 tablespoonful of cornstarch. When it thickens pour it over the fruit. Beat the whites of the eggs with a tablespoonful of pulverized sugar. Frost the pudding and brown it in the oven. You can substitute strawberries or peaches if you like.—*Sister Minnie E. Schultz, Lancaster, Pa.*

Orange Pudding.—Peel and cut in small squares 6 oranges, sprinkle with sugar. Let stand about 2 hours. Boil 1 pint of milk, beat the yolks of 3 eggs, 3 tablespoonfuls of sugar, a heaping tablespoonful of cornstarch. Stir into the milk while boiling. Cook until thick, or till it is done. When nearly cold, pour over the oranges. Beat the whites of the eggs stiff with ½ cup of sugar. Spread over the pudding. Set in the oven in a pan of cold water and let brown lightly. The reason for putting it in a pan of water is to keep the oranges from cooking.—*Sister Mary A. Rosenberger, Covington, Ohio.*

Peach Cobbler.—Make a crust of sweet milk, lard, baking powder, salt, and flour, almost but not quite as short as for pie dough. Line a bread pan or baking dish with the dough, put in a layer of peeled and stoned peaches, sprinkle with sugar and a little grated nutmeg. Roll out a piece of this dough and cut it into small squares and put in a layer of these; finish with another layer of peaches, over which sprinkle sugar, grated nutmeg, and a little flour. Add a few bits of butter and sufficient water to make plenty of juice. Put on a cover of the dough, with openings in the center for the steam to escape. Bake in the oven the same as chicken pie. To be served warm and eaten with rich milk and sugar. Canned peaches may be used when fresh ones cannot be obtained.—*Sister Lizzie D. Mohler, Falls City, Nebr.*

Peach Float.—Take 1 quart can of peaches from which the syrup has been drained, mash fine, add ½ cup sugar. Beat the whites of 2 or 3 eggs stiff and beat into the peaches. Bake 5 or 10 minutes; when cool serve with sugar and cream. Apples are very good served in the same way.—*Sister Frances Miller Leiter, Hade, Pa.*

Peach Pudding.—Two or three hours before mealtime pare, slice, and sugar very ripe peaches. Toast nicely thin slices of stale bread. Put alternate layers of the prepared peaches and bread into a deep dish. Set in a cool place. Serve with cream or rich whole milk.—*Sister Phoebe Zook, Mattawana, Pa.*

Peach Pudding.—Peel and cut about 1 quart of ripe peaches, put in a dish and pour over them a cup of white sugar; let a pint of milk get boiling hot by setting it in a pot of boiling water; add the yolks of 3 eggs well beaten, 1 tablespoonful of cornstarch made smooth with a little cold milk; stir all the time. As soon as thickened, pour over the fruit. Beat the whites to a stiff froth, adding a tablespoonful of sugar and spread over the top for frosting, set in the oven a few minutes to harden. Serve cold with cream. Berries or oranges can be substituted for the peaches.—*Sister Lydia Garber, Redfield, Kans.*

Persimmon Pudding.—Scald 1 gallon of persimmons, let stand over night in same water, then drain and rub them through a perforated sieve. Peel and grind or grate 1 quart of sweet potatoes, add 1 cup of molasses, 1½ cups of sugar, 3 eggs well beaten, 1 quart of fresh milk, not skimmed, 4 cups of flour, 2 tablespoonfuls of baking powder, 1 tablespoonful of ground cinnamon and 1 teaspoonful of grated nutmeg. Mix in granite pan, bake in a medium oven 2½ hours and serve with sugar and cream. This pudding will keep as fruit cake, if kept in a cool place.—*Sister Emmet Moore, Mooreland, Ind.*

Pineapple Pudding.—Take 1 cup of tapioca soaked over night, 1½ cups of granulated sugar dissolved in water, and cook almost to a syrup, add the juice of two lemons, 1 can of sliced pineapple chopped in pieces, the beaten whites of 2 eggs stirred in when cold.—*Sister Kate Whitaker, Red Cloud, Nebr.*

Pineapple Pudding.—Use 1 can of pineapple, or 1 fresh pine. Run through the grinder to make fine. If a fresh pine is used, cook it a few minutes and sweeten well; then put into a big dish. Over this fruit, pour a batter made of the yolk of 1 egg, ½ cup of sugar, ½ cup of milk, a pinch of salt, 2 tablespoonfuls of shortening, and ½ teaspoonful of baking powder, mixed in 1¼ cups of flour. When it is baked, cover with a meringue, made of the white of the egg and 1 tablespoonful of sugar. Brown in the oven.—*Sister Lillus E. Mahan, Omaja, Cuba.*

Baked Pieplant.—Cut 2 pounds of pieplant into a pudding dish, sprinkle over it ½ cup of sugar and two tablespoonfuls of flour, or what is better, ½ cup of rolled breadcrumbs. Add water until the pieplant is two-thirds covered. Bake in a quick oven thirty or forty minutes. This method of preparing pieplant removes the medicinal taste and makes an acceptable spring dish.—*Sister Martha V. Flory, Sterling, Ill.*

Plum Pudding.—Take 1 cup of suet chopped fine, 1 cup of molasses, 1 cup of raisins, 1 cup of sweet milk, 1 teaspoonful of soda, 1 egg, a little salt and enough flour to make the batter as stiff as for cake. Boil or steam two or three hours.—*Sister L. Clanin, Hicksville, Wash.*

Prune Dessert.—Beat the whites of 6 eggs stiff, add gradually 1 cup of sugar, ½ teaspoonful of vanilla, ½ cup of chopped English walnuts and 27 pitted prunes which have been cooked and hashed fine. Bake in a pudding dish a short time. Serve with whipped cream.—*Sister Kathryn Wingert, Kingsley, Iowa.*

Prune Dessert.—Cover the prunes with water and let soak over night. In the morning add sugar to taste, and stew slowly until soft, drain, remove the seeds, cut up fine. When cold, add the juice of a lemon, and grated rind also if desired. Beat the whites of 2 or 3 eggs to a stiff froth, mix thoroughly with the prunes and serve. The juice of the prunes may be used for another dessert: Bring the juice to a boil; dissolve 2 tablespoonfuls of cornstarch in a cup of milk, add this to the juice, stir till it thickens, remove from the fire, add the juice of a lemon, pour into cups to cool. Serve in the cups with milk or cream.—*Sister Adaline Hohf Beery, Elgin, Ill.*

Prune Pudding.—Take the whites of 5 eggs beaten to a stiff froth, 1 cup of stewed prunes chopped fine, 5 tablespoonfuls of sugar; add the seed kernels chopped fine, and mix all together; put into a pudding dish, set in a pan of boiling water and bake 40 minutes.—*Sister Clara Ringer, Oregon, Ill.*

Prune Whip.—Cook ½ pound of choice prunes until dry and tender. Remove the stones and mash the fruit. Add ½ cup of sugar, ½ teaspoonful cream of tartar, and the well-beaten whites of 5 eggs. Bake in a moderate oven 20 minutes. Serve either warm or cold with cream.—*Sister R. E. Arnold, Elgin, Ill.*

Raisin Pudding.—Take 3 cups of flour, 1 pound of raisins, 2 eggs, 1½ cups of suet, 2 teaspoonfuls of baking powder, 1½ cups of sugar and milk enough to make a stiff batter. Tie loosely in a cloth and drop in boiling water. Boil from 1½ to 2 hours, or spread a cloth on a steamer, and pour the pudding on it.—*Sister Sue Runk, Rockhill Furnace, Pa.*

Raspberry Pudding.—Take 2 eggs, 1 cup of sugar, 1 pint of sour milk, 1 teaspoonful of soda; beat well together, thicken with flour about as thick as cake batter; grease a baking pan, put in a layer of the batter, then a layer of the fruit, and so on; bake in a slow oven. Serve warm with cream.—*Sister Ida B. Hamilton, Springport, Ind.*

Raspberry Pyramid.—Wash ½ pint of good hard rice, put it into a quart of milk and cook in a double boiler till the rice is quite soft, season with ½ teaspoonful of salt; then while hot spread on a large plate ¼ of an inch thick and cover this with ripe raspberries; sprinkle with sugar, then another layer of rice and berries, making each layer smaller than the preceding one, so as to form a pyramid; let it stand until quite cold. Serve in perpendicular slices with sweetened cream or milk.—*Sister Hannah Ziegler, Royersford, Pa.*

Rhubarb Tapioca.—To 1 pint of chopped rhubarb add 2 dozen cooked prunes, ¼ cup of prune juice and ½ cup of sugar; boil for 5 or 10 minutes, then add ½ cup of any quick-cooking tapioca which has first been soaked for half an hour in ¾ cup of cold water; cook until the tapioca looks transparent. Serve either hot or cold with sugar and cream.—*Sister S. S. Blough, Batavia, Ill.*

Ribbon Pudding.—First Part: Take 1 pint of milk, 2 table-spoonfuls of cornstarch, the yolks of 2 eggs and vanilla and sugar to suit the taste. [About ¼ cup of sugar should be sufficient.—Ed.] Stir the egg yolks and cornstarch, wet with a little cold milk, into the remainder of the milk when nearly boiling. Boil a few minutes then flavor and pour into one large mold or divide into individual molds. While this is cooling and becoming set proceed with Second Part: Take 1 pint of milk, 2 tablespoonfuls of cornstarch and 1 tablespoonful of cocoa mixed with a little milk. Make as above, adding vanilla and sugar; perhaps a little more than above of latter. Pour this into the mold or molds on top of first part. Third part: Take cup of water, 1 tablespoonful of cornstarch, the whites of 2 eggs and sugar to sweeten. Wet the cornstarch with a little cold water and stir into the cup of water when boiling. Take from the stove and immediately stir in the stiffly beaten whites. Then pour this on top of second part in the mold.—*Sister Lizzie Andes, Ephrata, Pa.*

Rice Custard.—Cook done ½ cup rice seasoned with a little salt. Then add 2 cups cream. Beat the whites of 2 eggs, and ⅔ cup of sugar and beat again and when the rice and cream begin to boil, add the eggs and sugar and let boil a few minutes, then take off and flavor.—*Sister Lillie M. Blickenstaff, Cerro Gordo, Ill.*

Rice Pudding.—Take 1 cup of rice, wash and scald, but do not boil; let stand ½ hour, drain, then add 1 cup of sugar, 1 cup of raisins, 1 quart of sweet milk; flavor with nutmeg. Bake in oven until rice is done.—*Sister Mary Netzley, Batavia, Ill.*

Rice Pap or Pudding.—Take 2 quarts water, ½ teacupful rice, 1 teacupful flour, 1 egg, 2 quarts rich milk and ½ teaspoonful of salt. Boil rice in water till nearly dry, then have your milk boiling, and pour the rice into the milk. Keep back 1 teacupful milk, and make a batter of flour, egg, and milk; add salt and stir in batter. Stir till it comes to a boil, and it will be ready to eat with sugar. Maple sugar is fine if you have it.—*Sister Saaie Lichty, Waterloo, Iowa.*

Rice Pudding.—To a cup of rice boiled until dry in a pint of water, seasoned with salt, add a pint of milk in which a little cornstarch has been dissolved; boil again, add the yolks of two eggs beaten with half a cup of sugar, stir well together and lastly add the juice and grated rind of one lemon. Place in a dish and bake slowly in the oven. When done spread over the top the whites beaten with two tablespoonfuls of sugar and set in the oven to brown. A cup of raisins may be added just before baking, if liked.—*Sister Ella Snavely, Scottville, Mich.*

Steamed Roly Poly.—Take 1½ cups of sour cream, or sour milk and ½ cup butter and lard, a little salt and 1 teaspoonful of soda. Add flour to form a soft dough as for biscuit and roll out into one large sheet. Spread over this stewed, fresh or dried, peaches, apples or apricots, without juice, and sprinkle with sugar. Roll up like roll jell cake and close ends by pressing dough together. Place in a well greased steamer with large holes in bottom. Set over kettle half full of boiling water and keep boiling for 1½ to 2 hours, depending on fruit. Eat with sweetened milk or plain.—*Sister Lizzie Shirk, Mt. Morris, Ill.*

Sago Pudding.—To 2 cups of any kind of cold fruit juice add 4 tablespoonfuls of sago and cook until the sago is well swollen. Sweeten to taste and serve with cream and sugar, or whipped cream. Enough for four persons.—*Sister J. F. Thomas, Inglewood, Cal.*

Sago Pudding.—Take 4 tablespoonfuls of sago, 1 cup of sugar, and 1 pineapple chopped fine. Boil together or steam for two hours. A lemon may be added to it, if desired.—*Sister Mary C. Hoke, Goshen, Ind.*

Snow Cream.—Heat a quart of thick, sweet cream; when ready to boil, stir into it 3 tablespoonfuls of cornstarch blended with some cold cream; sweeten to taste. Allow it to boil gently, stirring for 2 or 3 minutes; add quickly the whites of 6 eggs beaten to a froth. Do not allow it to boil up more than once after adding the eggs. Flavor with any desired flavoring.—*Sister Sara Reese Eby, West Elkton, Ohio.*

Silver Pudding with Gold Dressing.—Take 4 tablespoonfuls of cornstarch dissolved in cold water, pour on enough boiling water to make a thick starch; beat the whites of 4 eggs to a stiff froth and stir in the starch while hot so as to cook the eggs. Dressing: Take the yolks of 4 eggs, ½ cup of sugar, 1 teaspoonful of vanilla; let come to a boil, then put in a separate dish and let cool. After the starch is dished in sauce dishes, serve the Gold Dressing. *Sister Lizzie E. Smith, Morrill, Kans.*

Spanish Cream.—To 1 quart of milk add ¾ of a box of gelatin dissolved slowly over the fire; then beat light the yolks of 3 eggs, 6 tablespoonfuls of sugar, vanilla to taste, add to the milk, let come to a boil; then beat the whites with 2 tablespoonfuls of sugar; pour the custard into the whites, stir well together and set away to cool. —*Sister Annie R. Stoner, Union Bridge, Md.*

Steamed Pudding.—Take 1 cup of sugar, 1 heaping tablespoonful of butter, 1 cup of sweet milk, 1 cup of seeded raisins, and ½ nutmeg grated. Use flour enough to make a stiff batter. Steam two hours and eat with sweetened cream.—*Sister Sarah A. Burger, Weiser, Idaho.*

Strawberry Custard.—To 1 pint of warm water add enough biscuit crumbs to thicken, then add 1 cup of milk, 2 eggs, 2 cups of sugar, and a teaspoonful of flavoring. Chop fine 1 pint of strawberries and add to above after mixing. Bake until brown. Cover the top with whole strawberries. Let cool and serve as dessert.— *Sister Amy V. Furry, Johnsville, Md.*

Suet Pudding.—Take 1 cup of suet chopped fine, 1 cup of raisins, 1 cup of brown sugar, 1 cup of milk, 1 pint of flour, 1 teaspoonful of baking powder; steam 3 hours. Sauce: Take 2 tablespoonfuls of flour, 4 tablespoonfuls of sugar, 2 tablespoonfuls of butter, water to make as thin as desired.—*Sister M. E. Wise, Myrtlepoint, Oregon.*

Suet Pudding.—Take 1 cup suet, 1 cup molasses, 1 cup sweet milk, 3 cups flour, 1 cup raisins, 1 teaspoonful soda, 1 teaspoonful

salt, and spice to suit taste. Steam about 3 hours. Sauce for same:
Take a small teacupful of water, and ½ pint maple sugar. Let simmer. Remove the scum. Take 4 tablespoonfuls butter, mix with a
level teaspoonful of flour, and 1 teaspoonful grated nutmeg. Boil a
few moments and serve with pudding while warm.—*Sister Susie M.
Brallier, Johnstown, Pa.*

Suet Pudding.—Take ½ cup of New Orleans molasses, ½
cup of chopped suet, ½ cup of raisins cut fine, ½ cup of sour milk,
½ teaspoonful of soda, 1 cup of flour; mix and steam. Sauce: Take
1 pint of water, 1 cup of sugar, 1 tablespoonful of vinegar, 1 tablespoonful of cornstarch, a lump of butter, vanilla to flavor,
bring to a boil, then let slightly cool. Serve pudding warm with
sauce.—*Sister Agnes K. Landis, Richland, Pa.*

Suet Pudding.—Take 4 eggs, 1 cup of milk, ½ cup of New
Orleans molasses, ½ cup of suet chopped fine, 1 teaspoonful salt, 2
teaspoonfuls of baking powder in 3 small cups of flour, cloves, cinnamon, nutmeg, and as much citron and raisins as you like. Steam
2 hours. Sauce: ½ cup of butter, 2 cups of sugar, ½ cup of boiling
water, nutmeg or brandy to flavor. Beat well together. Serve hot.
—*Sister Mary Kinsley, Elkhart, Ind.*

Suet Pudding.—Take 1 cup suet chopped fine, 1 cup sorghum, 1 cup raisins seeded, 1 cup sour milk, 3 cups flour, 1 scant teaspoonful soda, a little salt. Put pudding in bag, steam 3 hours.
Dressing: 1 pint water, 1 tablespoonful butter, 1 cup sugar; flavor
with cinnamon; thicken with tablespoonful of cornstarch.—*Sister
C. S. Eisenbise, Sabetha, Kans.*

Tapioca Pudding.—Soak 4 tablespoonfuls of tapioca in a
little water over night or 2 hours; boil 1 quart of milk and pour
over the tapioca while hot; when cool add ½ cup of sugar, 1 whole
egg and the yolks of 2 eggs well beaten; bake; when done, beat the
whites of the 2 eggs with 2 tablespoonfuls of sugar and spread on
top.—*Sister S. M. Romig, Fostoria, Ohio.*

Tapioca Pudding.—Take 1 teacupful of tapioca soaked 2 hours in 1 pint of milk. Then add a pinch of salt, sweeten to taste, and 1 egg beaten to a froth. Then boil till tender. Flavor to taste. It may be served warm or cold with sugar and cream.—*Sister Mary E. Halderman, Morrill, Kans.*

Tapioca Pudding.—Take 3 tablespoonfuls of tapioca, 1 quart of sweet milk, a little salt, 1 tablespoonful of butter, 2 eggs well beaten, sugar and flavoring to taste; mix tapioca with half of the milk, cold, put on fire and let boil until it thickens, then put in baking dish and add the rest of the milk, butter, eggs, sugar and flavoring; bake a nice brown.—*Sister C. N. Huff, Amsterdam, Va.*

Tapioca Pudding.—Soak 3 tablespoonfuls of tapioca over night in enough water to cover it; in the morning boil 1 quart of milk with the soaked tapioca and ⅔ of a cup of sugar; add a pinch of salt and cook for 10 minutes in a double boiler. Remove from the fire; thoroughly beat the yolks of 3 eggs and add to the tapioca, stirring rapidly for 5 minutes to prevent curdling. Flavor with vanilla and pour into a pudding dish. Beat the whites of the eggs to a stiff froth and pour over the top of the pudding; sift sugar over it and brown a few minutes in the oven. Serve cold.—*Sister H. I. Buechley, Carlisle, Ark.*

Vanilla Cream.—Take ½ pint of milk, 2 eggs, 2 tablespoonfuls of sugar; beat the eggs and sugar together; add to the boiling milk, stir till thick; do not allow it to boil; flavor with vanilla. Serve cold on sliced oranges, bananas, peaches or apricots.—*Sister Emma S. Andes, Lancaster, Pa.*

Vanilla Snow.—Cook 1 cup of rice in a covered dish to keep it white. When nearly done add 1 cup of cream, a pinch of salt, the beaten whites of 2 eggs, and 1 cupful of sugar; flavor with vanilla. Pile in a glass dish and dot with jelly. Serve with sugar and cream. —*Sister Etta Crumpacker, Roanoke, La.*

Velvet Cream.—Dissolve ½ package of gelatin in 1½ cups of water. Add 1½ cups of sugar. Set over the fire long enough to dissolve. When cool add ¾ pint of cream previously whipped and flavor with vanilla to suit taste.—*Sister I. M. Englar, Union Bridge, Md.*

Vinegar Jelly.—Take 1 cup of vinegar, 1 cup of sugar, and 1 cup of water, and put on in a double boiler. When it boils add to it 1 cup of flour, made smooth with 1 cup of water, and stir until it thickens. Flavor to suit the taste; ½ teaspoonful of ground cinnamon, ¼ teaspoonful of ground cloves mixed with the flour while dry, makes it very good. One cup of molasses may be used instead of the sugar.—*Sister Mary L. R. Davis, Dunn, Tenn.*

Whipped Cream.—Take 1 pint of sweet cream well beaten; add the whites of 2 eggs; beat very hard; sweeten and flavor to taste and serve in dessert.—*Sister Mary Rowland, Astoria, Ill.*—If cream to be whipped is first scalded and then cooled again it will swell more when whipped and keep sweet longer.—*Sister Blanche Lentz, Elgin, Ill.*

The Winter Pudding.—An excellent winter pudding may be made as follows: A cupful of finely-picked or chopped suet, kept cool, or it will not work right, 1 cup of any kind of sugar, 3 eggs well beaten, ¼ cup of sweet milk, a teaspoonful each of ground cinnamon and cloves, 2½ cupfuls of flour, a teacupful of raisins and 1 cupful of currants, 2 full teaspoonfuls of baking powder, and a teacupful of bread crumbs. Put in a pan the suet, the sugar and the bread crumbs, pour the milk over this and mix thoroughly. Then stir in the eggs and the fruit and all the other ingredients. Lastly stir in the baking powder with a half teacupful of flour. Mix thoroughly. Put in a well-greased pan, set in a steamer, over boiling water, cover tightly, and steam for 2½ hours, or till a broom splint will come out clean when the pudding is tested. For the sauce melt together in a pan a cupful of sugar, 3 or 4 tablespoonfuls of butter, 3 tablespoonfuls of flour; when these are not only melted, but hot, pour over all a quart of boiling water, and flavor with lemon or vanilla. The pudding left over can be resteamed as long as it lasts. This has been thoroughly tried and is excellent as a cold weather dish.—*Sister Ada L. Early, Macdoel, Cal.*

Woodford Pudding.—Take 1 cup of jam, 1 cup of sugar, 2 cups of flour, ½ cup of butter, 1 teaspoonful of soda dissolved in ¾ of a cup of sour cream, a little nutmeg, cinnamon and cloves. Bake slowly and serve with a sauce.—*Sister Nora B. Hufford, Rossville, Ind.*

Woodford Pudding.—Take 3 eggs, 1 cup jam or preserves (it is best to use something with small seeds, such as gooseberries or raspberries), ½ cup of sugar, ½ cup butter, 1½ cups flour, 1 teaspoonful soda dissolved in 3 teaspoonfuls of sour milk. Flavor with vanilla, cinnamon and nutmeg, and bake slowly. Sauce: 1 cup sugar, butter size of an egg, 1 tablespoonful flour, 1 cup boiling water. Flavor with vanilla. Pour the sauce over the pudding and serve while warm.—*Sister Sallie Shirkey, Rockingham, Mo.*

Woodruff Pudding.—Take 1 cup of sugar, ½ cup of butter, ½ cup of flour, ½ cup of jelly, 3 eggs, 3 teaspoonfuls of sweet or sour milk, ½ teaspoonful of soda, 1 teaspoonful vanilla and a little nutmeg. Pour the batter into a double boiler and boil one and one-half hours. Sauce: Take ⅔ cup of sugar, 1 tablespoonful of flour, ¼ cup of butter, and 1 cup of boiling water. Boil until clear and flavor to taste.—*Sister Emma Schildknecht, Rea, Mo.*

Where any recipe calls for both sugar and flour, always mix them dry before adding the milk or cream, and the mixture will be smooth,— no lumps, as is usually the case when milk and flour are mixed alone.—*Sister Sadie Finch, Portersville, Cal.*

PIES

The pie, it is said, is a strictly American invention or discovery. Some people think this is to be counted to our credit, while some think otherwise, each side being influenced by the nature of his acquaintance with the said invention. Those who have been favored with careful, skillful cooks, and to whose portion there has often fallen a generous wedge of delectable pie fruit, are unanimous in the opinion, that the discovery of pie should be classed with the other great discoveries of the world. Given a well-prepared pastry, for the making of which we have several recipes, and the next matter of importance is the baking. Often pies are either overdone or underdone. If you cannot trust the "smell" of the oven, test it with a bit of pie crust or a sprinkle of flour on the bottom of the oven. If it browns readily, the oven is in proper condition; if it turns black, it is too hot and if it colors slightly it is too slow. After the pie has been in for a few minutes the heat may be decreased slightly; especially should this be done where the filling is of raw material, so that it may have time to cook through before the crust becomes too brown. If stewed fruit is used, it should be perfectly cold so that it will not soak the crust. Brushing the lower crust with white of egg before putting in filling will also prevent soaking. For pies baked in the crust, such as cream, custard and pumpkin, it is well to partly bake the crust before putting in the filling. It is said that the use of cornmeal in pie crust, in the proportion of one-third to two-thirds of flour, makes it lighter and more digestible. The best way to prevent juicy pies from boiling over, is first to see that the filling does not insure a greater amount of juice than can well be accommodated; then see that there is ample opening in the top crust for the escape of steam, and lastly make the top crust large enough to extend a little beyond the edge of the pie plate and lower crust and double the extra edge under the edge of the lower crust. This when pressed down with fork or thumb will make a well-nigh unleakable seam.

Pie Crust.—Sift together 3 cups of flour, 1 tablespoonful of corn starch, and 1 teaspoonful of salt. Cut into this 1 cup of lard. Chop and mix with a knife, only using hands to toss lightly together. (Do not knead pie dough or it will be tough). Moisten with very cold water only just enough to roll out. Use as little dry flour as possible in the process. This will make three pies. If all is not wanted, do not add water to all the flour and lard, but set it away until another time.—*Sister W. H. Royer, Dallas Center, Iowa.*

Pie Crust (For Two Pies).—Take 1 cup of flour, ⅓ cup of lard and a little salt. Mix this with the hand, add enough water to make a dough stiff enough to roll out well.—*Sister Carrie Martin, Mankato, Kans.*

Pie Crust.—Take 3 cups of sweet milk, 2 cups of shortening, salt and flour to stiffen. This will make 10 or more pies.—*Sister Florence Hays Kline, Broadway, Va.*

Good Pie Crust.—Take 3 cups of flour, 1 cup of lard, ¾ cup of cold water, 1 teaspoonful of salt, and 1 level teaspoonful of baking powder. Sift the flour, salt and baking powder, rub in the lard till well mixed, make into a dough with the cold water and roll quite thin.—*Sister John D. Clear, Rockford, Ill.*

Healthful Pastry.—Put into a mixing bowl 3 cups of flour, 1 cup of melted lard, 1 cup of cold water and a pinch of salt. Stir well together with a spoon. This makes three pies with covers.—*Sister Milo H. Geyer, Syracuse, Ind.*

Healthful Pie Crust.—Mix salt in the desired amount of flour. Dissolve a very little soda in some rich sour cream, and mix all together to a soft dough. Never use much flour in rolling pie dough. This is more hygienic than the ordinary lard-and-water kind and looks much richer and better. Sweet cream and baking powder may be used with good results.—*Sister Nettie C. Weybright, Syracuse, Ind.*

Plain Pie Crust.—Take 3 pints of flour, 1 pint of lard, and ½ teaspoonful of salt; rub lard and salt thoroughly through the flour, then take as much cold water as will make a soft dough, mix with as little kneading as possible. This will make crust for 6 pies. —*Sister Ida M. Benner, Duncansville, Pa.*

Pie Dough.—Take flour, mix in lard and salt, then add 3 tablespoonfuls of bread sponge, add enough water to wet dough. Let set ½ hour before forming into pies.—*Sister G. R. Goughnour, Middlebranch, Ohio.*

Amber Pies.—Take the yolks of 3 eggs, 2 cups of sugar, 3 heaping tablespoonfuls of flour, 1 cup of seeded raisins, 1 level teaspoonful each of cloves, cinnamon and allspice, 2 cups of buttermilk, butter the size of a walnut, and a small pinch of salt. Mix and let thicken over a slow fire and pour into 2 baked crusts. Beat the whites of the eggs with 3 tablespoonfuls of sugar; spread on the top of pies and place in the oven until brown.—*Sister Laura Crutchley, Mulberry Grove, Ill.*

Apple Custard.—Take ½ cup of melted butter, 2 cups of sugar, 3 cups of stewed apples, and 4 eggs, whites and yolks beaten separately. Bake in pie plates in bottom crust.—*Sister Cora B. Ober, Mastersonville, Pa.*

Apple Butter Pie.—Take 1 pint of good sweet apple butter, 4 eggs, 2 cups of sugar, 4 heaping tablespoonfuls of flour, 4 pints of milk, and flavor with cinnamon. Bake like custard pies. This will make 4 pies.—*Sister Vinnie A. Weaver, Mound City, Mo.*

Dried Apple Pie.—Make pie dough, using 5 cups of flour, 2 cups of lard, salt, and water. Roll a crust, put over it dried apples, mashed and seasoned with sugar and cinnamon to suit taste. Grate orange peeling over the top.—*Sister Annie Young, Mount Joy, Pa.*

Family Apple Pie.—Make dough the same as for other pies, using about 1 pint of sweet milk for a good-sized pie. Have ready 3 quarts of thinly-sliced baking apples. Line a bread pan with the dough and fill half full of the apples. Sprinkle it with sugar enough to sweeten to suit the taste; then put in a thin layer of the dough and finish filling to the top with the apples and sweeten, after which place on the cover and bake an hour. Serve warm with sweetened cream or fresh butter.—*Sister Mary J. Huffman, Churchville, Va.*

Banana Pie.—Bake a crust; let it cool; slice 2 bananas into the crust. Boil 1 cupful of milk, ½ cup of sugar, yolks of 2 eggs, and 2 tablespoonfuls of flour until thick. Let it cool and then pour over the bananas. Beat the whites of eggs and spread over the top. Put in a quick oven to brown, but do not let pie get hot through.—*Sister F. J. Weimer, Greenville, Ohio.*

Bob Andy Pie.—Take ⅔ cup of butter, 2 cups of sugar, 3 tablespoonfuls of flour and mix together with the yolks of 3 eggs, 1 tablespoonful of cloves and 1 tablespoonful of cinnamon. Beat and add whites of eggs. Then add 3 small cups of milk. Bake like pumpkin pie. This will make two pies.—*Sister Laura Gibson, Virden, Ill.*

Boston Pie.—Take 1 cup of sugar, 1 egg, ½ cup of sour cream, ½ cup of sweet milk, 2 cups of flour, 1 small teaspoonful of soda dissolved in the milk, and 2 teaspoonfuls of cream of tartar sifted in the flour. Bake in 2 jelly pans. When done, as soon as cool, split with a sharp knife, and spread with a custard made as follows: Take 1 cup of sweet milk, 1 large tablespoonful of cornstarch, 1 egg, sweeten well, and a pinch of salt. For the top take 1 square of chocolate, 6 tablespoonfuls of sugar, and 2 tablespoonfuls of sweet cream; melt gently over boiling water. When it comes to a boil, remove from the fire and beat until cool. This will make 2 pies.—*Sister Jas. M. Rowland, Hagerstown, Md.*

Buttermilk Custard.—Take 2 eggs, 1 cup of sugar, 2 tablespoonfuls of butter, 2 tablespoonfuls of flour, and 2 cups of buttermilk. Beat all together and boil 5 minutes; flavor with lemon, pour into baked crusts. Beat the whites of 2 eggs to a stiff froth and add 2 tablespoonfuls of sugar; spread on top of custard and brown in a quick oven.—*Sister Joannah Keedy, Darlow, Kans.*

Buttermilk Pie.—Take 4 cups of buttermilk, 1 cup of sugar, 2 eggs, 2 heaping tablespoonfuls of flour, 1 level teaspoonful of soda, and a little nutmeg. Bake the same as custard.—*Sister Margaret Henrick, Kidder, Mo.*

Butter Scotch Pie.—Bake a crust for one pie. For the filling take 1 cup of brown sugar, 1 tablespoonful of butter, the yolk of one egg, and 2 tablespoonfuls of flour. Mix all together and then stir in one cup of sweet milk. Put over the fire and cook until thick. Flavor with a little vanilla. For frosting use the white of the egg beaten with a little sugar. Cover the pie with this and return to the oven to brown.—*Sister Amanda Widdows, Hagerstown, Ind.*

Butter Scotch Pie.—Take 2 cups of brown sugar and 2 tablespoonfuls of butter. Let boil on the back of the stove until the filling is prepared. Filling: One cup of boiling water, the yolks of 4 eggs, 2 heaping tablespoonfuls of cornstarch or flour, and 1½ cups of sweet milk. Mix the boiling water, cornstarch, or flour, and eggs together, and add to the milk which has been brought to a boil. Add the filling to the wax on the back of the stove, then put into the shells, which have been previously baked. Beat the whites of the eggs stiff, put on the pies and set in the oven to brown.—*Sister Mary Christner, Cerro Gordo, Ill.*

Butter Scotch Pie.—Take 2 cups of brown sugar, 2 tablespoonfuls of butter and ½ cup of hot water. Boil this until it scorches. (This is very important as it gives it the butter-scotch flavor.) Make a custard with 3 heaping tablespoonfuls of flour, 2½ cups of milk and 2 eggs. Pour the butter-scotch into the custard, stirring continually until well mixed. Then pour into two baked crusts. If desired the whites of the eggs may be beaten, a little sugar added, and spread over top of pies. This adds to the appearance of the pie but not to the flavor.—*Sister Effie F. Gnagey, West Milton, Ohio.*

Caramel Pie.—Take 1 cup of granulated sugar and butter the size of a walnut. Put into a frying pan and stir constantly until melted, then add 1 quart of milk and melt again. Have ready the yolks of 2 eggs, mixed with 2 tablespoonfuls of flour, and stir into the milk, and cook until it thickens. Pour into the previously baked crusts and cover with the whites of the eggs beaten stiff with a little granulated sugar.—*Sister Milo H. Geyer, Syracuse, Ind.*

Caramel Pie.—Take 5 eggs beaten separately, 1 cup of butter, 1 cup of damson preserves, seeded, or blackberry jelly, 2 cups of sugar, and 1 cup of sweet milk, vanilla to taste; beat whites in last; bake with 1 crust.—*Sister Lula O. Trout, Hollins, Va.*

Caramel Pie.—One cup of brown sugar, 1 cup of sweet milk, 1 egg, 2 heaping tablespoonfuls of flour, and butter the size of a walnut. Stir till thick, then take from the fire, flavor with vanilla and pour into open crust that has been baked. Use the white of the egg for icing. This makes one pie.—*Sister Ida Younce, Goshen, Ind.*

Caramel Pie.—Take 1 cup of damson preserves, ¼ cup of butter, 1 cup of sugar, and 2 or 4 eggs. Beat all together, then pour over mixture 1 cup of boiling water and add 2 teaspoonfuls of vanilla. This makes 2 pies.—*Sister Luverna Sheets, Mt. Solon, Va.*

Carrot Custard.—Cook carrots until tender, then mash and rub through a fruit sieve. To 2 cupfuls of carrot add ½ cup of sugar and a pinch of salt; stir into it till smooth 2 tablespoonfuls of flour, then add 3 pints of new milk and 4 well-beaten eggs; put in a baking dish and set in a shallow pan of boiling water and bake in a moderate oven until light brown. If spice is desired, half a spoonful of ginger and cinnamon may be added. This can be used for pies also, and is a good substitute for pumpkin.—*Sister Emma Whisler Click, Tekoa, Wash.*

Chess Pie.—Take 4 eggs, 2 cups of sugar, 1 cup of sweet cream, ⅔ cup of butter and 1 tablespoonful of flour. Bake in a pie. —*Sister J. M. Mangus, Roanoke, Va.*

Cheese Cakes.—Take 1 cupful of cocoanut, 1 cupful of milk curd, 1 cupful of cream, yolks of 5 eggs, 1 cupful of sugar, and 1 teaspoonful of extract of rose. Place cream, curd, eggs, sugar, and cocoanut on the stove in a thick saucepan, and when thick remove from fire; add the extract when cold; fill pie pans lined with crust and bake in a steady oven 10 minutes.—*Sister Annie Sell, McKee Gap, Pa.*

Chocolate Pie.—Line a deep pie pan with a rich pie crust and bake in a quick oven. Grate ½ cup of chocolate, place in a sauce pan with 1 cup of hot water, butter the size of an egg, 1 teaspoonful of vanilla, 1·cup of sugar, the beaten yolks of 2 eggs, and 2 tablespoonfuls of cornstarch dissolved in as much water. Mix well and cook till thick, stirring constantly. Pour into the pie crust and let cool. Make a meringue of the two whites beaten stiff with 2 tablespoonfuls of powdered sugar, spread on top of the pie and brown lightly in oven.—*Sister Emma S. Critchfield, Friedens, Pa.*

Chocolate Pie.—Mix together ½ cup grated chocolate, 6 tablespoonfuls of sugar, 3 of flour, with a little sweet milk. Stir this into 2 cups of boiling milk till thick. Add the beaten yolks of 3 eggs and 1 teaspoonful vanilla. Bake the crust first, then fill, put the beaten whites of the eggs on top and slightly brown. This makes 2 pies.—*Sister E. J. Longanecker, East Lewistown, Ohio.*

Chocolate Pie.—Cover the outside of a pie tin with a rich pie dough and bake with the pan upside down. Let one pint of sweet milk come to the boiling point, then stir in and let come to a boil, 1 heaping tablespoonful of corn starch, 1 tablespoonful of cocoa or chocolate, 3 tablespoonfuls of sugar, the yolk of one egg and a few drops of vanilla stirred all together with a little sweet milk. Pour into the baked crust. Beat light the white of 1 egg, add 1 tablespoonful of sugar and several drops of lemon extract. Put on top and set pie in the oven until a light brown.—*Sister Jennie Wampler, Falks Store, Idaho.*

Cinnamon Pie.—Line a pie tin with dough, sprinkle cinnamon over it, sugar, flour and a little butter, add water. Bake without top crust. Nutmeg may be used instead of cinnamon if desired.—*Sister Sarah A. Crowl, Nappance, Ind.*

Cocoanut Pie.—Bake two crusts and let them cool. Take 2 pints of milk, 1 cup of sugar, ½ cup of flour, and 3 eggs, reserving the whites of 2 for frosting. Boil together in a double kettle until thick; then put one layer of this into the crust and sprinkle it well with cocoanut. Fill in another layer, then cocoanut again. Then spread with frosting.—*Sister Victoria Stoneburner, Magley, Ind.*

Cocoanut Pie.—Grate one cocoanut, add 3 eggs, 2 cups of sugar and one quart of sweet milk. Bake with two crusts. This is sufficient for 4 pies.—*Sister Katie B. Blanch, Annville, Pa.*

Cocoanut Cream Pie.—Bake crust when convenient. Take 1 cup milk and bring to boil. Stir together 3 tablespoonfuls sugar, ⅓ cup of cream, and 2 tablespoonfuls of flour. Add to the boiling milk and let all come to a boil. Remove from fire, flavor, add ½ cup of shredded cocoanut and pour into the previously baked crusts. Sprinkle the top liberally with shredded cocoanut.—*Sister Florence Neff, Clovis, N. M.*

Cocoanut Custard Pie.—Take 1 tablespoonful of flour, 2 tablespoonfuls of sugar, 2 eggs, 1½ pints of sweet milk and ½ teaspoonful of lemon. Bake slowly until it begins to thicken, then sprinkle ½ cupful of cocoanut over top and bake until done.—*Sister Gertrude Stoner, Hutsonville, Ill.*

Cream Pie.—Beat the white of 1 egg to a stiff froth; add 2 heaping tablespoonfuls of sugar, 1 tablespoonful of flour, mix well, then add 1 cupful of rich milk. Pour into a shallow crust, grate nutmeg on top, and bake in a moderate oven.—*Sister M. Jane Stauffer, Polo, Ill.*

Cream Pie.—To 1 pint of sweet milk, add 1 cup of sugar and let come to a boil; then take 2 eggs, reserving the whites for frosting, and to the yolks add 1 large tablespoonful of flour and enough milk to beat up smoothly, and pour into the boiling milk. Bake the crust, then put the filling into the crust and bake. Beat the whites well and add 2 tablespoonfuls of sugar and 1 teaspoonful of vanilla. After putting on frosting, return the pie to the oven again to brown a little. This is for one pie.—*Sister Leah S. Gauby, Washington, Kans.*

Cream Pie.—Take one heaping tablespoonful of flour, the yolk of one egg and one large spoonful of sugar. Mix the above ingredients in a little cold milk, then stir into milk (enough for one pie) which has been previously heated. Boil all until thick and flavor with vanilla. Beat the white of egg light, sweeten and cover top of pie. Set in oven a few minutes to brown.—*Sister Ida Brubaker, Conway, Kans.*

Cream Pie.—Take 2 tablespoonfuls of sugar, 2 tablespoonfuls of flour, and 1 teacupful of very rich sweet cream. Bake with lower crust only.—*Sister Laura E. Goetze, Saratoga, Wyo.*

Cream Pie.—Take ½ cup of butter, 1½ cups of sugar, 1 cup of milk, 4 tablespoonfuls of flour and whites of 4 eggs well beaten and stirred in lightly.—*Sister Esther M. Brown, Whitewater, Ind.*

Fruit Cream Pie.—Line a deep pie pan with crust. Now put in good, ripe blackberries or peaches, then a large handful of flour (sprinkled on evenly as possible), then sugar to taste and pour over it a cup of sour cream, wetting the flour as much as possible so it will not be dry when done.—*Sister L. Clanin, Hicksville, Wash.*

Raisin Cream Pie.—Take 1 cup of good sour cream, 1 cup raisins, without seeds, 1 cup sugar, 1 egg. Bake with 2 crusts, and this will make 2 pies.—*Sister Etta Eckerle, Lanark, Ill.*

Crumb Cake.—Sift together 1 quart of flour and 2 teaspoonfuls of baking powder, add 1 cup of sugar, ½ cup of butter, rub well together. Have pie tins lined with pie dough. Stir 2 tablespoonfuls of molasses into 1 cup of cold water, dip 2 tablespoonfuls of this on the crust, sprinkle on a layer of crumbs, alternating with the water until the tin is full. Bake till nicely brown.—*Sister Sarah A. Crowl, Nappanee, Ind.*

Grandma's Crumb Pie.—Take ½ cup of sugar, a little over ½ cup of flour, and a piece of butter the size of a walnut. Mix these well together, then take out 2 tablespoonfuls of mixture to put on top of the pie; to the rest add ½ teaspoonful of baking powder and milk enough to make a batter, and put them into the pie crust, sprinkling the 2 tablespoonfuls of crumbs on top.—*Sister Lucile Royer, Dallas Center, Ia.*

Old-fashioned Crumb Pie.—Take ¾ cup of butter, 1 cup of sugar; mix sugar and butter and sufficient flour to crumb nicely; after it is crumbed by rubbing together with the hands, take about ⅓ of the crumbs, mix the remainder with a cup of buttermilk and 1 teaspoonful of soda, flavor with vanilla or lemon; mix to the con- sistency of a thin cake dough or a thick batter; have a lower crust prepared in 2 pie plates, put ½ of the dough into each plate and sprinkle the remaining crumbs on top; bake in a quick oven.—*Sister F. Alice Davidson, Centropolis, Kans.*

Custard Pie.—Take 8 tablespoonfuls of sugar, 2 heaping tea- spoonfuls of flour, 5 eggs, and 2½ pints of milk, flavor with nutmeg. Mix flour and sugar together before adding milk and eggs. This will make two pies.—*Sister Lydia Flory, South English, Iowa.*

Custard Pie.—Beat 3 eggs with 2 tablespoonfuls of flour, add 2 pints of sweet milk, and sweeten and flavor to suit taste. Pour into two deep crusts and bake.—*Sister Luverna Sheets, Mt. Solon, Va.*—In making custards some cooks allow 1 tablespoonful of sugar to each egg used. But where flour is also used perhaps more sugar would be necessary.—*Sister Blanche Lentz, Elgin, Ill.*

Boiled Custard Pie.—Take the yolks of 4 eggs, 4 pints of sweet milk and 4 tablespoonfuls of flour. Moisten the flour with a little of the cold milk, add the eggs, beat well. Let the milk come to a boil on the stove then stir in the batter. Boil, stirring to keep from burning, remove from fire, add 1 teacupful of sugar, and flavor with nutmeg. Pour custard into 4 baked crusts. Beat the whites to stiff froth, sweeten, spread over the tops of the custards and put in the oven a few minutes to brown.—*Sister Eliza A. Weaver, Hopkins, Mo.*

Cheap Custard Pie.—Take 2 eggs, 2 tablespoonfuls of sugar, 1 of cornstarch or flour and 1 pint of milk; flavor to taste. This is for one pie.—*Sister John H. Rinehart, Union, Ohio.*

A Good Milk Pie.—Mix well ⅔ cup of brown sugar and the same amount of flour. Place in the lower pie crust. Add 1 pint good creamery milk, but do not stir, sprinkle with cinnamon and bake. It is best eaten while yet warm.—*Sister Nettie C. Weybright, Syracuse, Ind.*

Cookie Dough Pie.—Take 1 lemon, 1 cupful of seeded raisins chopped and mixed with the lemon, 1 cupful of sugar, 2 cupfuls of water, and 2 tablespoonfuls of cornstarch. Boil until clear. Dough part: ½ cupful of sugar, lump of butter size of a walnut, 4 tablespoonfuls of sweet milk, 2 teaspoonfuls of baking powder, 1 egg, and flour enough to make it as thick as cookie dough. This will make 2 pies. Spread out on plates with spoon; bake in a quick oven. When cold, have the boiled part well cooled and spread on top of the cookie.—*Sister J. P. Holsinger, Mt. Morris, Ill.*

Date Pie.—Take 3 eggs, 3 tablespoonfuls of sugar, a pinch of salt and 1 pint of milk. Cook 1 pound dates, squeeze through masher and mix with the above. Bake with one crust.—*Sister Edna Eisenbise, Lanark, Ill.*

Elderberry Pie.—Take a handful of elderberries, put in a pie crust, then take 1 teacupful clabber and sour cream, 1½ tablespoonfuls of sugar, 1 tablespoonful of flour. Stir flour and sugar in cream, put on top lid and bake till done.—*Sister Luverna Sheets, Mt. Solon, Va.*

Foam Pie.—Stir (not beat) together the yolks of 5 eggs, 1 cup of butter, and 1 cup of sugar. Bake with lower crust in a moderate oven. Take the whites of the eggs and beat stiff and put on top of the pie. This makes two pies.—*Sister Grace Roberts, Frederic, Ia.*

Granger Pie.—Make a pie crust and line 4 pie pans. Put 1 cupful of baking syrup in a bowl, 1 teaspoonful of soda, and 1 cupful of boiling water. Stir well and divide in the 4 pans. Now take 3 cupfuls of flour, 1 cupful of sugar, ½ cupful of lard, rub well and put over the top of the syrup. Bake in a moderate oven.— *Sister Sarah A. Sell, Newry, Pa.*

Fruit Granger Pie.—Stew 2 cups of raisins. Thicken with cornstarch or flour and sweeten to taste. Now take 3 cups of flour, 1½ cups of sugar, ½ cup of shortening, and 2 teaspoonfuls of baking powder; mix together. Take out ⅔ of a cup of crumbs and add enough sweet milk to roll. Now put the raisins in pie crust. Roll this dough the size of the pie, put on top of raisins and sprinkle remaining crumbs on top. This makes 4 pies.—*Sister Minnie Baker, Hollidaysburg, Pa.*

Huckleberry Pie.—Take the amount of huckleberries desired for 1 pie, add 1 tablespoonful of vinegar, 2 tablespoonfuls of granulated sugar, and 1 tablespoonful of flour; bake between 2 crusts.—*Sister Hattie Kline, Augusta, W. Va.*

Jam Pie.—Take 1 cup of jam, 1 cup of butter, 1 cup of sugar, 1 cup of cream and 5 eggs. This makes 3 pies.—*Sister Nora B. Hufford, Rossville, Ind.*

Jelly Pie.—One cup of any kind of jelly, 2 cups of sugar, 4 eggs, ½ cup of butter. Cream, sugar and butter, beat eggs last and mix in jelly and bake. This makes 3 pies.—*Sister Carrie A. Smith, St. Peter, Minn.*

Lemon Custard.—Dough part: Take ½ cup of sugar, lump of butter size of walnut, 5 tablespoonfuls of sweet milk, 2 teaspoonfuls of baking powder, 1 egg and flour to make as stiff as cookie dough. Spread this in pie pans with a knife and bake. This will make 3 pies. Top part: Grate the rind and extract juice of 1 lemon. Dissolve 4 tablespoonfuls of cornstarch in a little water, add the yolks of 3 eggs well beaten, 2 cups of white sugar, a small lump of butter, and last the grated rind of lemon. To this add 1 quart of boiling water, and cook. Use white of eggs for frosting.—*Sister Clara Custer, Windber, Pa.*

Lemon Pie.—Take the grated rind and juice of 1 lemon, 1 cup of sugar, 2 tablespoonfuls of cornstarch, 1 cup of boiling water and 1 egg. Cook on top of the stove and pour into a pie tin lined with a baked crust. Frost with the white of the egg and a little sugar beaten to a stiff froth. Put in the oven a few minutes to brown slightly.—*Sister Della Funderburg, Surrey, N. Dak.*

Lemon Pie.—Take 6 eggs, 1½ cupfuls of sugar, 4 heaping teaspoonfuls of cornstarch or flour, 3 cups of warm water, the grated rind and juice of 1 lemon, and butter the size of an egg. Beat the yolks of the eggs, flour and sugar together, add water, lemon juice, and butter (melted). Mix well together and bake in 4 pie plates without upper crusts. Add 6 heaping teaspoonfuls of granulated sugar to the whites of the eggs, beat to a froth, flavor with vanilla. Spread on top of custards and brown.—*Sister J. P. Bowman, Jonesboro, Tenn.*

Lemon Pie.—Take 1 large lemon, 1 cup of sugar, ⅔ cup of flour, 2 cups of cold water, 2 eggs, a piece of butter the size of an egg. Put the flour, sugar and eggs together, then add the juice, grated rind and water, and butter (melted). Bake in a deep plate without an upper crust.—*Sister D. F. Lepley, Connellsville, Pa.*

Lemon Pie.—Take 1 egg, 2 teacups of white sugar, 2 teacups boiling water, 1 tablespoonful of butter, 2 small tablespoonfuls of cornstarch and 2 lemons. Dissolve the cornstarch in a little cold water, then put it in the boiling water. Add the sugar and let it boil a few minutes. Set aside, and when cool add the butter, egg, and juice and grated rind of the lemons. This makes 3 small pies. —*Sister Ella Moore, Chicago, Ill.*

Lemon Pie.—Take the grated rind and juice of 1 lemon, 3 tablespoonfuls of flour, 3 cups of water, 2½ cups of sugar, 3 eggs and butter the size of a walnut. Boil together and let cool.—*Sister Anna Showalter, Lattasburg, Ohio.*

Lemon Pie.—Take 4 eggs, 2 cups of sugar, 2 tablespoonfuls of flour, ½ cup of butter, 2 pints of water, 1 large lemon, grated (peel before grating) ; boil the custard until thick, pour into 2 baked crusts, and bake.—*Sister Dora Studebaker, Whitewater, Ind.*

Lemon Pie.—Take the juice and grated rind of 1 lemon, 1 cup of sugar, 1 egg, 2 tablespoonfuls of flour and 2 cupfuls of water. Cover with a crust. This makes 2 pies.—*Sister Hazel Fahrney Fausnacht, Twin Falls, Idaho.*

Lemon Pie.—Take 1 grated lemon, 1 pint water, 1 egg, 1 cup sugar, 1 cup sugar syrup, 1 tablespoonful of flour, then cook 2 minutes. Then divide in 5 ordinary-sized pie plates lined with pastry. Dough for top: Take 1 cup of white sugar, 1 teaspoonful soda, ½ cup butter, ½ cup of sour milk, flour to make stiff, roll and cut in strips.—*Sister Anna Martin, Weaverland, Pa.*

Lemon Pie.—Take 2 cups of sugar, juice and grated rind of 2 lemons, 2 cups of sweet milk, ½ cup of butter, yolks of 4 eggs and 1 slice of bread broken fine without crust. Mix these ingredients together, put in 4 pie plates lined with pastry and bake. When done, beat the whites of the eggs with 4 tablespoonfuls of sugar and a few drops of lemon juice. Spread on top of the custards and return to the oven to brown lightly.—*Sister Fannie Wenger, Mt. Sidney, Va.*

Lemon Pie.—Take 2 cups of white sugar, yolks of 4 eggs well beaten, 3 tablespoonfuls of cornstarch, 2 tablespoonfuls of butter, juice and rind of 2 lemons, 2½ cups of boiling water. Let thicken over a slow fire, pour the mixture into baked crusts. Beat the whites of the eggs, add 4 tablespoonfuls of sugar. Spread on top of pies and place in the oven till brown.—*Sister J. E. Price, Dallas Center, Iowa.*

Lemon Tarts.—Take 1 lemon, 1 cup of good sour cream, 2 cups of thick milk, 3 eggs, 1 teaspoonful of baking soda, 1½ cups sugar, 1 tablespoonful of flour, if the eggs are small. Put strips of pie crust on top and pie crust in bottom.—*Sister Mattie O. Weaver, Hinkletown, Pa.*

Lemon Tarts.—Line dishes with dough and fill with 1 cup of molasses, 1 cup of sugar, 1 pint of boiling water, 1 tablespoonful of cornstarch, and 1 lemon. For strips: Take ½ cup of sugar, ½ cup of sweet milk, ¼ cup of lard, ½ teaspoonful of baking powder, and flour enough to roll. This will make three pies.—*Sister Hettie E. Gibble, Mechanicsburg, Pa.*

Lemon Tarts.—Top part: Take 2 eggs, 2 cups of granulated sugar, ½ cup of butter and lard mixed, 1 cup of water, 2 teaspoonfuls of baking powder, and 2 cups of flour. Mix these ingredients together. Lower part: Take the juice and grated rind of 1 lemon, or 1 tablespoonful of essence of lemon, 1 egg, 1 cup of soft white or light brown sugar, 1 cup of molasses, 1¼ pints of water, and 2 tablespoonfuls of flour. Mix these ingredients together. Have six pie plates lined with dough and put the lower part in them. Pour the top on the lower part and bake in a moderate oven. These will look like a cake when done.—*Sister Harriet Baugher, Brodbecks, Pa.*

Mock Lemon or Vinegar Pie.—Stir into 2 heaping tablespoonfuls of flour, 1 cup of sugar, 4 tablespoonfuls of vinegar and 2 eggs. Stir until all ingredients are thoroughly mixed. Add butter the size of a walnut and 2 cups of boiling water. Set on the stove and stir to prevent lumps. Let boil a few minutes, add 1 teaspoonful of lemon extract, remove and pour into two baked pie crusts. This is enough for medium-sized pie-tins.—*Sister Mary Sherfy, Mont Ida, Kans.*

Mock Cherry Pie.—Take 2 cups of cranberries and 1 cup of raisins. Chop fine and add ¾ cup of sugar and ½ water.—*Sister Sarah Deutschman, Elwood, Ill.*

Mince Pie.—Take 1 cup of sugar, 1 cup of bread crumbs, 1 cup of water, ½ cup of raisins, ½ cup of vinegar, a small piece of butter, ½ teaspoonful each of cinnamon, cloves, allspice and grated nutmeg. Cook before baking, and bake with 2 crusts.—*Sister Sarah Blocher, Pearl City, Ill.*

Countryside Mince Meat.—Take 5 pounds of lean beef, cover with boiling water, salt as for table use, boil until tender. Have ready 2 gallons of pared apples (canned ones will do), 2 pounds of suet, 3 pounds of seedless raisins and 1 large home-canned citron. Chop the beef, apples, suet, raisins and citron very fine. Add 1 quart of canned cherries or seeded grapes, 1 quart of dried apples (stewed), 1 quart of sorghum, 1 quart of boiled cider, 1 pint of cider vinegar, 2 tablespoonfuls ground cinnamon, and 1 teaspoonful ground cloves. Mix thoroughly, sweeten to taste, heat until scalding hot. It requires great care to prevent scorching. Seal in glass jars and keep in a cool place. When ready to make pies, thin to the proper consistency with fruit juices, grate a little nutmeg over filling and add a small lump of butter to each pie. Bake between crusts.—*Sister Mary P. Ellenberger, Turney, Mo.*

Mock Mince Pie.—Take 1 cup of seedless raisins, 1 cup of chopped apples, ½ cup of vinegar, ¾ cup of sugar, ½ cup of broken crackers and ½ teaspoonful each of cloves, allspice, and cinnamon. Mix the above, and thin with water, some thinner than mince meat. This will make 2 pies.—*Sister D. M. Miller, Milledgeville, Ill.*

Mock Mince Pie.—Take 1 cup of buttermilk, 1 cup of sugar, 1 cup of raisins chopped fine, 1 tablespoonful of vinegar, 2 eggs, cloves, cinnamon and allspice. For 2 pies; bake with 2 crusts.—*Sister N. E. Lilligh, Mulberry Grove, Ill.*

Mock Mince Pie.—Take 1 large cup of sugar, 1 of sour cream, ½ cup bread crumbs, butter the size of a walnut, yolks of 2 eggs, 3 tablespoonfuls of vinegar, 1 teaspoonful of cinnamon and 1 of cloves (ground), and ½ cup of raisins or jam. Bake with lower crust only. Beat the whites of eggs and spread on the top of pie as soon as taken from oven. This makes 2 pies.—*Sister Mary E. Teeter, Bells, Tenn.*

Mock Mince Pie.—Take 1 cup of sugar, ½ cup of vinegar, 1 cup of molasses, 1 cup of raisins, 1 cup of boiling water, 1 tablespoonful of cornstarch, 1 teaspoonful of cinnamon, ½ teaspoonful of cloves, ½ teaspoonful of nutmeg, and 2 eggs. Bake with 2 crusts.—*Sister Nettie Stine, Leaf River, Ill.*

Montgomery Pies.—Top Part: Take 3 eggs, 2½ cups of granulated sugar, ¾ cup of lard and butter, 1½ cups of sweet milk, about 3½ cups of flour and 3 teaspoonfuls of baking powder. Lower Part: Grate 1 lemon and add 1 egg, 2 tablespoonfuls of flour and 1 cup of brown sugar. Beat thoroughly, then add 1 cup of molasses; beat again and add 1 pint of cold water. Divide this in 5 large crusts, then spread top part over and bake in a moderate oven. They are fine.—*Sister Nora E. Zimmerman, Big Timber, Mont.*

Molasses Pie.—Take 2 cups of molasses, 1 cup of sugar, 3 eggs, 1 tablespoonful of melted butter and 1 lemon. Beat all together and bake in pastry with a lower crust and strips of the pastry over the top, same as tarts. In the absence of the lemon leave out the sugar also.—*Sister J. A. Sell, McKee Gap, Pa.*

Orange Pie.—Take 1 cup of sugar, 2 tablespoonfuls of flour, yolks of 2 eggs, grated rind of 1 orange and juice of 2 oranges, a little salt, and 2 cups of milk. Put on stove to get warm before putting into crust. Beat whites of eggs to stiff froth, spread over pie when baked and put back in oven to brown. This makes 2 pies. —*Sister Stella A. Parret, Lordsburg, Cal.*

Orange Pie.—Take the juice and ½ the grated rind of 1 orange, ¾ cup of sugar, yolks of 2 eggs and 1 teaspoonful of flour. Heat these together, then add 1 cup of cream that has been boiled. Let cool, then add last the whites of 2 eggs beaten to a stiff froth. This makes 1 pie.—*Sister Susan C. Ressler, Altoona, Pa.*

Peach Pie.—Stew the peaches before placing them in crusts. For 6 pies, take ½ gallon of peaches, 1 teacupful of sugar and 2 nutmegs to season. Make the pie crust short, put in fruit, cover with upper crust and bake in a quick oven.—*Sister Bettie E. French, Shanks, W. Va.*

Peach Pie.—Line a pie tin with puff paste, with pared peaches in halves or quarters well covered with sugar. Put on an upper crust and bake, or leave off the upper crust and make a *meringue* of the whites of 2 eggs beaten to a stiff froth with 2 table-spoonfuls of powdered sugar. Spread on pie after it is baked, return to oven and brown.—*Sister Sallie Brubaker, Beryl, Pa.*

Pineapple Pie.—Take 1 grated pineapple, its weight in sugar, ½ its weight in butter, 1 cup of cream, and 5 eggs. Beat butter to a creamy froth, add sugar and yolks of eggs and continue to beat until very light. Add the cream and pineapple, and last the whites of the eggs beaten to a stiff froth. Bake with an under crust. Serve cold.—*Sister Emma M. Zug, Lebanon, Pa.*

Pineapple Pie.—Take 1 large pineapple, and grate or grind. Add to this 3 eggs which have been well beaten, 2 cups of sugar and ½ cup of butter. Bake with lower crust. This makes 2 pies. —*Sister Esther M. H. Brown, Omaja, Cuba.*

Pineapple Pie.—Line a pie tin with crust, sprinkle 1 table-spoonful of flour over bottom, add 1 cup of sugar, 1 pint of grated pineapple, a little lemon juice, and water if necessary. Cover and bake in quick oven.—*Sister L. U. Kreider, Omaja, Cuba.*

Plum Pie.—Line a pie tin with ordinary pie crust, dust with a little flour and about half the amount of sugar to be used. Fill with a layer of plums, flour again and add the remainder of the sugar. Then cover with jelly-cake batter, spread quite thin, and it is ready to bake. This makes a delicious pie and is best served cold. Other sour fruits may be used but plums or cranberries are preferable.—*Sister Alice Funderburg, Gildford, Mont.*

Potato Pie.—Line a pie tin with crust same as for other pies. Slice raw potatoes very thin, season with salt, pepper and butter the size of a walnut, put in a little hot water and bake until done. Serve with lamb or veal stew gravy.—*Sister L. A. Eshelman, Los Angeles, Cal.*

Potato Pie.—Take 1 cup of well-mashed potatoes, 1½ cups of sweet milk, 3 tablespoonfuls of sugar, 1 teaspoonful of butter, 3 well-beaten eggs, season with nutmeg and cinnamon, to taste. Bake same as custard pie. Serve hot with sweet cream flavored with vanilla. This is delicious. This will make 1 pie.—*Sister Annie Bolender, Dayton, Ohio.*

Potato Pie.—Line a pudding dish with good pie paste. Pare about four potatoes, slice them into the pudding dish, add parsley, salt, pepper and butter. Bake about ½ hour. Then heat milk and butter to pour over this when you eat it.—*Sister Jos. H. Johnson, Royersford, Pa.*

Sweet Potato Pie.—Stew 3 cupfuls of sliced sweet potatoes in 1 quart of water. When done, add 1½ cups of sugar, ⅔ cup of butter, and a teaspoonful of grated nutmeg. For the dough take a scant quart of flour, 1 teaspoonful each of salt and soda. Sift, work in a small cup of lard and moisten with 1⅔ cups of buttermilk. Knead 2 minutes. Roll out ⅔ of it to line a deep 3-quart pudding dish or baking pan; put in the potatoes and the water in which they were stewed with the seasoning. Roll out remainder of dough and cover, being careful to have the edges pressed together. Bake quickly to light brown and serve in the pan in which it is baked.—*Sister Annie Pitzer, Cordell, Okla.*

Sliced Sweet Potato Pie.—Boil the potatoes until done; peel, slice and place in a deep pan lined with dough. Fill the pan with rich milk or cream, sugar enough to make it good and sweet, and flavor with nutmeg or cinnamon. Put on a top crust and bake. Serve while hot.—*Sister Lizena Hylton, McComb, Mo.*

Prune Pie.—Line a pie tin with puff paste; fill with seeded prunes well covered with sugar; put on an upper crust of the paste and bake quickly.—*Sister Sallie Brubaker, Beryl, Pa.*

Kentucky Pudding Pie.—Take 4 eggs, 1 quart of sweet cream and milk, 1 teacupful of sugar, ½ teacupful of melted butter, 1 tablespoonful of flour. Flavor with vanilla, and bake without an upper crust.—*Sister M. Kate Crist, Timberville, Va.*

Pumpkin Pie.—Boil a quantity of pumpkin until quite soft, and press through a sieve to make it fine and smooth. Take 1 quart of the fine pumpkin to make 4 large custards. Add to it the yolks of 4 eggs, 4 tablespoonfuls of sugar and 4 tablespoonfuls of flour. Beat thoroughly and season with salt, pepper, and nutmeg or other spices as desired. Add to this 4 pints of sweet milk, and lastly the whites of the 4 eggs beaten to a froth. Pour the custard into 4 pie pans lined with the pie dough and bake in a hot oven.—*Sister Mary Elizabeth Replogle, Roaring Spring, Pa.*

Pumpkin Pies (Made of Canned Pumpkin).—Take 1 can of pumpkin, and 5 eggs well beaten with 1 cup of sugar. Put all together and add nutmeg, allspice, or any preferred seasoning. Then add enough milk to make five pies.—*Sister Catharine Allan, York, N. Dak.*

Pumpkin Pie.—For each pie wanted take 2 eggs and beat; then add 1 tablespoonful of flour and as much sugar as is liked and mix together. Add also 2 tablespoonfuls of cooked pumpkin and 1 pint of sweet milk. Flavor with ground allspice.—*Sister L. Clanin, Hicksville, Wash.*

Grated Pumpkin Pie.—To 1 quart of grated pumpkin add 6 eggs, 1 cup of sugar, a pinch each of salt and pepper, and ginger and cinnamon to suit taste. Mix all together and add enough sweet milk to fill pie crusts, and bake in a slow oven until a nice brown. This will make two large pies, or three small ones.—*Sister Lizzie A. Dunger, Mount Carroll, Ill.*

Raspberry Pie.—Pick 1 pint of berries clean, rinse in cold water. Line a greased pie tin with pie paste, put in prepared berries, dredge with 1 teaspoonful of flour, add nearly ½ cup of sugar and 1 tablespoonful of water. Moisten edges, cover pie with a crust, press edges with hands. Bake.—*Sister Effie Gnagey, Fruita, Colo.*

Rhubarb Custard.—Pour boiling water over 2 teacupfuls of chopped rhubarb, drain off the water after 4 or 5 minutes. Mix with rhubarb, 1 teacupful of sugar, the yolk of 1 egg, 1 tablespoonful of butter and 1 tablespoonful of flour, moistening the whole with 3 tablespoonfuls of water. Bake with lower crust only. Make a *meringue* of the white of the egg with 3 tablespoonfuls of sugar. Spread over the top of the pie and return to the oven to brown.—*Sister Emma Detweiler, Johnstown, Pa.*

Rhubarb Custard.—Take 1 cup of stewed rhubarb, 1 cup of white sugar, 1 tablespoonful of flour, yolks of 2 eggs, season with lemon extract. Beat this mixture thoroughly and bake in 1 crust. Frost with the beaten whites of the eggs.—*Sister Sue Sisler, Dallas Center, Iowa.*

Rhubarb Pie.—Peel rhubarb and cut very fine, pour boiling water over it and let stand awhile. Take 1 teacupful of sugar to 1 pie. Put half the sugar on the bottom crust with some flour, put in the rhubarb from which the water has been drained, and cover with a little more flour and the remainder of the sugar.—*Sister J. W. Brooks, Independence, Oregon.*

Rich Man's Pie.—Take 4 tablespoonfuls of melted butter, spread on a crust, spread over top of butter ½ cup of sugar, grate on a little nutmeg, then spread on top of all 2 heaping tablespoonfuls of flour. Now set the pie in the oven and pour over enough sweet milk to make it full enough, and bake. Bake with lower crust only. Put the ingredients in just as this is written, beginning with butter and ending with milk. It will make a queer-looking pie to those who have never seen it, but will taste far better than it looks. Try it.—*Sister Mary E. Crofford, Martinsburg, Pa.*

Smearcase Pie.—Work your smearcase fine and salt to suit the taste. For each pie take 1 cup of the cheese, 1 egg, 1 tablespoonful of flour and sugar to suit the taste. Thin the mixture with sour cream. Flavor with nutmeg or cinnamon and bake without upper crust.—*Sister Anna Wise, Bradford, Ohio.*

Squash Pie.—Take 1 pint of squash, boiled dry, 1 cup of brown sugar, 3 eggs, 1 tablespoonful of melted butter, spices to suit the taste, and 1 pint of sweet milk. This makes 2 pies.—*Sister J. J. Stowe, Girard, Ill.*

Squash for Pies.—Cut a squash in pieces, remove the seeds, pare the same as for pumpkin, put in a kettle on the stove and stew until tender. When done, rub through a fruit sieve. For each pie, add 1 egg, ½ teaspoonful of ginger, ½ teaspoonful of cinnamon, a little nutmeg, and sugar to taste; add milk to make as thin as for pumpkin. A little molasses adds very much to the flavor. Beat the eggs before mixing with the squash.—*Sister Mary Stutsman, Muscatine, Iowa.*

Syrup Pie.—For 2 pies. Beat 3 eggs very light, add 2 cups of syrup, 1 cup of milk or water and 1 rounding teaspoonful of baking powder. Flavor to taste. Bake without upper crust.—*Sister J. D. Teeter, Rex, Fla.*

Tailor Pie.—Take the yolks of 4 eggs, 1 cup of sugar, ½ cup of butter, 1 large cup of sweet cream seasoned with nutmeg. Beat well together and bake in crusts. Beat the whites of the eggs very light and add ½ cup of sugar. When the pies are done, spread the beaten whites over the top, and put in oven to brown. This makes 3 pies.—*Sister Elsie Huff, Ft. Defiance, Va.*

Green Tomato Pie.—Peel and slice 9 pounds of green tomatoes, add 3 pounds of sugar and 1 sliced lemon; cook until soft. Put in glass cans and it will keep until wanted. Make pies with upper and lower crusts.—*Sister Lulu O. Trout, Hollins, Va.*

Green Tomato Pie.—Slice green tomatoes very thin and put into a crust. Add 1 tablespoonful of vinegar, about 3 tablespoonfuls of sugar, a little flour, and spice to taste. Bake with 2 crusts.—*Sister Laura E. Goetze, Saratoga, Wyo.*

Green Tomato Pie.—Take 1 pint of green tomatoes pared and sliced; line a pie pan with pie paste and put in the tomatoes. Then sprinkle over them 5 tablespoonfuls of sugar, add 1 tablespoonful of vinegar, 1 teaspoonful of flour; season with allspice, cloves, and cinnamon. Put on top crust and bake in a moderately hot oven. —*Sister Sue Wire, Acton, Okla.*

Tart Pies.—Take 1 cup of molasses, 1 cup of sugar, 1 cup of sour cream, 1 cup of thick milk, 2 eggs, 4 tablespoonfuls of flour, cinnamon, nutmeg and cloves to taste and 1 teaspoonful of soda.—*Sister Lottie Wine, Enders, Nebr.*

Transparent Pie.—Take 3 eggs, ½ cup butter, 1 cup of sugar, ½ cup of milk. Beat butter and sugar to a cream, add the yolks. Stir all together, add flavoring and milk. Bake in 2 crusts. Beat the whites of the eggs, put on top and brown slightly.—*Sister Sara Reese Eby, West Elkton, Ohio.*

Transparent Pie.—Take 3 eggs, ½ glass of cream, 1 teaspoonful of lemon essence, 1 cup of butter and 2 cups of sugar. This makes 2 pies.—*Sister Nora B. Hufford, Rossville, Ind.*

Vinegar Pie.—Take 1 egg, 1 heaping tablespoonful of flour, 1 teacupful of sugar. Beat all well together, then add vinegar to make it taste real sharp, and 1 cup of cold water; flavor with lemon essence and bake with 2 crusts.—*Sister Cora B. Byer, Albert City, Iowa.*

Vinegar Pie.—Take 1 cup sorghum, 1 cup of sugar, 1 cup of flour, 1 teaspoonful of soda, 1 teaspoonful each of cloves and cinnamon, 1 cup of vinegar, and 4 cups of water. Bake with under-crust and strips of crust on top. This makes 4 pies.—*Sister Stella G. Turner, Iliff, Colo.*

Whipped Cream Pie.—Prepare a nice, crisp pie crust, prick well with a fork to prevent puffing, bake quickly and put aside to cool. Mix 1½ cups of thick, sweet cream, at least 24 hours old, with ½ cup of granulated sugar, all of which has been previously thoroughly chilled, and in a cold place beat it with a spoon, egg or cream beater, until it stands up stiff, and fine. Then add ½ teaspoonful of lemon extract and pour the cream into the cold crust.—*Sister Lula Goshorn, Ladoga, Ind.*

A good many things enter into the art of successful cake making and one can hardly hope for invariable success without having spent more or less time in the school of experience. All ingredients should be fresh and pure. Flavorings and the process of baking will not be able to destroy the natural effects of rancid butter, stale eggs, etc. The mixing bowl, measuring cup, spoon, beater and all ingredients should be collected before the mixing begins. In cold weather it will aid the mixing process greatly if the bowl is warmed and the spoon scalded with boiling water. The eggs, however, should be perfectly cold. Lay them in the refrigerator some time before you are ready to make the cake, or drop them into cold water. The whites will then whip up much more readily and perfectly. A pinch of salt will also aid in this. The general order for mixing the ordinary cup cake is: Cream shortening and sugar together (if these ingredients are cold two tablespoonfuls of hot water will hasten the creaming, and afterward an equal amount of liquid may be deducted from that called for in the recipe); add yolks and beat well; then add flour and milk alternately and lastly the beaten whites which should be folded in. The flour should be sifted before measuring and again with the baking powder, if the latter is used. It is said a tablespoonful of flour added to the creamed butter and sugar before any liquid is added will prevent curdling. Line the pans with greased paper, using two or three layers for pound cakes and fruit cakes. If you are not an adept at judging the temperature of an oven with the hand, test it with a small amount of the prepared batter. Rich loaf cakes and thick batters should be baked slowly; layer cakes, sponge cakes and most little cakes require a quick oven. A cake is done when it shrinks from the pan and stops hissing. When taken from the oven the pan should be set for a few minutes on the stove hearth or shelf where you can barely hold your hand. A very light, delicate cake will fall if cooled too quickly or shaken while hot.

Bow Knots.—Beat 2 eggs, add ⅓ cup of sugar, 1 tablespoonful each of cream and melted butter, ⅛ teaspoonful of soda, ½ teaspoonful of cream of tartar, ¼ teaspoonful each of salt and mace, and flour enough to make a stiff dough. Roll into pieces the shape of a pencil; tie in bow knots. Fry in deep fat, and dust with powdered sugar.—*Sister Zura L. Peck, Meyersdale, Pa.*

Crulls.—Four good-sized potatoes cooked and mashed without cream, butter the size of a walnut, 1½ cups of sugar and 1 teaspoonful of nutmeg. Stir this together, then add 1 cup of sweet milk, 2 eggs and 3 teaspoonfuls of baking powder. Use flour enough for a soft dough. Roll thin, cut and fry in hot lard.—*Sister Lizzie Angle, Bringhurst, Ind.*

Maryland Crullers.—Take 2 eggs, 2 cups of sugar, 1 cup of lard, 1½ pints of sour milk, 1 teaspoonful of soda, 1 teaspoonful of cream of tartar and enough flour to roll nicely. Cut, and fry in boiling lard to which has been added 1 teaspoonful of vinegar.—*Sister A. Roop Shaw, Westminster, Md.*

Crullers.—Take 2 eggs, 1 cup of sugar, 1 cup of sour milk, 1 level teaspoonful of soda dissolved in the milk, 3 tablespoonfuls of melted butter or lard, and 4 cups of flour.—*Sister Amanda Brown, Whitewater, Ind.*

Doughnuts.—Take 2 cups of sugar, 1½ cups of sweet milk, 5 eggs, 3 tablespoonfuls of butter, 3 tablespoonfuls of baking powder, and enough flour to mix soft. Bake in hot lard, and roll in soft "A" sugar when taken from lard, if desired to give snowy appearance.—*Sister Charles Schubert, Alvada, Ohio.*

Doughnuts.—Take 1 cup of sugar, 1 egg, 1 cup of sour milk, 1 teaspoonful of soda, 1 teaspoonful of salt, and flavor with nutmeg. Flour to roll.—*Sister Ina Herbert, Fostoria, Ohio.*

Doughnuts.—Take 3 eggs, 1 cup of milk, 1 cup of sugar dissolved in the milk, 3 tablespoonfuls of melted lard, 3 pints of flour, 3 heaping teaspoonfuls of baking powder, a pinch of salt, and nutmeg to flavor. Fry in hot lard.—*Sister Annie Sell, McKee Gap, Pa.*

Doughnuts.—Take 1 cup of sugar, 2 eggs, 2 tablespoonfuls of melted butter, ⅔ cup of milk, 2 even teaspoonfuls of cream of tartar, 1 even teaspoonful of soda, flour enough to roll, salt and nutmeg. Fry in hot lard.—*Sister Lizzie M. Lichty, Meyersdale, Pa.*

Doughnuts.—Take 1 cup of sugar, 1 tablespoonful of butter, and 1 egg well beaten together. Grate half a nutmeg into this, and add 1 cup of milk, 2 teaspoonfuls of baking powder in 2 cups of flour. Add as much more flour as may be needed to make a soft dough. Do not roll, but pat out with the hands. Fry in hot lard.—*Sister Lillus E. Mahan, Omaja, Cuba.*

Doughnuts.—Take 1 cup of granulated sugar, 4 tablespoonfuls of butter, 1 cup of sweet milk, 2 eggs, and 3 cups of unsifted flour, sifted with 3 teaspoonfuls of baking powder. Add ½ teaspoonful of salt, 1 teaspoonful of vanilla, and sufficient flour to roll out. Fry in lard, and roll in sugar while warm.—*Sister Allie M. Jones, Arcanum, Ohio.*

Fried Cakes or Doughnuts.—Take ½ cup of sugar, 1 cup sweet cream, a piece of butter the size of a walnut, 2 eggs, a pinch of salt, 1 teaspoonful of soda and enough flour to make a stiff dough. Roll out about twice as thick as pie dough and cut in any shape desired. Drop the cakes one by one into boiling lard in which put several dried apple snitz to keep it from getting too brown.—*Sister Mary Snively, Lanark, Ill.*

Corn Meal Doughnuts.—Take 2 cups of sifted corn meal, 1 cup of white flour, 1 tablespoonful of sugar, 1 teaspoonful of salt, 3 eggs, 1 cup of sour or buttermilk, and 1 teaspoonful of soda dissolved in the milk. Drop from a spoon into hot lard. Fry brown on both sides and serve warm with molasses.—*Sister Mary Hilderbrand, Walkerton, Ind.*

Excellent Doughnuts.—Mix, by sifting 2 or 3 times, 2 heaping teaspoonfuls of baking powder with 1 quart of flour. Beat 2 eggs with 1 coffeecup of sugar, adding a teacupful of new milk (or better if at hand, half milk and half cream), and flavor with nutmeg. Mix all together, reserving a little flour for rolling out. Fry in hot lard, and when cold roll in powdered sugar.—*Sister Flora Weigle, Shannon, Ill.*

Fastnacht Cakes.—Take 1 egg, 2 cups of sugar, 1 cup of lard, 1½ pints of sour milk, 1 teaspoonful of soda, 1 teaspoonful of cream of tartar, and enough flour to roll nicely. Cut, and bake in boiling lard.—*Sister Amy Roop Shaw, Westminster, Md.*

Fat Cakes.—Take 3 tincupfuls of sweet cream, 1 tincupful of sour cream, 3 eggs, 1 teaspoonful of soda, 2 tablespoonfuls of salt, 1 teaspoonful of cream of tartar. Use 8 tincupfuls of flour, or enough to make a dough stiff enough to handle without sticking to the fingers. Then roll out in squares and fry in hot lard. Cut dough with cake cutter, using something round to cut holes in the middle of the round cakes. Make diamond-shaped holes in the square cakes.—*Sister Mary Murray, Laurel Hill, Pa.*

Funnel Cakes.—Take 1 quart of sweet milk, 3 pints of flour, 2 eggs well beaten, 1 teaspoonful of soda, and salt to taste. Heat the milk in a granite pan until a skin is formed on it. Then stir it into the sifted flour, which you have in a gallon crock and add the eggs and the soda. Beat until very light. Have 3 pints of hot lard in a round-bottomed iron kettle on the stove. Now put 3 or 4 large spoonfuls of batter into a funnel, holding the front finger of the left hand over the small hole. Then remove the finger, holding the funnel with the right hand over the hot lard and move the funnel slowly around in rings, till the batter has all run out. Be careful not to let the rings of batter cross each other. When the rings rise in the hot grease, turn with a flesh fork to brown on the other side. Use your judgment as to when to remove from the grease. They are fine served with syrup. If you do not get them coiled just right the first time, try again. We used to make gallons of these funnel cakes in Pennsylvania for harvest hands, for a nine o'clock piece. The batter ought to be just a little thicker than for pancake batter; just so it runs out nicely. Some like a funnel with a one-inch hole, so that the cakes will be large and round.—*Sister Katie E. Keller, Enterprise, Mont.*

Raised Doughnuts.—Take 1½ cups of bread sponge, add a tablespoonful each of melted lard, melted butter, and sugar, and a little salt. Mix with less flour than for bread. Roll and cut in strips, twist and fry in hot lard.—*Sister Grace Hileman Miller, Lordsburg, Cal.*

Snow Balls.—Take 1 cup of cream, 2 eggs beaten well and stirred in with the cream, and lard about the size of an egg. Rub the lard in the flour as for pie dough, and add a little salt. Make the dough about as stiff as pie dough. Roll out thin and cut in pieces about 4 or 5 inches square, then cut with a dough cutter, and tangle. Drop into hot lard and bake a light brown. Sprinkle with sugar while warm.—*Sister D. B. Puterbaugh, Lanark, Ill.*

Snow Ball.—Break 2 or more eggs in flour enough to make a stiff dough, work smooth and roll out a portion like pie dough, only much thinner. Now cut in strips, about a finger's width, but do not cut out to the edge within an inch. Keep the whole joined together, lay aside and prepare all the dough the same way; let dry a little. Have ready hot lard or grease in a shallow frying kettle. Now with both hands gather up one piece at a time and lay in the hot grease. Have ready two forks, one in each hand, and stir and shape as crinkled as you can without breaking, then turn quickly, fry till done, or light yellow (it will take but a few seconds to fry one piece), lift out and lay on a plate and sprinkle each piece with powdered sugar. Proceed with all in the same way. When done the mass should be high and look like a bunch of tangled ribbons. It is good to the taste, and also for a novelty on special occasions, for instance, a wedding.—*Sister Amanda Witmore, McPherson, Kans.*

Trifles.—Work 1 beaten egg and 1 tablespoonful of sugar into as much flour as will make a stiff paste. Roll as thin as a silver dollar, and cut into small cakes. Drop a few at a time into hot lard, and cook till they rise to the surface. Turn over, remove with skimmer and drain.—*Sister Mary E. Whitney, Kearney, Nebr.*

Cheese Straws.—A dainty dish and a good way to use left-over pie crust: Roll out the pastry to ¼ inch in thickness, sprinkle thickly ½ of it with grated cheese and a dash of salt, fold over the other half, press the edges together, roll out, and sprinkle with cheese as before. Fold again, and roll ¼ inch thick. Cut into strips as straw-like as possible and bake about 8 minutes. Make some of the strips in rings and bake, then place the straws through them and arrange on a plate to serve.—*Sister Evelyn T. Keiser, Lordsburg, Cal.*

Peanut Butter Sandwiches.—Spread slices of thinly-cut graham bread with peanut butter, and then with chopped dates or figs. Finely-minced celery is excellent used in the same manner.—*Sister Tuda Haines, North Manchester, Ind.*

Table Dainties.—Take 1 quart flour mixed with 2 table-spoonfuls of baking powder, an even teaspoon of salt and 1 cup of butter and lard mixed. Wet with milk and roll out as for biscuit. Take a small egg, mix with brown sugar and spread over dough like jelly roll. Roll and slice about an inch thick. Spread more of the mixture over slices and sprinkle currants over this. Bake in a quick oven.—*Sister C. D. Bonsack, Union Bridge, Md.*

Butter Scotches.—Take 1 pint of New Orleans molasses, 2 pounds of brown sugar, 6 ounces of butter, 2 teaspoonfuls of soda, 1 grated cocoanut and flour to make stiff.—*Sister Mary J. Long, Mechanicsburg, Pa.*

Cracker Jacks.—Take 2 cups of sugar, 1 tablespoonful of vinegar, and enough water to cover the sugar. Boil till it will roll in a ball by putting it in water. Have the whites of 2 eggs beaten to a stiff froth, into which beat the syrup. Take a teacup full of any kind of nuts desired (black walnuts are good), roll and stir into the above. Spread on the top of crackers and set in the oven to brown lightly.—*Sister J. W. Miller, Hereford, Tex.*

Cocoanut Puffs.—Take 2 cups of grated cocoanut, 1 cup of powdered or fine granulated sugar, beaten whites of 2 eggs, and 2 tablespoonfuls of flour or cornstarch. Drop on buttered tins and bake quickly.—*Sister Ella Eckerle, Chicago, Ill.*

Cream Puffs.—Take 6 ounces of flour, ¼ pound of butter, ½ pint of hot water, and 5 eggs. Boil butter and water together and stir in flour while boiling. When cool, stir the well-beaten eggs in and beat all well, the same as pound cake. Drop on tins and rub tops of cakes with 1 egg beaten. Bake in quick oven. Cream part: ½ pint of sweet milk, 2 eggs, 1 cup of sugar and ¼ cup flour. Boil the milk, add the sugar, eggs and flour, stirring all till boiled. Flavor with vanilla. Open the puff at one side and put the cream in. —*Sister Amy Roop Shaw, Westminster, Md.*

Cream Puffs.—Add ½ cup of butter to 1 of hot water, and while boiling stir in 1 cup of flour. When cool stir in 3 eggs, 1 at a time, without previous beating. Drop in spoonfuls on buttered tins, and bake in a moderate oven, till a light brown. When done, each one will be hollow. Fill with whipped cream. or cornstarch filling flavored with extract or grated chocolate. This amount makes 18 puffs.—*Sister Mary L. Tannreuther, Waterloo, Iowa.*

Cream Puffs.—Take 1 cup of hot water and ½ cup of butter. Boil water and butter together and stir in 1 cup of flour while boiling. When cold add 3 eggs not previously beaten. Mix well and drop by spoonfuls into buttered tins. Bake in a quick oven twenty-five minutes. Don't open the oven for fifteen minutes at the first. You can use whipped cream or the following for a filling: One cup of sweet milk, ½ cup of sugar, 1 egg, and 3 tablespoonfuls of flour. Cook in double boiler till thick. Flavor with lemon. Open the puffs and insert filling.—*Sister Viola Sheeler, Kingsley, Ia.*

Cookies.—Take 4 eggs, 1½ cups of white sugar, 1 cup of butter, 4 cups of sifted flour, and 1½ teaspoonfuls of baking powder. Mix all together with the hand. Roll out as soft as possible. Bake in a quick oven. Flavor to taste.—*Sister Jennie A. Stephens, Corvallis, Oregon.*

Cookies.—Take 2 cups of sugar, 2 eggs, 1 cup of sweet milk, 1 cup of half butter and half lard, a little lemon flavoring, 2 tablespoonfuls of baking powder, and enough flour to make a soft dough. Roll out thin. Bake in a hot oven. They will keep good for weeks. —*Sister Mary A. Himes, McCune, Kans.*

Boston Cookies.—Take 1 cup of sugar, ½ cup of butter, ½ cup of lard, 2 eggs, twelve teaspoonfuls of sweet milk, 1 teaspoonful of soda, 2 cups of flour, 1 teaspoonful of cinnamon, one cup of raisins and 2 cups of oatmeal added last with a pinch of salt. Mix with a spoon and drop by spoonfuls into a greased pan like cookies.—*Sister Geo. Wrightsman, Virden, Ill.*

Boston Cookies.—Cream together ½ cup of butter, ½ cup of lard, and 1 cup of sugar. To this add 2 well beaten eggs, 1 teaspoonful of cinnamon, 1 teaspoonful of soda, a pinch of salt, 2 cups of flour, 1 cup of chopped raisins, and last of all 2 cups of rolled oats. This makes a very stiff dough. Take a small spoon and spread in small cakes in a greased pan. Bake in a quick oven. This does not make very pretty cakes, but they are very palatable if let set a couple of days before using.—*Sister D. H. Brubaker, Hereford, Tex.*

Cake Squares.—Measure 2 cups of sifted pastry flour, sifting well, add 1 rounding teaspoonful of baking powder, sift three times and set to one side. Cream 1 cup of granulated sugar and ¼ cup of butter. Then add the whites of 3 eggs well beaten and ½ cup of milk; also add the flour and beat well. Bake in two-inch square cake pans thirty or thirty-five minutes. Put plain icing in a bowl over the teakettle and dip the squares into it.—*Sister Bertha Allan, York, N. Dak.*

Cream Cookies (Within Everyone's Reach).—Take 3 cups of good sour cream, 3 eggs, a pinch of salt, 3 cups of white sugar, 3 small teaspoonfuls of soda, and any kind of flavoring desired and flour enough for a soft dough. Roll out and sprinkle with granulated sugar.—*Sister Mary E. McVicker, Spencer, Ohio.*

Sour Cream Cookies.—Take 1 pint of sour cream, ¾ of a pint of butter and lard mixed, 3 cups of light-brown sugar, 2 eggs, and 1 rounding teaspoonful of soda. Flavor as liked and mix as soft as can be handled.—*Sister Amanda Widdows, Hagerstown, Ind.*

Drop Cakes.—Take 2 cups of sugar, 1 cup of lard, 1 cup of water, 4 cups of flour, 4 eggs and 4 teaspoonfuls of baking powder. Stir lard and sugar together and add the beaten yolks of the eggs, then the water, flavor, and the whites. Put the baking powder in the flour and add last. Bake in well-greased gem pans, or drop the batter a teaspoonful at a time in rows, on flat greased tins.—*Sister Pearle F. Benner, Duncansville, Pa.*

Drop Cookies.—Take 2 cups of sugar, 1 cup of butter or lard, 4 eggs well beaten separately, 1 cup of sweet milk, and 4 teaspoonfuls of baking powder. Flavor to suit the taste and add as much flour as is needed to make like cake dough.—*Sister Susie M. Bere, Lanark, Ill.*

Deacon Cookies.—Take 3 eggs, 1 cup of sugar, 1 cup of butter and lard mixed and 2 teaspoonfuls of baking powder. Add enough flour to make a soft dough. Roll thin, cut out, and bake in a quick oven.—*Sister Ada M. Gnagey, West Milton, Ohio.*

Eggless Cookies.—Take 2 cups of brown sugar, 1 cup of sweet milk, ½ cup of lard, and ½ teaspoonful of soda. Use flour to make a dough not too stiff.—*Sister Eveline Skiles, Rossville, Ind.*

Eggless Cookies.—Take 2 cups of soft white sugar, or 1½ cups of granulated, 1 cup of butter or lard not melted, 1 cup of sour cream, 1 teaspoonful of soda dissolved in the cream. Flavor with nutmeg, if desired, and sift in enough flour to make a stiff dough, cut, and sprinkle with sugar. Put a raisin in the center of each cookie.—*Sister G. R. Goughnour, Canton, Ohio.*

Eggless Cookies.—Take 2 cups of flour, a scant cup of butter (or other good shortening; lard and butter mixed do nicely), 1 cup of sweet milk and 1 teaspoonful of soda. Flavor as you like and mix with flour enough for a soft dough.—*Sister Elsie Oliver, Kinross, Iowa.*

Fig Cookies.—Make a rich fig jam, then make your favorite plain or sugar cookie dough, roll thin, spread fig jam on half, fold the other half over this and cut with a sharp knife into sized pieces desired. Bake as any other cookies.—*Sister J. I. Miller, Roanoke, La.*

Filled Cookies.—Make any good sugar cookies, roll very thin and bake quickly. To 1 cup of chopped dates add ½ cup of chopped nuts, ½ cup of water, 1 tablespoonful of sugar, and 1 teaspoonful of flour. Cook all together till smooth and use as filling between the cookies. Another to be used in the same way: The juice and grated rind of one lemon, 1 cup of seedless or seeded raisins, ½ cup of chopped nuts, 2 tablespoonfuls of water and 1 teaspoonful of sugar. Cook the same as above. Fine for school lunch. —*Sister C. S. Colony, York, N. Dak.*

Frosted Creams.—Take 1 cup of sugar, 1 cup of butter and lard, mixed to a cream, 1 cup of molasses, 1 cup of cold water, 1 teaspoonful of soda and 1 tablespoonful of ginger. Mix soft and roll. Bake on under side of dripping pan. Ice while warm with the following: Take 2 cups of granulated sugar, dampen with water and boil until it threads. Pour it over the whites of 2 eggs well beaten. Cut the creams into squares with a sharp knife.—*Sister Lizzie Chamberlain, Yale, Iowa.*

Frosted Creams.—Take 2 cups of molasses, 1 cup of sugar, ½ pint of shortening, ½ teacupful of water, 1 tablespoonful of soda, 2 tablespoonfuls of cinnamon, yolks of 3 eggs and the white of 1 egg. Knead in flour to roll out easily, and cut in squares the size of soda crackers. Bake in a quick oven. Frosting: Take 1⅓ cups of white sugar dissolved in 4 tablespoonfuls of water, and boil until it threads. Pour it over the beaten whites of the 2 eggs, and beat until smooth. Season with vanilla, and spread on each square with a knife.—*Sister Bertha Brunskill, Minneapolis, Minn.*

Frosted Creams.—To make extra good cookies, take 1 egg, 1 cup of molasses, 7 tablespoonfuls of lard, 6 tablespoonfuls of water, 1 tablespoonful of ginger, 1 teaspoonful of soda, and flour enough to roll. Leave dough ½ inch thick. Bake on the bottom of a large bread pan. After it is baked, put on frosting which is made as follows: 1 cup of sugar and ¼ cup of water. Boil till it hairs. Pour in beaten white of egg and beat till it hardens. After the frosting is on, cut in squares the size you like.—*Sister M. A. Wolf, Libertyville, Iowa.*

Fruit Cookies.—Take ¾ cup of butter, 2 cups of sugar, 3 eggs, 1¼ cups of lard, 10 tablespoonfuls of sweet milk, 2 cups of raisins, 4 cups of rolled oats, 4½ cups of flour, sifted beforehand, 1 teaspoonful of cinnamon, ½ teaspoonful of salt, 1 level teaspoonful of soda dissolved in milk. Mix very stiff, drop in a pan and bake.—*Sister Eunice Early, South Bend, Ind.*

Fruit Cookies.—Take ½ cup of butter, 1 cup of sugar, 1 egg, 1 cup of chopped and seeded raisins, ½ cup of currants, ½ cup of sour milk, 1 teaspoonful of cinnamon, 1 level teaspoonful of soda. Flour the fruits and add spices, then mix in the order given. Mix soft, roll thick, cut out and bake quickly.—*Sister Annie Taylor, Brazil, N. Dak.*

Fruit Cookies (Excellent).—Take 1 cup of sugar, ½ cup of butter, ½ cup of sweet milk, ½ cup each of raisins, currants and figs chopped fine, 3 eggs, 1 teaspoonful of vanilla, 2 teaspoonfuls of baking powder and flour to make dough that can be easily handled. —*Sister John D. Clear, Rockford, Ill.*

Brighton Rocks.—Take 4 cups of flour, 2 cups of sugar, 2 teaspoonfuls of cinnamon, 2 cups of seeded raisins, 1 cup of butter, 4 eggs, 2 tablespoonfuls of sweet milk and 1 even teaspoonful of soda; put together in order as given, mould with your hands and flatten. Bake in a quick oven.—*Sister Sarah Cook, Sabetha, Kans.*

Chocolate Cookies.—Take 2 eggs, 2 cups of sugar, 1 teaspoonful of soda dissolved in ½ cup of warm water, 1 cup of grated chocolate, ½ cup of butter and ½ cup of lard. Melt chocolate, butter and lard. When cool add to sugar and eggs. Flour enough to stiffen. Roll thin. When baked, ice with white icing.—*Sister Katie B. Blouch, Annville, Pa.*

Chocolate Jumbles.—Take 2 cups of sugar, 1 cup of butter, 1 cup of grated chocolate, 4 eggs, 1 teaspoonful of soda, 1 teaspoonful of cream of tartar, and 3 cups of flour. Roll thin and cut in any pattern desired.—*Sister Katie Geib, Mastersonville, Pa.*

Ginger Cookies.—Take 1 cup of sugar, 1 cup of butter, 2 cups of molasses, 1 tablespoonful of ginger, 3 eggs, 2 teaspoonfuls of soda dissolved in 1 cup of buttermilk. Beat well together the sugar and butter. Then put in molasses and ginger, thoroughly mixing them. Then put in the eggs after they have been well beaten. Put in the milk. Use enough flour to make a dough as soft as you can easily work. Roll about ⅙ inch thick and bake in a quick oven. The softer you keep the dough, the better the cookies will be.—*Sister Mattie Wertz, Johnstown, Pa.*

Ginger Cookies.—Take 1 cup of sugar, 1 cup of butter, 1 egg, 1 cup of baking molasses, ⅓ cup of vinegar, 1 teaspoonful each of salt and soda, and 1 tablespoonful of ginger. Dissolve soda in the vinegar, then add to the molasses. Use flour enough for soft dough.—*Sister E. W. Hollopeter, Rockton, Pa.*

Drop Ginger Cakes.—Take ½ cup each of butter and sugar, 1 cup of molasses, 2 eggs, 1 teaspoonful each of cinnamon and ginger, ½ cup of boiling water, 1 teaspoonful of soda, and a pinch of salt mixed in 3 cups of flour. Mix the ingredients in the order named; drop small spoonfuls 2 inches apart in a well-greased pan and bake in a quick oven.—*Sister M. Jane Stauffer, Polo, Ill.*

Grandmother's Ginger Cookies.—Take 1 quart of molasses, 1 pint of buttermilk, ½ pint of lard; have all warm, and mix 3 tablespoonfuls of soda with buttermilk, 1 tablespoonful of ginger; stir in 6 pints of flour. When cold, roll. Wash with beaten egg before baking.—*Sister Laura B. Reiff, Idaville, Ind.*

Good Ginger Cookies.—Take 1 cup of molasses, 1 cup of sugar, 1 cup of shortening. 1 tablespoonful of ginger, ½ cup of made coffee, 2 teaspoonfuls of soda dissolved in the coffee, flour enough to roll out. Roll medium thick and bake in a rather hot oven.—*Sister Sarah Witmore Harnly, McPherson, Kans.*

Soft Ginger Cookies.—Take 1 pint of molasses, 1 cup of lard, 1 cup of sour or buttermilk, 1 tablespoonful of soda, 1 teaspoonful of ginger. Stir the soda and ginger in the molasses, add the other ingredients, stir in enough flour to make a soft dough. Roll a little thicker than sugar cookies. Cut into cakes, bake in a moderate oven.—*Sister Lizzie Bagwell, Bremen, Ohio.*

Ginger Snaps.—Take 7 cups flour, 1 cup sugar, 2 cups molasses, 1 cup butter, 1 egg, 1 tablespoonful good vinegar, 1 teaspoonful soda, and 1 teaspoonful ginger If the ingredients are cold, it may seem hard to mix in the full amount of flour, but it should be in if possible. These, if properly baked, very much resemble those in the bakeries.—*Sister Kittie Neher, Ark.*

Ginger Snaps.—Take 2 cups of molasses, 3 tablespoonfuls of melted lard, 1 tablespoonful of soda dissolved in 2 tablespoonfuls of warm water, 1 tablespoonful of ginger, 1 tablespoonful of cloves, and flour to make a stiff dough.—*Sister Lizzie Allbright, North Manchester, Ind.*

Ginger Snaps.—Take 1 cup of molasses, 1 cup of dark sugar, 1 egg, ½ cup of lard and butter mixed, 1 teaspoonful of soda, 2 teaspoonfuls of ginger, 4 cups of flour; dissolve soda in 1 tablespoonful of boiling water. Pinch off small bits of the dough, roll in palm of the hand, flatten a little, lay in pan not too close and bake.—*Sister Katie Shetter, Morrill, Kans.*

Ginger Snaps.—Of all the cakes one loves to eat perhaps none charms the palate like good ginger snaps.

And if to make the best you'd wish to know,
Why, study well the lines you find below:
Melt of butter half a pound; also of lard;
Then add sugar brown a half a pound.
Stir in a quart of 'lasses, not too hard,
Four tablespoons of ginger nicely ground.
Into this mixture sift two quarts of flour,
Then, to insure the cake shall not be sour,
Dissolve in milk four teaspoonfuls of soda;
(Saleratus is advised, but I like not the odor).
Mix either with milk; it surely makes no matter,
So that you pour the milk into the batter.
Add more flour and roll out thin the dough;
Then cut in cakes, but this you surely know.
Bake them well in an oven cooks call "slow,"
And when they are baked they will not last long, I know.
    —*Sister Alice Funderburg, Gillford, Mo.*

Ginger Snaps.—1 cup of sugar, 1 cup of molasses, 1 cup of lard or butter, 2 eggs, 1 teaspoonful of ginger, 1 teaspoonful of cinnamon, 1 tablespoonful of soda dissolved in a little warm water, 1 tablespoonful of vinegar, and a little salt. Add the vinegar to the dissolved soda, let it foam well, then add to the dough, mix hard, roll thin and bake quickly.—*Sister Geo. Wrightsman, Virden, Ill.*

Round Ginger Snaps.—Take 1 cup of brown sugar, 1 cup of molasses, 1 cup of butter, 2 teaspoonfuls of ginger, 1 teaspoonful of soda dissolved in ¼ cup of water, flour enough to make a very stiff dough. Do not roll as thin as sugar cookies, cut with a small round cutter and bake in a quick oven.—*Sister Barbara Wolf, Mayville, N. Dak.*

Hermits.—Take 2 cups of brown sugar, 1 cup of butter or lard, 1 cup of raisins seeded and chopped, 3 eggs, ½ nutmeg, ½ teaspoonful each of cinnamon and cloves, 1 teaspoonful of soda dissolved in ½ cup of sweet milk, flour enough to roll without sticking. Roll ½ inch thick and cut with round cake cutter; bake in a rather quick oven. These will keep a month.—*Sister Louella Hitchings, Warriorsmark, Pa.*

Hermits.—Take 2 cups of " C " sugar, 2 eggs, ½ cup of butter, ½ cup of sweet milk, 1 cup of chopped raisins, 1 cup of chopped nuts, 1 teaspoonful of soda, 1 teaspoonful of cinnamon and 1 teaspoonful of cloves. Mix as stiff as possible, just so it can be stirred with a spoon. A teaspoonful of dough makes 1 good-sized cake. Frost with boiled icing.—*Sister Nettie Stine, Leaf River, Ill.*

Pepper Nuts.—Mix into a baking pan 3 pounds of molasses 1 pound of sugar, ½ pound of lard or butter, 4 teaspoonfuls of cinnamon, and 2 each of cloves and ginger. Place on the stove and bring to a sharp heat, then take from the stove and stir in 3½ teaspoonfuls of soda dissolved in boiling water. Lastly stir in 4½ pounds of flour, and let stand in a cool place over night. In the morning work out into half-inch rolls, cut in inch lengths, place in pans not too close and bake in a moderate oven.—*Sister Minnie Barkdoll, Warrenville, Ill.*

Rock Cookies.—Take 2 beaten eggs, 2 cups of sifted flour, 1 cup of butter, 2 cups of rolled oats, 2 cups of brown sugar, 1 cup of seedless or seeded raisins, ½ teaspoonful of salt, 1 teaspoonful of soda, 1 teaspoonful of cinnamon and the same of cloves if liked. Mix all together and form in little balls as large as a hulled walnut. Place on the under side of a dripping pan with plenty of room to spread and bake a light brown. Remove with a knife.—*Sister Bertie Cullen, Beatrice, Nebr.*

Lemon Cookies.—Take 2 cups of sugar, 1 cup of butter or lard, 1 cup of buttermilk, 1 teaspoonful of soda and flour to mix stiff. Flavor with lemon. Before baking brush the top of the cookies with this mixture: The yolk of 1 egg, 2 teaspoonfuls of sweet milk and 3 of water.—*Sister Mary C. Hoke, Goshen, Ind.*

French Lemon Cakes.—Take ¼ pound of butter, 4 eggs, 1 pound of sugar, 1 pound of flour, and 2 teaspoonfuls of baking powder. Flavor with lemon. Roll very thin and cut with a cake cutter.—*Sister Anna Danner, Knoxville, Md.*

Lemon Hearts.—Take ½ cup of butter, cream it, and mix gradually 1 cup of granulated sugar, add 2 well-beaten eggs, 1 teaspoonful of milk, 1 teaspoonful of lemon extract. Mix a heaped teaspoonful of baking powder in with the former preparation, adding enough flour to enable one to roll. Roll very thin, sprinkle granulated sugar on top, cut with a heart-shaped cutter and bake to a brownness desired.—*Sister Kate H. Zug, Elizabethtown, Pa.*

Molasses Cookies.—Take 2 cups of molasses, 3 eggs, 1 cup of lard, 3 teaspoonfuls of soda, 2 tablespoonfuls of ginger and flour enough to roll. Flavor with vanilla.—*Sister Cora Shaffer, Odell, Nebr.*

Molasses Cookies.—Put into a bowl 1 cup of shortening (drippings and lard), 2 cups of New Orleans molasses, 2 tablespoonfuls of boiling water, and 2 teaspoonfuls of soda, stir until "bubbly." Then add ½ teaspoonful of salt, a tablespoonful of ginger, a teaspoonful of cinnamon, 1 beaten egg, and flour to roll as soft as possible. Cut out perfectly round and lift carefully with a broad-bladed knife into a floured dripping pan, being careful not to crowd them. Bake a rich brown in a moderately hot oven. When done, lift out carefully and lay on a smooth surface till cold.—*Sister Grace R. Sell, McKee Gap, Pa.*

Cheap Molasses Cookies.—Take 1 cup of molasses, 1 cup of sugar, ¾ cup of lard cold, ½ teaspoonful each of ginger, cloves, nutmeg and cinnamon and the yolk of 1 egg. Mix all together and stir until very light; then add ½ cup of cold water, and 1 heaping teaspoonful soda. Sift soda and flour together, add enough flour to mix nicely and roll out. Mix in the evening, let stand in a cool place over night and bake the next day. Beat the white of the same egg and brush over the tops of the cookies before baking.—*Sister Emma Fisher, Baltic, Ohio.*

Good Plain Cookies.—Take 4 cups of white sugar, 2 cups of melted butter and lard, 4 eggs, 12 tablespoonfuls of cold water, 2 teaspoonfuls of soda, and flour to make a soft dough. Roll thin. *Sister Florence Inman, Bradford, Ohio.*

Oatmeal Cookies.—Take 1 cup of sugar, 1 cup of molasses, ¾ cup of lard, ¾ cup of butter, 3 cups of oatmeal, 2 teaspoonfuls of ginger, or if you like flavor with other spice, 1 teaspoonful of soda. Dissolve with ½ cup of boiling water. Take flour enough to make stiff. Roll and bake in a moderate oven. Turn pan upside down to bake.—*Sister Maude O. Fahrney Flora, Twin Falls, Idaho.*

Oatmeal Cookies.—Take 2 eggs, 1 small cup of butter, 1 cup of sugar, ½ cup of sour milk, in which is dissolved 1 teaspoonful of soda, 2 cups of oatmeal, 2 cups of flour, and 1 cup of chopped raisins (seeded or seedless). Mix into a soft batter and drop from a spoon on buttered pans.—*Sister Lora Marsh, Williston, N. Dak.*

Oatmeal Cookies.—Mix as for pie dough 3 cups of rolled oats, 2 cups of flour, ¾ of a cup of lard, ¾ of a cup of sugar, ½ teaspoonful of salt, 1 teaspoonful of soda, ¼ of a cup of raisins, 1 teaspoonful each of cloves, cinnamon and allspice, and ½ cup of sweet milk. Roll thin and bake.—*Sister Lida Hershberger, Salem, Ill.*

Snowballs.—Take the whites of 5 eggs, 2 cups of sugar, ¾ cup of lard, ¾ cup of sweet milk, 3 cups of flour and 2 tablespoonfuls of baking powder. Bake in gem pans. Then take 1 cup of sugar, enough water to melt it and boil until stringy. Stir this into the white of an egg well beaten and spread over gems, and sprinkle shredded cocoanut over them. Place in oven a few minutes for icing to harden.—*Sister Ella Miller, Versailles, Ohio.*

Sugar Cookies.—Take 1 cup of butter and 2 cups of sugar creamed together, 5 eggs beaten (to make extra nice, beat whites and yolks separately), 2 teaspoonfuls of baking powder, flavor to suit taste, flour to make a soft dough. Roll and bake in a quick oven. Just before baking, sprinkle with granulated sugar.—*Sister Alice S. Wallick, Cerro Gordo, Ill.*

Sugar Cookies.—Take 2 cups of brown sugar, 1 cup of butter, 1 cup of sour milk, 1 teaspoonful of soda. Flavor, roll thin and sprinkle with white sugar before baking.—*Sister N. E. Lilligh, Mulberry Grove, Ill.*

Sugar Cookies.—Take 1½ cups of sugar, 2 eggs, 1 cup of butter or lard, ½ cup of sweet milk, 1 teaspoonful of soda, 1 teaspoonful of ginger, and flour enough to allow you to handle, not stiff. Roll thin, cut and bake in a hot oven.—*Sister Minerva Kintner, Bryan, Ohio.*

Sugar Cookies.—Take 2 cups of sugar, 1 cup of butter or lard, 1 cup of sour cream, 1 teaspoonful of soda, and 6 cups of flour. Flavor to taste.—*Sister Dora Studebaker, Whitewater, Ind.*

Sugar Cookies.—Take 2 heaping cups of light-brown sugar, 1 cup of lard, and 2 eggs. Cream together till light, then add 1 cup of sour cream, 2 teaspoonfuls of soda, dissolved in the cream, and flour enough to roll. Sprinkle granulated sugar over the top, cut out and bake in a hot oven.—*Sister Martha Ross, Sidney, Ind.*

Bakery Sugar Cookies.—Take 4 cups of flour, 1 cup of sugar, ½ cup of sweet milk, ½ cup of melted lard, 2 eggs and 3 teaspoonfuls of baking powder. Bake in cookies.—*Sister Eldora Thomas, Warrensburg, Mo.*

Sugar Cakes.—Take 1½ cups of sugar, ¼ cup of lard, 1 cup of sour milk, 1 teaspoonful of baking soda, and ½ nutmeg. Add flour enough to roll. Sprinkle granulated sugar over the top. They are best if the batter is stirred up in the evening and allowed to set until morning.—*Sister Alice K. Trimmer, York, Pa.*

Sugar Drop Cookies.—Take 2 eggs, 2 cups of sugar, 2 cups of shortening, 2 cups of sour milk, 1 teaspoonful of salt, 2 teaspoonfuls of soda dissolved in the milk. Add 6½ cups of sifted flour and stir well. Drop pieces about the size of a walnut on greased tins, allowing space for them to spread as they bake. Flavoring of any kind liked may be added.—*Sister Sallie C. Cline, Castleton, Kans.*

Plain Sugar Cookies.—Take 2 cups of sugar, ½ cup of butter, ½ cup of lard, 1 cup of cold water, ½ teaspoonful of salt, 2 eggs, 2 heaping teaspoonfuls of baking powder, and flour to the consistency for rolling. Flavor with vanilla. Sprinkle with sugar. Bake in a quick oven.—*Sister Della Lehmer, Los Angeles, Cal.*

Scotch Cookies.—Take 2½ pounds of sugar, 1¼ pounds of butter or part lard, 4 eggs, ½ pint of molasses, 1½ ounces of soda, and 3¾ pounds of flour. Flavor with allspice. Mix in rotation.— *Sister Emma J. Weaver, Mound City, Mo.*

Fruit Crackers.—Required: 1 pound of dates, 1 pint of rich cream, graham flour. Seed the dates. Cut them in small pieces. Take first-class graham flour, sift into the cream till it forms a paste thick enough to roll out. Roll out 2 layers, ¼ inch thick. Sprinkle the cut dates over one of these pieces, lay the other thereon, and then roll out smooth. Cut into squares, about 3 inches each way, prick deeply with a fork, and bake till not too crisp.—*Sister J. H. Moore, Elgin, Ill.*

Graham Crackers.—Take 1 cup of sour cream, ½ cup of sugar, 1 tablespoonful of butter, 1 teaspoonful of soda and graham flour enough to make a stiff dough, so that it can be rolled and cut the same as sugar cookies. Bake in a hot oven.—*Sister Mary Wampler, Dayton, Va.*

Lemon Crackers.—Take 2½ cups of sugar, 1 cup of lard, 2 eggs, 1 pint of sweet milk, five cents' worth of oil of lemon, and 1 ounce of carbonate of ammonia. Beat the sugar and lard well together, then add the eggs well beaten. Pulverize the ammonia and dissolve in sweet milk, then add the lemon and stir in flour until it is real stiff. Knead well, roll thin as pie crust, cut in squares, stick with a fork, and bake in a quick oven.—*Sister M. Kate Crist, Timberville, Va.*—Pound the dough until light.—*Sister Lizzie M. Blickenstaff, Cerro Gordo, Ill.*

Oatmeal Crackers.—Take ⅔ cup of sugar, ½ cup of butter, 1 egg, ½ cup of sweet milk, 1 level teaspoonful of soda, 2 cups of wheat flour, and 3 cups of oatmeal. The dough should be as stiff as it can be rolled, and if necessary add a little more milk. Roll and cut in squares, or any desired shape and bake.—*Sister H. Kurtz, Hebron, Iowa.*

Oatmeal Wafers.—Take 2 cups of oatmeal, 3 cups of flour, ½ cup of shortening, 2 cups of sugar, ½ cup of cold water, and ½ teaspoonful of soda. Roll thin.—*Sister Laura Hass, Mechanicsburg, Pa.*

Vanilla Wafers.—Take 1 cup of sugar, ⅔ cup of butter, 4 teaspoonfuls of milk, 1 tablespoonful of vanilla, 1 egg, 1½ teaspoonfuls of cream of tartar, ⅔ teaspoon of soda and flour to roll very thin.—*Sister Ethel Mishler, South Whitley, Ind.*

Vanilla Wafers.—Take 1 egg, 1 cup of sugar, ⅔ cup of butter and lard mixed, 1 tablespoonful of vanilla, 1½ teaspoonfuls of cream of tartar, and ⅔ teaspoonful of soda mixed with 4 tablespoonfuls of milk. Stir all together and use flour enough to roll very thin. Cut in small shapes and bake on slide in the oven.—*Sister Mazie Clippinger, Shippensburg, Pa.*

Ginger Bread.—Cream a cup of butter with ½ cup of sugar, add 1 cup of molasses, 1 teaspoonful of cinnamon, ½ teaspoonful of salt, and 1 teaspoonful of ginger. Mix well and add 1 cup of boiling water, into which a teaspoonful of soda has been dissolved. Sift in 3 cups of flour, and 1 teaspoonful of baking powder. Bake three-fourths of an hour in a large pan. If desired, put in a cup of raisins. —*Sister Mary C. Beard Eshelman, Elgin, Ill.*

Ginger Bread.—Take 1 quart of New Orleans molasses, ¾ pint of melted lard, add flour to thicken and stir in 2 tablespoonfuls of ginger, 1 teaspoonful of pulverized alum dissolved in a tablespoonful of cold water. Dissolve 2 tablespoonfuls of soda in ¾ of a pint of boiling water, and pour it over the mixture; then add flour enough to make it very stiff. Grease pans well and dredge white with flour to prevent sticking. Spread batter evenly in pans. This will make 2 cakes.—*Sister Jennie A. Crofford, Martinsburg, Pa.*

Ginger Bread.—Take 1 cup of sugar, 1 cup of molasses, 1 cup of cream, 4 cups of flour, 1 egg, 1 small teaspoonful of soda, butter the size of a walnut, and ginger to taste.—*Sister Barbara Wolf, Mayville, N. Dak.*

Gingerbread.—Take ½ cup of butter and 1 cup of sugar; cream together. Add 1 cup of molasses, beat again. Then add 2 eggs and beat again, lastly add 1 cup of sour milk, 3 cups of flour, 1 teaspoonful of soda, 1 teaspoonful of ginger, and 1 teaspoonful of cinnamon. Beat thoroughly. The beating is what makes it good.—*Sister Landonia B. Saul, Octavia, Nebr.*

Soft Ginger Bread.—Take 3 eggs, ½ cup of sugar, ¼ cup of shortening, 1 cup of sorghum molasses, 1 cup of buttermilk, 1 tablespoonful of ginger, 1 teaspoonful of soda and 3 teacupfuls of flour. This will make 2 small loaves.—*Sister Ella E. Leedy, Cerro Gordo, Ill.*

Soft Ginger Bread.—Take 1 cup of molasses, 1 egg, 5 tablespoonfuls of melted shortening, 1½ cups of flour, 1 teaspoonful of ginger, 1 teaspoonful of soda mixed with the molasses, and ⅔ cup of hot water added last.—*Sister Emma Carstensen, Girard, Ill.*

Ginger Cake.—Take 1 pint of sour milk, ¾ pint of sugar, ¾ pint of molasses, lard or butter size of an egg, 1 egg, 2 teaspoonfuls of soda, 2 teaspoonfuls of ginger, and 1 pint of raisins does not spoil it, but can be left out. Bake in bread pans and serve with jelly.—*Sister Ida Wampler Mohler, Leeton, Mo.*

Ginger Cake.—Take 1 cup of baking molasses, 1 cup of sugar, ½ cup of lard, 3 cups of flour, 3 eggs, and 1 teaspoonful of ginger. Beat this well, then add 1½ teaspoonfuls of soda. On the batter now pour 1 cup of boiling water, and stir well. Bake in a moderate oven.—*Sister Sarah A. Sell, Newry, Pa.*

Ginger Cake Without Milk or Eggs.—Take 1 cup of sugar, 1 cup of butter, 1 cup of molasses, ½ cup of made coffee, 2 teaspoonfuls of soda, 1 tablespoonful of ginger and flour enough to make a good batter.—*Sister Lizzie D. Mohler, Miami, N. M.*

Angel Food Cake.—Whites of 10 eggs, 1¼ cups of sugar, 1 cup of flour sifted 3 times, 1 level teaspoonful of cream of tartar. Add the cream of tartar to the eggs when half beaten, add a pinch of salt, beat until very stiff, put in the sugar and flour, stirring lightly. Put in an ungreased cake pan and bake from 35 to 50 minutes in a moderate oven.—*Sister E. E. Scroggs, Centerview, Mo.*

Angel Food Cake.—Take the whites of 11 eggs, 1½ cups granulated sugar, 1 cup of pastry flour measured after sifting 4 times with 1 teaspoonful of cream of tartar, and 1 teaspoonful of vanilla. Beat the whites to a stiff froth, beat the sugar into the eggs, add the vanilla and flour, stirring quickly and lightly. Beat until ready to put in the oven. Bake 40 minutes in a moderate oven. Do not grease the cake pan.—*Sister Lillie M. Ulrey, Canton, Kans.*

Angel Food Cake.—Take the whites of 8 eggs, 1½ cups of sugar, 1 level cup of flour (sift flour before measuring), and a scant half teaspoonful of cream of tartar. Add a pinch of salt to the whites of the eggs before whipping. Flavor to suit the taste. Sift, measure and set aside the flour and sugar; whip the eggs to a foam; add the cream of tartar and whip till very stiff. Add the sugar and beat in with a spoon; then add flavoring and beat again. Lastly, fold in the flour lightly. Do not beat after adding flour, except just enough to mix it in well. Bake in a moderate oven forty minutes.— *Sister Fannie Hollar, Hardin, Mo.*

Dried Apple Cake.—Cut in small pieces dried apples enough to fill 2 cups, wash, cover with water, let stand over night. In the morning add 1 cup of Orleans molasses, cook until tender, let cool. Take 1 cup of sugar, 2 eggs, ⅔ cup of shortening (butter and lard mixed), 1 teaspoonful of soda, 2 cups of flour, 1 teaspoonful each of ground cloves, cinnamon, and other spices if you like. Stir all together and bake in a loaf 1 hour. Lay a greased paper in the bottom of cake pan, as it will separate in removing if baked otherwise. —*Sister Sarah J. Johnsonbaugh, Hagerstown, Ind.*

Dried Apple Cake.—Boil together 2 cups of molasses and 3 cups of dried apples, which have been soaked over night. When cool, add 2 cups of raisins, 1 cup of nut-meats, and 1 teaspoonful each of cloves, cinnamon and nutmeg. Add this to a batter made of 2 cups of sugar, 2 well-beaten eggs, 1 cup of butter, 1 cup of milk, 1 teaspoonful of soda, and 3½ cups of flour. Bake one and one-half hour.—*Sister Edna Eisenbise, Lanark, Ill.*

Apple Butter Cake.—Cream together 1 cup sugar, ½ cup butter and 4 eggs well beaten. Then add 4 tablespoonfuls of sour milk, 1 teaspoonful soda, 1 teaspoonful each of ground cinnamon and cloves. Add 2 cups of flour. Beat this well together. Then add 1 cup of good apple butter. To be baked as layer cake.—*Sister Susie Heestand, Smithville, Ohio.*

Dried Apple Fruit Cakes.—Soak 3 cups of dried apples over night, in the morning chop them, put on the stove with 3 cups of molasses, stew almost soft; add 1 cupful of raisins and stew a few minutes; when cold, add 3 cups of flour, 1 cup of butter, 3 eggs and 1 teaspoonful of soda, spice to taste. Bake in a steady oven.—*Sister J. A. Sell, McKee Gap, Pa.*

Applesauce Cake.—Take 1½ cups of sugar, 1½ cups of apple-sauce, ½ cup of butter and lard, 2 tablespoonfuls of grated chocolate, 1 teaspoonful each of cloves, cinnamon and nutmeg, 1 scant teaspoonful of soda, and 1 cup of raisins. Add enough flour to make a stiff batter and bake in three layers, or in a loaf. The spices may be left out.—*Sister R. F. Brubaker, San Dimas, Cal.*

Applesauce Cake.—Take 1 cup of sugar, ½ cup of butter, 1½ cups of apple sauce, 1 cup of raisins, 1 teaspoonful each of cinnamon and cloves, 2 teaspoonfuls of soda, and 2¾ cups of flour. Bake slowly one hour.—*Sister Mary Butterbaugh, Polo, Ill.*—Lard may be used instead of butter. The apple sauce should be tart. Dissolve the soda in the sauce.—*Sister Blanche Lentz, Elgin, Ill.*

"Brownstone Front" Cake.—For the dark part: Add ½ cup of grated chocolate to 1 cup of sweet milk; boil until well dissolved and add the yolk of one egg in a little milk. Light part: Take ½ cup of butter creamed with 1½ cups of sugar, ½ cup of milk, 1 teaspoonful each of baking powder and soda, 2 eggs, 2 teaspoonfuls of vanilla, and 2 cups of flour. Mix light and dark parts together and bake in a moderate oven. This baked in a loaf and covered with white icing is excellent.—*Sister Rosa May Miller, Roanoke, La.*

Blackberry Jam Cakes.—Take 3 eggs, 1 cup of sugar, ⅔ cup of butter, 2 cups of flour, and 1 cup of blackberry jam, 2 large tablespoonfuls of sour cream, and 1 even teaspoonful of soda. Bake in layers and put together with white icing. Raspberry or strawberry jam may be used instead of the blackberry jam if preferred.—*Sister Lizzie D. Mohler, Miami, N. M.*

Bread Dough Cake.—Take 2 cups of bread dough before the bread is worked stiff; add 2 cups of sugar, 1 cup of lard, 1 cup of seedless raisins, 2 eggs, 2 cups of flour, 1 teaspoonful of soda, 1 teaspoonful each of all kinds of spices.—*Sister Anna Miller, Versailles, Ohio.*

Buttercup Cake.—Take ¾ cup of butter, 1½ cups of sugar, yolks of 8 eggs, 1 whole egg, 1 cup of sweet milk, 2 cups of flour, ½ teaspoonful of soda, 1½ teaspoonfuls of cream of tartar, 1 teaspoonful of lemon essence. Golden frosting: Beat the yolks of 3 eggs very light and stir in powdered sugar until stiff enough to spread. Flavor with vanilla.—*Sister M. A. Peacock, Mt. Morris, Ill.*

Buttermilk Cake.—Take 1 cup of buttermilk, 1 pint of molasses, ½ cup of sugar, ⅔ pint of lard, 2 eggs, 2 scant teaspoonfuls of saleratus, and flour enough to make a batter a little stiffer than common cake batter if it is baked in jelly tins; if baked as drop cakes, mix stiff enough so they will not run.—*Sister Effie Hoover, Milford, Ind.*

Caramel Cake.—Take 2 eggs, 2 cups of sugar, 1 cup of sweet milk, ½ cup of shortening, 3 cups of flour and 2 teaspoonfuls of baking powder. Icing: 1½ cups of brown and white sugar mixed, ½ cup of sweet cream, butter size of a walnut; boil all together until thick enough to spread between the layers and over the cake. Just before removing the icing from the fire, add 1 teaspoonful of vanilla. —*Sister Sue C. Foutz, Waynesboro, Pa.*

Caramel Cake.—Cream 1 cup of butter with 2 cups of sugar, add slowly 1 cup of sweet milk, 3 cups of flour in which 3 teaspoonfuls of baking powder have been well sifted, and last the well beaten whites of 8 eggs. Flavor with vanilla. Filling: Take 2 cups of light-brown sugar, 1 cup of cream, and 3 tablespoonfuls of melted butter; boil until the mixture will hold together in cold water: when done, add 1 or 2 teaspoonfuls of vanilla. Spread between layers and on outside of cake.—*Sister Orpha Bolinger, Lanark, Ill.*

A Cheap Cake.—Take ½ cup of butter, 2 cups of granulated sugar, 3 eggs well beaten, 1 cup of sweet milk; mix all together, then add 3 cups of flour and 3 teaspoonfuls of baking powder. Bake in loaf or layer.—*Sister Mattie E. Hylton, Troutville, Va.*

A Good Cheap Cake.—Take 2 cups of brown sugar (or granulated), 1 tablespoonful of lard, 2½ cups of sifted flour, 1 cup of chopped raisins, 1 teaspoonful each of cinnamon and cloves, 1 teaspoonful of soda, and 1¼ cups of sour milk, preferably buttermilk. Put all excepting the milk into the mixing bowl and mix thoroughly with the hand. Then stir in the milk and bake in four layers. Put together with caramel filling. This is excellent when butter and eggs are expensive.—*Sister M. A. Snyder, Bradford, Ohio.*

Very Cheap Cake.—Take 3 eggs beaten very light, add 1 cup of sugar, beat again, add 1 cup of flour, 1 teaspoonful of baking powder, and ⅔ cup of almost boiling water. Bake in a quick oven. —*Sister Mary E. Whitney, Kearney, Nebr.*—Pour in the water slowly while stirring. Do not move or jar while baking.—*Sister Mary Strickler, Octavia, Nebr.*

Colorado Chocolate Cake.—Take 2 cups of granulated sugar, ½ cup of butter, 1 cup of milk, 3 level cups of flour, 5 eggs beaten together, 3 squares of chocolate, 2 teaspoonfuls of cinnamon, ¼ teaspoonful cloves, 1 teaspoonful vanilla, 2 teaspoonfuls of baking powder, ½ nutmeg. Mix in ½ cup of walnuts and bake in two thick layers. Add 1 cup of nuts to a cream filling. Half of this recipe makes one common-sized cake. A nice icing: Boil 1 cup of sugar in ¼ cup of water, four minutes. Beat until cool, and spread on cake quickly. Then spread over that butter and chocolate melted together.—*Sister Sarah Winger Merrill, The Dalles, Ore.*

Checkerboard Cake.—Light part: Take 1½ cups of sugar, ½ cup of butter, ½ cup of sweet milk, 2 cups of flour, whites of 4 eggs, 2 teaspoonfuls of baking powder, flavor with extract. Dark part: Take 1 cup of brown sugar, ½ cup of butter, ½ cup of sweet milk, yolks of 4 eggs, 2 cups of flour, 2 teaspoonfuls of baking powder and flavor with spices. Mix in separate tins. Put a ring of the light, then a ring of the dark, then a ring of light in 2 jelly tins; then in 2 other jelly tins put a ring of the dark, then a ring of the light then a ring of the dark. This makes 2 tins each with a light edge and center, and 2 each with a dark edge and center. Put together in layers alternately.—*Sister Mina H. Bosserman, Dayton, Ohio.*

Chocolate Cake.—Take 1½ cups of granulated sugar, ½ cup of butter, ½ cup of milk, 4 eggs, 1 teaspoonful of baking powder, 1 teaspoonful of vanilla and 1 square of chocolate; dissolve chocolate in a tablespoonful of hot water and add to cake. Bake in layers and put together with icing.—*Sister Lora Roop, Warrensburg, Mo.*

Chocolate Cake.—Take ½ cup of grated chocolate, ½ cup of sweet milk, ½ cup of brown sugar. Cook until smooth and when cool mix with the following: 1 cup of white sugar, ½ cup of butter, ½ cup of milk, 2 eggs, 2 cups of flour, and 1 teaspoonful of soda dissolved in warm water. Put the flour in last.—*Sister Edna Eisenbise, Lanark, Ill.*

Chocolate Cream Cake.—Cream 2 cups of sugar with ¾ of a cup of butter (lard may be used instead of butter). Add the yolks of 3 eggs, 1 cup of milk, 3 cups of flour, and 2 teaspoonfuls of baking powder. Beat well and fold in the beaten whites of 3 eggs. Flavor with vanilla. Cream filling: Scald 1 pint of milk and stir into it 3 tablespoonfuls of cornstarch moistened in a small portion of the milk. Add ½ cup of sugar beaten light with the yolk of one egg, a pinch of salt and ½ teaspoonful of vanilla. Spread between the layers of cake. Ice the top with an icing made by boiling 1 cup of sugar with 2 teaspoonfuls of water until it strings. Pour this over the beaten white of the egg and add 1 square of melted chocolate. Flavor with vanilla.—*Sister Maud M. Click, Fairfax, Va.*

Chocolate Cake or Devil's Food.—Take 2 cups of dark-brown sugar, ⅔ cup of sour milk, 2 eggs, ½ cup of butter, ⅓ cup of chocolate, ½ cup of boiling water over the chocolate, 1 teaspoonful of soda, 1 tablespoonful of vanilla and flour to make a rather stiff batter. Bake in layers in a slow oven. Spread chocolate icing between layers.—*Sister D. W. Inman, Bradford, Ohio.*

Eggless Chocolate Cake.—Mix 1 cup of sugar with 1 tablespoonful of butter or lard. Add ½ cup of milk or water, and one teaspoonful of soda dissolved in hot water. Then in a small pan mix 2 heaping tablespoonfuls of ground or grated chocolate, 1 level teaspoonful of cornstarch and ½ cup of milk or water, and cook until it thickens. Add this to the first mixture while hot. Flavor with ½ teaspoonful of vanilla and sift in 1½ cups of flour with 1 teaspoonful of baking powder.—Caramel Frosting: 1 cup of sugar and 5 tablespoonfuls of milk. Boil until when a little is dropped in cold water it will form a soft ball. Take from the fire, flavor with a few drops of vanilla and beat until the mixture begins to thicken. Spread quickly between layers and on top.—*Sister Edith Riley, Highland, Ohio.*

Eggless Devil's Food Cake.—Take 2 cups of dark brown sugar, ½ cup of butter, ½ cup of hot water, ½ cup of sour milk, 6 teaspoonfuls of cocoa, 1 teaspoonful of soda and flour to thicken. Bake in a square pan.—*Sister Nannie Byer Newcomer, South Bend, Ind.*

Chocolate Layer Cake.—Take 2 eggs, ½ cup of butter, 1 cup of sweet milk, 1½ cups of sugar, 2 teaspoonfuls of baking powder and 3 cups of flour. Filling: Take ½ cup of sweet milk, 1 cup of sugar, 1 teaspoonful of butter, 1 tablespoonful of chocolate and ½ teaspoonful of vanilla. Boil until it threads.—*Sister Jennie Neher, Mountain Grove, Mo.*

One-egg Chocolate Cake.—Take the yolk of one egg, ½ cup of milk, and ½ cup of either grated chocolate or cocoa. Beat well and put on the stove to cook slowly until a little thick. Then take off and add ½ cup of milk, 1 cup of sugar, 3 teaspoonfuls of baking powder and 1¾ cups of flour, sifted twice. Bake in two layers. For filling and frosting: White of the egg beaten light and on it pour the syrup made of one cup of sugar and a little water boiled until it threads.—*Sister Verna Cooney, Enders, Nebr.*

Layer Chocolate Cake.—Take 1½ cups of sugar, ½ cup of butter, 1 cup of milk, 3 eggs, whites and yolks beaten separately, 3 teaspoonfuls of baking powder mixed with 3 cups of flour, 1 teaspoonful of vanilla, and a little salt. When done, ice with the following: Take the white of 1 egg beaten to a froth, 1 cup of powdered sugar, 1 tablespoonful of melted chocolate and 1 tablespoonful of cream. Flavor with vanilla.—*Sister Sarah A. Haines, Huntington, Ind.*

Chocolate Loaf Cake.—Take 1 cup of brown sugar, ½ cup of butter, ½ cup of sour milk, 2 eggs, 1 teaspoonful of soda, 1 teaspoonful of vanilla and 2 cups of flour. Mix all well together. Put in a pan ½ cup of grated chocolate, ½ cup of brown sugar and ½ cup of sweet milk. Boil this and pour into the cake boiling hot. Mix well and bake slowly. Icing: Take 2 cups of granulated sugar, 6 tablespoonfuls of boiling water, 2 tablespoonfuls of vinegar or lemon juice. Boil together 8 minutes and pour slowly over the well-beaten whites of 2 eggs. Beat until cool, and flavor to taste.—*Sister Barbara Culley, Elgin, Ill.*

Chocolate Marble Cake.—Put 1 ounce of chocolate and 1 tablespoonful of butter into a cup, and place in a tin of boiling water. Beat to a cream 2 tablespoonfuls of butter and 1 cup of sugar. Beat in gradually ½ cup of milk; next add the whites of 6 eggs beaten stiff, 1 teaspoonful of vanilla, 1½ cups of sifted flour and 1 teaspoonful of baking powder mixed with the flour. Put ⅓ of the batter into a bowl and stir into it the melted chocolate. Put one mixture into a pan, then the other. Bake about 40 minutes.—*Sister Elmer Snowberger, Roaring Spring, Pa.*

Chocolate Nut Cake.—For the cake part take 1 cup of granulated sugar and ½ cup of butter. Beat to cream, then put in 2 eggs, 1 at a time, ½ cup of sweet milk, 1½ cups of flour, putting 1 teaspoonful of baking powder with the last ½ cup of flour. Bake in 2 layers. For the filling, take 1½ cupfuls of sugar, 1 cupful of milk, 2 bars of grated chocolate, butter the size of a walnut; put in a granite pan and cook to the soft ball state, stirring occasionally, then remove from the fire and add 1 teaspoonful of vanilla. Take about ⅓ of this mixture and add 1 teacupful chopped nut meats, stir until cool enough to spread. Put this between the layers, and spread the remaining icing on top and sides of cake. Save some of the whole nut meats and arrange on top of cake. Use English walnuts or hickory nuts. Grease the pan that the icing is cooked in to prevent scorching. This is excellent if the recipe is followed closely.—*Sister Pearl Jackson, South Bend, Ind.*

Sclid Chocolate Cake.—Take 2 cups of brown sugar, ½ cup of butter, 1 cup of sour milk or black coffee, 2 eggs, 1 teaspoonful of soda dissolved in ½ cup of hot water, ⅓ cake of grated chocolate, and 2 heaping cups of flour.—*Sister Lydia Jordon, Wiley, Ohio.*

Christmas Cake.—Take ½ cup of molasses, 1 cup of brown sugar, 1 cup of very sour cream, 3½ cups of pastry flour, 1 tablespoonful each of allspice and cinnamon, 1 teaspoonful of soda dissolved in two tablespoonfuls of hot water, and 1 pound of raisins. Bake one and one-half hours.—*Sister Ida Talley, Kingsley, Iowa.*

Cinnamon Layer Cake.—Take 1 cup of sugar, ⅓ cup of butter, the whites of 3 eggs, ½ cup of milk, 1½ cups of flour, and 1½ teaspoonfuls of baking powder. Filling: The yolks of 3 eggs, 1 cup of brown sugar, and 1 teaspoonful of ground cinnamon. Beat until light and foamy, and put between and on top of layers.—*Sister Emma Schildknecht, Rea, Mo.*

Clove Cake.—Take 1 cup of sugar, ½ cup of butter, 1 cup of milk, 2 cups of flour, 1 cup of raisins, 1 egg, 1 teaspoonful of soda and 1 teaspoonful each of cinnamon and cloves. Mix and bake.—*Sister J. A. Sell, McKee Gap, Pa.*

Cocoanut Pound Cake.—Take 1 pound of sugar, ½ pound of butter, 6 eggs, ¾ of a pound of flour, 1 pound of fresh grated cocoanut, and 2 teaspoonfuls of baking powder.—*Sister Anna Danner, Knoxville, Md.*

Excellent Cake or Cocoanut Cake.—Take 2 cups of sugar, ¾ cup of butter, 1 cup of sweet milk, 4 cups of flour, whites of 6 eggs, and 2 teaspoonfuls of baking powder. Bake in layers.—*Sister Lora Roop, Warrensburg, Mo.*

Coffee Cake.—Take 1 cup of light-brown sugar, 1 cup of molasses, 1 cup of cold coffee, 1 cup of shortening (lard and butter), a big teaspoonful of soda, 1 level teaspoonful of cinnamon and 1 of ground cloves, and 1 cup of chopped raisins. Dissolve the soda in the coffee. Put all together before stirring. Add enough flour to make stiff. Bake. This cake should be made several days before using. We prefer it made a week before eating. Keep it well wrapped to prevent drying out.—*Sister Hattie Y. Gilbert, Daleville, Va.*

Cornstarch Cake.—Take 2 cups of granulated sugar, 1 cup of butter, ¾ of a cup of milk, the whites of 6 eggs, ¾ of a cup of cornstarch, 2 full cups of flour and 3 teaspoonfuls of baking powder. Flavor with lemon. This makes four layers.—*Sister Ettie Holler, Hagerstown, Ind.*

Cream Cake.—Take 2 cups of white sugar, 2 tablespoonfuls of butter, 3 eggs beaten separately, ½ cup of sweet milk, 2 tablespoonfuls of cold water, 2 rounding cups of flour, and two teaspoons rounding full of baking powder. Bake in three jelly pans.—*Sister Mary L. Miller, North Manchester, Ind.*

Cream Cake without Eggs.—Take 3 cups of flour, 2 cups of sugar, 1 cup of sweet cream, 1 cup of sweet milk, ¼ cup of lard or butter, and 2 heaping teaspoonfuls of baking powder. Flavor to taste.—*Sister Leona Shively, Newville, N. Dak.*

French Cream Cake.—Take 1 cup of sugar, 3 eggs beaten together, 1½ cups of flour, 2 teaspoonfuls of baking powder sifted with the flour and 3 tablespoonfuls of water. When baked, split each layer and spread with custard. Custard: Heat 1 pint of milk and when nearly boiling stir in 2 tablespoonfuls cornstarch that have been mixed with cold milk, 1 beaten egg; ¾ cup sugar, and butter size of an egg. Flavor to suit taste.—*Sister Grace Moats, Polo, Mo.*

Plain Cream Cake.—Take 2 eggs well beaten, 1 cup of sugar, 1 cup of sour cream, 1 teaspoonful of baking powder and a pinch of soda dissolved in the cream. This makes a small three-layer cake and is delicious. Frosting: Take 1 cup of sugar and ½ cup of sweet milk. Boil until it threads when dropping from spoon, then beat until it will spread without running. Flavor to suit taste.—*Sister Zelma Bosserman, Burkey, N. Dak.*

Fig Cake.—Light part: Take 1½ cups of sugar, ½ cup of butter, ½ cup of sweet milk, ½ cup of cornstarch, whites of 4 eggs, 1¾ cups of flour, and 1½ teaspoonfuls of baking powder. Dark part: Take 1½ cups of sugar, yolks of 4 eggs, ¾ cup of butter, ½ cup of water, ½ pound of seedless raisins, ½ teaspoonful each of nutmeg and cinnamon, ½ pound of figs split the broad way, ½ teaspoonful of soda, 1 teaspoonful of cream of tartar and 2 cups of flour. Put together when baked, using light and dark layers alternately, with or without icing.—*Sister Sue C. Foutz, Waynesboro, Pa.*

Fig Cake.—Take 1 cup of white sugar, ½ cup of butter, 1 cup of sweet milk, 2 cups of flour, with 2 teaspoonfuls of baking powder sifted into it, and the whites of 3 eggs. Fig filling for cake: Put ½ pound of figs, chopped fine, in a saucepan with 1 pint of cold water and 1 cup of sugar. Cook slowly until thick enough to spread without running, then let cool; then with the whites of 3 eggs and 2 tablespoonfuls of water mix powdered sugar enough to make stiff, spread on cake rather thick, then a layer of figs and on top of figs spread another layer of eggs. This makes a filling about 1 inch thick, and is a very good, rich cake.—*Sister Emma Kindig, Inglewood, Cal.*

Fig Cake.—Take 1½ cups of sugar, ½ cup butter, ½ cup sweet milk, 1½ cups of flour, 1 teaspoonful baking powder, ½ cup cornstarch and the whites of 6 eggs. Bake in layers and fill with fig filling, which is made as follows: Chop 1 pound of figs, add ½ cupful of sugar and 1 cup of water. Stew until soft and smooth. Spread between layers and ice the whole cake with boiled icing.—*Sister Josie Sloniker, Burroak, Kans.*

Fruit Cake.—Take 2 cups of sugar, 1 cup of butter, 4 eggs, 1 cup of sour milk, 1 teaspoonful of soda, 1 tablespoonful each of cinnamon, allspice and cloves, 1 nutmeg, 2 pounds of raisins, 1 pound of currants and flour enough to make a stiff batter.—*Sister A. W. Hawbaker, Kenmare, N. Dak.*—Instead of sugar and sour milk use 1 cup of brown sugar, 1 cup of baking molasses, and sweet milk with cream of tartar and soda.—*Sister Mandelia E. Eaton, Baltimore, Md.*

Fruit Cake.—Take 1 large cupful of sour cream, 1¼ cupfuls of brown sugar, 4 eggs, one teaspoonful of soda, 1 teaspoonful of cinnamon, ½ teaspoonful of cloves, ¼ pound of citron, 2 cupfuls of raisins and 2 cupfuls of currants. Mix the fruit in a little flour to keep it from settling, and put as much flour in as you think it will take to mix it thick enough to hold the fruit up. If your cream is rich, do not take any butter, but if not, you will have to take a little. —*Sister Lizzie G. Arnold, Albert City, Iowa.*

Fruit Cake.—Take 1 pound of sugar, 1 pound of flour, ½ pound of butter, 7 eggs, ½ pound of currants well washed and dried, 1 pound of raisins, 1 pound of dates seeded, ¼ pound of citron sliced, 1 teaspoonful of ground cinnamon, 1 teacupful of buttermilk, 1 teaspoonful of soda and the juice and grated yellow rind of 1 lemon. Dredge the fruit with flour, cream the butter and sugar together, add the beaten yolks, the milk and soda, then the spices, and last the beaten whites alternately with the flour, fruit, and lemon juice. This amount requires a 7-pound mould and 2½ hours for baking in a moderate oven, or it can be divided into parts and baked in 2 hours.—*Sister N. E. Shickel, Roanoke, Va.*

Imitation Fruit Cake.—Take 3 cups of sugar, 1 cup of molasses, 1 cup of buttermilk, 2 teaspoonfuls of soda, 7 eggs, 1 cup of lard and butter and 1 level tablespoonful each of cinnamon, cloves and allspice. This makes 3 large cakes.—*Sister Effie Hoover, Milford, Ind.*

Gem Cake.—Break 2 eggs into a cup and fill with rich, sweet cream. Add to this in a mixing bowl, a lump of butter the size of a walnut, 1 cup of white sugar, nearly 1½ cups of flour and 2 teaspoonfuls of baking powder. Bake in gem pans or two layers.— *Sister Anna Miller, Versailles, Ohio.*

A Good Cake.—Take 9 eggs, 2 cups of soft white sugar. Beat them together 1 hour; then add 2 cups of flour and ½ teaspoonful of baking powder. Bake 1 hour.—*Sister Josiah Clapper, Salemville, Pa.*

Gold and Silver Cake.—Gold part: The yolks of 4 eggs, ¼ cup of butter, 1 cup of sugar, ¼ cup of milk (sweet), 1½ cups of flour and 1 teaspoonful of baking powder. Silver part: The whites of 4 eggs, ¼ cup of butter, 1 cup of sugar, ¼ cup of milk (sweet), 1½ cups of flour, and 1 teaspoon baking powder.—*Sister L. Clanin, Hicksville, Wash.*

Hickorynut Cake.—Take 2 cups of white sugar, 1 cup of butter, 1 cup of rich sweet milk, whites of 4 eggs, 3½ cups of flour, 2 teaspoonfuls of baking powder and 4 cups of chopped nut meats. Flavor with vanilla. Bake in layers or loaf.—*Sister M. Alice Mumma, Sharpsburg, Md.*

Hurry Cake.—Take 1 cup quite full of unsifted flour, the same cup three-fourths full of granulated sugar, and 2 even teaspoonfuls of baking powder. Stir all of these together dry in a dish. Take the same cup, break into it 2 eggs, beat well with teaspoon and fill cup with thin sweet cream. Pour this over dry mixture and beat rapidly till smooth. Pour into baking pan, sprinkle with granulated sugar and bake quickly. Very nice for loaf or layer cake.—*Sister L. M. Funderburgh, Morrill, Kans.*

Ice Cream Cake.—Take 2 cups of sugar, 3 cups of flour, ¾ cup of butter, whites of 6 eggs, and 3 teaspoonfuls of baking powder. Bake in 4 layers.—*Sister Elmira Shoemaker, Eaton, Ind.*

Ice Cream Cake.—Take 1½ cups of white sugar, ½ cup of butter, 1 cup of sweet milk, whites of 5 eggs thoroughly beaten and 3 teaspoonfuls of baking powder sifted in 3 cups of flour. Flavor with lemon.—*Sister Mary A. Albright, North Manchester, Ind.*

Ice Cream Cake.—Cream well 1 cup of sugar and ½ cup of butter. Add ½ cup of sweet milk, 2 cups of flour, 1½ teaspoonfuls of baking powder, whites of 3 eggs and flavor with vanilla. Bake in layers in a hot oven. Frosting: Beat together the yolks of 2 eggs, ⅔ cup of sugar and ½ teaspoonful of vanilla, 15 minutes. Spread between layers and on top of cake, wrap a greased paper around cake, set in the oven for a few minutes till the frosting sets, remove and set away to cool.—*Sister Anna Sherfy, Mont Ida, Kans.*

Jam Cake.—Cream ¾ cup of butter, 1 cup of sugar and yolks of 3 eggs together. Add first 1 teaspoonful of cinnamon, 1 teaspoonful of allspice, ½ nutmeg and 3 tablespoonfuls of sour cream. Next add 1 cup jam and 1½ cups of flour in which has been mixed 1 teaspoonful of soda. Add the beaten whites. Bake in layers and put together with soft icing.—*Sister Kittie Keim, Rockingham, Mo.*

Lemon Jelly Cake.—Cream 1½ cups of sugar, butter the size of an egg, and 3 eggs. Add ½ cup of sweet milk, 2½ cups of flour and 2 teaspoonfuls of baking powder. Bake in 4 layers. Filling: Take 1 cup of boiling sweet milk, 1 egg, 1 tablespoonful of sugar and 2 tablespoonfuls of flour moistened with cold sweet milk. Let boil. Flavor with lemon and spread between layers.—*Sister Sarah A. Crowl, Nappanee, Ind.*

Roll Jelly Cake.—Take 3 eggs well beaten, 1 cup cf sugar beaten in after the eggs are beaten, sweet milk in amount to equal one egg and 1 large cup of flour sifted with 2 teaspoonfuls of baking powder. Bake in one large pan, spread with jelly or icing and roll.—*Sister Lola Fausnight, Canton, Ohio.*

Roll Jelly Cake.—Beat 3 eggs until light then add a scant cup of sugar. Beat with the beater until well mixed. Add 1 cup of flour minus 1 tablespoonful, and when mixed add 3 tablespoonfuls of cold water. Lastly add the tablespoonful of flour mixed with 2 teaspoons of baking powder, and 1 teaspoonful of lemon or vanilla. Bake in a large greased and floured pan in an oven a little hotter than for sponge cake.—*Sister Carrie A. Smith, St. Peter, Minn.*

Layer Cake.—Take 1½ cups of sugar, ½ cup of butter, ½ cup of sweet milk, 2 cups of flour, 2 teaspoonfuls of baking powder and 3 eggs.—*Sister Lizzie W. Kilhefner, Ephrata, Pa.*

Layer Cake.—Take 2 cups of sugar, 2 eggs well beaten, 1 cup of milk, 1 cup of cream, 2 heaping teaspoonfuls of baking powder sifted in 2 large cups of flour. Flavor to taste. Mix up cake in evening and let rise over night, and bake in the morning. The cake will seem stiff but do not thin or beat. Cakes made in this way will be light and feathery. Any cake can be made in this way, except Angel Food.—*Sister Cassie Martin, Bloom, Kans.*

Layer Cake.—Take 2 eggs, ¼ cup of butter, 2 cups of sugar, ¾ cup of sweet milk, 1 heaping teaspoonful of baking powder, and 2½ scant cups of flour. Bake in layers, flavoring with lemon or vanilla. Then take 1 cup of milk. Put in a pan and let come to a boil. Then mix 1 tablespoonful of flour and 1 of sugar. Put in a pan and boil, and flavor with lemon or vanilla. Spread between layers and sprinkle with shredded cocoanut.—*Sister Florence Myers, Goshen, Ind.*

Layer Cake.—Take 1 cup of sugar, 1 cup of sour cream, 2 eggs well beaten, 2 cups of flour, 1 teaspoonful of soda dissolved in the cream, and 1 teaspoonful of cream of tartar. Put together with cream filling.—*Sister Alice Fausnight, Canton, Ohio.*

Leap Year Cake.—Take 1 cup of white sugar, ½ cup of butter, whites of 3 eggs, ½ cup of sweet milk, 2 cups of flour, 2 teaspoonfuls of baking powder, and 1 teaspoonful of vanilla. Frosting: Beat the yellow of the eggs with at least 15 teaspoonfuls of pulverized sugar. Ice while cake is hot.—*Sister J. T. Myers, Philadelphia, Pa.*

Layer Cake.—Take ½ pound figs and stew quite tender. Cream together 1½ cups of sugar, 2 teaspoonfuls of butter, then add 1 egg well beaten, 1 teaspoonful of soda dissolved in 1 cup of sweet milk, 3 cups of sifted flour, and with the last cup mix 2 teaspoonfuls of cream of tartar. Make your frosting with the white of 1 egg and sugar, and spread on the cake. Then put on a layer of figs well mashed, then another layer of cake, frosting and figs, until all are added. The last layer is simply frosted. Raw bananas sliced fine, and used instead of figs, make a fine cake.—*Sister Cassie Bowser, Lineboro, Md.*

New England Layer Cake.—Place on the stove where it will not burn, 1 cup of sweet milk, 1 cup chocolate grated (stir slowly in the milk until it is dissolved), then add 1 cup sugar, yolk of 1 egg beaten, then let cool. When the custard is cool, add 1 cup sugar, ½ cup butter, ½ cup sweet milk, 2 eggs well beaten, 1 teaspoonful soda dissolved in 1 tablespoonful water, 2½ cups of flour. Bake in a moderate oven.—*Sister Ella Moore, Chicago, Ill.*

Lemon Cake.—Take 3 cups of flour, 2 cups of sugar, ½ cup of butter, 1 cup of sweet milk, whites of 5 eggs, 2 teaspoonfuls of baking powder, and flavor with essence of lemon. Icing: Take the juice and grated rind of 1 lemon, 1 large cup of pulverized sugar, 1 egg and 1 tablespoonful of butter. Beat well together and then boil for 5 or 10 minutes.—*Sister Clara A. Mullendore, Gapland, Md.*

Loaf Cake.—Take 2 cups of raised dough, 2 cups of sugar, 1 cup of butter or lard, 2 eggs, 2 tablespoonfuls of cinnamon, ¼ spoonful of nutmeg and 1 cup of raisins or currants. Mix well. Put in a pan to bake. Let it rise like bread, and bake in moderate oven 1 hour.—*Sister Winnie West, Leesburg, Ohio.*

Mahogany Cake.—Take 1½ cups of sugar, ½ cup butter, ½ cup of sweet milk or coffee, 2 cups of flour, 3 eggs, 1 teaspoonful of soda dissolved in the milk, 1 teaspoonful of baking powder, and ½ cup of chocolate in ½ cup of milk or coffee; cool and stir in last. Filling: 1½ cups of sugar cooked in ½ cup of milk; beat until cool. —*Sister Sue B. Heiny, Carleton, Nebr.*

Lunch Cake.—Take ½ cup of sugar, ½ cup of butter, ½ cup of sweet milk, 1 egg, 2 cups of flour and 1 teaspoonful of baking powder. Flavor to suit taste.—*Sister L. M. Funderburgh Morrill, Kans.*

Marble Cake.—White part: Take the whites of 4 eggs, 1 cup of white sugar, ½ cup of butter, ½ cup of sweet milk, 2 table-spoonfuls of baking powder, 1 teaspoonful of vanilla or lemon and 2½ cups of sifted flour. Dark part: Yolks of 4 eggs, 1 cup of brown sugar, ½ cup of cooking molasses, ½ cup of butter, ½ cup of sour milk, 1 teaspoonful of ground cloves, 1 teaspoonful of cinnamon, 1 teaspoonful of mace, 1 grated nutmeg, 1 teaspoonful of soda (soda to be dissolved in a little milk and added after a part of the flour has been stirred in), and 1½ cups of flour. Drop a spoonful of each kind in a well-buttered cake dish, first the light part then the dark part, alternately.—*Sister Lella E. Sanger, Bays, W. Va.*

Marble Cake.—White part: Take the whites of 4 eggs, 1 cup of sugar, ½ cup of sweet milk, 2 teaspoonfuls of baking powder and butter size of a large egg. Dark part: Take the yolks of 4 eggs, 1 cup of sugar, ½ cup of milk, butter the size of an egg, 2 teaspoonfuls of baking powder, spices to taste, and flour enough to make a stiff batter. Bake in layers.—*Sister Lydia Brubaker, Argos, Ind.*

Marshmallow Cake.—Take 2 cups of powdered sugar, 1 cup of butter, 1 cup of milk, 3½ cups of flour, whites of 6 eggs and 3 level teaspoonfuls of baking powder. Filling: Take 1½ cups of sugar, 2 eggs, 10 cents' worth of marshmallows and 7 tablespoonfuls of water. Put marshmallows in oven to melt before adding to the other ingredients.—*Sister Lydia Jordan, Wiley, Ohio.*

Molasses Loaf Cake without Eggs.—Take 1 cup of sorghum molasses, 1 cup of sugar, ½ cup of lard, 1 cup of raisins, 1 teaspoonful of cinnamon, 1 teaspoonful of ginger, 1 teaspoonful of soda, 1 cup of hot water, and flour enough to make a stiff batter. Place in pan, and bake in quick oven.—*Sister Lizzie A. Wagoner, Charles City, Iowa.*

Molasses Loaf Cake.—Take 1 cup of sour milk, 1 cup of molasses, 2½ cups of flour, 1 level teaspoonful of soda, and ½ cup of shortening.—*Sister J. T. Myers, Philadelphia, Pa.*

Marie Cake.—Take 1 scant cup of granulated sugar, 1 egg, 1 cup of sour cream, 2 teaspoonfuls of baking powder, 1 level teaspoonful of soda and flour enough to make a stiff dough.—*Sister Lizzie Angle, Bringhurst, Ind.*

Mountain Cake.—Take 1 cup of sugar, ½ cup of butter and 2 eggs beaten together. Add ½ cup of milk or water, 2 cups of flour and 2 teaspoonfuls of baking powder in the flour.—*Sister W. J. Swigart, Huntingdon, Pa.*

Old Maid's Cake.—Take 1 cup of sugar, ½ cup of butter and lard. Mix well together, then add 1 cup of sweet milk, 2 cups of flour, 1½ teaspoonfuls of baking powder, ½ teaspoonful of cream of tartar, and add last the well-beaten whites of 5 eggs. Do not stir much after the eggs have been added. Bake in 3 layers. Icing: Take ⅔ cup of sugar, 5 tablespoonfuls of milk and flavor with lemon. Boil till thick.—*Sister Mary A. Diehl, Polo, Ill.*

New Mexico Cake.—1 cup of sugar creamed with ½ cup of Fairbank' cottolene; add the yolks of 2 eggs, 1 cup of milk, 2 cups of flour, a pinch of salt, and flavoring to taste. Beat thoroughly. The success of your cake lies largely in the beating. Lastly add well-beaten whites of the 2 eggs. Use the same cup to do all the measuring. For icing pour ½ cup of boiling water over 1 cup of sugar, let boil till it hairs, remove from stove and add the beaten whites of two eggs, stirring briskly. Beat till all is a creamy mass. —*Sister Florence Neff, Clovis, N. M.*

Nutmeg Cake.—Take 2 cups of sugar, 1 cup of butter, 3 eggs, 1 cup of milk, 1 nutmeg, 4 cups of flour, 2 teaspoonfuls of cream of tartar, 1 teaspoonful of soda, and the grated rind of 1 lemon. Beat the sugar and butter together, then add half of the flour and half of the milk, then the beaten eggs, grated nutmeg and grated rind of the lemon. Then add the remainder of the flour, having the cream of tartar mixed in it, and lastly, add the remainder of the milk, with the soda dissolved in the milk. Beat all together and bake in buttered bread pans.—*Sister Ida E. Yoder, Spencer, Ohio.*

Oatmeal Cake.—Take 1 cup of shortening, 1 cup of sugar, 1 cup of raisins, 2 cups of oatmeal, 2 eggs, 2 cups of flour, 1 cup of sour milk, 1 teaspoonful of cinnamon, 1 teaspoonful of salt, and 1 teaspoonful of soda. Icing: Boil 1 cup of sugar in a little water until it spins a hair. Pour over a well beaten egg. Stir until it cools and begins to thicken, then spread on the cake.—*Sister Martha C. Senger, Franklin Grove, Ill.*

Orange Cake.—Cream 2 cups of sugar with ⅔ cup of butter and add 3 eggs beaten separately. Squeeze the juice of 2 oranges into a cup (use only ¼ cup of orange juice) and add cold water to fill the cup. Add this to above and lastly 3½ cups of flour, a little orange grated, and 2 heaping teaspoonfuls of baking powder.—*Sister Emma E. Kindig, Inglewood, Cal.*

Orange Cake.—Cream 2 cups of sugar, ½ cup of butter and the yolks of 4 eggs. Add 1 cup of sweet milk. Mix by sifting twice 2 heaping cups of flour and 2 teaspoonfuls of baking powder, stir into the milk and sugar. Add the beaten whites of 4 eggs last, and flavor to taste. Bake in a quick oven. Filling: Take the juice of 2 oranges, the grated peeling of 1 orange, 1 cup of sugar and 1 tablespoonful of butter. Boil, and stir in 1 tablespoonful of flour mixed with cold water. When cool, add 1 teaspoonful of orange extract. —*Sister Ida M. Fesler, Longmont, Colo.*

Plain Cake.—Take 1½ cups of sugar, 3 eggs, ½ cup of lard or butter, ⅔ cup of sweet milk, 3 teaspoonfuls of baking powder, and flavoring to suit the taste.—*Sister Adaline Huston, Mishawaka, Ind.*

Pound Cake.—Take 1 cup of sugar, ½ cup of butter, 1¼ cups of flour, 4 eggs, the whites and yolks beaten separately. Beat them together for 10 minutes, and add ¼ teaspoonful of baking powder.—*Sister Clara Ringer, Oregon, Ill.*

Old-time Pound Cake.—Take 1 pound each of butter, sugar and flour, 10 eggs, and 1 small teaspoonful of baking powder. Bake one and one-half hours in a moderate oven.—*Sister Anna Zimmerman, Mt. Solon, Va.*

Peanut Cake.—Remove the brown hulls from 2 cupfuls of shelled peanuts, chop them fine and slightly flour. Cream 1 cup of sugar and ½ cup of butter together; beat the white of 1 egg until it will pile up, beat the yolk, add to the butter and sugar and beat. Add 1 cup of sweet milk, 2½ cups of flour, and 2 heaping teaspoonfuls of baking powder. Flavor to taste, and add the nuts last.—*Sister Grace Gaffin Price, Oregon, Ill.*

Potato Cake.—Take 2 cups of sugar, 1 cup of butter, 2 cups of flour, 2 cups of warm mashed potatoes, ½ cup of sweet milk, 4 eggs, beaten separately, 1 cup of grated chocolate, 1 cup of chopped walnuts. ½ teaspoon each of cinnamon, allspice and nutmeg, and 2 teaspoonfuls baking powder.—*Sister Myrtle Blocher, Greenville, Ohio.*

A Quick Cake.—Break 2 eggs in a teacup, then fill up with rich sour cream; add 1 teacupful of sugar, 1 of flour, and a level teaspoonful of soda. Mix all together and beat thoroughly. Bake in layers and dress it with ½ teacupful of sugar wet with sweet cream, put in a pan and boiled thick. Stir to keep it from burning, and flavor with vanilla or banana.—*Sister Almeda Caskey, Corning, Iowa.*

Raised Cake.—Take 2 cups of bread sponge, 1 cup of shortening, 2 cups of sugar, ⅔ cup of raisins (chop or grind them fine), 2 cups of flour, 4 tablespoonfuls of milk, 2 eggs, 1 teaspoonful of soda dissolved in the milk, and 1 teaspoonful each of cloves and cinnamon. Mix all together and bake. Do not let it rise. Do not have the oven too hot. It is better baked slowly.—*Sister Lottie E. Perry, Dodge City, Kans.*

Prince of Wales Cake.—White part: Take 1 cup of white sugar, ½ cup of butter, ½ cup of sweet milk, 2 cups of flour, whites of 4 eggs, 1 teaspoonful of baking powder. Dark part: Take 1 cup of brown sugar, ½ cup of molasses, ½ cup of butter, ½ cup of sour milk, 2 cups of flour, yolks of 3 eggs, 1 teaspoonful of soda dissolved in the milk, 1 teaspoonful each of spices, 1 pound of raisins, and ¼ pound of citron. A small amount of black pepper improves it. Bake in layers and put together with icing.—*Sister Barbara Culley, Elgin, Ill.*

Raisin Loaf Cake.—Take 1 cup of bread sponge, 1 cup of sugar, 1 egg, butter the size of an egg, and 1 cup of raisins. Add flour as needed and bake in a mould.—*Sister John E. Metzger, Rossville, Ind.*

Rebel Cake.—Take 3 eggs, 2 teacups of sugar, ½ cup of butter, 1 cup of sour milk, 3 cups of flour, 2 teaspoonfuls of cream of tartar, and 1 teaspoonful of soda. Flavor to suit the taste. Bake in jelly tins.—*Sister M. Kate Crist, Timberville, Va.*

Ribbon Cake.—Cream well together 1 cup of butter with 2 cups of sugar; add 5 eggs beaten separately, 1 cup of milk, 4 cups of flour well sifted with 2 teaspoonfuls of baking powder, and flavor with vanilla. Take ⅓ of the cake batter and add to it 1 cup of chopped raisins and citron, and a little spice. Bake in 3 jelly tins, and place the fruit layer in the middle.—*Sister L. H. Funk, Kansas City, Mo.*

Delicate Ribbon Cake.—Take 2 cups of sugar, ½ cup of butter, 1 cup of sweet milk, 3 cups of flour and 3 teaspoonfuls of baking powder. Divide in 5 parts; for the brown put in a teaspoonful of grated chocolate or cocoa; for the pink, a teaspoonful of red sugar; for the yellow, the yolk of 1 egg; for the salmon, the yolk of 1 egg and a teaspoonful of red sugar. The white leave as it is without any addition.—*Sister Medora Wright, Cottage Grove, Ind.*

Rubber Cake.—Take 2 cups of flour, 2 cups of sugar and 2 teaspoonfuls of baking powder. Sift together 12 times. Then add 1 cup of boiling water and beat quite awhile. Add the beaten whites of 7 eggs, stir lightly and bake in layers. Filling: Take ⅓ cup of cold sweet cream, stir in enough powdered sugar to make stiff enough to spread, and spread between the layers. Flavor with vanilla.—*Sister Glennie Williams, Richland, Iowa.*

Ribbon Cake.—Take 1½ cups of granulated sugar, or 2 cups of soft white, and ¾ cup of butter and lard; beat well, then mix in 1 cup of sweet milk, followed by 3 cups of flour, sifted with 4 even teaspoonfuls of baking powder. Beat all together, then add the beaten whites of 4 eggs, and mix in after the other ingredients are all mixed. Take out 5 spoonfuls of batter and put in separate dishes, and put the rest in a long, flat pan well greased and sprinkled with flour. For the red part, melt a tablespoonful of red sugar on the stove in a very little water; for the salmon, take a little melted red sugar in one dish of dough and put part of the yolk of an egg with it. Mix well. For yellow, take yolk of 1 egg and mix well in one part. For spiced part, mix in cloves, nutmeg and cinnamon. For the remaining part put a heaping teaspoonful of chocolate or cocoa on the stove to melt in a little water, just enough so it will not burn. Mix thoroughly. To each colored part, except the spiced, add a little more flour. I put red in the center lengthwise on top of the white batter. Next beside the red I put spiced, and chocolate color lengthwise. On the other side of spiced and chocolate I put yellow and salmon. Then put into the oven and bake. When baked cover the top with icing. This cake is nicest cut in slices crosswise.—*Sister G. R. Goughnour, Canton, Ohio.*

Favorite Snow Cake.—Beat ½ cup of butter to a cream, add 1 cup of flour and stir thoroughly together. Add ½ cup of corn-starch, and ½ cup of sweet milk in which 1½ teaspoonfuls of baking powder have been dissolved. Last add the whites of 4 eggs and 1 cup of sugar well beaten together. Flavor to taste, and bake in a loaf cake.—*Sister Lizzie Chamberlain, Yale, Iowa.*

A Simple Cake.—Take 1 cup of sugar, 1 egg beaten, 1 scant cup of milk, 6 tablespoonfuls of melted butter, and 2 cups of flour sifted with 2 teaspoons of baking powder. Flavor to taste. I often divide this into three parts and put 2 teaspoons of powdered chocolate in one, a little red fruit coloring in another, and with the plain this makes a very pretty cake and pleases the children very much for picnic. A nice icing for this is 2 cups of brown sugar, 1 scant tablespoonful of butter, and just enough milk to wet the sugar. Put on the stove and let come to a boil. Then beat till it begins to harden, and spread on the cake.—*Sister Lulu Haddon, Bremerton, Washington.*

Snow Cake.—Take 1 cup of sugar, ½ cup of butter, ½ cup of sweet milk, 1½ cups of flour, 1½ teaspoonfuls of baking powder, and the whites of 3 eggs. Flavor with lemon.—*Sister Susie C. East, South English, Iowa.*

Spice Cake.—Take 4 eggs, leaving out the whites of 2, 2 cups of brown sugar, ½ cup of melted butter, ½ cup of sour milk, 1 teaspoonful of soda, 2 teaspoonfuls of cinnamon, 1½ teaspoonfuls of cloves, ½ teaspoonful of nutmeg and 2 cups of flour. Dissolve the soda in the sour milk. Bake in layers. Make an icing, using the 2 whites of the 2 eggs and spread between the layers.—*Sister Katie Shetter, Morrill, Kans.*

Spice Cake.—Take of the sponge of bread just ready to stiffen 1½ cupfuls, 1½ cupfuls of sugar, 1½ cupfuls of flour, ½ cup of lard and butter, and 2 eggs. Put sugar, lard and eggs in sponge and add 2 teaspoonfuls of cinnamon, 1 teaspoonful of cloves and ½ nutmeg. Mix well and add 1 teaspoonful of soda, 1 cupful of raisins, 1 cupful of currants, and the flour last. This makes a large loaf and should be baked nearly an hour in a moderate oven. Try with a splint.—*Sister Maggie E. Harrison, Conemaugh, Pa.*

Spice Cake.—Take 2 cups of sugar, 1 cup of lard, 1½ cups of buttermilk, 1 big teaspoonful of soda, 1 teaspoonful of cinnamon, 1 teaspoonful of nutmeg, ½ teaspoonful of ground cloves and 1 cup of raisins. Dissolve the soda in the milk and add 3 cups of flour. This cake should be made several days before using. Keep it well wrapped to prevent drying out.—*Sister Belle Porter, Abbyville, Kans.*

Spice Cake.—Take 2 cups of brown sugar, ½ cup of butter, 2¾ cups of flour, 1 cup of sour milk, 1 teaspoonful of soda, 1 teaspoonful of baking powder, 2 teaspoonfuls of ground cinnamon, 1 teaspoonful of ground cloves, ½ nutmeg grated, white of 1 egg and yolks of 2 eggs. Bake either in layers or in a loaf.—*Sister Sara Reesc Eby, West Elkton, Ohio.*

Spice Cake.—Take 1 cup of thick milk, and in part of the milk dissolve 1 teaspoonful of soda; take 2 cups heaped full of dark-brown sugar (if you do not have brown sugar you can use ¾ cup of molasses and 1½ cups of white sugar, but brown sugar is better), and mix with the milk, then stir in 4 eggs, keeping out the whites of 2 eggs to make the icing, and add 1 cup of melted butter and lard. (The lard should not be hot.) Now take 4 even cups of flour and mix in it 2 teaspoonfuls of good baking powder, 1 teaspoonful each of cinnamon and cloves, and ½ teaspoonful of nutmeg. Then mix all together until it becomes a smooth, thick batter. You need not grease the pan in which it is to be baked, but instead place into the pan some nice clean paper, sufficient to cover both bottom and sides of the pan, after which pour in the batter and place in a good oven until thoroughly baked. When taking the cake out of the pan, lift it out with the paper. This will make a large cake and should be very light and moist when baked. Mix the whites of the 2 eggs with pulverized or confectioners' sugar and spread over the top of the cake while hot. This is a very elegant cake.—*Sister Lovena Andes, Elgin, Ill.*

Spice Cake.—Take 2 cups of brown sugar, ½ cup of butter, ½ cup of sweet milk, 1 teaspoonful of allspice, 1 teaspoonful of cinnamon, 2 teaspoonfuls of baking powder, 2 cups of flour, yolks of 4 eggs, and the whites of 2.—*Sister Dora Studebaker, Whitewater, Ind*

Spice Cake.—Take 1 pint of maple syrup, 1 cup of good thick sour cream, 2 eggs, 1 teaspoonful of soda, 1½ teaspoonfuls each of cinnamon, cloves, ginger, nutmeg, and allspice. Flour to make a thick batter.—*Sister Elta Ross, Sidney, Ind.*

My Choice Spice Cake.—Take 2 cups of sugar, and ⅔ of a cup of lard, beaten to a cream; then add the yolks of 3 eggs and beat these well together. Next add 1 cup of thick milk or buttermilk with 1 teaspoonful of soda dissolved in it, 1 large teaspoonful of cinnamon, 1 teaspoonful of nutmeg, 3 teaspoonfuls of cocoa, a pinch of salt and 2 cups of flour, sifted with 2 teaspoonfuls of baking powder. Lastly, add the beaten whites of 3 eggs. Bake a sample so as to get the correct amount of flour.—*Sister Dora Snyder, Brookville, Ohio.*

Sponge Cake.—Take 2 eggs, beat the whites stiff, add most of a cup of sugar, and beat again. Beat the yolks, add the rest of the cup of sugar and beat more. Then put the whites and yolks together and beat. Add a cup of flour and a teaspoonful of baking powder, and sift together. Stir into the eggs until smooth. Add any flavoring that is liked, and ½ cup of boiling water. Beat quickly and pour into an ungreased pan. Bake 20 minutes and when baked turn upside down to cool.—*Sister Etta Martin, Laurens, Iowa.*

Sponge Cake.—Take 1 pint of sweet milk and cream together, 2 cups of sugar, 3 eggs, well beaten together, 2 teaspoonfuls of baking powder, a pinch of salt, lemon to flavor. Stir in necessary amount of flour, sugar and baking powder together, then add milk and eggs.—*Sister Jennie G. Dugan, Listie, Pa.*

Sponge Cake.—Take 3 eggs, whites beaten to a stiff froth, then beat the yolks. Put them together and beat again. Add 1½ cups of sugar and beat again. Add 1 teaspoonful of baking powder sifted into 1½ cups of flour, sift 3 times. Lastly add ½ cup of boiling water, stirring in a little at a time. Flavor with lemon or vanilla. Bake either in sheet or layers.—*Sister Kate Riley, Highland, Ohio.*

Simple Sponge Cake.—Beat long and well 6 eggs with a teaspoonful of salt. Then slowly add 1 cup of sugar, and in the same manner 1 cup of flour. Flavor to suit the taste.—*Sister Nora M. Gauby, Washington, Kans.*

Cream Sponge Cake.—Take 4 eggs, 1 cup of sweet cream, 2 cups of sugar, 2 cups of flour, and 2 tablespoonfuls of baking powder.—*Sister Emma A. Miller, Sharpsburg, Md.*

Surprise Cake.—Take 1 whole egg and the yolk of another, 2 cups of sifted sugar (1½ cups of granulated), 1 tablespoonful of soft butter, 1 cup of sweet milk, 3 cups of flour measured after sifting with 2 large teaspoonfuls of baking powder, and 1 cup of hickory-nut kernels chopped fine and mixed in last. Bake in three layers. Filling: One cup of sweet milk, 1 teaspoonful of cornstarch and the yolk of 1 egg. Flavor and sweeten to suit taste. If outside of cake is covered with icing, save some of the nuts to put in it.—*Sister G. R. Goughnour, Canton, Ohio.*

Thanksgiving Cake.—Take 8 eggs (beaten separately), 1 pound of butter, 2 pounds of dark sugar, 1 pound of raisins, 1 pound of figs, 1 pound of currants, ½ pound of citron, ½ cup of molasses, ½ cup of coffee, 2 pounds of flour, 2 teaspoonfuls of soda, 1½ teaspoonfuls of cinnamon, 1½ teaspoonfuls of nutmeg, 1½ teaspoonfuls of cloves, 1 teaspoonful of pepper and 1 teaspoonful of salt. This will keep 3 months if kept in a proper place.—*Sister Nettie Stine, Leaf River, Ill.*

Tilden Cake.—Take 1 cup of butter, 2 cups of sugar, 1 cup of sweet milk, 3 cups of flour, ½ cup of cornstarch, 4 eggs, 2 teaspoonfuls of baking powder and 2 teaspoonfuls of flavoring.—*Sister J. T. Myers, Philadelphia, Pa.*

Tried and True Cake.—White Part: The whites of 12 eggs, 3 cups of sugar, ¾ of a cup of butter, 1½ cups of sweet milk, 4½ cups of flour, and 4½ teaspoonfuls of baking powder. Yellow Part: The yolks of 12 eggs, 3 cups of sugar, ¾ of a cup of butter, 1½ cups of sweet milk, 4½ cups of flour, and 4½ teaspoonfuls of baking powder. Beat the eggs thoroughly, add the butter and sugar thoroughly mixed and beat again until light. Flavor to suit the taste. This will make two large, or three-medium sized cakes. Bake in layers and put together, alternating the white and the yellow parts.—*Sister Esther Horner Baker, Baltic, Ohio.*

Quick Tea Cake.—Break 2 eggs into a large teacup. Put in with the eggs 1 tablespoonful of butter and then fill up the cup with sweet milk. Pour into a vessel and add 1 cup of sugar and 1¾ cups of flour with 2 teaspoonfuls of baking powder. Do not stir until all the ingredients have been added, then beat thoroughly. Bake in layers and put jelly or other filling between layers.—*Sister Dessa A. Kreps, Independence. Oregon.*

Union Cake.—Take 2 cups of sugar, the whites of 4 eggs, 1 cup of sweet milk, ½ cup of cornstarch, 2½ cups of flour, and 2 teaspoonfuls of baking powder. Fold the beaten whites in last.—*Sister Mary C. Hoke, Goshen, Ind.*

Velvet Cake.—Take 2 cups of sugar, ½ cup of butter, 2 eggs, 1 cup of sweet milk, and 3½ cups of flour sifted with 2 heaping teaspoonfuls of baking powder. Flavor with nutmeg or lemon.—*Sister Alice Roberts, Ligonier, Pa.*

Cold Water Cake.—Take 2 cups of sugar, butter the size of a duck egg, 1 cup of cold water, whites of 6 eggs, and 3 teaspoonfuls of baking powder. Use flour enough to make a batter as for loaf cake and flavor to suit the taste.—*Sister Ira Miller, North English, Iowa.*

Whipped Cream Cake.—Take 1 cup of sugar, 2 eggs, 2 tablespoonfuls of softened butter, and 4 tablespoonfuls of milk. Beat all well together, then add a cup of flour in which 1 teaspoonful of baking powder has been sifted. Bake in a small square dripping pan. When the cake is cool, have ready ½ pint of sweet cream whipped to a stiff froth, sweeten and flavor to taste; spread over cake and serve while fresh. Or bake the same in small round gem pans, and when cool split open and put in each a few slices of ripe banana. Put in a dessert dish and put the whipped cream over. A little more cream will have to be used in the latter case.—*Sister Sarah Witmore Harnly, McPherson, Kans.*

White Cake.—Take 1½ cups of soft sugar, a piece of butter as big as a duck egg; cream the butter and sugar, add 1 cup of water, flour enough to make a good batter, 2 teaspoonfuls of baking powder and the whites of 4 eggs beaten stiff. Bake in a moderate oven.—*Sister Nola Graves, Cottage Grove, Ind.*

White Cake.—Take 1½ cups of flour, sifted seven times, 1 cup of sugar, 1 cup of boiling water. Beat these together thoroughly and let cool. Then add 2 heaping teaspoonfuls of baking powder. While the above cools beat the whites of four eggs very stiff and then just fold into the above batter, stirring as lightly and little as possible. Have your cake tins lined with buttered paper and bake in a quick oven. This is much like angel food but much cheaper.—*Sister Martha E. Lear, Cerro Gordo, Ill.*

White Cake.—Take the whites of 4 eggs, 2 cups of sugar, ½ cup of butter, 1 cup of sweet milk, 3 cups of flour, and 2 teaspoonfuls of baking powder. Mix well sugar and butter, and the whites well beaten, add milk, then flour with baking powder. Can be used as jelly or solid cake.—*Sister Iva C. Metzger, Rossville, Ind.*

White Mountain Cake.—Take 2 cups of sugar, ⅔ cup of butter, 2 cups of flour. Mix in 2 teaspoonfuls of baking powder, 1 cup of cornstarch, ⅔ cup of sweet milk, and last put in the whites of 7 eggs well beaten. Bake in layers and put on icing and cocoanut.—*Sister Ida E. Gibble, Lykens, Pa.*

White Layer Cake.—Beat 1½ cups of sugar and ½ cup of butter together, then add ¾ cup of milk. After adding 2 cups of flour, beat the whites of 4 eggs and put in 3 teaspoonfuls of baking powder and 1 teaspoonful of vanilla.—*Sister Etta Fox Kreider, Shannon, Ill.*

Cream for Cake.—Take 1 pint of sweet cream, 1 cup of sugar, the juice of 1 lemon, 2 tablespoonfuls of cornstarch and 2 eggs. Boil together.—*Sister F. Alice Davidson, Centropolis, Kans.*

Burnt Caramel.—Pour 1 cup of sugar into a granite saucepan and stir over fire until sugar melts and becomes a liquid throwing off a smoke. Have ready 1 cup of boiling water. Remove the pan from fire and pour in water and then place it on the fire and stir rapidly until it becomes like a syrup. Put in glass jar for future use. This is enough caramel for 6 cakes.—*Sister Minerva M. Metzger, Cerro Gordo, Ill.*

Made Cream for Layer Cake.—Take 1 cup of milk, ½ cup of sugar, 1 tablespoonful of flour, and flavor with vanilla. First heat the milk and sugar to boiling, then moisten the flour with cold milk and stir into the boiling milk. When partly cold, add the vanilla and spread on the cake.—*Sister M. C. Whitesel, Wayside, Wash.*

Boiled Icing.—Take 4 tablespoonfuls of sweet milk to ½ cup of granulated sugar. Boil till it threads, beat thoroughly and spread on cake.—*Sister Mary C. Hoke, Goshen, Ind.*

Boiled Icing.—As soon as the cake is taken from the oven, break the whites of 2 large fresh eggs into a medium-sized meat platter. When beaten stiff, place a scant teacupful of granulated sugar with 3 tablespoonfuls of hot water on the stove, and boil quickly until it will harden in cold water. Then pour it slowly over the beaten whites, beating quickly all the time until perfectly mixed. Flavor to suit taste, and spread on cake immediately. It will be as smooth as satin in a few minutes.—*Sister Mary P. Ellenberger, Turney, Mo.*

Caramel Icing.—Take 1 cup of brown sugar, ½ cup of milk, and butter the size of an egg; boil till thick and flavor with vanilla.—*Sister Mary C. Hoke, Goshen, Ind.*

Caramel Filling.—Take 5 tablespoonfuls of cream to 1 cup of sugar; boil till thick.—*Sister Cora Shaffer, Odell, Nebr.*

Chocolate Filling.—Take 5 fablespoonfuls of chocolate dissolved in a little cream, 1 egg, and 1 cup of sugar. Boil until it bubbles, and flavor with vanilla.—*Sister Lydia Jordan, Wiley, Ohio.*

Chocolate Filling for Cake.—Take 1 cup of soft white sugar, ¼ cake of chocolate, 1 egg unbeaten and 1 tablespoonful of sweet cream. Mix all together and put on to cook in a double boiler before you begin your cake. If it gets too thick add more cream. This will get smooth and glossy and will not crumble when cake is cut.—*Sister Anna E. Underwood, Fleming, Pa.*

Cocoa Filling.—Take 1 cup of powdered sugar, 2 tablespoonfuls of cocoa, 1 teaspoonful of butter and enough coffee to wet; add vanilla and spread on cake.—*Sister Sarah Deutschman, Elwood, Ill.*

Frosting for Burnt Sugar Cake.—Place in a sauce pan 1 cup of granulated sugar, 3 tablespoonfuls of water, and 2 tablespoonfuls of burnt sugar syrup (see recipe for burnt sugar cake). Boil until it forms a ball of wax when dropped into cold water. Have the white of 1 egg beaten to a stiff froth so stiff that you can pile it up. Now pour the syrup over the egg very slowly, beating briskly all the while. If the frosting appears too thin, continue beating until the right consistency, or until it is entirely cold. If quite stiff to begin with, it should not be beaten much. Place between and on top of layers with a silver knife dipped in water.—*Sister Minnie Replogle, Mount Morris, Ill.*

Fruit Filling for Cake.—Take 4 tablespoonfuls of citron cut very fine, the same amount of raisins, ½ cup of nuts, and ¼ pound of figs. Have all cut up very fine. Put just enough water over the fruit to soak it. Let stand for an hour, then simmer slowly, until it seems cooked enough. Beat up 1 egg, then add 1 cup of sugar, with 1 heaping teaspoonful of cornstarch mixed in it. Put the nuts, egg, sugar and cornstarch into the fruit and let scald well, then cool and spread on the cake. It is fine.—*Sister J. P. Holsinger, Mount Morris, Ill.*

Icing for Cake.—Take the white of 1 egg, 1 cup of sugar, and 1 cup of berries. Whip to a cream. One cup of grated apple may be used instead of the berries.—*Sister Sadie Shank, Notus, Idaho.*

Good Cake Filling.—Take 1 cup of pulverized sugar, 1 table-spoonful of butter, and 1 teaspoonful of melted chocolate. Cream this together and add 1 teaspoonful of vanilla and just enough strong coffee to make it the right consistency to spread.—*Sister D. E. Yeager, Franklin Grove, Ill.*

Hickorynut Icing.—Take 1 cup of ground nut meats, 1 cup of sweet cream and 1 cup of sugar. Cook slowly until it thickens. Be careful not to scorch.—*Sister Mary Butterbaugh, Polo, Ill.*

Icing without Eggs.—Take 1 cup of granulated sugar and dampen with ¼ cup of sweet milk. Stir till it boils. Let it boil 4 minutes without stirring, then remove it from the fire and set the dish in another of cold water, and add flavoring while cooling. Stir or beat it until it becomes a thick, creamy frosting.—*Sister Lizzie Chamberlain, Yale, Iowa.*

Lemon Cake Filling.—To the grated rind and juice of 1 lemon add 1 egg, 1 cup of sugar, and 1 tablespoonful of butter. Boil till thick and spread between layers and on top of cake.—*Sister Stella G. Turner, Iliff, Colo.*

Malaga Filling.—Seed and chop fine 1 cup of raisins, mix with icing and place between the layers of cake.—*Sister Edna Crowe, Des Moines, Iowa.*

A Nice Cake Filling.—Boil together 1½ cups of light brown sugar and ½ cup of sweet cream. Flavor with vanilla.—*Sister L. Clanin, Hicksville, Wash.*

Nut Filling for Cake.—Take 1 cup of nuts, chopped (not too fine), 1 cup of sour cream, 1 cup of sugar, 2 tablespoonfuls of flour. Mix flour and sugar, add cream, then let come to a boil, stirring constantly, if not in a double boiler. Add nuts just before removing from the stove. Let cool slightly before dressing the cake.—*Sister Addie Bales, Ollie, Iowa.*

Sea Foam Icing.—Take 2 cups of brown sugar and the white of 1 egg. Add a little water to sugar and let boil until it will spin a thread in cold water. Have white of egg beaten stiff, add the boiled sugar to the egg slowly and beat.—*Sister Mary Christner, Cerro Gordo, Ill.*

Burnt Sugar Cake.—First make the burnt sugar syrup: Put ½ cup of granulated sugar into a granite saucepan, stir continuously over the fire until sugar first softens, then melts and, finally, becomes liquid and throws off an intense smoke. It really must burn. Have ready ½ cup of boiling water, remove saucepan a moment, pour in the water and stir rapidly, allowing it to boil until you have a syrup. Cake Part: Cream together ½ cup of butter and 1½ cups of granulated sugar. Add 2 well-beaten eggs and 1 cup of milk; then add 2 cups of flour and ½ cup of the burnt sugar syrup. Lastly, add 1 teaspoonful of vanilla and another ½ cup of flour, sifted with 2 teaspoonfuls of baking powder. Beat well before putting it in the pans. Bake in loaf or layer. This is excellent if the recipe is followed closely.—*Sister Mae Gish, Rydal, Kans.*

PICKLES

Pickles possess very little food value, their chief service being that of a stimulant or relish, and their part in the bill of fare should therefore not be large. A porcelain-lined kettle or one of good granite should be used in making pickles. Use good cider vinegar, if possible, as other vinegar frequently softens or eats the pickles. Do not have the vinegar too strong; it is injurious to the lining of the stomach. Mustard seed, used in seasoning pickles, helps to prevent mould. Horseradish also has the same effect and helps to preserve the strength of the vinegar. Grape leaves assist in keeping the pickles green and also tend to keep them firm. Scalding the vinegar and pouring it over the pickles for successive days also makes them firm and crisp. If one does not wish to seal pickles in glass jars they may be kept in earthen jars. After the pickles are made and put in the jars, cover with a layer of grape leaves; then cover the jar with a layer of sheet wadding cut large enough to extend over the edge and tie down with a cloth or paper over the top of it. The jars may also be tied up with a cloth spread thickly with mixed mustard. With some pickle recipes the pickles will keep in earthen jars indefinitely without these precautions.

Pickled Artichokes.—Wash and scrape about ½ gallon of artichokes, cutting the larger in two. Cover with water, drain the water and measure it. Take the same quantity of vinegar; if too sharp, dilute it; add 1 tablespoonful of salt, 1 teaspoonful of black pepper, ½ cup of sugar, 1 teaspoonful of cinnamon (the latter may be whole or ground), and pour over the artichokes in a granite kettle. Boil about 5 minutes. If wanted for immediate use, put in a crock the same as beet pickles. If desired to be kept indefinitely, put in air-tight jars.—*Sister Sarah Hohf, Mt. Morris, Ill.*

Apple Pickles.—Make a syrup in the proportion of 2 cups of sugar, 2 cups of vinegar, and 1 cup water. Boil your apples in this until tender enough to pierce with a fork. Fill jars with the apples, cover with the hot vinegar, and seal. Sweet apples make the best pickles.—*Sister E. S. Moore, Eldora, Iowa.*

Spiced Apples.—Select perfect, round and well-matured sweet apples. Take ½ pint of vinegar, 1 pint of sugar, 1 pint of water, and place in an earthen or agate vessel. Boil for 10 or 15 miuutes, then add 3 drops each of cinnamon and clove oil, and drop in the apples. Boil until the apples are soft through. Cinnamon bark and whole cloves can be used in place of the oil, as preferred. If vinegar or oil is not strong, use enough to season.—*Sister Lottie Replogle, Roaring Spring, Pa.*

Pickled String Beans.—Boil beans in water to which has been added a little salt, till just a trifle tender, and drain very carefully. Put into glass cans, and after filling them stand them upside down, to be sure to get all the water out. Then cover with hot vinegar flavored with whole spices. Seal up while hot.—*Sister Laura E. Goetze, Saratoga, Wyo.*

Pickled Beets.—Wash and trim the tops from as many beets as desired; drop them into hot water and boil rapidly until they can easily be pierced with a broom straw; then peel and quarter or slice as preferred; have ready vinegar enough to cover them, place on the fire and heat thoroughly; add 3 tablespoonfuls of sugar to each quart of vinegar; salt and pepper to taste. Let come to a boil, then pour over the beets.—*Sister Clara Kreighbaum, South Bend, Ind.*

Beet Pickles.—Cook the beets till tender. To one quart of water take 3 cups of good vinegar, 4 cups of sugar, and ground allspice and cloves to taste. Peel and slice the beets, put them into the boiling vinegar, let them heat through, then put them into hot jars, cover with the vinegar and seal. When cold set in a cool, dark place. These are as good as any fruit.—*Sister R. D. Kirendall, Niotaze, Kans.*

Beet Pickles.—Take 1 quart of cabbage chopped or ground, 1 quart of beets chopped or ground, 1 cup of horse-radish, 1 cup of vinegar, 1 cup of sugar, 1 teaspoonful of black pepper, and salt and red pepper to taste. Red cabbage is preferred for this. Seal up cold.—*Sister Orvilla C. Ogle, Adams, Nebr.*

To Can Red Beets.—Cook the beets first, then peel and slice in slices about half inch thick, more or less, just as you like. Then heat one quart vinegar, 2 cups of sugar, 1 teaspoonful of salt and pepper as you like. Put the beets in this and let come to a boil, then put in glass jars, pour the vinegar over them and seal up as fruit. This amount of vinegar and seasoning will can four quarts of beets. —*Sister Della Smith, Eldora, Iowa.*

Canned Young Beets.—Cook young beets till tender, peel and fill glass jars, sprinkling with a little salt. Take 1½ cups of sugar and 1 quart of vinegar; let boil and pour over the beets. This is for 2 quarts of pickles. These are as fine as fresh beets.—*Sister Jennie Sheeler, Kingsley, Iowa.*

Beet Chow Chow.—Cook the beets until tender, then chop real fine and mix with finely-chopped cabbage. Take equal parts of beets and cabbage and to 1 quart of the mixture add 1 cup of sugar; 1 tablespoon of salt and 1 teaspoonful of black pepper. Mix thoroughly, put in glass jars and then fill the jars with cold vinegar and seal tight. This will keep like any other chow chow.—*Sister L. C. Beam, Elgin, Ill.*

Red Beet Relish.—Take 1 quart of chopped red beets, 1 quart of chopped cabbage, 1 cup of grated horse-radish, 2 cups of sugar, 1 tablespoonful of salt and 1 teaspoonful of pepper. Pour on vinegar and mix thoroughly. Can cold. None of the ingredients is cooked except the red beets which should be cooked before they are chopped.—*Sister John D. Clear, Rockford, Ill.*

Beet Salad.—Take 2 quarts of cooked beets chopped when cool, 2 quarts of raw cabbage chopped fine, 1 cup of ground horse-radish, 3 cups of brown sugar, 1 tablespoonful of salt, 1 teaspoonful of ground cinnamon and cloves, or other 'spices, to suit the taste; 1 cup of vinegar to each quart of ingredients. Mix beets, cabbage and horse-radish together and sprinkle over a little pepper. Boil the spices and sugar in the vinegar about five minutes. Pour over the mixture and can. This is extra good.—*Sister Salome Bausman, Sabetha, Kans.*

A Good Pickle.—Cut a head of cabbage into neat pieces, plunge into briskly boiling water and boil rapidly until tender. Drain and cover with sweetened vinegar, with pepper or celery seed as flavoring. Then putting into boiling water and rapid boiling, will prevent the cabbage from discoloration.—*Sister M. A. Snyder, Bradford, Ohio.*

Canteloupe Pickle.—For 7 pounds of canteloupe take 4 pounds of sugar and 1 pint of vinegar. Cut the canteloupe in pieces about 5 inches long and 2 inches wide, lay in weak vinegar over night, and drain in a colander for ½ hour. Boil the vinegar and sugar for 3 mornings. The third morning put the canteloupe in the vinegar and boil until tender. Spice to taste with cinnamon.—*Sister W. S. Reichard, Hagerstown, Md.*

Celery Pickle.—Chop fine enough cabbage to fill a quart bowl, after it is salted slightly and all the water pressed out. Chop enough celery to fill a quart bowl, but do not press. Now put the two in a mixing bowl with ½ cup of white sugar, a tablespoonful of salt, a dessert spoon of Jamaica ginger, and a tablespoonful of white mustard seed. Mix well and add a pint of good vinegar.—*Sister N. J. Roop, Warrensburg, Mo.*

To Pickle Celery.—Take good bleached celery, cut in pieces about 2 inches long, boil in water till tender. Take out and drain, then pour over the celery boiling vinegar which has been sweetened a little. Put in glass jars and it is ready for use any time.—*Sister Perry Broadwater, Lonaconing, Md.*

Pickles.—Put fresh cucumbers in warm brine and let stand 24 hours, then dry them with a towel and put them in a stone jar. Put in a layer of the cucumbers, then a layer· of horseradish cut lengthwise, with a few grape or bay leaves. Take vinegar enough to cover the pickles, season with brown sugar and mixed spices to taste; heat to boiling point, skim and pour over pickles. Repeat heating vinegar 3 mornings. Cover with grape or bay leaves and tie up for use. Pickles put up this way will keep all winter.—*Sister Amanda Brown, Whitewater, Ind.*

Pickles.—To pickle cucumbers for winter, take 1 gallon of vinegar, 3 gallons of water, 3 quarts of fine salt, and ½ pound of alum. Wash the cucumbers and cover with this pickle. When wanted for use wash and put in vinegar.—*Sister Cora Sell Brubaker, Hollidaysburg, Pa.*

Best Cucumber Pickles.—Take 1 cup of salt, 2 cups of sugar, 1 cup of ground mustard, and 1 gallon of vinegar. Wash the cucumbers and put in cold. Let stand a couple of days, and they are ready for use.—*Sister Lauren T. Miller, Elgin, Ill.*

Canning Cucumbers.—Wash the cucumbers, place in a kettle and cover with cider vinegar. Add 3 large tablespoonfuls of sugar, mixed spices, peppers, and to each can of cucumbers add 8 onion sets. Heat gradually till hot through. Fill the cans with cucumbers, then heat the vinegar to a boil and fill up the can. Seal at once.—*Sister Mollie Conway, Bradford, Ohio.*

Canned Pickles.—Take vinegar and water equal parts, add salt according, put the pickles in and let them come nearly to a boil. Then put them in jars and take proportions of 1 pint of water and 2 of vinegar. Let boil, pour over pickles and seal.—*Sister D. F. Kelly, North Georgetown, Ohio.*

To Can Cucumber Pickles.—Take small green cucumbers, wash and place in salt water over night, then remove from the salt water and put into boiling vinegar. Let them get hot through, but not boil. Place in glass cans and pour the boiling vinegar with spices to suit taste over the cucumbers, and seal.—*Sister Adaline Huston, Mishawaka, Ind.*

To Can Cucumber Pickles.—Fill a jar with cucumbers just from the vine, cover with salt water, let stand over night and in the morning drain. Take about 3 pints of vinegar, about ½ cup of sugar (use sugar according to taste), and some horseradish. Let vinegar and sugar come to a boil; then pour over pickles and seal while hot.—*Sister F. Alice Davidson, Centropolis, Kans.*

To Can Cucumber Pickles.—First you must have good, sour vinegar, or the pickles will not keep. Wash cucumbers as soon as possible after picking and put them in a porcelain kettle. Take two-thirds vinegar and one-third water, pour over the cucumbers and add sugar, salt and spices to suit the taste. We like them sweet; also celery cut up fine and put in. Now put all over the fire, stir the cucumbers while heating all the time, and just as soon as they begin to change color from green to yellow, take the kettle off the fire and pack the pickles in cans tightly. Then put the kettle with the vinegar back on the fire, let boil five minutes and pour over pickles and seal up, and you will have good, crisp, solid pickles that will keep. The main points are to use strong vinegar and not let the cucumbers get too hot before packing in cans. The large cucumbers we peel and slice one-half inch thick and proceed same as with whole cucumbers. We like them 'most better than the whole cucumbers.—*Sister Martin Moyer, Goshen, Ind.*

Cold Pickles.—One cup of yellow mustard, 1 cup of sugar, 1 cup of salt. Put all in a stone jar with 1 gallon of vinegar. Wash the pickles and put in the jar, stirring them every day for a week. Tie a cloth over them.—*Sister Bernice Ashmore, St. Peter, Minn.*

Cucumber Pickles.—Take 1 gallon of cold vinegar, 1 cup of salt, 1 cup of sugar, and 1 cup of ground mustard. Mix the mustard with a little of the vinegar and work it to a smooth paste before stirring it in. Wash your cucumbers and put them into this cold mixture. Place a plate on top to hold the cucumbers under the vinegar. They need not be sealed and will keep a long time if the ingredients are good.—*Sister Katie Moore Strickler, Eldora, Iowa.*

Cucumber Pickles.—Take a teacupful of salt to 1 gallon of cucumbers, pour boiling water over them enough to cover, and let stand over night. Then rinse and drain. Heat cider vinegar almost to boiling, put in the cucumbers, heat through and put in glass jars. If wanted quite sour, have other vinegar heated to boiling and pour over them. Put in spices and also horseradish to keep from moulding, then seal.—*Sister Mary Reddick, Sheridan, Mo.*

To Pickle Cucumbers.—To every gallon of vinegar (strong) add 1 cup of salt and 1 tablespoonful of powdered alum. Mix these well in the vinegar. Wash the cucumbers and pack in stone jars. Around the jar and between each layer put grape leaves, also between each layer put cloves, cinnamon, and horse-radish. Then pour on the vinegar (not heated).—*Sister C. D. Bonsack, Union Bridge, Md.*

Ripe Cucumber Pickle.—Take ripe cucumbers, pare, and remove the seeds, and soak over night in salt water with a little alum in it. Steam till tender, not soft. Boil 3 pounds of sugar and 2 quarts of vinegar 15 minutes, and pour over the cucumbers.—*Sister Flora Doughty, Eldora, Iowa.*

Spiced Ripe Cucumbers.—Pare, remove seeds, and cut in small pieces one-half dozen cucumbers. Parboil in salt water and drain. Prepare syrup of 2 pints of vinegar, 5 pints of sugar, and 1 teaspoonful each of cloves, cinnamon and allspice. Tie the spices in a bag. Boil the cucumbers in the syrup till they can be pierced easily with a fork, leaving spices in the syrup. Seal in fruit jars while hot.—*Sister Grace Holsinger Butterbaugh, Elgin, Ill.*

Cucumber Sweet Pickles.—Gather small cucumbers fresh from the vines, wash them and put into gallon jars. To each gallon put a small cup of salt, then cover with hot water and let stand over night. In the morning drain, and to each gallon take 2 quarts of vinegar, 1 cup of sugar, 2 tablespoonfuls of mixed spices, or "spice to suit taste." Put this over the fire, let come to a boil, then put in the cucumbers. Let them heat through, *not boil*. Can while hot.—*Sister Carrie Martin, Mankato, Kans.*

Spiced Currants.—To 1 gallon of prepared currants take 3 pounds of white sugar, 1 pint of good vinegar and 1 tablespoonful each of ground cloves, cinnamon, allspice and ginger. Put the vinegar in a porcelain stewpan; add the sugar and melt. Put the spices in a thin muslin bag and drop into the syrup. Bring to a boil, skim, and put in the ripe fruit. Let come to a boil, then skim the fruit out, and boil syrup thick. Pour over the fruit and put spice bag on top.—*Sister M. E. Rothrock, Hartland, Wash.*

Pickled Eggs.—Boil 12 eggs 20 minutes, then place them into cold water a few minutes so they will peel easily. After they are peeled put in a jar. Take 1 quart of vinegar, 1 teaspoonful of mustard, 1 teaspoonful of salt and ¼ teaspoonful of pepper. Bring this to a good boil and pour over eggs in jar and seal.—*Sister L. Clanin, Hicksville, Wash.*

Pickled Grapes.—Take ripe grapes, pick off carefully so as not to burst them if possible. Wash them, fill glass jars and put 3 or 4 cloves on top of grapes. Make a syrup of 2 pints of vinegar, ½ pint of water and 4 pints of sugar, and pour into filled jars while syrup is hot and seal. This will make 4 to 6 jars (quart). To serve, put grapes with some of the juice into side dishes and eat with meats.—*Sister W. J. Haynes, Moorefield, Nebr.*

Sweet Pickled Muskmelon.—Take any kind of good ripe melon, peel and slice, not too thin. Boil together five or ten minutes 1 quart of vinegar and 1 quart of sugar. Drop in the sliced muskmelon and boil till tender. Last of all, drop in whole cloves and cinnamon bark. Let all boil a few minutes longer, then put in jars and seal, and you have as nice a pickle as peaches.—*Sister Susie Smith, Conway Springs, Kans.*

Pickled Onions.—Cook onions in salt water till tender, and put into a jar. Take vinegar, sugar and spices to taste. Heat the vinegar, pour over the onions hot until they are covered, then seal up. Vinegar of red beets gives them a nice color.—*Sister C. B. Smith, Red Cloud, Nebr.*

Peach Mangoes.—Take good, firm peaches, wash and cut into halves, removing the pit. Make a mixture of grated horse-radish and mustard seed. Fill ½ the peach and put together by sticking a toothpick through, or tie together. Prepare the vinegar as for any spiced fruit.—*Sister Guy E. Foresman, Lafayette, Ind.*

Spiced Peaches.—To 7 pounds of peaches take 3 pounds of sugar and 1 quart of vinegar; spice with cinnamon bark. Boil the sugar, spice and vinegar together. After these are well boiled, put in the peaches and leave in until tender enough, then pour them into either a jar or crock as desired. When cold they are ready for use. —*Sister D. A. Thomas, Hagerstown, Md.*

Sweet Peach Pickle.—Take ½ gallon of peaches, washed and peeled, 1 quart of vinegar, 1 pound of sugar, and 1 tablespoon-ful of cinnamon buds. Put vinegar, sugar and peaches over the fire and bring slowly to a boil; then put in a jar and seal.—*Sister Mary Gibbel, Inavale, Nebr.*

Spiced Pears.—Pare the pears with a very sharp knife. To 8 pounds of fruit take 4 pounds of the best brown sugar, 1 quart of cider vinegar and 1 cupful of mixed spices (whole), cassia buds, cloves, stick cinnamon, mace and allspice. Tie the spices in a bag, and boil with the vinegar and sugar; skim. Pack the fruit in a jar, and pour the boiling syrup over it. Repeat this for 3 mornings, unless pears are hard, when they should be boiled in the syrup 3 minutes. They can be canned, but will keep in a jar. Leave the bag of spices in the syrup.—*Sister S. E. Chafin, Roanoke, Va.*

Pickled Pears.—Take 1 pint of the best vinegar, 4 pounds of sugar, 8 pounds of pears, and spices to taste. Boil the pears in the mixture until soft, then take them out, and boil the syrup until quite thick, then pour it over the pears.—*Sister John Barker, Fairview, Oregon.*

Mango Recipe.—Cut fine the amount of cabbage needed, salt it and work well with the hands, press the water out, then mix in plenty of brown mustard seed. Fill the mangoes (which should be previously salted over night in scalding water). Place them in a jar and take strong vinegar enough to cover them. For a gallon jar take a pint of sugar and dissolve in a little hot water, then add to the vinegar.—*Sister Kate Royer, Celina, Ohio.*

Sweet Pickle.—To 7 pounds of fruit take 3 pounds of sugar and 1 quart of vinegar, 1 ounce of cinnamon and 1 ounce of cloves. Put the fruit into a jar and make a syrup of the vinegar and sugar. Strain, and pour it over the fruit boiling hot. Let them stand 24 hours, then pour off the syrup, boil it and pour it on them again and let stand another 24 hours. Then pour fruit and all into a kettle and simmer slowly until done.—*Sister Hettie Engel, Darlow, Kans.*

Sweet Pickles.—Take 9 pounds of fruit, 3 pounds of sugar, 1 pint of best cider vinegar, 1 ounce of cloves and 1 ounce of cinnamon. Make syrup of sugar and vinegar; heat, with spices tied in a loose cloth; then put fruit in and make hot. Can up for future use. Very delicious.—*Sister Mary Gibson, Des Moines, Iowa.*

Sweet Pickles.—Take 25 small cucumbers, 1 quart of small onions, 1 quart of green tomatoes (cut fine), 1 quart of string beans (cooked tender), 2 heads of celery and 2 heads of cauliflower. Sprinkle with salt enough to make a weak brine, cover with cold water and let stand 24 hours. Let come to a boil in the same water and drain in a colander. Let 3 quarts of vinegar come to a boil, mix ½ ounce of tumeric and 3 cups of sugar. Let boil again, and while hot pour over the vegetables.—*Sister Martha Reiff Tobias, Camden, Ind.*

Spiced Plums.—Take 8 pounds of plums (we use Miners), 4 pounds of sugar, 2 quarts of good cider vinegar, 1 ounce of cloves, and 1 ounce of cinnamon. Boil the syrup thick, then put in the plums and boil until done.—*Sister E. S. Moore, Eldora, Iowa.*

Chow Chow.—Take 1 peck of green tomatoes, ½ peck of onions, 3 heads of cabbage, ¼ peck of carrots and 10 heads of celery. Chop fine, salt and let stand over night. Drain carefully. Take vinegar enough to cover, and 2 cups of sugar. Mix celery and mustard seed with ingredients and other mixed spices tied in a piece of muslin. Boil all together until tender. Can while hot.—*Sister Emma Carstensen, Girard, Ill.*

English Chow Chow.—Take 1 quart of small cucumbers not over 2 inches long, 2 quarts of small white onions, 2 quarts of tender string beans each one cut in halves, 3 quarts of green tomatoes sliced and chopped very coarsely, and 2 heads of cauliflower cut in small pieces, or 2 heads of cabbage. Put all into a stone jar. Mix together and sprinkle salt between sparingly; let stand 24 hours, then drain off the brine and put in a kettle over the fire. Add 1 ounce of tumeric, 6 red peppers chopped coarsely, 4 tablespoonfuls of mustard seed, 2 tablespoonfuls each of celery seed, whole cloves, and whole allspice, 1 cup of sugar and ⅔ cup of ground mixed mustard. Pour on enough vinegar to cover well, cover the kettle and simmer until all is tender, stirring often. Seal in bottles or glass jars.—*Sister W. S. Reichard, Hagerstown, Md.*

French Chow Chow.—Take 1 quart of cucumbers cut not very fine, 1 quart each of small cucumbers, onions, green tomatoes and 4 sweet peppers. Put all together and cover with a brine made of 1 gallon of water and 1 cup of salt. Soak 4 hours, then scald them in the same brine and drain. Dressing: Take 6 tablespoonfuls of ground mustard, 1 tablespoonful of tumeric, 1 cup of flour, 2 quarts of vinegar and 2 pounds of white sugar. Mix this all together with a little vinegar and scald until smooth. Now put in the pickles, and it is ready for use.—*Sister Sadie Stover, Lanark, Ill*

Sweet Chow Chow.—Take 1 gallon of cabbage, 2 quarts of green tomatoes, 1 pint of onions, ¼ cup of green peppers. Chop all fine, and add 1½ pounds of sugar, 1 tablespoonful of mustard, 1 tablespoonful of ginger, 2 tablespoonfuls of cloves, 2 tablespoonfuls of salt, 3 tablespoonfuls of cinnamon, and 1½ quarts of vinegar. Boil until cabbage is tender.—*Sister Lisetta Brown, Whitewater, Ind.*

Chop Pickles.—Take green tomatoes and cabbage, about equal parts ground together. Salt well and let stand in wooden or earthen vessel 24 hours, then press out all juice, add weak vinegar, and bring to boiling point and let cool. After it is cool, press out all juice again and put in enough good strong vinegar to make as thin as desired. To 4 gallons of pickle add 2 ounces cinnamon, 2 ounces of cloves, 2 ounces of celery seed, 4 tablespoonfuls of ground pepper, and 2 pounds of brown sugar, and mix well. Do not boil again, but pack in glass or earthen vessels cold.—*Sister Geo. B. Holsinger, Bridgewater, Va.*

Chowder Recipe (For Two Gallons).—Take 3 heads of cabbage, 1 peck of green tomatoes, 1 quart of vinegar, ½ cup of salt, 6 onions, 8 mangoes, and 2 red peppers. Chop all fine and boil ½ hour. Drain in a colander. Then add 2 quarts of vinegar, 2 pounds of light brown sugar, and 1 tablespoonful each of ground cinnamon, cloves, allspice, and mustard seed, and 1 pint of grated horse-radish. Boil all together till tender and seal up in fruit jars.—*Sister Edith Warstler, Goshen, Ind.*

Green Tomato Pickles.—Take 1 peck of green tomatoes, 6 onions, sliced together, 1 cup of salt over both. Mix thoroughly and let remain over night. Then pour liquor off in the morning; throw it away. Mix 2 quarts of water, and 1 of vinegar, boil 20 minutes, drain, and throw liquor away. Take 3 quarts of vinegar, 2 pounds of sugar, 1 tablespoonful each of allspice, cloves and cinnamon, and 3 green peppers chopped fine. Boil from 1 to 2 hours.

This recipe will make 1 gallon of pickles.—*Sister Hannah F. Dunning, Denbigh, N. Dak.*

Green Tomato Pickles.—Take 1 peck of tomatoes, 1 quart of vinegar, 1 pound of sugar, 3 large onions, 4 tablespoonfuls of whole cloves and 4 sweet green peppers. Boil the vinegar, sugar, cloves and peppers together 10 minutes. Slice the tomatoes, onions and peppers. Put in enough at a time to be covered, boil till pierced easily with a fork; take out and put in more until all are cooked. Then add 1 quart of vinegar to the liquid left in the vessel and boil 20 minutes, then pour it over the tomatoes. These are crisp and light in color; if cooked too long they get soft and dark.—*Sister E. A. Dunn, Oaks, Pa.*

Green Tomato Pickles.—Take only firm green tomatoes, slice thin and steam them until soft, drain off all the water and make a syrup as follows: To 3 pints of good vinegar take 1 pint of sugar, and boil 20 minutes, then add 1 ounce of cloves, 1 ounce of cinnamon bark, and ½ ounce of mustard seed. Pour over the tomatoes. *Sister Eliza A. Wenger, Long Glade, Va.*

Mixed Pickles.—Take ½ peck of green tomatoes, 25 small cucumbers whole, 15 large onions, 2 large heads of cabbage, 1 pint of onion sets, 1 pint of grated horse-radish, ½ pound of white mustard seed, ¼ pound box of mustard, 1 ounce of ground cinnamon, 1 ounce of celery seed, some celery stalks cut in small pieces, and 2 tablespoonfuls of black pepper. Slice tomatoes not too thin, cut the cabbage coarse, and if cucumbers are large cut in pieces about 1 inch long. Salt over night, and in the morning drain and put in weak vinegar. Let stand a day or two, then press out and pack in a jar and sprinkle in the spices excepting the mustard while packing. Heat 1½ gallons of good vinegar and pour over. Heat the vinegar for 3 mornings, and the last time add the brown sugar. When cold, stir the ground mustard through and pour over the mixture.—*Sister Martha L. Fitz, Panora, Iowa.*

Mixed Pickles.—Take 1 peck of green tomatoes, 1 peck of onions, 1 large head of cabbage and 1 large head of cauliflower. Cut these in small pieces, stew in salt water, drain over night. The same evening put to soak in salt water ½ peck of small beans, ½ peck small cucumbers. In the morning heat 1 gallon of vinegar and add 1 pound of brown sugar, to which add mustard, cloves, a little red pepper and horse-radish to taste. Now mix 1 box of English mustard with a little vinegar and 2 teaspoonfuls of tumeric. Stir all into the vinegar. Let come to a boil and pour over pickle.— *Sister J. A. Sell, McKee Gap, Pa.*

Mixed Pickles.—Take string beans and cook until tender, salt to taste. Take green tomatoes, slice, sprinkle salt over them. Take young muskmelons and watermelons, very young and green; slice in suitable pieces, for pickles; cucumbers size for pickles. Let all stand in salt over night and drain well next morning. Take a barrel, or whatever is wanted to put the pickles in. First cover the bottom with large cabbage leaves, then put in a layer of each of the above-named vegetables; then sprinkle all kinds of spices over them. Then add small heads of cabbage or the sprouts that gather around where the head has been cut out. Then begin over again, putting in a layer of the vegetables, then the spices and some green peppers. When all are in, pour good vinegar over and cover with cabbage leaves. Put on a weight heavy enough to keep all under the vinegar. It is ready for use in a few days. When kept in a cool place it will keep until all is used up.—*Sister Rachel E. Gillett, Camp Verde, Ariz.*

Mixed Pickles.—Take 12 stalks of celery cut fine, 6 quarts of very small pickles, 2 quarts of large cucumbers sliced, 5 quarts of very small onions, 2 quarts of green tomatoes diced, 3 heads of cauliflower, and 6 large peppers chopped fine, soak all separately in brine over night. In the morning cook all separately in same brine until just tender. Dressing: Take 1 gallon of vinegar, 24 tablespoonfuls of ground mustard, 2 cups of flour, 4 cups of light " C " sugar, and 5 cents' worth of tumeric. Heat the vinegar, keeping out just enough of it cold to mix up the last 4 ingredients smoothly, and add this to the hot vinegar. When it has boiled up well, add all the prepared vegetables and stir thoroughly until all are heated through. Use a pan or kettle to heat them in large enough to hold all with plenty of room for stirring.—*Sister Permelia A. Greenwood, Granger, Ind.*

Fancy Mixed Pickles.—Take 1 large head of cauliflower, 2 quarts of pickling onions, 2 quarts of small cucumbers or larger ones cut into small pieces and 1 or 2 quarts of nice, tender, yellow-pod beans. Pick the cauliflower into small pieces and soak in salt water over night; also the onions, beans and cucumbers should be soaked over night in salt water, then all drained. Cauliflower, beans and onions should be boiled until just tender, but firm. Put in the colander to drain. Then mix all together. Take vinegar enough to cover all and bring to a boil. Add 1 pound of sugar and 1 ounce of mixed spices. Pour over the pickles, and they will soon be ready for use.—*Sister Jno. D. Bonsack, Rock Lake, N. Dak.*

Mustard Pickles.—Take 1 quart of small cucumbers, 1 quart of small onions, 1 quart of green tomatoes, 6 green peppers and 1 quart of chopped cauliflower. Put all in salt water and soak for 24 hours, and then heat in the same water. Dressing: Take 6 tablespoonfuls of mustard, 1 tablespoonful of tumeric, 1 cup of flour, ½ cup of sugar and 2 quarts of vinegar. Stir constantly until heated. Pour over pickles and seal.—*Sister E. Hodgden, Huntington, Ind.*

Mustard Pickles.—Take 2 quarts each of cucumbers, green tomatoes, cabbage, and onions; chop not too fine and mix all together. Boil in weak salt water until tender, then drain over night. Dressing: Take 2 quarts of vinegar, 2 pounds of sugar, ¼ pound of ground mustard, ½ cup of flour, and 1 tablespoonful of tumeric. Boil, and pour over pickle.—*Sister Mary Rowland, Polo, Ill.*

Piccalilli.—Take ½ peck of green tomatoes, 2 medium-sized heads of cabbage, 12 cucumbers, 12 large sweet peppers and 1 quart of celery. Cut all very fine, salt, let stand over night, and drain. Then add one tablespoonful of mustard seed, 1 teaspoonful each of cinnamon and cloves, 1½ cups of sugar, ½ gallon of vinegar and pepper to taste. Heat all together and put in jars.—*Sister Alice Trimmer, York, Pa.*

Spanish Pickle.—Take one peck of green tomatoes, 4 good-sized heads of cabbage, 1 dozen onions, 3 ounces of mustard seed, 2½ pounds of brown sugar, 2 good bunches of green celery, ½ ounce of tumeric, and ½ box of Coleman's mustard. Chop the tomatoes and cabbage. Mix with a pint of salt and let stand a few hours, or over night, then drain or squeeze out and add the onions and celery chopped. Also add 2 quarts of pickles, when they are ready for use. Cut the pickles in pieces lengthwise. Mix all together and simmer one hour. Put in vinegar to suit taste, as you would for piccalilli. Then can up.—*Sister Mary C. Beard Eshelman. Elgin, Ill.*

Tomato Soy.—Take 2 gallons of green tomatoes sliced without peeling, 12 large onions sliced, 1 tablespoonful each of salt, pepper, allspice and ground cloves, 2 tablespoonfuls of ground mustard, 1 quart of sugar, and 2 quarts of vinegar. Mix all together and cook until tender, stirring often to keep from burning.—*Sister Sadie Shank, Notus, Idaho.*

Watermelon Pickle.—Boil the white rind of the melon until it is soft enough to run a broom straw through, then lay it on a plate to drain dry. Boil together 1 pint of vinegar and 2 pints of sugar. Drop into this the melon and spice to suit the taste.—*Sister Levi Bear, Hagerstown, Md.*

Watermelon Pickle.—Peel and cut the white rind of the melon into pieces, soak in strong salt water twelve hours then soak in clear water another twelve hours. Boil in fresh water until tender and easily pierced with a straw. For 5 pounds of rind make a syrup of 2 pounds of sugar, 1 pint of vinegar, 1 pint of water, ½ cup of mixed spices (whole), cloves, cinnamon, allspice. If desired the spice may be tied in a bag boiled in the syrup, and placed in jar with the pickle. Pack rinds in jar, pour boiling syrup over them. Repeat this for three mornings. Boil syrup down the last time until it barely covers rinds. May be canned, but will keep in a jar if set in a cool place.—*Sister Katherine Newsom, Chicago, Ill.*

Watermelon Sweet Pickle.—Prepare the rind as you like. Weigh the rind as soon as you cut it, then leave in salt water over night. The next day soak in fresh water, changing it now and then for twenty-four hours. Put in a brass kettle one layer of grape leaves and one of rind, until the rind is all in. Add alum the size of an egg, cover with water and boil ½ hour. Then take out rind and soak in fresh water again, changing the water often for twenty-four hours. To each pound of rind take ¾ of a pound of sugar, ½ pint of strong vinegar; spice with ginger, mace, cinnamon and a few cloves. Boil the rind in the vinegar and sugar till it is clear, then put in jar and boil syrup till it gets the least thickened and add to melon.—*Sister Luverna Sheets, Mt. Solon, Va.*

Catsup.—To 1 gallon of ripe tomatoes, take 4 tablespoonfuls of salt, 1 tablespoonful of black pepper, 1 teaspoonful of allspice, and 3 tablespoonfuls of mustard. Peel the tomatoes, slice and cook soft, then strain through a colander. Add the other ingredients and boil all together 1 hour. Can, and seal tightly.—*Sister Effie Hoover, Milford, Ind.*

Cold Catsup.—Take ½ peck of tomatoes, peel, cut fine, and pour off the juice. Add 1 teacupful of grated horseradish, 1 cup of ground mustard seed, 1 cup of nasturtium seed cut fine, 1 tablespoonful of celery seed, ½ cup of salt, pepper to taste, and ½ gallon of vinegar. Put it in a jug or bottle, and it is ready for use. Peel the tomatoes cold, and do not put anything warm about it.—*Sister Alice Trimmer, York, Pa.*

Grape Catsup.—Take 1 quart of grape juice, 1 pint of vinegar, 1 pound of sugar, and ground cloves to suit your taste. Boil until quite thick.—*Sister Amy Roop Shaw, Westminster, Md.*

Cucumber Catsup.—Pare and grate 24 medium-sized cucumbers, also 3 onions. Strain all through cheese cloth and add to the pulp sugar, salt, pepper, and celery seed to taste. Add vinegar to make as before straining. Seal for keeping as canned fruit. Serve with meats in winter. If properly made it has the flavor of fresh cucumbers.—*Sister Mary C. Cline, Stuarts Draft, Va.*

Tomato Catsup.—Boil 1 gallon of tomatoes until soft, strain through a sieve; add 1 quart of vinegar, 1 pound of sugar, 1 teaspoonful of cayenne pepper, 1 teaspoonful of black pepper, 4 teaspoonfuls of ground cloves, 4 teaspoonfuls of ground mustard, and 4 teaspoonfuls of salt. Boil down to ¼ of its bulk and add 4 teaspoonfuls of cinnamon. Bottle and seal.—*Sister Elmer Snoberger, Roaring Spring, Pa.*

Tomato Catsup.—Wash the tomatoes, boil a few minutes, and when cool put them through a sieve. To 4 quarts of pulp add 4 tablespoonfuls each of salt and black pepper, 3 tablespoonfuls of mustard, 1 each of cinnamon and cloves, ½ teaspoonful of cayenne pepper, and 1 quart of vinegar, and boil down one-half.—*Sister Susan Rouzer, New Paris, Pa.*

Cold Tomato Catsup.—Peel and remove seeds from 1 gallon of ripe tomatoes. Mash fine and add 1 teacup of salt, 1 teacup of sugar, 1 tablespoonful of mustard, 2 tablespoonfuls of pepper, 1 tablespoonful of celery seed and 1 quart of vinegar. Mix well, bottle and seal.—*Sister Mary C. Cline, Stuarts Draft, Va.*

Chili Sauce.—Take ½ bushel of ripe tomatoes, 4 good-sized onions, 4 red peppers chopped fine. Add 10 tablespoonfuls of sugar, 5 tablespoonfuls of salt and 9 teacupfuls of cider vinegar. Boil 1 hour, and bottle.—*Sister Perry Broadwater, Lonaconing, Md.*

Chili Sauce.—Take 12 ripe tomatoes, 3 onions, 3 bunches of celery cut fine, sweet and sharp peppers, 1 cup cider vinegar, a little salt, and cinnamon if liked. Boil all together not too soft.—*Sister Lizzie Pehlman, Millersville, Pa.*

Chili Sauce.—Take 36 large ripe tomatoes, 6 green peppers, seeds and all, 5 large onions, 3 tablespoonfuls each of salt and sugar, 2 tablespoonfuls each of cinnamon and mustard, 1 tablespoonful of cayenne pepper, and 7 cups of vinegar. Scald and skin the tomatoes; then boil them 15 minutes. Add peppers and onions chopped fine and your seasoning, and boil 2 hours, or till thick enough to bottle.— *Sister Alverna E. Butterbaugh, Carthage, Mo.*

Bordeaux Sauce.—Take 2 gallons of chopped cabbage, 1 gallon of chopped green tomatoes, 1 gallon of vinegar, 1½ pounds of brown sugar, ½ pound of white mustard seed, 1 dozen onions, ¾ ounce of tumeric, 1 ounce each of celery seed, cloves, and allspice, and 1 gill of salt.—*Sister Myra Troyer, Baltic, Ohio.*

Peach Sauce.—Take 1 peck of peaches, wash and wipe dry: put ½ of the quantity in a kettle and cover with boiling water and boil until tender. Take them out and cook the remaining peaches. Add to the syrup 1 pint of vinegar, and 3 pints of white sugar. Let come to a boil, and put the peaches in again and let boil, then put in jars and seal tight.—*Sister S. C. Smucker, Timberville, Va.*

Tomato Relish.—Take 1 peck of ripe tomatoes, peel, slice, and drain well; chop 6 large onions, 1 cup of celery, and 4 small peppers; mix all together. Add 1 ounce of mustard seed, 2 pints of sugar, 1 pint of vinegar, 2 teaspoonfuls of cinnamon (more if liked), ½ ounce of celery seed, and salt to taste. Do not cook. This will make about 6 quarts. Can and seal, and it will keep until late in the spring.—*Sister Mary Royer, Mt. Morris, Ill.*

Green Tomato Sauce.—Take 8 pounds of green tomatoes and chop fine or grind on a sausage grinder; add 4 pounds of sugar and boil down 3 hours. Then add 1 quart of vinegar and 1 ounce each of mace, cinnamon and cloves, all ground, of course, and boil about 15 minutes. Let cool and put in jars or other vessels. Try this once and you will make it again.—*Sister Martha Jane Ikenberry, Gowrie, Iowa.*

Corn Salad.—Take 2 dozen ears of corn, 8 onions chopped fine, 4 green peppers, 1 cup of sugar, 2 cabbage heads chopped fine, 1 teaspoonful each white and black mustard seed and celery seed, 1 gallon of vinegar and 1 tablespoonful of ground mustard. Scald and can hot. We like it fine for winter use.—*Sister Clara Clark, Palisade, Colo.*

Corn Salad.—Take 1 gallon of corn, ¾ gallon of cabbage, 2 large sweet peppers, 1 onion, 2 tablespoonfuls of flour, 2 tablespoonfuls of salt, 1 teaspoonful of mustard, or more if desired, 1 tablespoonful of celery seed, 2 cups of sugar, 1½ quarts of vinegar, and 1 pint of water. Boil together all but the flour and mustard for thirty minutes. Then add these and boil twenty minutes. Seal hot.—*—Sister D. E. Yeager, Franklin Grove, Ill.*

Good Vinegar.—A family using much canned fruit and berries may keep themselves provided with excellent vinegar by rinsing each jar after the fruit or berries have been removed a'nd pouring it into another jar, crock, or demijohn used for the purpose. The many kinds of juices cause it to become a very fine-flavored vinegar. While the first jar made is being used, another jar can be filled.—*Sister Rachel Michael, Myrtle Point, Ore.*

PRESERVING AND CANNING

With the present knowledge of canning and preserving open to all, no family need be without wholesome fruits any time during the year, if they are to be had in their season. The two essentials to successful canning are sterilizing of fruits, jars, etc., and exclusion of air. Directions are given in the recipes that follow. Excellent jellies may be made from parings, cores, etc., of fruit prepared for canning. Jellies should be cooked rapidly and preserves slowly. Cream of tartar added to preserves and jams just before they are quite cooked, in the proportion of one teaspoonful to one gallon of fruit, will prevent sugaring. If one does not wish to seal preserves, jams and jellies, cover them when cold with about one-half inch of melted paraffin. Keep preserves, jams, jellies and canned fruit in a cool, dark, dry place. Paraffin that has been used to cover jellies, etc., may be cleaned by boiling it rapidly in water, then setting it aside to cool, when the dust will settle to the bottom and any fruit juice in it will be dissolved, and it will be ready to use again. A good sealing wax may be made of one pound of resin and one ounce each of lard, tallow and beeswax. Melt together and apply hot.

Apple Butter.—Take 12 gallons of cider, 1 bushel of apple snitz, and 20 pounds of sugar. Put the apples in as soon as the cider has been skimmed, and boil 3 hours. This recipe has proved successful and produces a larger quantity and better quality than when made the old way.—*Sister Sue C. Foutz, Waynesboro, Pa.*

Twentieth Century Apple Butter.—For 10 gallons take 20 gallons of cider; 20 pounds of sugar and a 3-hooped tub of quartered apples. Boil and skim the cider and put in the apples as fast as the cider boils down to make room. When the apples are cooked very soft, add the sugar, dipping out some of the butter to dissolve the sugar, as the cold sugar would fall to the bottom and burn. This butter can be made between breakfast and supper, and no hurry or night work.—*Sister N. J. Roop, Warrensburg, Mo.*

Egg Butter.—Put a cup of molasses in a skillet and a lump of butter the size of an egg. Then add 2 well-beaten eggs and a little nutmeg, stirring briskly all the time or the eggs will cook in big pieces. Take up as soon as the eggs are all stirred in. Serve the same as apple butter.—*Sister Susie Peters, Emporia, Kans.*

Lemon Butter.—Take 3 lemons grated and seeds removed, 3 eggs, 1 pint of sugar, butter size of a walnut and ½ cup of water; boil all together for 15 minutes. Best boiled in a double boiler. This makes an excellent butter.—*Sister J. P. Holsinger, Mt. Morris, Ill.*

Lemon Butter.—Take 1½ cups of sugar, ½ cup of butter, the whites of 3 eggs and the yolk of 1 egg. Grate the yellow off of 2 medium-sized lemons, then squeeze in the juice and mix all together. Cook twenty minutes by setting the pan containing the mixture into a pan of boiling water.—*Sister Bertha Kauffman, Williston, N. Dak.*

Pear Butter.—Take six heaping buckets of pear snitz (our bucket holds fourteen quarts even full) and four buckets of water. (This is the way we make it of harvest pears.) Boil the pears till mushy, then put in forty or forty-five pounds of brown sugar. The light brown is best, as it helps to give the butter a nice color. Now boil till it gets that peculiar bubble which apple butter also gets when it is done. Of course, do not boil it too hard. A little experience will tell you how fast to cook it. This gives a nice amount and it is good. We boil this amount in about five hours.—*Sister Mattie Weaver, Ephrata, Pa.*

Sugar Butter.—Take 2 cups of brown sugar, 1 cup of good sweet cream and 1½ teaspoonfuls of alum, to keep it from sugaring. Then boil till the right consistency.—*Sister K. Westrick, Belleville, Kans.*

Tomato Butter with Apples.—Steam ripe tomatoes and rub them through a sieve. Stew apples and treat them the same way. Thicken the tomatoes with the stewed apples and sweeten to taste.

Cook until quite thick. Spices may be added if desired.—*Sister Perry Broadwater, Lonaconing, Md.*

Honey Recipe.—Put ⅓ ounce of alum in 1½ pints of water and bring to a boil; then add **4 pounds of white sugar** and boil about 3 minutes. Strain while hot, and add a teaspoonful of the following: 5 drops of rose oil into 1 pint of alcohol (or a proportionate quantity of each). This makes about ½ gallon.—*Sister W. K. Conner, Bridgewater, Va.*

Homemade Honey.—Boil together for 3 minutes the following: Five pounds of white sugar, 1½ pints of water, and alum the size of a hickory nut. Strain through a white cloth, and when partly cool stir in 1 tablespoonful of rose water.—*Sister Minnie Barkdoll, Warrenville, Ill.*

Pineapple Honey.—Take 3 pounds of sugar and 1 pint of water boiled together until clear. Then add 1 pint of grated pineapple and boil seven minutes. It can be made of quinces or apples, and is excellent when fruit is ground through a food chopper.—*Sister Amy V. Furry, Johnsville, Md.*

Pineapple Honey.—Put the peeling and core of 1 pineapple into 2 cups of water. Let stand a few hours. Then bring to a boil and strain. Add 3 cups of sugar to 1 cup of pineapple. Boil again for ten minutes. Keep in a dark, cool place.—*Sister Cassie Martin, Bloom, Kans.*

Quince Honey.—Take 4 large or 6 small quinces and grind in a small grinder or food chopper. Put in a kettle 4 pints of sugar and 1 quart of water and boil a few minutes. Then put in the ground quince and boil 20 minutes. Put in jelly cups.—*Sister Bernice Ashmore, St. Peter, Minn.*

Quince Honey.—Take fully ripe, juicy quinces. Pare, halve, core and grate them. Weigh the grated fruit, and to the half pound take three cups of sugar and a cup of water. Boil the sugar and water until it spins a thread; add the grated quinces and continue boiling until thick as honey. Bottle and seal the honey while hot and it will keep indefinitely.—*Sister Margaret Fox, Sidney, Ind.*

Quince Honey.—Take 2 pints of sugar, 1 pint of water and 1 grated quince. If a bit of alum is put in it will not sugar so readily. Boil to a syrup.—*Sister Katie Moore Strickler, Eldora, Iowa.*

Seedless Blackberry Jam.—Run through a sieve 1 gallon of blackberries, add about 2 pounds of sugar, or enough to suit the taste, and boil to a thick jam. Then put in glass jars and seal.—*Sister Kate Moomaw, Versailles, Mo.*

Grape Jam.—Take 2 qts. of hulled grapes, 8 cups of sugar, and 1 lb. of seeded or seedless raisins. Cook 20 minutes. Stir in 1 cup of English walnut meats just before taking off.—*Sister Bernice Ashmore, St. Peter, Minn.*

Wild Red Plum Jam.—Take one gallon of plums, drop into a granite kettle, cover with cold water, add 1 tablespoonful of baking soda, set on the stove and let boil till the plums crack open. Then drain off all the water, take out the seeds and replace plums on the stove with a little water. Let boil five minutes, then add four pints of sugar and boil twenty minutes more. If you would prefer the plums whole, make a syrup of the sugar and drop the plums in without taking out the seeds. Let simmer till done, or the syrup will jell.—*Sister Catharine A. Walker, Lovejoy, Pa.*

Raspberry Jam.—Take equal parts of raspberries and sugar (white sugar preferred). Put a little water on the sugar and let come to a boil. Mash the berries well and put them in the syrup; let boil slowly until it jells, then put in glass jars and keep in a dry, cool place.—*Sister Maggie Bosserman, Carrington, N. Dak.*

Strawberry Jam.—Take 1 quart of granulated sugar and ½ pint of water. Let it boil, then add 2 quarts of mashed strawberries and let boil 30 minutes.—*Sister Emma Amick, Idaville, Ind.*

Sunshine Jam.—Take 1 pint of berries or any kind of fruit you wish, mash as fine as you can, then take 2 pints of granulated sugar, mix thoroughly and boil 5 minutes.—*Sister Emma Fisher, Baltic, Ohio.*

Crab Apple Jelly.—Take as many crab apples as wanted, put in a kettle, cover with water and boil until tender. Put in a colander or jelly bag, let stand and drain over night. Take 1 pint of sugar to 1 pint of juice and boil rapidly until it jells.—*Sister J. W. Brooks, Independence, Oregon.*

Crab Apple Jelly.—Quarter the apples, and allow sufficient water to cover them; cook till soft, and strain. To 1 quart of juice add the juice of 1 lemon. Take equal parts of sugar and juice and cook until it jells. Equal parts of apple and plum juice make a good jelly.—*Sister Mary E. Whitney, Kearney, Nebr.*

Cherry Jelly.—The Morello is the best cherry for jelly. Stone the fruit, put it into a stone jar in a kettle of water; cover the top of the jar with a plate and place on the stove, where the fruit will gradually heat through. When soft, pour it into small jelly bags and hang it up to drain out the juice; do not squeeze until no more jelly will run out, then press all remaining juice out by squeezing the bag, but use this juice for a second grade of jelly. Measure the juice, and to each pint allow a pound of granulated sugar. Do not cook more than 2 quarts of juice at one time; let the juice boil rapidly for 10 minutes. Have the sugar heating in the oven, but do not let it brown; skim the juice as it boils and at the end of the 10 minutes add the heated sugar. Stir until dissolved and let it boil for 10 minutes longer. After adding the sugar it may not require 10 minutes' boiling; if the fruit is in prime condition for jelly-making, it may jell at the first hard boiling. If it clings in drops from a spoon it is done. Have glasses heated and stand them on a folded cloth. Fill almost to overflowing and let get perfectly cold before covering them.—*Sister Emma R. Armey, Silver Lake, Ind.*

Currant Jelly.—Take any desired quantity of well-ripened currants, wash in cold water and mash fine. For best results in pressing out the juice, put about 1 pint at a time into a sack or cloth. Press well, so as to get all the juice, then add 1 pint of granulated sugar to each pint of juice. Put all together into a kettle and boil quickly for 15 or 20 minutes.—*Sister Lizzie F. Miller, Roanoke, Va.*

A Good Jelly.—When canning pears add a liberal quantity of water and stew a good while. Save the juice that is left over. Now take some crabapples, stew as for jelly, also stew several quinces; add all the juices together. Make as other jellies.—*Sister Sarah Early, Salem, Oregon.*

Loquat Jelly.—Pit the loquats and cover the pulp with water, cook until soft, and strain in a close sack. To 1 pint of juice take 1 pint of sugar. It is best tó make it in small quantities, as it gets clearer. Always cook in a granite saucepan, never use tin. Cook until a little tried in a saucer will' jell.—*Sister Barbara Kindig, Inglewood, Cal.*

Rhubarb Jelly.—Cut young rhubarb in short lengths, and allow 2 tablespoonfuls of water to 1 pint of the fruit; cook till soft, and strain. Combine with ⅓ currant juice, and use sugar in the ordinary proportion.—*Sister Mary E. Whitney, Kearney, Nebr.*

Pie Plant Jelly.—Wash the rhubarb and cut it into small pieces. To 2 gallons of rhubarb add 1 quart of water, boil until tender, drain through a cheese cloth; boil this juice down ½ after which add an equal quantity of sugar, then boil 10 minutes more. Dissolve 1 box of good gelatine and add to the jelly, then remove from the fire; let sit 10 minutes, strain and pour into jelly glasses, cover with paraffine wax when cool; keep in a dark place, not too damp.—*Sister Maggie Stambaugh, Carrington, N. Dak.*

Pineapple Jelly.—When canning pineapples, after removing the outer, rough peeling, punch out the eyes into a separate vessel, cover with water and cook slowly for 15 or 20 minutes. Then strain and can up and later use with currant juice or other fruit juices that jell easily to make jelly. By this method a nice lot of finely flavored jelly is obtained without robbing the canned pineapple of any of its juice. This juice may also be used with gelatine in making dainty dessert.—*Sister Blanche Lentz, Elgin, Ill.*

Rhubarb Jelly.—To 9 cups of rhubarb, take 9 cups of sugar, 3 oranges cut up fine and ½ cup of almonds. Crack the almonds and scald the goodies so you can remove the brown hull, and cut up fine. Put sugar on the rhubarb which has been cut up fine and let stand over night. Put all together in the morning and boil, strain and continue to cook like any other jelly until thick.—*Sister Stella Smith, Eldora, Iowa.*

Marmalade.—Take 2 gallons of fresh cider and boil down to 1 gallon. Then take 1 gallon of stewed apples and 1 quart of granulated sugar and put them into the boiling cider. Boil until it becomes very thick. Flavor with allspice or cinnamon.—*Sister Jas. Hatcher, Fairview, Oregon.*

Orange Marmalade.—Take equal parts of sour oranges and sugar. Grate the yellow rind from $\frac{1}{4}$ of the oranges, cut all the fruit in halves, pick out all the pulp and free it from seeds. Drain off all the juice you can and put it on to boil with the sugar. Let it come to a boil, skim and simmer for 15 minutes. Then put in the pulp and grated rind and boil 15 minutes longer.—*Sister Jas. F. Thomas, Inglewood, Cal.*

Orange Marmalade.—Take 6 oranges, 4 peeled and 2 with peeling. For every pound of fruit take 1 quart of cold water and let stand 24 hours, then set on stove and let boil for $\frac{1}{2}$ hour. Take off and weigh. For every pound of fruit add 1 pound of sugar; cook until done. Test by putting a little in a dish, and when cool it will be like jelly.—*Sister E. E. Aschenbrenner, Covina, Cal.*

Pear Marmalade.—Boil pears till soft, when cold rub the pulp through a sieve and boil it to a jelly, allowing 1 pound of sugar to 2 pounds of pears.—*Sister Amy V. Furry, Johnsville, Md.*

Corncob Molasses.—Take about a dozen corncobs (sweet corn preferred), and boil about $\frac{3}{4}$ hour in 3 pints of water. Take out cobs; strain, add a pound of good brown sugar to the juice and boil down enough to make a syrup. This is a very good substance for maple molasses, the cobs giving it this flavor.—*Sister Maggie Berkley Bail, Washington, Pa.*

To Preserve Cherries.—Carefully seed wax cherries. Take equal parts of cherries and sugar, and make a syrup with just enough water to dissolve sugar. Let syrup come to a boil, then put in fruit and boil slowly until the syrup is ropy and fruit well preserved.—*Sister Mary C. Cline, Stuarts Draft, Va.*

Peach Preserves.—After preparing the peaches for preserving, slice the fruit in thin slices or cut in small blocks as preferred. Then take 1½ pounds of the fruit to 1 pound of granulated sugar. I sugar the fruit over night; in the morning I take the syrup that has gathered on the fruit and boil that until it commences to thicken, then put the fruit in the syrup until it foams up well. Then they are ready to be put away until wanted for use.—*Sister Callie Beachley, Hagerstown, Md.*

Pear Preserves.—Boil the pears soft in water, then add as much sugar as fruit. Boil until the jelly thickens. I prefer the Kiefer pears for preserving.—*Sister Mary Shinham, Cearfoss, Md.*

Tomato Preserves.—To 7 pounds of tomatoes use 4 pounds of brown sugar, the juice of 1 lemon and about 2 dozen whole cloves. Cook as other preserves.—*Sister Florence Hays Kline, Broadway, Va.*

Watermelon Preserves.—Pare off the green rind, cut the melon or white rind into pieces and weigh them. Cook in clear water until partly transparent, but not until likely to break. Take out the melon in a dish; there will be nearly enough juice that drains from the melon; if not, add a little water. With the juice add sugar to the amount of ½ pound to 1 pound of fruit as it weighed when raw. When the sugar is well dissolved, put in the melon and cook until even and clear. Flavor as desired, and can.—*Sister Wm. Lichty, Darlow, N. Dak.*

Watermelon Preserves (or Butter).—Grate white part of melon rind on the horse-radish grater. Then take same amount of sugar and boil till done. Stir frequently or it will settle and burn.

Flavor with lemon or wintergreen.—*Sister L. Clanin, Hicksville, Wash.*

To Can Fruit.—After the jars are cleaned, pour boiling water from the tea-kettle inside and out at the same time, to scald them thoroughly, then scald again inside with boiling water; have the lid filled with boiling water and sitting on the stove while filling the jar with boiling fruit; then empty the water and put the lid on quickly. If the lid does not fit down smoothly, put on another rubber, as the fruit is of more value than the extra rubber.—*Sister Almeda Caskey, Corning, Iowa.*

To Can Fruit in Self-Sealers.—Have the can lids and ribbons perfectly clean; have a little syrup in the kettle made of sugar and water; drop enough fruit in to fill 1 can; let boil until cooked through. Skim off the froth and put into the can. Clean the top of the can with a cloth that has not been used for dishwashing. Let the juice cover fruit well, but not come near the top of the can. Put lid on tight and press down with the handle of a case knife, turn jar over to see if the juice will run out, if it does, turn lid a little tighter and press again with the knife. If it still runs out, remove the lid, wipe clean and ascertain the cause, perhaps can was too full or steam wanted to get out, or there may be a piece of glass hindering the lid which can be knocked off; put lid on again, press down, and when partly cool turn upside down until cold, then put in a dark cool place. Aluminum lids are soft and will not bear turning as tight as other lids.—*Sister Sarah C. Goughnour, Canton, Ohio.*

To Can Green Beans.—Prepare ready to cook 1 gallon of green beans, and boil in clear water until tender. Add 1 teacupful of good sour vinegar, and boil a few minutes, then can same as fruit. To prepare them for the table: About 3 hours before meal-time put on the stove to boil a good-sized piece of bacon, enough to season beans well; boil 1 hour. Open a can of beans, pour off all the liquor and put beans in the kettle with meat and enough water to cover. Salt and pepper to taste.—*Sister Harriet E. Menear, Postoak, Texas.*

Canned Beans.—String and cut beans as for cooking. Boil till nearly soft. Then put in jars and pour over boiling salt water, and seal.—*Sister W. G. Lint, Meyersdale, Pa.*

Canned Baked Apples.—Cut apples in halves and core, place in baking pan, sweeten and season to taste. Put enough water on them to make a syrup to cover them when placed in jars. Bake until done and seal while hot.—*Sister Lottie Miller, South English, Iowa.*

To Can Beef.—Take fresh beef that has not been frozen or washed in water and cut it off the bones. Then take half gallon fruit jars that are fresh and clean, with good lids and rubbers (old rubbers will do). Cut the meat into strips small enough to put into these jars, and salt and pepper them enough to season. Fill the jars with meat, put on rubbers and lids, and screw part way down. Leave the lids loose enough, so the steam can escape. Put the boiler on the stove with the bottom covered inside with boards. Set the jars in, fill the boiler with cold water until it reaches nearly to the tops of the cans. Bring to a boil and continue hard boiling for four hours. If the water boils away, refill with boiling water. When the time is up, take out the jars, wipe clean, put on new rubbers and screw the lids down tight. Place in a cool cellar and it will keep all summer. To prepare it for the table, take the meat out of the jars and put it in a little water and heat through. It is then ready to eat. It is also good cold.—*Sister Sovilla Schwab, Grundy Center, Iowa.*—Use seasoning in the proportion of 4 tablespoonfuls of salt, 2 of sugar and 1 of pepper. To tell when the meat is done, remove the top from a can and try with a fork. When done remove fire or remove boiler from stove with the can in it and let cool a little to prevent jars from burning when taken out of the water. In preparing for the table make a gravy of the broth.—*Sister Carrie Martin, Mankato, Kans.*

Canned Cabbage.—Cut the cabbage into as large pieces as can be put into the jars, cook in salty water till tender, put in jars, stand the jars top down and let all the water drain out; then fill the jars with boiling vinegar, containing spices (cloves are best), and sweetened to suit the taste. Seal while hot. It is then ready for the table at any time.—*Sister L. V. Forehand, Gerster, Mo.*

To Can Cabbage.—Cut the cabbage very fine on the slaw cutter, and steam quickly with ½ pint of water and 1 tablespoonful of salt. When tender, put in glass cans. Let the cabbage contain as little of the water as possible. Seal up tight and it will keep fresh until late in the winter. To prepare it for the table: Drain all the water from the cabbage that has been contained in canning, and put over to heat. Make a dressing with 1 teaspoonful of flour, 1 tablespoonful of sugar, 4 tablespoonfuls of rich cream, ½ cup of vinegar and a dash of pepper, and it is ready to serve.—*Sister Eliza A. Wenger, Longglade, Va.*

Canned Corn.—Gather the corn early, the same day it is to be used, husk, silk, and cut from the cob carefully. Use corn not too old, cut the corn in a shallow pan; if the pan is held on the lap, put a board under it to prevent heat from the body reaching the corn. Fill quart or half-gallon jars with the corn, putting in a little at a time, and pressing it firmly with some blunt instrument. As soon as it can be reached with the fingers press down until the can is very full. Wipe the can, put on new rubbers, screw cover as tight as you can with thumb and fingers; it must not be too tight, as the air that accumulates must escape. Fill only as many cans as your boiler or kettle will hold, wrap each can in a cloth to prevent breaking; place the cans in kettle either horizontally or upright, cover entirely with cold water, place cover on kettle; bring to a boil and boil steadily 3 hours; if half-gallon jars, boil 4 hours; keep the water boiling steadily and the jars well covered with water; replenish with hot water as the water evaporates. When done, let the fire go out or remove from the stove; leave the cans in the water till cool enough to bear the hands in it, then with a can screw, screw the covers on as tight as possible. Set the cans in a cool place, tighten at night and in the morning. Wrap in dark papers and put in a cool, dark, airy place.—*Sister Ella Stutsman, Clayton, Ind.*

Canned Cherries.—Prepare the cherries by picking off the stems; wash them well, sort, and remove the seeds with the thumb and finger so as not to mash them as much as by using the cherry seeder. To 2½ cups of seeded cherries take ¾ cup of sugar. Let them come to a boil, and skim. This will fill 1 quart can. Use no water only the juice of the cherries and the sugar. Can in glass cans, seal with sealing wax. It is best not to cook more cherries at one time than enough to fill 2 quart cans. If the juice will not all go in the cans, save it till you have enough to fill a can or bottle. Strain it, then let come to a boil, skim, and can.—*Sister Nancy Martin, Covington, Ohio.*

To Can Corn.—Take 10 cups of corn, 1 cup of sugar and ½ cup of salt. Mix and let stand over night; then boil 15 minutes and can while boiling hot.—*Sister Mollie Zarger, Franklin Grove, Ill.*

To Can Corn.—Take 12 cups of corn, 1 cup of sugar and 1 cup of salt. Let stand one hour. Boil 5 minutes, press lightly in glass jars and seal. This corn will form its own juice.—*Sister L. E. Kindig, Holmesville, Nebr.*

To Can Corn.—To 9 pints of corn take 1 pint of salt, 1 pint of sugar, and 1 pint of water. Cook till done, stirring often. Do not put in any more water while cooking. Put in jars, seal tight, and when cool wrap in paper and put in a cool, dark place. To prepare it for the table take the corn from the can, drain off the brine, soak in 1 gallon of water three or four hours, or over night, drain and cook a few minutes, seasoning with butter and pepper and a little sugar.—*Sister R. D. Kirkendall, Niotaze, Kans.*

To Can Corn without Acid.—After cutting corn from the cob, put it into a granite sauce kettle, with enough water to cover, and boil as for table. When nearly done, add ¾ pint of salt for every 8 pints of corn and boil 10 minutes longer. Can in glass cans. Be sure to have brine enough in each can to cover corn; if this is neglected the corn will spoil. To prepare it for the table: Take the corn from the can, drain off the brine and cover to about 2 inches with water. Boil 10 minutes and drain again; then add 1 pint of sweet milk, 1 tablespoonful of sugar, and season with butter and pepper.—*Sister D. P. Miller, Emma, Ind.*

Canned Dandelion.—Boil dandelion until tender. While hot pack in a can, disregarding the water. Fill the can with boiling vinegar, and seal the same as fruit.—*Sister Catharine Wampler, Dayton, Va.*

Canned Grapes.—Wash your grapes and fill your jars. Stand the jars in a warm place. I set mine on the back of the range, where they gradually get quite hot and form some juices of their own. Make a syrup in the proportion of 2 cups of sugar to 1 quart of water. Let boil and pour over the grapes. Have good lids and new rubbers. Seal and pack away as you do your fruit. They are like fresh grapes and are fine for the sick.—*Sister C. S. Colony, York, N. Dak.*

To Can Grapes So They Will Not Harden.—To every gallon of grapes add 1 pint of sugar. Boil until the seed and pulp have separated; the seed will settle to the bottom of the kettle. Seal up in glass jars and keep in a cool dark place.—*Sister Eliza A. Wenger, Long Glade, Va.*

Canned Peaches.—Select fine freestone peaches, wash, pare, cut in two and stone them, taking care not to break the fruit. See that the peaches are not over-ripe. Put in a kettle 1 quart of cold water and 1 cup of sugar; put in this 2 quarts of the cut peaches; bring slowly to a boil. As soon as they are easily pierced with a fork, put them in the can, fill up with the juice, and seal.—*Sister Mary Gibbel, Inavale, Nebr.*

Excellent Canned Peaches.—Prepare peaches as usual. Put on in water and boil until about half done. Have ready another kettle containing a pint of water and ½ cup of sugar. Have this boiling. Dip the half-cooked fruit into this, let boil through and put in jars and seal. This par boiling rids the fruit of the red—next the seed; also the bitter taste. Peaches canned this way are far superior to those canned in the ordinary way.—*Sister Susie M. Hout, Sharpsburg, Md.*

Canned Plums.—To every pound of plums allow ¼ pound of sugar. Put the sugar and plums alternately into the preserving kettle, first pricking the plums to prevent their breaking. Then put them over a moderate fire and let come to a boil. Skim and pour at once into jars, running a silver spoon handle around the inside of the jar to break the air bubbles. Cover and screw down the tops. —*Sister Pearle F. Benner, Duncansville, Pa.*

Canned Plums.—Have ready plenty of boiling water. Put plums into earthen or porcelain vessels. Pour over boiling water, set on the back of the stove or hearth and cover. Let stand twenty minutes; then pour off the water and cover again with boiling water. Let stand twenty minutes longer. Have ready a vessel with syrup, allowing a cup of sugar to a quart of fruit, or more sugar if desired very sweet. Dip the plums into jars, being careful to drain the water from them. Pour over the boiling syrup and seal. Plums canned this way will keep without bursting and breaking the fruit, and will be of excellent flavor, all the undesirable qualities being taken from them.—*Sister Susie M. Hout, Sharpsburg, Md.*

Canned Pineapple.—Take 6 pineapples, peel and slice into quite thin slices, add 4 cups of sugar and let stand over night. In the morning, put on and boil slowly for one hour, then can in glass jars. You can use half rhubarb if you wish. In this case, you should cook the rhubarb separate and, when done, add it to the cooked pineapple and can.—*Sister Jennie Sheeler, Kingsley, Iowa.*

Canned Pineapple.—Take nice sound fruit—large pineapples pay better than small ones—cut in thin slices and pare them. Be sure to get out all the little specks of skin. After paring cut in pieces and grind through the meat grinder, or, chip it in small pieces, or, grate fine. Have your cans clean and well heated. Use one cup of sugar to every quart of fruit, cook as long as you do any other kind of fruit, fill cans, and seal.—*Sister D. L. Miller, Mt. Morris, Ill.*

When preparing pineapple for canning wash the hands frequently in soda water and they will not get sore.—*Sister Mollie Zarger, Franklin Grove, Ill.*

To Can Raspberries.—Carefully clean the raspberries and wash. To 1 quart of berries add a large tablespoonful of sugar and enough hot water nearly to cover them. Let them come to a boil, fill the can and seal at once.—*Sister Mollie Conway, Bradford, Ohio.*

To Can Raspberries and Grapes.—Have the fruit picked over, washed, and drained. Have the teakettle full of fresh water boiling. Have a granite pan, as wide as the height of the jar, standing on the stove, with hot water in. Roll the jar in this till very hot, then stand upright in the water. Lay the jar cap and rubber ring in the pan until wanted. Now fill the jar one-fourth full of berries, using a wide-necked funnel; pour boiling water from the teakettle to the level of the berries. Make the jar half full of berries, and pour boiling water to their level. Shake down the berries as you go. Then make it three-fourths full, and pour again. Lastly fill the jar, and pour until the water overflows freely. With a fork lift the rubber ring and cap, adjust quickly. Lift out on a wet cloth or a board and finish the screwing-up process. In canning this way, have everything as hot as possible. You will be pleased with the result.—*Sister Adaline H. Beery, Elgin, Ill.*

To Can Rhubarb without Cooking.—Wash but do not remove the skin. Cut in rather small pieces, and fill a clean glass jar, shaking down several times during the operation. Press in the top pieces with the fingers. Fill with freshly-drawn cold water, allowing it to overflow till the air-bubbles have disappeared. Lift the rubber and cap out of clean cold water. Screw up tightly and set away in the cellar at once.—*Sister Judith Beery, Elgin, Ill.*

Canning Sauerkraut.—Boil kraut till done, put in jars, press down solid, and seal while hot. Season when opened.—*Sister D. F. Kelley, Homeworth, Ohio.*

To Make Sauerkraut.—Cut cabbage in halves or quarters, according to size. Then wash it and let it drain; cut with kraut cutter or knife. Have ready the vessel: put 4 gallons of cut cabbage in the vessel, sprinkle over 1 tablespoonful of salt; then stamp with a kraut stamper. Repeat this until the amount of kraut desired is in the vessel; then put clean cabbage leaves over the top; have a lid to fit the vessel, then put on a heavy press and let it ferment.—*Sister Lizzie Kimmel, Elklick, Pa.*

Canned Strawberries.—Take 4 pints of strawberries, and 1 pint of sugar; let them come to a boil, skim and can while hot. Let stand a few days, then wrap paper around the can and keep as dark as possible.—*Sister Nancy Martin, Covington, Ohio.*

Canned Strawberries.—Take 1 cupful of granulated sugar with enough water to dissolve it. Let it come to a boil, then add 3 pints of strawberries. Boil 2 minutes, then add 1 teaspoonful of cornstarch dissolved in water. This will fill a 1-quart jar. If there is any juice left, use it to dissolve the sugar for the next 3 pints of berries, instead of adding water.—*Sister Emma Amick, Idaville, Ind.*

To Dry Green Pod Beans.—Gather the beans in the evening, and string them. In the morning wash them, and boil them about twenty minutes, or until well heated through. Then remove from the fire, drain all the water off, and dry in the sun. When cooked with meat they are nearly as good as fresh green beans.—*Sister Mary E. Ritter, Crescent, Okla.*

To Salt Sweet Corn.—Boil the corn till heated through, cut if off the cob and let get cold; to 7 cups of corn add 1 cup of salt; mix well together and pack in an earthen jar; put cloth and weight on top. Freshen when used.—*Sister Flora Doughty, Eldora, Iowa.*

Mock Mince.—Pare green tomatoes and when you have 2 gallons, slice and boil them in salt water. When done drain and add 1 quart of strong vinegar, 1 quart of water, 4 pounds of raisins,

2 pounds of English currants, which were previously soaked in water or boiled a little, if not seeded ones, 4 pounds of light brown sugar and cinnamon to suit the taste. Boil all together 10 minutes and can. Will keep same as fruit.—*Sister S. E. Fausnight, Hartville, Ohio.*

ICE CREAM AND DRINKS

In making ice cream, the finer the ice is broken the sooner the cream will freeze. Use salt—"Diamond C" rock salt is best—in the proportion of three pints to ten quarts of fine ice. This is sufficient to freeze one gallon of cream. When the cream is frozen remove the beater, if a regulation freezer has been used, and pack the cream into a compact mass. If it is to stand for several hours—and it is better if it stands awhile—repack with fresh ice and salt and cover with a heavy carpet or blanket. If ice is scarce, use many thicknesses of newspaper in repacking, wrapping them closely about the can. When through with the freezer, drain the water from the salt dry and use again. The ice may easily be reduced to proper fineness by placing the large pieces in a sack—a good gunny sack will do—and pounding with a large hammer or the side of an ax.

Ice Cream.—To make 1 gallon, let 1 quart of milk come to a boil, and thicken with cornstarch, Let cool, then add 1 quart of milk, 1 quart of cream, 2 eggs well beaten, and 1 pound of sugar. Favor to taste.—*Sister Malinda S. Geib, Mastersonville, Pa.*

Ice Cream.—Take 3 pints of milk, 1 pound of granulated sugar, 3 eggs and 1 quart of cream. Boil milk, sugar and eggs together until the custard thickens and set aside to cool. When cold, flavor with vanilla and lemon mixed. Do not add the flavoring until cream is about half frozen, as it retains its strength better; but if chocolate is used, boil it in the milk.—*Sister Rachel Myers, Ore Hill, Pa.*

Ice Cream.—To 1 quart of milk just coming to a boil add 2 tablespoonfuls of dissolved cornstarch. Let it boil 20 minutes, then strain and put in a freezer. When cool, add 1 quart of cream and 2 teaspoonfuls of flavoring and freeze.—*Sister A. W. Hawbaker, Kenmare, N. Dak.*

Ice Cream.—Mix thoroughly 1½ pints of sugar with ⅔ pint of flour. Add a little cold milk and 6 eggs beaten very light; stir the whole together. Have 1 quart of sweet milk in a double boiler, let come to the boiling heat, and stir in the above mixture, stirring constantly till it thickens. Strain and add 2 quarts of cream, 1½ quarts of sweet milk and 1 teaspoonful of vanilla or lemon. Freeze, and let it stand 4 or 5 hours before using.—*Sister Sue Sisler, Dallas Center, Iowa.*

Ice Cream.—Take 6 or 8 eggs, 2 cups of sugar, ½ teaspoonful of any flavoring liked. Beat well together, then add 1 gallon of rich milk and freeze hard.—*Sister Sarah A. Taylor, Pierson, Iowa,*

Ice Cream.—Take 1½ quarts of sweet imlk, 2 quarts of sweet cream, 1½ cups of sugar, 3 eggs and scant teaspoonful of salt. Heat to a scald 1 pint of the cream with the sugar and yolks of eggs. Cool and flavor to taste. Stir in whites of eggs beaten to a stiff froth just before freezing, and add the milk. If a richer cream is desired we leave out all or a part of the milk, just to suit the taste of the one making it. I like a rich cream.—*Sister Ida Salsbury, Barron, Wis.*

Economical Ice Cream.—Take 3 quarts of milk, 3 pints of cream, 2 eggs, 2 cups of sugar, 2 tablespoonfuls of flour, not cornstarch. Beat the eggs and add 1 quart of milk. Cook in double boiler; when hot, add the sugar and flour well mixed. Cook 5 minutes, stirring often so it will be smooth; cool, add the remainder of the milk and cream, flavor to taste and freeze. This will make 6 quarts when frozen, and will not melt readily.—*Sister Ella Stutsman, Clayton, Ohio.*

Frozen Fruit.—Take 1 quart of peaches or apricots, 1 pint of sugar, 1½ pints of water, 1 tablespoonful of gelatin, the juice of 1 lemon, and the whites of 2 eggs. Put the fruit through a sieve. Dissolve the gelatin in a small amount of water. Have the remainder of the water boiling and pour over the gelatin; add sugar, stir and let come to the boiling point. Cool, add the fruit, lemon juice, and ½ teaspoonful each of vanilla and lemon extract, if preferred.

Put into a freezer. When just beginning to thicken, add the two beaten whites of eggs. Churn until done. Remove the flyers from the freezer and pack the fruit. In two or three hours, if well packed, it will be nice and firm, and ready to serve.—*Sister J. P. Holsinger, Mount Morris, Ill.*

Orange Cream.—Take 1 quart of milk, 1 pint of cream, 2 cups of sugar and 4 oranges. Grate rind and squeeze juice of oranges—putting sugar with them and let stand one hour; add milk and cream and freeze in the usual way.—*Sister Jos. H. Johnson, Royersford, Pa.*

Orange Ice.—Take the juice of 6 oranges, 1 quart of water, 1 tablespoonful of good gelatine, 1 pint of sugar, and the whites of 3 eggs. Soak the gelatine in ¼ of the water for 5 minutes; boil the remainder of the water and add the gelatine, sugar, and strained juice. Set aside to cool, and when very cold add the whites of the eggs beaten stiff. Turn in freezer and freeze in usual manner.— *Sister F. O. Burket, Topeka, Kans.*

Peach Ice Cream.—Take 3 pints of cream, 3 pints of milk, 6 eggs, 3½ cups of sugar, 2 heaping tablespoonfuls of cornstarch, 2 teaspoonfuls of vanilla and 1 can of peaches. Cook cornstarch, milk and the yolks of the eggs together. Let cool, then add the cream, peaches and whites of the eggs, and freeze.—*Sister Zura L. Peck, Meyersdale, Pa.*

Tutti Frutti Ice Cream.—To 2 quarts of rich cream add 1 pound of pulverized sugar and 4 eggs well beaten; mix together well, then place on the fire, stirring constantly until brought to the boiling point. Remove immediately and continue to stir until cold. Add vanilla to taste, place in a freezer and when about half frozen mix thoroughly into it 1 pound of preserved fruits in equal parts of peaches, cherries, pineapple, orange, banana, etc. All these fruits are to be cut into small pieces and mixed well with the frozen cream. If you desire to mold this cream, sprinkle with a little carmine dissolved in a little water with 2 drops of spirits of ammonia. Mix a color in this, so it will be in veins like marble.—*Sister Rose E. Smith, Dunlap, Kans.*

Lemon Sherbet.—Take the juice of 6 lemons, 5 pints of water, 3 teacupfuls of sugar. Squeeze the lemons and strain. Add sugar and water, and freeze. When frozen to mushy ice, add the well-beaten whites of 4 eggs, and finish freezing.—*Sister Emily Shirky, Rockingham, Mo.*

Pineapple Sherbet.—For 1 gallon of sherbet grate 2 pineapples, add the juice of 1 lemon. Sweeten with 1½ pints of sugar and add sufficient water to make a gallon. Leave stand in freezer until thoroughly chilled, then turn freezer every few minutes. When about frozen, remove stirrer from can and leave stand for 1 hour. Serve in sherbet glasses.—*Sister J. J. Keim, Elklick, Pa.*

Chocolate.—Take 1 pint of water, let come to a boil, then stir in ¾ cup of grated chocolate. Let boil 2 or 3 minutes, remove from the stove, and add 2 quarts of fresh milk, and sugar to suit the taste. Put back on the stove, let get scalding hot, but be careful not to let it boil, as boiling spoils it. This will make about 8 cups.—*Sister Jennie A. Crofford, Martinsburg, Pa.*

To Make Chocolate.—Take the amount of shaved or grated chocolate, an equal amount of sugar, and as much flour as will lie on a nickel for each cup to be made. Mix well. Now take equal amounts of water and rich milk and put the above-mentioned ingredients in it and boil, stirring continuously. In the countries where the chocolate comes from they use a pinch of ground cinnamon to the chocolate, and then boil. Enough must be used to give it a cinnamon flavor. It will probably suit the taste of our readers better if, when the drink is made, it is slightly flavored with extract of vanilla, added just after the pot is taken from the fire. It should be stirred in. The trick of putting the flour in should not be forgotten. Its use is in holding the chocolate in suspension.—*Sister Bessie Royer Bates, Elgin, Ill.*

Buttermilk Coffee.—Boil together 1 quart of buttermilk and 1 pint of sweet milk. Make a thin batter, using 1 egg, 3 tablespoonfuls of flour, and sweet milk. Add to the boiling milk, sweeten, and serve as coffee.—*Sister Sarah A. Crowl, Nappanee, Ind.*

Hygienic Coffee.—Take good clean wheat, wash and dry it and put it in a large dripping pan in a hot oven; roast until a golden brown, stirring often. Then to every quart of wheat add 1 table-spoonful of butter and 2 tablespoonfuls of molasses and finish roasting to a nice brown, but do not burn. It must be watched closely as it will burn easily when the butter and molasses are added. Do not grind but use the whole grain; the boiling will burst the grain and thus the nutriment will be obtained and the flavor will be better and the coffee clearer than if ground. Like other hygienic coffee, the longer the boiling the better.—*Sister Amanda Witmore, Mc-Pherson, Kans.*

Making Coffee.—No person can make a cup of good coffee out of an inferior grade of the berry. The best is a mixture of ½ Mocha and Java, half and half, ground together. The coffeepot must be rinsed clean, and a cup of ground coffee put in it, then add either 6 or 8 cups of water that has been freshly boiled. Then set where it is as near the boiling point as possible without actually boiling. It should remain on the stove, steeping, for 20 minutes, and an hour will not hurt it. The secret of making good coffee is not allowing it to boil. Use no so-called extract of coffee, which is nothing but burned sugar and does nothing but color the decoction. To make *cafe au lait,* take half as much strong coffee as may be needed and pour in the pot as much more rich, sweet milk. Let this just come to the boil and serve.—*Sister Bessie Royer Bates, Elgin, Ill.*

Lemonade.—Take 2 lemons, 4 tablespoonfuls of sugar, and 2 quarts of water. If you have no lemon squeezer, slice the lemons in round slices, put the sugar on and press out the juice with a potato masher.—*Sister Mary Wampler, Dayton, Va.*

Lemonade.—For 1 quart of lemonade take 2 lemons. Wash the lemon, slice fine into a pitcher, add 2 large tablespoonfuls of sugar, stirring in with the lemon well before putting in the water. Fill up with cold water to make 1 quart.—*Sister Annie Lint, Quinter, Kans.*

Lemonade Syrup.—Take 2 pounds of granulated sugar, 1 ounce of citric acid, and 1½ pints of boiling water. Stir until thoroughly dissolved. Add sixty drops of oil of lemon. Bottle. For a drink put about 3 tablespoonfuls in a tumbler and fill up with fresh water. This is cheaper than lemons and a very good substitute.—*Sister Judith Beery, Elgin, Ill.*

Cream Mead.—Take 3 pounds of soft sugar dissolved in 1 quart of water, whites of 3 eggs beaten stiff, 1½ ounces of tartaric acid, dissolved in ¾ of a pint of water, and flavor with oil of lemon. —*Sister Jennie Brown, Whitewater, Ind.*

Raspberry Vinegar.—Mash 1 pound of berries and put them into 1 quart of vinegar. Put the same amount of berries into this same vinegar for 3 successive mornings, then drain through a cloth and add 1 pound of sugar to every pint of the strained juice. Let simmer and skim; when cold, bottle. Can be used any time adulterated with ⅔ water.—*Sister Annie R. Stoner, Union Bridge, Md.*

A Refreshing Drink.—Take 3 tablespoonfuls of root beer; add 1 lemon sliced and sugar to suit the taste. Place in a gallon jar, add a large lump of ice and fill the jar with water.—*Sister Willoughby Felker, Leaf River, Ill.*

Soda Water.—Take 2 ounces of tartaric acid, the juice of 1 lemon, 2 pounds of white sugar, 3 pints of water; boil together 5 minutes. When nearly cold, add, after beating together, the whites of 3 eggs, ½ cup of flour made smooth with a little water, and 1 ounce of wintergreen essence. Mix well, put in glass jars or pint bottles and keep in a cool place. For a drink, take 2 tablespoonfuls of the syrup to ⅔ tumbler of cold water, and ¼ teaspoonful of soda. Stir until creamy with foam. This is very refreshing in hot weather.—*Sister Adaline Hohf Beery, Elgin, Ill.*

To Boil Water for Drinking.—Rinse out the teakettle clean; fill with freshly-drawn water. Bring to a boil quickly, and as soon as it reaches the boiling point, pour out into cups and serve. This is more palatable than water that has been boiling a long time.— *Sister Adaline H. Beery, Elgin, Ill.*

Unfermented Wine.—Place twenty pounds of stemmed and washed grapes into a four-gallon jar, scald with six quarts of boiling water, stir thoroughly and let stand until cool. Strain through a jelly bag, bring to a boil, sweeten to suit taste and can in mason jars.—*Sister Nora E. Petry, Westminster, Md.*

In the making of candy as well as most other products of the kitchen, book knowledge will hardly insure success unless coupled with more or less actual experience. If the materials used in candy are pure, it possesses no little food value; the evils resulting from its use may usually be traced to overeating or eating at ill-timed hours. If we are to be safe on the point of purity and wholesomeness in the candy we eat it is best to know the nature of all ingredients used and then learn to put them together successfully for ourselves.

Candy.—Beat the white of one egg until stiff, add 2 table-spoonfuls of water and mix in powdered sugar until enough to knead like dough. Use this to make different kinds of candy. Dip balls of it in chocolate, put nuts in it or sprinkle shredded cocoanut through it.—*Sister Orvilla C. Ogle, Adams, Nebr.*

Caramel Candy.—Take one pound of glucose, 2 pounds of sugar, and 1 quart of milk. Boil until thick, then add 1 more quart of milk and ¼ pound of butter, and boil until it hardens in water. Then put in chopped nuts and pour into a buttered pan. Stir all the time while cooking.—*Sister Mary C. Beard Eshelman, Elgin, Ill.*

Cocoanut Candy.—Take 2 cups of granulated sugar, ½ cup of water. Boil 6 minutes and add 1 grated cocoanut. As soon as the sugar is soft, spread on white greased papers, and when cold cut in squares.—*Sister S. S. Blough, Pittsburg, Pa.*

Cream Candy.—Take ½ pound of glucose and 2½ pounds of sugar. Moisten the sugar with water, then add ½ pint of milk. Do not stir while boiling. When it has boiled enough to make a stiff taffy, set the cooking vessel in cold water and beat until it is creamy; then flavor to taste.—*Sister Mary C. Beard Eshelman, Elgin, Ill.*

Christmas Candy Loaf.—Take 2 pounds of glucose, 4 pounds of granulated sugar and 1 cup of boiling water. Boil until it will form a soft ball when dipped in cold water. Beat until cool enough to stir in beaten whites of four eggs, 2 or 3 teaspoonfuls of vanilla and 1 pound of shelled almonds. If properly stirred and then placed in a deep custard tin it can be sliced off like cake. Should be made several days before wanted.—*Sister Lauren T. Miller, Elgin, Ill.*

Cream Candy.—Take 1 pound of confectioner's sugar, 1 tablespoonful of cream, the white of 1 egg, and 1 teaspoonful of vanilla. Beat egg, add cream and vanilla, and beat in sugar until you cannot beat. Then mix like pie dough. Shape with the hand and put nuts on for nut candy; for chocolate candy dip in melted chocolate; for cocoanut candy mix in cocoanut.—*Sister Emma H. Snyder, Royersford, Pa.*

Cream Candy.—Take 4 cups of sugar, 2 cups of water, ¾ cups of vinegar, 1 cup of sweet cream, a piece of butter the size of an egg, 2 teaspoonfuls of vanilla and a pinch of soda. Boil until it hardens when dropped in cold water. Pour into buttered pans to cool, and when cool pull until white.—*Sister Nellie Hostetler, South English, Iowa.*

Cream Candy.—Take 2 cups of sugar, ⅔ cup of water and a pinch of cream of tartar; boil till it hardens when dropped into cold water. Set pan into a pan of hot water to cool. When cool enough to bear fingers in it, stir briskly till it leaves the pen. Put on kneading board and knead thoroughly with a knife. Put into molds. Colorings and flavorings may be used as desired.—*Sister Emma Carstensen, Girard, Ill.*

Divinity Candy.—Take 3 cups of granulated sugar, ½ cup of molasses (table syrup) and ½ cup of water. Mix and boil until it hardens in cold water. Stir till cooled a little, then pour over the beaten whites of two eggs, beat hard till thick, then pour on platter. Nuts or cocoanut may be used, if desired.—*Sister Mollie Zarger, Franklin Grove, Ill.*

Divinity Candy.—Take 2 cups of sugar, ½ cup of syrup (lily white or any good corn syrup), ¼ cup of water, and ½ cup of finely chopped nuts. Boil the sugar, syrup and water until it hairs, when dropped from the spoon. Then stir it into the beaten whites of two eggs. Flavor with 1 teaspoonful of vanilla and add the nuts. When getting stiff, pour into buttered pans and cut into squares before cold.—*Sister Katie E. Keller, Enterprise, Mont.*—Chopped figs or raisins may be used instead of the nuts or in addition to them.—*Sister J. E. Peck, Reserve, Kans.*

Marshmallow Candy.—Part One: Dissolve 1 box of gelatine in 12 tablespoonfuls of cold water. Part Two: Take 4 cups of granulated sugar and 12 tablespoonfuls of boiling water; boil until it threads. Pour part two into part one and beat. Beat for 15 minutes with Dover egg-beater, flavor and then beat 20 minutes with a flat beater. When it gets too stiff to beat any more, pour out on a plate which has been lined with pulverized sugar, then turn it over onto the bread board which has been covered with pulverized sugar. Pat and knead slightly then flatten out and cut in squares.—*Sister Thomas Jordan, Lordsburg, Cal.*

Real Marshmallows.—Soak ½ pound of gum Arabic in a pint of water. When dissolved, add 1 pound of powdered sugar. Stir in a double boiler. When thick and white try in water. If it is soft and not in hard lumps, then stir in gradually the whites of 2 eggs. Pour in cornstarch molds.—*Sister Maude Fahrney Flora, Twin Falls, Idaho.*

Molasses Candy.—Take 1 cup of molasses, 2 cups of sugar, 1 tablespoonful of vinegar, and a lump of butter the size of an egg. Flavor with vanilla. Boil 10 minutes; then cool it enough to pull. —*Sister Susie Peters, Emporia, Kans.*

Sea Foam Candy.—Put in a kettle 2 cups of sugar with ½ cup of water, and stir in the beaten white of 1 egg. Stir constantly until it boils enough to thread slightly. Take from the stove, and beat briskly until cool. Pour on a buttered plate and cut in squares. —*Sister Ada P. Huffman, Churchville, Va.*

Plain Homemade Candy.—Take 2 cups of light brown sugar, 1 cup of sweet cream, and as much cream of tartar as will lie on a nickel. Boil all together, stirring constantly, until it hardens when a few drops are tried in cold water. Flavor, remove the kettle from the fire and continue stirring until somewhat cool. Pour it out on a buttered plate or pan and when it begins to harden, with a buttered knife cut into squares or other figures. For chocolate candy add 2 tablespoonfuls of grated chocolate to the above. To make cocoanut candy add cocoanut to the above after removing from the fire, or add 1 cup of finely-chopped nut meats and you will have nut candy. —*Sister Rachel Dyck, Moundridge, Kans.*

Sea Foam Candy.—Put 3 cups of light brown sugar, 1 cup of water and 1 tablespoonful of vinegar in a saucepan. Heat it slowly until it boils, stirring it only until the sugar dissolves; then boil till it hardens in cold water. Take from the fire and when it stops bubbling pour in slowly the stiffly beaten whites of two eggs. Keep beating until it will hold its shape, then add a teaspoon of vanilla and a cup of pecan, walnut or hickory nut meats and drop in rough piles on buttered paper.—*Sister Lina Riddlesbarger, Belleville, Kans.*

Vinegar Candy.—Take 2 cups of sugar, ½ cup of vinegar and a piece of butter the size of an egg. Boil 20 minutes or till it hardens in water; then pour into greased plates to cool. Flavor, but do not pull.—*Sister Susie Peters, Emporia, Kans.*

Caramels (Mexican).—Put 1 cup of granulated sugar into a clean, iron skillet and stir constantly over a slow fire until sugar is melted. Then add 1 cup of rich milk or cream and stir until sugar is dissolved. Add next 1 cup each of granulated sugar and light brown sugar and boil steadily until the mixture forms a soft ball when tested in cold water. Take from the fire and add 1 cup of coarsely-chopped nuts, stir to creamy consistency and pour into a buttered dish.—*Sister J. F. Thomas, Inglewood, Cal.*

Chocolate Caramels.—Take 2 cups of brown sugar, 1 cup of molasses, 1 cup of cream or milk, ½ cup of butter, ½ pound of grated chocolate, and 2 tablespoonfuls of flour. Boil the molasses, butter, sugar and flour for 15 minutes, stir the chocolate into the cream, pour it into the boiling syrup, and boil till it hardens when dropped in cold water. Before pouring it out on buttered plates add a teaspoonful of vanilla. As it cools, crease it in small squares, keep in a cool place.—*Sister J. E. Price, Dallas Center, Iowa.*

Chocolate Caramels.—Take 1 cup of grated chocolate, 1 cup of brown sugar, 1 cup of molasses, and ½ cup of sweet milk. Boil till it hardens when dropped in water. Then add a piece of butter the size of an egg and 1 cup of chopped English walnut meats. Pour into buttered pan, and when partly cool cut into squares.—*Sister Maggie C. Stauffer, Polo, Ill.*

Chocolate Creams.—Take 2 cups of granulated sugar, and ½ cup of sweet cream, and boil them together for just 5 minutes from the time they begin to boil. Remove from the stove, add a teaspoonful of vanilla, and stir constantly until cool enough to work with the hands. Roll into little balls and lay on buttered papers to cool. Put ¼ of a cake of Baker's chocolate in a bowl and put the bowl in hot water. Do not add water. When the chocolate is melted, roll the balls in the melted chocolate with a fork, and replace them on the buttered papers. This makes a most rich and delicious candy. When the white mixture has partly cooled, it may be dropped on buttered papers, and nut meats put on top, making it a pleasing variety.—*Sister Rhoda E. Price, Polo, Ill.*

Chocolate Creams.—Take 2 pounds of granulated sugar, 1½ cups of water and boil until it will form a soft ball when dropped in cold water; pour on a buttered plate to cool. When cool enough that it can be handled without burning your hands, knead it as you would bread dough, when it will form into a soft creamy mass somewhat resembling powdered sugar icing. It is then ready to shape. Form into cones, oblong, or any desired shape. Now prepare by scraping some chocolate into a small dish and set the dish in a pan of boiling water until melted. Do not add a drop of water to the chocolate. Dip the candy into the chocolate, using a knitting needle or hat pin to handle it with; drop on buttered or oiled paper.—*Sister Katie R. Trostle, San Gabriel, Cal.*

Fudge.—Take ¼ cup of butter, 1 cup of white sugar, 1 cup of brown sugar, ¼ cup of molasses, and ½ cup of sweet cream. Boil for three minutes after it begins to boil. Beat till cool.—*Sister Mollie Zarger, Franklin Grove, Ill.*

Candy Fudge.—Take 2 cups of granulated sugar, ½ cup of milk, butter the size of a walnut, and Baker's chocolate to suit the taste. Boil until it hardens in water. Beat and put in buttered tins. Cut in squares.—*Sister Gladie Swartz, Goshen, Ind.*

Chocolate Fudges.—Take 1 cup of sugar, ⅓ cup of sweet cream, and 1 heaping tablespoonful of grated chocolate; boil till it hairs from the tines of a fork. Stir briskly till cool, pour into a pan and cut into squares.—*Sister Emma Carstensen, Girard, Ill.*

Delicious Fudge.—Boil together two cups of either maple or table syrup, 1 cup of water, and a tablespoonful of vinegar. When it will thread add a teaspoonful of vanilla and remove from the fire. While this mixture has been boiling, a cup of granulated sugar should have been put over the fire in a saucepan with ½ cup of cold water and boiled without stirring until it thickens. This should then be beaten up with the stiffly-whipped whites of two eggs, and then stirred into the first preparation. Beat it hard for twenty minutes and add two cups of nuts, or in place of nuts one may use shredded cocoanut.—*Sister Verna Cooney, Enders, Nebr.*

Taffy Candy.—Take 1 pound of glucose and 2 pounds of sugar. Mix with water and boil until brittle. Do not stir while cooking. Pour into pan and when cool enough pull like other taffy. —*Sister Mary C. Beard Eshelman, Elgin, Ill.*

French Taffy.—Take 2 pounds of glucose and 1 pound of sugar. Dissolve 1 ounce of gelatin in a little water and ½ pint of cream. When a little warm, put in 1 ounce of paraffine. Stir paraffine, gelatin and cream all together until it is dissolved. Then put in the glucose and sugar and boil until it hardens in water. Pour into a buttered pan, and pull when cold enough. Flavor with vanilla.—*Sister Mary C. Beard Eshelman, Elgin, Ill.*

Taffy Made of Lily-White Syrup.—Take 1 quart of lily-white syrup, [Any good table syrup might be used.—Ed.] 2 tablespoonfuls of granulated sugar, and 1 tablespoonful of butter. Boil until it hardens in cold water. Flavor with ½ teaspoonful of vanilla. Pour out and let get cool enough to pull. When pulled, cut into pieces, after twisting or braiding.—*Sister Katie E. Keller, Enterprise, Mont.*

Pop Corn.—Take 1½ cups of granulated sugar, ½ cup of molasses and a lump of butter the size of an egg. Boil the above ingredients together until they harden in cold water, then stir into this syrup ½ gallon ground popped corn. Stir well together, then put in an earthen dish, press well with the hands, and set in a cool place over night. Add flavoring to the syrup before taking from the stove.—*Sister Lottie P. Snavely, Kearney, Nebr.*

To Sugar or Crystallize Pop Corn.—Put into an iron kettle 1 tablespoonful of water and 1 cup of white sugar. Boil until ready to candy, then put in three quarts of corn nicely popped. Stir briskly until candy is evenly distributed over the corn. Set the kettle away from the fire and stir until a little cooled, and you have each grain separate and crystallized. Care should be taken not to have fire too hot lest the corn be scorched. Nuts of any kind prepared in this way are delicious.—*Sister Katie B. Blouch, Annville, Pa.*

SUNDAY MENUS.

Breakfast
Fruit
Cornflakes   Omelet
Coffee

Dinner
Roastbeef cold   Gravy
Potatoes   Cabbage
Pickled eggs   Olives
Pie   Cake   Fruit
Ice tea or Cocoa

Lunch
Pie   Fruit   Cookies
Milk

Breakfast
Oatmeal   Potato cakes
Gravy   Pie   Coffee

Dinner
Pressed chicken   Gravy
Mashed potatoes   Tomatoes
Salad
Cocoanut-puffs   Pie
Lemonade or Tea

Lunch
Egg or ham sandwiches
Fruit   Cake   Tea

I have given the subject of Sunday meals more study than those of any other day, for the reason that I greatly oppose much cooking on the Lord's Day, and too, company at our home is a very common occurrence, and a third reason, I need to prepare the meals so as to be able to reach Sunday-school on time and then to get dinner quickly after our return from church. You will notice that the Sunday dinner can be very largely prepared on Saturday. The beef or chicken can be cooked or roasted, the pie and cake will of course be baked beforehand, the eggs pickled. The potatoes can be pared before going to Sunday-school, and I have known some of our best cooks to pare them on Saturday evening. The gravy is quickly made and with our family is almost indispensable, and in my experience, when carefully made, I find it relished by company. I suppose most housewives know the little details that go to make it appetizing; viz.,—thicken the grease from the meat with flour, not too stiff, pour in a cup or two of cold water, then milk enough to make it the required thickness. Stir constantly and be sure not to salt until after the milk in it has boiled; otherwise the milk will curd more or less and spoil a good flavor.

—*Sister J. Z. Gilbert, Los Angeles, Cal.*

Dinner

Delicious pot-roast   Browned potatoes   Green string beans
Pickled red-beets or salad
Cake   Pie   Cheese
Coffee or Tea
(The dessert and drink may be left to choice of family.)

Delicious Pot-Roast.—On Saturday procure a five-pound rump-pot roast. Have the bone taken out and ask butcher to use several skewers to hold meat together while cooking. Place in refrigerator till Sunday morning. While getting breakfast ready, start the meat cooking, and, if a tender piece, you will be surprised to learn in what a short time it will be done ready to set on the back part of the stove. Take a good-sized iron kettle and place on the stove where it may become very hot. Into this hot kettle cut in small pieces of either suet or bacon, or, use fryings, not much of either; let fry a little while. After the meat has had a sufficient amount of salt rubbed over it place into the hot grease and let cook rapidly. Watch closely lest it burn. Every few minutes turn the meat until the surface is brown. At this point begin to add water. just a small quantity as it boils away. The object is to cook the meat with as little water as possible. The juice from the meat will make quite a little moisture when first put on to cook. You will find that by the time breakfast is over and your morning work done your meat has cooked enough to set on the back part of stove where there will be no danger of burning. Remove lid that steam may escape; otherwise you will have a very rusty iron pot to look at. This will furnish enough meat for about eight persons.

Browned Potatoes.—After your return from church start meat to cooking. Take the potatoes you have pared—they must be of an even size—and place them in the kettle, under the meat. If water is needed put a little in so that potatoes do not burn. Cover and cook briskly. By the time your table is set you will find potatoes a golden brown, almost ready to be eaten. When done, place meat on platter, potatoes in a dish, and set in a warm place till ready for use. Be very sure to watch closely lest you have a burned dinner.

Brown Gravy.—Take two or more tablepoonfuls of flour and mix with milk or water, pour into the kettle where your meat and potatoes have been cooked and stir until you have the desired thickness. If not salty enough season to your taste. Use pepper if you like. Remove from the fire and serve while hot.

Green Beans.—Gather a half peck of beans on Saturday, string, wash and cook either Saturday or Sunday morning. Cook in salt water, season with butter, pepper and salt and dress with flour and milk dressing, or use a small piece of bacon instead of butter. Either way is very good.

Salad.—Take six small beets and cook tender. When cold cut in small pieces by slashing across the beet. Take three fair- sized solid ripe tomatoes, squeeze seeds out and cut in small, chunky pieces. To this add a few stalks of lettuce also cut in small pieces. Season with pepper, salt, and a light sprinkle of sugar. Mix together very lightly or tomatoes will be mushy. Use pure cider vinegar. Put in a cool place till ready for use. Do not use vinegar until ready for use. Use mayonnaise dressing if preferred to vinegar. Pickled beets may be used instead of the salad, if preferred.

—*Sister D. L. Miller, Mt. Morris, Ill.*

Summer—Breakfast

Cantaloupe

Well-cooked cereal   Omelet with cracker crumbs

Sliced tomatoes

Graham Gems   Cereal coffee

Dinner

Casseroled beef   Brown gravy   Sweet potatoes   Corn

Cabbage salad

Chocolate pie   Peaches

Cake   Coffee

The beef should be prepared in the morning and can be left slowly baking while the family is at church.

Omelet (with cracker crumbs).—Take 4 eggs well beaten, 1 cup of rolled cracker crumbs, 2½ cups milk and salt. Pour into a buttered skillet and bake slowly till brown on both sides.

Casseroled Beef.—Select a nice roast, from the rump preferred. Into an iron pan put sufficient suet to brown the roast on both sides. When the suet is very hot place in the meat and sear it well on both sides. Then take out the meat and put it into the casserole; season with salt and dredge with flour. (A little tomato sauce, celery seed and onion is a good seasoning.) Pour water into the pan in which the meat was browned and when it has boiled up pour the brown gravy into the casserole. Bake in a very slow oven for three or four hours. A casserole is a glazed earthenware pan with a tight cover of the same material. This method of cooking does not call for a high degree of heat, but is slow cooking at a moderate heat, which does not destroy flavors of the food that are usually lost in the escaping steam where other methods are employed. Various and delicious combinations of meats and vegetables consisting of almost an entire meal may be cooked and served together, thus making the casserole an every day friend to the busy housewife.

Winter—Breakfast

Oranges   Cooked cereal

Crisped bacon   Rice pancakes   Maple syrup

Coffee

Dinner

Noodle soup

Sliced cold beef   Mashed potatoes   Creamed lima beans

Apple salad   Spiced pears

Cake   Canned fruit

Pie   Coffee

The meat should be cooked on Saturday and broth saved for the noodle soup.

Rice Pancakes.—Two cups of well-cooked rice to which a little butter has been added while rice was warm. To the rice when cool, add 2 cups of flour, 3 eggs well-beaten, 2½ cups of milk, salt and 2 teaspoonfuls of baking powder, if sweet milk is used.

To Cook Rice.—Take four parts of water to one part rice. Cook slowly till rice has absorbed all the water. Then place in double boiler and cook half hour longer. The rice will be white and dry. Then prepare as desired for table.

—*Sister R. E. Arnold, Elgin, Ill.*

Summer—Breakfast

Muskmelon   Cream of wheat
Graham gems   Maple syrup
Coffee

Dinner

Cold sliced beef heart or tongue
Mashed potatoes   Green beans
Gravy from stock   Fruit salad
Tapioca pudding   Lemonade

Supper

Sandwiches   Iced tea
Cake   Fruit

The greater part of the dinner can and should be prepared on Saturday. The meat stock can be saved for the gravy on Sunday. The beans can be cooked on Sunday morning while preparing breakfast. Thus much Sunday work can be avoided. The sandwiches for supper can be made of finely-chopped dinner meats left over and covered with a mayonnaise. Garnish meat platter with lettuce leaves or parsley.

Winter—Breakfast

Oranges or canned fruit
Buttered toast with poached eggs
Oatmeal porridge   Cocoa

Dinner

Roast beef or chicken with dressing
Baked beans with tomatoes
Stewed apples   Cake
Coffee

Supper

Bread and butter and jelly
Chocolate cake   Apples
Tea

The heavier part of the winter menu can also be prepared on Saturday. Have your beef or chicken prepared then. While finishing up your early morning work, put your roast in the oven, so that it may be about baked till time to attend church services. Leave in the oven to keep warm till your return. Remove meat, reheat stove, place your dressing in roasting pan and let it bake while preparing other parts of the dinner. Bake beans on Saturday and reheat for Sunday dinner. Stewed apples may also be reheated. Save yourself all unnecessary Sunday labor. Have meals on time and regular if possible. Avoid elaborate display and over-feeding.

—*Sister Flora E. Teague, Lordsburg, Cal.*

WEEK-DAY MENUS

Breakfast

Oatmeal   Cream

Breakfast bacon   Fried potatoes   Scrambled eggs

Bread   Butter

Coffee

Dinner

Cured pork   Mashed potatoes   Scalloped corn

Bread   Butter   Plum preserves   Pickles

Apple Pie

Supper

Scalloped potatoes   Rice

Bread   Butter   Jelly

Canned peaches   Cake

Tea

Oatmeal should be covered with hot water the night before so that it can easily be well cooked. Stir frequently and salt to taste.

—*Sister Olive O. Ball, Belleville, Kans.*

Breakfast

Rolled oat mush   Beefsteak   Fried potatoes
  Cornmeal pancakes   Butter   Syrup

Dinner

Boiled beef and dumplings   Potatoes boiled and fried whole   Peas
                    Mustard salad
        Butter   Preserves   Jelly

Supper

Vegetable soup   Scalloped potatoes
        Tomato salad
        Pie   Fruit

Breakfast

Graham mush   Fried bread (using eggs)
        Fried potatoes   Ham
            Butter   Jam

Dinner

Chicken potpie   Mashed potatoes   Green beans
      Stewed tomatoes   Pickled beets
            Butter   Jelly
            Cookies   Pie

Supper

Mush and milk   Potato cakes   Celery
        Cottage pudding

In preparing the fried potatoes, chop them finely and fry nicely.
Then pour in a little water and cover closely to steam a little.

For supper I usually prepare the things left over from dinner
in as appetizing way as I can. Then add a new dish or two such as
shortcake, rice custard, cake, and sometimes soup.

Green Mustard Salad.—Gather tender green mustard, pick it over, wash, cut quite fine and place in a dish. Put 2 tablespoonfuls of lard or butter in a frying pan. Then beat an egg and pour into ⅔ cup of vinegar, stir and pour into frying pan which is hot. Stir until the mixture thickens, then pour over mustard. Season with salt. This is very good in the spring when the appetite is poor.

—Sister Mary M. Michael, Myrtle Point, Oregon.

Breakfast

Breakfast food   Fried eggs
Buns   Butter   Jelly
Postum and cream

Dinner

Stewed chicken   Gravy   Mashed potatoes
Rice (cooked in chicken broth)
Pickles   Pie

Supper

Fried potatoes   Sliced tomatoes
Peaches   Cake

Breakfast

Corn cakes   Butter   Honey
Postum

Dinner

Boiled beef   Noodles   Potatoes
Pickles
Tapioca pudding

Supper

Rice soup   Potato cakes
Butter   Crackers

—Sister Gay McDannel Nill, Hollister, Okla.

Breakfast

Fruit

Poached eggs Toast

Cocoa Cinnamon cake

Dinner

Boiled fish Mashed potatoes

Baked rice Cabbage slaw Olives

Lemon custard

Coffee

Supper

Soup Crackers

Cold meat Potatoes with brown butter

Apple sauce

Junket

Breakfast

Oatmeal Cream

Frizzled beef

Hot cakes Honey

Postum

Dinner

Roast meat Dressing

Potatoes roasted with meat

Macaroni Tomato sauce

Lettuce Pickles

Chocolate custard

Supper

Rice boiled in meat dressing

Spice cantaloupe

Fried potatoes Peas

Apple tapioca Whipped cream

Coffee

Breakfast
Fruit

Cereal   Cream

Omelet

Cocoa   Buns

Dinner
Boiled Chicken   Dressing

Bread filling   Fried sweet potatoes   Mashed potatoes

Corn pudding   Sliced tomatoes   celery

Sliced peaches   Cream

Sponge cake

Supper
Hot biscuits   Maple syrup

Boston baked beans   Ketchup   Potato salad

Strawberry tart

Tea

Breakfast
Cantaloupe

Milk   Toast

Frankfurters

Stewed potatoes

Postum

Dinner
Beefsteak   Dressing

Corn on ear   Potatoes in jackets   Lima beans

Sliced tomatoes   Apple sauce

Watermelon

Supper
Soup   Croutons

Succotash   Stewed sweet potatoes

Potato salad

Doughnuts

Tea

Omelet.—Beat 6 eggs, add 6 tablespoonfuls of cold water, salt and pepper to taste and beat a little more. Put a tablespoonful of butter and cottolene in a skillet; when hot pour in eggs, fry a delicate brown and turn. Serve immediately. Bacon cut in small pieces and fried brown will give a fine flavor and can be used instead of butter and cottolene. Small bits of dried beef spread over the eggs as soon as poured in pan will make a driedbeef omelet. A ham omelet is made in the same way with left-over ham chopped fine and spread on eggs. If you have stale cheese grate it and put on eggs and you have a cheese omelet.

Christ said gather up the fragments that nothing be lost. We as Christian sisters should make use of the fragments as we all have some at times. By using common sense and a little judgment we will often be able to get a good meal from fragments. Save all the bits of vegetables from today's dinner and use them for tomorrow's vegetable soup. If you made too much biscuit dough, cover and put in cellar, then drop little bits in your soup tomorrow and see how good it is. Keep the bits of stewed crackers, mashed potatoes, rice, macaroni and use them for your batter cakes next morning.

—*Sister Emma Andes Zobler, Lancaster, Pa.*

Breakfast
Fried ham   Poached eggs   Fruit
Home-made bread   Butter
Coffee

Dinner
Boiled beef   Potatoes (cooked in beef broth)
Cabbage salad
Pie   Fruit

Supper
Rice soup (made of broth left over from dinner)
Mixed pickles   Fruit

If the broth is not rich enough for soup add butter to make it as rich as desired.

Breakfast

Fried mush   Fish   Fruit
Home-made bread   Butter
Cocoa

Dinner

Sausage   Beans   Fried potatoes
Fruit   Pie

Supper

Roast potatoes   Lettuce salad
Fruit

If green beans are wanted for dinner, put the kettle on the fire, let it get hot and then put in 1 tablespoonful of lard and butter mixed and 1 tablespoonful of flour. Let brown a little, add cold water, a pint or more, the prepared beans and salt according to amount of beans. Boil slowly for one and a half or two hours. Never boil beans fast as they will not have as good flavor as when boiled slowly. Before serving add 1 cup of sweet cream.

If soup or lima beans are wanted, parboil and drain; then cook till tender and dress with butter and cream.

You will notice I have fruit with each meal. I consider it so important to the health of most people that it should not be omitted. People who must buy everything they eat often consider fruit too expensive, but I would do without meat before I would do without fruit. It does not need to be the most expensive kind; apples are very good—even dried apples when they cannot be had otherwise.

—*Sister J. B. Miller, Curryville, Pa.*

Breakfast

Oatmeal with cream and sugar
Bacon   Cornbread   Honey or syrup

Dinner

Baked beans   Hot cabbage slaw
Plain boiled potatoes   Pork (baked with beans)
Pie

Supper

Fresh fried potatoes   Shirred eggs
Fruit or tapioca cream   Cookies

Hot Slaw.—Cook the cabbage in salt water. When tender drain and add dressing made of the yolk of 1 egg, 1 teaspoonful of flour, 2 tablespoonfuls of sugar, 1 cup of sour cream and vinegar to suit the taste. Do not add dressing till nearly time to serve and merely let come to a boiling heat.

Shirred Eggs.—Put a small piece of butter in a frying pan, break in the eggs and to each egg add 1 tablespoonful of sweet cream, with salt and pepper. Bake in the oven or cover closely and let cook slowly on top of stove.

—*Sister Emma Newcomer, Lanark, Ill.*

A MENU FOR THE " SIMPLE LIFE."

Sunday—Breakfast

Poached eggs on toast   Cream of wheat
Grain-o or postum
Bread and butter

Dinner

Mashed potatoes   Sausage
Cold slaw
Bread   Butter   Lemon butter
Strawberries   Cake

Supper

Cold cream of wheat
Bread   Butter   Preserves
Bananas

Monday—Breakfast

Hominy   Oatflake
Bread   Butter
Grain-o

Dinner

Potatoes boiled and fried whole   Stewed onions
Lettuce
Graham gems   Butter   Syrup
Apple sauce   Cookies

Supper

Boiled rice   Prunes   Shredded wheat biscuit
Bread   Butter   Jam
Chocolate

Tuesday—Breakfast

Fried mush   Wheat flake
Bread   Butter   Syrup
Grain-o

Dinner

Soup beans   Stewed tomatoes
Radishes   Bread   Butter   Apple butter
Raspberries   Graham wafers

Supper

Boiled macaroni   Cold wheat flake
Bread   Butter   Jelly
Bananas   Peppermint tea

Wednesday—Breakfast

Fried bread   Cream of wheat
Syrup   Bread   Butter
Grain-o

Dinner

Quirled potatoes   Dandelion   Frizzled dried beef
Bread   Butter   Apple butter
Cranberries   Molasses cake

Supper

Potato cakes   Cold cream of wheat
Milk   Cheese   Crackers
Bread   Butter   Preserves

Thursday—Breakfast

Scrapple Grape-nuts

Bread Butter Syrup

Grain-o

Dinner

Potatoes baked in their skins Green beans

Corn bread Butter Watermelon pickle

Cherries Cinnamon rolls

Supper

Fried eggplant Pumpkin sauce

Bread Butter Jelly

Bananas Sage tea Crackers

Friday—Breakfast

Omelet Graham mush

Bread Butter Syrup

Grain-o

Dinner

Fish Quirled potatoes Peas

Bread Butter Apple butter

Rhubarb sauce Little sponge cakes

Supper

Boiled rice Celery Toasted corn flakes

Bread Butter Jelly

Chocolate

Saturday—Breakfast

Hominy Wheat flake

Bread Butter

Grain-o

Dinner

Noodles Beet sauce

Bread Butter Apple butter Chow chow

Peaches Oatmeal crackers

Supper

Stewed oysters   Cold wheat flake

Bread   Butter   Jelly

Bananas   Milk

Mashed Potatoes.—Cook the potatoes till thoroughly done, drain, and set on the back of the stove or in the oven uncovered till the moisture is all evaporated. Squeeze them through a vegetable press into a warm vessel, add sufficient milk which has been heated in a tin cup, and with a four-tined fork beat vigorously until the mass grows white and light. Turn into a hot vegetable dish and serve immediately.

Tomato Salad.—Cook the tomatoes to pieces, and press through a wire sieve to remove the seeds. To the liquid add, to taste, salt, pepper, sugar, and ground cloves. When reheated to the boiling point, add one envelope of Plymouth Rock gelatine, which has previously been dissolved according to directions. Pour into cups to congeal. Turn into pretty dessert dishes and serve with any good salad dressing.

Patronize the green grocery and the milkman rather than the meat shop. Raisins are nourishing and palatable. Keep them on the table all the time. Eat two or three dates at supper. Two vegetables are usually sufficient for dinner. Do not worry about pie, but serve the fruit in dessert dishes. Be sure and have some kind of fruit for dinner every day, especially apples, if they are plentiful. Fruit is not so wholesome for supper. Be sparing of pickles. Eat a few nuts at the end of dinner, and a peppermint lozenge. Avoid concoctions that involve much time, trouble, and expense. You may save broiling yourself and burning extra fuel on a hot day by buying a few things at the bakery. Waste nothing. Some delectable supper dishes can be contrived from " left overs." Extravagance is the sin of the poor as well as the rich. At table be calm and courteous, eat slowly, chew thoroughly, and impart to the meal the dignity that you would to any other social function, and the family board will be the scene and source of the simple joys of normal man.

—*Sister Adaline H. Beery.*

MENUS FOR A WEEK.

Sunday—Breakfast

Toast   Boiled eggs   Stewed prunes
Coffee   Cream

Dinner

Roast chicken   Sweet potatoes
Potato salad   Currant jelly
Chocolate pudding   Pie
Coffee

Supper

Thin-sliced ham   Stewed fruit
Cake   Tea

Monday—Breakfast

Shirred eggs   Bacon
Biscuit   Coffee

Dinner

Noodle soup (from left-over chicken)
Boiled beef   Macaroni   Baked potatoes
Apple tart

Supper

Sliced cold beef   Cottage cheese
Corn bread
Tea

Tuesday—Breakfast

Oatmeal   Stewed dried peaches   Graham gems
Coffee

Dinner

Vegetable soup
Baked beans   Cold slaw
Tapioca pudding

Supper

Creamed dried beef   Tomatoes
Cinnamon rolls   Tea

Wednesday—Breakfast

Oatmeal   Baked eggs
Biscuits   Coffee

Dinner

Fried steak   Stewed cabbage   Baked potatoes
Canned fruit   Cookies

Supper

Beef and potatoes hashed
Strawberry shortcake   Cream

Thursday—Breakfast

Hot corn mush   Omelet
Fruit   Coffee

Dinner

Boiled ham   Dandelion greens   Mashed potatoes
Fruit pie   Coffee

Supper

Boiled rice with raisins   Cream
Brown bread   Fruit

Friday—Breakfast

Oatmeal   Cream   Omelet
Biscuits   Coffee

Dinner

Vegetable soup
Canned peas   Escalloped potatoes
Cold slaw
Jelly   Tarts

Supper

Cottage cheese   Stewed fruit
Rolls   Tea

Saturday—Breakfast

Fried mush   Scrambled eggs
Fruit   Coffee

Dinner

Stewed chicken   Dumplings and gravy   Mashed potatoes
Rice   Fruit salad   Cake

Supper

Salmon salad   Lettuce sandwiches
Cocoa   Cake

Picnic Dinner

Fried chicken   Baked beans   Potato chips
Lettuce sandwiches
Potato salad   Pickled eggs
Burnt sugar cake

—*Sister Minerva Metzger, Cerro Gordo, Ill.*

[Meals of office girls who board themselves. Lunch on week days was taken at the office.]

Sunday—Breakfast

Stewed prunes   Post toasties
Poached eggs on toast

Dinner

Veal chops   Mashed potatoes   Gravy
Stewed squash   Cold slaw
Snow pudding   Fig bars

Monday—Breakfast

Cream of wheat   Stewed prunes
Potato cakes   Gravy

Dinner

Plain boiled potatoes   Stewed tomatoes   Fried noodles
Peach tapioca

Tuesday—Breakfast

Graham mush   Sliced bananas
Pancakes   Cocoa

Dinner

Noodle soup   Hot slaw   Fried potatoes
Pumpkin pie

Wednesday—Breakfast

Rolled oats   Cranberry sauce
Chipped beef gravy   Fried potatoes

Dinner

Tomato soup   Potatoes boiled in jackets
Beet salad   Tapioca pudding

Thursday—Breakfast

Post toasties   Apple sauce
Omelet   Cocoa

Dinner

Green beans   Browned sweet potatoes
Celery
Grape gelatine with whipped cream   Cake

Friday—Breakfast

Post toasties with bananas sliced in same dish
Pancakes   Fried potatoes

Dinner

Boiled cabbage and potatoes   Macaroni and tomatoes
Stewed rhubarb.

Saturday—Breakfast

Graham gems   Syrup   Potatoes boiled in jackets
Stewed apples   Cocoa

Dinner

Fried sweet potatoes   Stewed celery
Rice pudding

—Sisters Maude Newcomer and Blanche Lentz, Elgin, Ill.

[Boarding Club Bethany Bible School, Chicago.]

Sunday—Breakfast

Rice and raisins
Dry toast
Fried potatoes   Beet pickles
Bananas

Dinner

Roast beef with brown gravy
Mashed potatoes   Peas
Apricots   Cake

Monday—Breakfast

Cream of wheat
Baked potatoes   Gravy
Pickles
Oranges

Dinner

Creamed potatoes   Stewed turnips
Corn bread   Onion salad
Blueberry pie

Tuesday—Breakfast

Cornflakes
Creamed dried beef   Hominy grits
Baked apples

Dinner

Tomato soup
Kidney beans   Scalloped potatoes
Creamed cold slaw
Apple butter

Wednesday—Breakfast

Oatmeal

Fried mush   Syrup

Stewed prunes

Dinner

Potpie   Baked dumplings

Hot beet salad

Tapioca custard

Thursday—Breakfast

Browned rice

French toast   Syrup

Cottage cheese   Apple butter

Dinner

Noodles   Whole fried potatoes

Sliced onions

Brown Betty

Friday—Breakfast

Rice patties   Tomato sauce

Baked potatoes

Stewed raisins

Dinner

Halibut steak   Mashed potatoes

Stewed tomatoes

Lemon pie

Saturday—Breakfast

Creamed toast   Baked potatoes

Pickles

Grapes

Dinner

Potato soup

Corn fritters   Syrup

Pickled celery

Apple dumplings

Browned Rice (Cereal).—Take 1 cup of rice, 2 cups of cold water and 1 teaspoonful of salt. Brown the dry rice in oven until golden yellow; then put rice, water and salt into a tightly-covered granite pan or cooking crock and set in oven until soft and dry,— about ½ hour. Do not stir.

—*Sister Sarah Rothrock, McPherson, Kans.*

THANKSGIVING AND CHRISTMAS MENUS.

Roast turkey and dressing

Cranberry sauce (or baked apples)

Escalloped corn

Mashed potatoes and gravy

Cabbage salad   Mixed pickles

Brown and white bread

Celery

Mince pie

Sliced oranges and bananas   Devil's food cake.

Nuts

The dressing for the turkey is greatly improved if the bread is first browned. Have ready, in a large baking pan or a deep dinner kettle, some hot drippings of lard and butter. Put in the diced bread and stir until all is nicely browned. Add to this sufficient broth or sufficient rich milk to make quite soft. Add a beaten egg if you wish a rich dressing. Season with salt, pepper and a bit of sweet marjoram.

Baked Apples.—Fill a baking dish with pared and halved apples. Bake until they can be pierced with a toothpick. Have ready a syrup made of one cup of sugar, one-half cup of water and a small piece of butter. Pour this over the half baked apples and bake until done.

Escalloped Corn.—Cover the bottom of a baking dish with fine cracker crumbs, dot with bits of butter and add a layer of canned corn. Then use more cracker crumbs and so on until the ingredients are used. Pour over all sufficient hot milk to cover well. Bake until it browns on the top. Dried corn can be used in place of the canned. It should be stewed and seasoned the same as if prepared for the table in that form.

Cabbage Salad.—Chop together one-half head of cabbage and twelve stalks of celery. Salt to suit taste. Have ready a dressing made of one egg, two tablespoonfuls of cream, one tablespoonful of butter, one-half cup of sugar and one-half cup of vinegar. Put this over the fire and let it come to the boiling point. It must be constantly stirred or it will curdle. When cold add to the chopped cabbage and stir thoroughly.

—*Sister Oma Karn, Covington, Ohio.*

The dining room and table can be decorated as the hostess sees best. I like some holly and ferns.

Roast duck or turkey (*we will have duck*)
Dressing and gravy
Cranberry sauce
Mashed potatoes   Sweet potatoes
Dried or canned corn and celery
Scalloped oysters   Apple salad
Pickles   Coffee
Mince pie   Pumpkin pie
Nut cake   Peaches and cream
A dish of homemade candies

Nut Cake.—Take 2 cups of sugar and 1 cup of butter, creamed together, 1 cup of sweet milk, 3 cups of sifted flour, 2 teaspoonfuls of baking powder, the whites of 3 eggs well beaten and added after rest are mixed and lastly stir in carefully 1 cup of any preferred nut kernels dredged with flour. Bake in loaf or layers in a moderate oven.

Apple Salad.—Take 4 medium-sized apples, chopped not too fine, ½ the amount of chopped celery, and 1 cup of English walnut kernels broken in pieces. Mix all this together and make a dressing of 2 tablespoonfuls of sugar, 1 tablespoon of butter, and 1 teaspoonful each of flour, salt and mustard. Mix in this 1 well-beaten egg. Turn on all 1 cup of boiling milk, stir briskly and add ½ cup of vinegar, not too sour. Pour dressing over other ingredients and serve.

Nearly all remaining dishes in menu are found in the cook book.
Sister I. Bruce Book, North Manchester, Ind.

Turkey with dressing   Mashed potatoes
Baked sweet potatoes   Lima beans with white cream sauce
Apple and banana salad
Mince pie   Coffee
Oranges   Nuts

Apple and Banana Salad.—Slice three apples and two bananas rather fine. Have a dressing made the day before of ¼ cup of vinegar and water, 1 tablespoonful of sugar, a pinch of mustard and a small piece of butter. Place this over the fire and pour in 1 well-beaten egg. Add cream to thin when put in the fruit. Serve individually on lettuce leaf.—*Sister Harry Fahrney, Elgin, Ill.*

FOR THE SICK

Before serving food bathe the patient's hands and face with a cloth wrung out of hot water. Arrange the food as daintily as possible, having the dishes, napkins and tray perfectly clean. Serve at one time only as much food as comes well within the limit of amount allowed. Often the sight of a large amount of food will cause nausea and make it impossible for any to be taken. Do not leave food standing by patient in order to arouse an appetite; that end is seldom accomplished in that way. Remove at once when not wanted and serve again, in fresh dishes, if necessary. Dishes should be heated if the food is to be served hot and kept cold if it is to be served cold.

Apple Tapioca Pudding for the Convalescent.—Take a small teacupful of tapioca, soak it in water over night. Then take 3 ripe cooking apples, pare, cut in halves, and put in a pudding dish with a little butter and sugar, then pour over them the tapioca and bake ¾ hour. Serve with sugar and milk.—*Sister C. Harley, Ephrata, Pa.*

Beef.—Get a small round steak and lay it on a plate. Take a table knife and scrape the tender meat out of it. Place it in a saucer and form it into a cake. Broil it in a hot buttered pan quickly, on both sides, and serve on a hot plate. The fibers which you cannot scrape, put in a stew dish with cold water and boil well. It will make a nice cup of broth for the sick.—*Sister Fannie E. Light, Pasadena, Cal.*

Rennet Custard.—Take 1 pint of sweet milk made lukewarm, add 2 tablespoonfuls of rennet liquid, 1 teaspoonful of sugar. Mix and let set 1 hour to thicken. Eat with sugar and milk.—*Sister Fannie E. Light, Pasadena, Cal.*

Prepared Beef (For Weak Stomach).—Take good beefsteak, cut about again as thick as for an ordinary fry, broil both sides lightly, then cut in small bits and press the juice out with a good lemon squeezer. The fluid will look like blood and is very nutritious. Cool, add a little salt, and it will be quite palatable. Given in small portions at a time, this will remain on the stomach when all other foods fail.—*Sister Amanda Witmore, McPherson, Kans.*

Broth.—Take a whole chicken, clean, and pick the meat off the bones in small pieces. Put it in a glass jar without water, cover tight, put in a kettle of cold water, and boil for 1 day. Take the broth for the sick, and the meat can be used for chicken salad for the other members of the family.—*Sister Fannie E. Light, Pasadena, Cal.*

Broth for the Sick (Chicken, beef or squirrel).—Put the meat into a glass jar, salt and pepper to suit the taste and seal airtight. Put the jar into a vessel of cold water, put on the stove and let boil till thoroughly tender, drain the broth from the meat and give to the sick. No water is added to the meat in the can.—*Sister L. V. Forehand, Gerster, Mo.*

Eggnog.—To ½ glass of milk add the yolk of 1 fresh egg; beat well together, sweeten and flavor to taste and then stir through the mixture the white of the egg beaten to a stiff froth. The result will be a pleasant and nourishing food for invalids. To add to its strengthening qualities, 2 teaspoonfuls of wine or brandy may be added if desired.—*Sister Hannah White, Altoona, Pa.*

Eggnog.—Take 1 egg, put it in a glass, beat well, then fill the glass with sweet milk, 2 tablespoonfuls of good wine and sugar to taste, stir well and set in a cool place. Give from 1 to 2 tablespoonfuls at one time.—*Sister Susan Coblentz, Peru, Ind.*

Boiled White of Egg.—When the yolk of egg disagrees with the patient, the white may be prepared, viz.: Beat the white of an egg until stiff and boil for 15 minutes in salted boiling water. Some prefer flavoring and a little sugar rather than salt.—*Sister Ida Wagner Hoff, Maywood, Ill.*

Milk and Eggs.—Bring a bowl of milk to a scalding heat (not boil). Break an egg into a dish, pour over it the scalding milk, stir with a fork, and add a little salt. Break in a few crackers or a slice of well toasted bread. This is nourishing and quite palatable. —*Sister Amanda Witmore, McPherson, Kans.*

Poached Eggs in Shell.—Place the eggs in a pan or kettle, pour boiling water over them and set on back of the stove 8 or 10 minutes, according to the amount and size. Do not let them boil. When just right they will drop out (when broken) like a lump of jelly.—*Sister Amanda Witmore, McPherson, Kans.*

Soft Boiled Egg.—The only way to prepare an egg that the sick will not tire of it. Place an egg in a tin cup, cover over with boiling water, set on the back of the stove from 5 to 10 minutes; do not let it boil. When the egg is just right, it will drop from the shell when broken. Have a hot dessert dish to serve it in.—*Sister Lizzie McNelly, Cincinnati, Ohio.*

Fruit Pudding.—Take the juice of any kind of berries, heat on the stove. Mix cornstarch with a little cold water, add it to the juice and boil until it thickens. Sweeten to taste, let cool, and eat with cream and sugar.—*Sister Fannie E. Light, Pasadena, Cal.*

Gruel.—Gruel can be made with oatmeal, corn meal, or farina. These should be mixed first with cold water, then add hot water. Two tablespoonfuls of meal is enough to make 1 pint when boiled.—*Sister Fannie E. Light, Pasadena, Cal.*

Corn Meal Gruel.—Take ½ cup of corn meal moistened with cold water; then stir into 1 quart of boiling water and let the boiling continue for 30 minutes or 1 hour; season with salt and butter. Cinnamon or nutmeg may be added if liked.—*Sister Ida Wagner Hoff, Maywood, Ill.*

Indian Meal Gruel.—Mix ½ cup of Indian meal with a very little water until perfectly smooth. Add the meal to 3 cups of boiling water, salted, stirring it in slowly, let it boil ½ hour. This can be retained in the stomach when almost everything else is rejected. —*Sister Elizabeth Rainer, Beatrice, Nebr.*

Irish Moss.—Buy 10 cents' worth of Irish sea moss in the drug store, then take a piece the size of a dollar and wash it in cold water, and put it in ½ pint of sweet milk and boil it till it thickens like cream. Stir all the time. Then strain, and season with a little sugar. Serve while warm. As soon as it cools it gets stiff, but it can also be eaten cold with cream and sugar.—*Sister Fannie E. Light, Pasadena, Cal.*

Panada.—Break in a bowl a piece of toast bread, add a little salt, and pour boiling water over the bread. Cover it up a few minutes, then add 4 or 5 spoonfuls of cream.—*Sister A. N. Renseyer, Halstead, Kans.*

Panada.—Take the white part of the breast and wings, freed from skin, of either roasted or boiled chicken, or the under side of cold sirloin or roasted beef, or cold roasted leg of mutton, and pound in a mortar with an equal quantity of stale bread. Add either the water in which the chicken has been boiled, or beef tea, until the whole forms a fluid paste, and then boil for 10 minutes, stirring all the time.—*Sister Gertrude E. Rowland, Reid, Md.*

Another Mode of Panada.—Take of pearl barley or rice 2 ounces, wash and put in a saucepan with ½ pound of veal or mutton cut in small pieces, and ½ pint of water. Simmer gently for 2 hours, then pound it in a mortar and rub through a fine sieve. Add a little cream to make it as thin as desired, with seasoning to taste, and serve hot or cold.—*Sister Gertrude E. Rowland, Reid, Md.*

Potato Soup.—Pare a few good-sized potatoes, cut in squares, boil them in 1½ pints of water until tender, season with salt and pepper and 1 tablespoonful of butter. Before removing from the fire, add 1 cup of sweet cream and let come to a boil. Pour them into a dish into which have been broken some bread crumbs, serve hot.—*Sister Lizzie McNelly, Cincinnati, Ohio.*

Cracker Soup.—Place a dozen crackers in a bowl, grate a little nutmeg over them, add 1 teaspoonful of butter and 1 tablespoonful of granulated sugar. Pour over boiling water enough to cover the crackers; cover and let steam a few minutes. Serve hot.—*Sister Lizzie McNelly, Cincinnati, Ohio.*

Sour Cream Soup.—Break a slice of stale bread toast or some tea crackers into a bowl. Add about 3 tablespoonfuls of rich sour cream and a sprinkling of salt. Fill up with boiling water, give it a stir and cover closely, and let stand for a few minutes.—*Sister Nannie H. Strayer, Johnstown, Pa.*

Tomato Soup.—Pare 1 tomato the size of a small teacup, cut and boil in a teacupful of water until very tender. While boiling add pepper and salt to season, 1 tablespoonful of butter and a pinch of soda. Before removing from the fire, add 1 pint of fresh milk, let come to a boil only, and serve with broken crackers.—*Sister Lizzie McNelly, Cincinnati, Ohio.*

For a Weak Stomach.—Beat the yolk of an egg thoroughly, gradually pour on it a cup of hot tea, stirring all the time, and sweeten to taste. This will often ease the stomach and be retained when nothing else will.—*Sister Mary E. W. Martin, Larned, Kans.*— Break a fresh egg in scalded—not boiled—milk and beat with a fork. Salt and pepper to taste.—*Sister Mary B. Peck, Manvel, Texas.*

Corn Meal Tea.—Parch common corn until browned through, grind; pour on boiling water. Excellent for nausea, vomiting, and diarrhœa.—*Sister Ida Wagner Hoff, Maywood, Ill.*

Toast.—Take a tablespoonful of currant or grape jelly, beat up the white of 1 egg and add 1 cup of boiling water, a little sugar, and a slice of toast bread.—*Sister Fannie E. Light, Pasadena, Cal.*

Egg Toast.—Brown a slice of bread, dip in hot water slightly salted, butter it and lay on top of the toast an egg that has been broken into hot water and cooked until the white is hardened. Season egg with a bit of butter and a little salt.—*Sister Chas. Hawbaker, Franklin Grove, Ill.*

Good, Rich Toast.—Toast a piece of bread to a light brown, butter it well on both sides while it is still hot, and break it into a bowl. Make a good tea, sweetened and with good cream in it, pour over the toast, and serve while hot. For the tea I prefer a mixture of Ceylon, Black, and Imperial.—*Sister Lizzie McNelly, Cincinnati, Ohio.*

Toast Water or Crust Coffee.—Toast a slice of bread a nice brown, but be careful not to burn it. Put it into a bowl and pour over enough boiling water to cover it. Cover bowl and let stand; then add a piece of ice, and when cool give to the patient by tea-spoonful.—*Sister Chas. Hawbaker, Franklin Grove, Ill.*

Raspberry Vinegar.—To 1 gallon of fruit add ½ gallon of water. Mash fruit well and set it in a cool place to sour; stir the fruit once or twice daily. Let fruit set about 4 days, then strain juice off the fruit, put in a kettle and cook. Skim off carefully what comes to the top. Then add 1 pound of sugar to it, let it boil for ¼ hour, and put in bottles. A couple of spoonfuls of the juice in a glass of ice water is a cooling drink.—*Sister A. N. Ramseyer, Halstead, Kans.*

Barley Water for Fever.—Take ½ cup of pearl barley and wash well. Take ½ gallon of cold water, put it over the barley, set it on the stove and let cook for 1 hour, then strain the liquid of the barley and put it to cool. Squeeze the juice of 1 lemon and sugar to taste in the barley water, and add a piece of ice. This is cooling and nourishing.—*Sister A. N. Ramseyer, Halstead, Kans.*

LIQUID DIET.

Egg Albumin (plain).—Put the white of one egg in a tumbler, with half a glass of cold water and a little crushed ice. Cover tumbler and shake well, or use an egg beater or milk shaker, until the egg and water are fully blended.

Albuminized Milk.—This is made the same way as the above, using milk instead of water, and shaking or beating until egg and milk are blended. Salt, sugar or flavor may be added. Serve very cold.

Albuminized Fruit Juice.—Beat the white of the egg light; then add equal parts cold water, and any preferred fruit juice,—orange, grape, lemon or pineapple, sweeten to suit the taste, and blend well together. Should the froth disagree with the patient, strain through a fine strainer. Serve very cold.

Beef Broth.—Cut two pounds of lean beef into small pieces and cover with three pints cold water. Let simmer for three hours. Strain, cool and remove all fat. Salt to taste. Veal broth can be made the same way.

Beef Juice.—See page 382.

Chicken Broth.—See page 382.

Chicken Broth.—Clean and cut into small pieces the fowl (a nice, fat hen about one year old is best). Cover it with about two quarts of cold water. Add one teaspoonful of salt and one teaspoonful of rice. Simmer gently for three hours, after it comes to the boiling point. Strain, cool, and remove all fat.

Egg Nog.—Sister Hannah White's, page 382.

Egg Nog.—Sister Susan Coblentz's, page 382.

Oatmeal Gruel.—Take two tablespoonfuls of oatmeal and three cups of cold water. Let come to a boil; then set back on stove and let it simmer for one hour. Strain and add salt and sugar to taste, or the sugar can be omitted. Should be made about half rich milk or cream. Serve either warm or cold.

Toast Jelly.—Take three slices of well-browned toast and put in a sauce pan with one quart of cold water. Let simmer for two hours. Then strain through a fine strainer, add sugar and a little lemon juice. Put in a cool place until it has set.

Lemonade.—Two tablespoonfuls of lemon juice (strained), one tablespoonful of sugar and one tablespoonful of crushed ice. Stir well, and fill up glass with cold water.

Milk.—Milk, either hot or cold should be sipped slowly to prevent an indigestible curd from forming in the stomach. Hot milk should be hot but not boiled. A pinch of salt in it may make it more palatable for some people. For a very delicate digestion, diluting the milk with water will sometimes render it more digestible.

Milk Shake.—Take a glass two-thirds full of rich milk or cream, sweeten and flavor to taste. Fill up glass with crushed ice, and shake well. Serve at once.

Orangeade.—This can be made the same as the above, using two tablespoonfuls of orange juice, to one of lemon.

Orange Flip.—Beat one egg very light with two teaspoonfuls of sugar; add one-third of a glass of orange juice. Fill up glass with crushed ice and cold water. Stir well and serve.

Corn Meal Tea.—See page 385.

Barley Water.—See page 386.

Rice Water.—Take two tablespoonfuls of rice, three cups of water and boil gently for one hour. Strain and cool, salt or sweeten, as preferred. A little lemon juice in it is relished by some. A few raisins can be boiled along with the rice if desired.

Toast Water.—See page 386.

—Sister Anna Mitchel, Newburg, Pa.

For the Convalescent.

An Appetizer.—For the invalid who likes something tart, the following might be relished: Chip into small, thin bits, a good, ripe apple, or part of one, into a dessert dish, also a portion of orange, pineapple, peach, plum or grapes, removing all skins and seeds. Squeeze a little lemon juice over it, and cover with sugar. Let stand a while until some juice is extracted. The patient can then be given the juice in small quantities, or if not restricted in diet, some of the fruit also.

Oatmeal Mush.—One cup of oatmeal, two cups of cold water, a saltspoon of salt. Let come to a boil, then set back on stove and let boil gently for twenty minutes. It is best well covered while cooking.

Toast Cream Soup.—Butter a slice of well-browned toast, break into a bowl, add one teaspoonful of sugar, a little grated nutmeg, and cover with boiling water. Cover closely for a couple minutes, then add one-half cup of cream.

—Sister Anna Mitchel, Newburg, Pa.

Diet List for Obstetrical Patients.

This list is suitable for patients having normal temperature and normal digestion. Where fever is present the diet should be restricted to liquid nourishments, such as milk, strained gruels, fruit juices, soups and broths, tea and coffee, the latter two well diluted with milk and cream. Also plenty of pure water should be given, preferably between the other nourishments, rather than with them.

First Twenty-four Hours.—One cup full of any of the liquids given under Liquid Diet should be taken every three of four hours.

Second Day.—Breakfast: Oatmeal gruel (strained), buttered toast. Dinner: Bowl of toast cream soup, orange juice. Supper: Milk toast, stewed prunes.

Third Day.—Breakfast: Corn meal mush with cream, toast, prunes, coffee. Dinner: Poached egg on toast, stewed peaches (dried), tea. Supper: Oyster soup (strained) with crackers, or toast cream soup, orange juice.

Fourth Day.—Breakfast: Oatmeal mush with cream, soft-boiled egg, toast, prunes, coffee. Dinner: Beef or chicken-broth with rice and crackers, baked apple, tea. Supper: Milk toast. Stewed fruit, cocoa.

Fifth Day.—Breakfast: Orange or grape fruit, cream of wheat with cream, poached egg on toast, coffee. Dinner: Small piece rare beefsteak, vegetable soup (strained) with crackers, baked potato, bread, currant jelly, tea. Supper: Soft boiled egg, toast, prunes, cocoa.

Sixth Day.—Breakfast: Shredded wheat biscuit with cream, bacon, toast, fruit, coffee. Dinner: Broiled beefsteak or chicken, beef or chicken broth with potato and crackers, boiled beets, bread, jelly, tea. Supper: Poached egg, toast, graham crackers, fresh or stewed fruit, cocoa.

Seventh Day.—Breakfast: Oatmeal mush with cream, omelet, toast, fruit, coffee. Dinner: Rare roast beef, mashed potato, baked apple, bread and butter, tea. Supper: Cracker soup, bread, jelly, fresh or stewed fruit, chipped dried beef, chocolate.

Eighth Day.—Breakfast: Corn meal mush (or any preferred breakfast cereal) with cream, broiled Hamburg steak, fruit, toast, coffee. Dinner: Stewed chicken, broth with rice and crackers, baked potato, fresh or stewed tomato, gelatine pudding, tea. Supper: Oyster stew, or chicken broth, toast, fruit, milk or cocoa.

Ninth Day.—Breakfast: Shredded wheat biscuit with cream, broiled beefsteak or fish, fruit, toast, coffee. Dinner: Rare roast-beef, cream tomato soup, baked potato, baked apple, tapioca pudding, bread, tea. Supper: Soft boiled egg, toast, fruit, chocolate custard, milk.

Tenth Day.—Breakfast: Oatmeal mush with cream, omelet, bacon, fruit, toast, coffee. Dinner: Roast beef or mutton, vegetable soup, mashed potato, lettuce, ice cream. Supper: Egg on toast, graham crackers, fruit, chocolate, puffed rice with cream.

—*Sister Anna Mitchel, Newburg, Pa.*

HOME REMEDIES

(Some of these have been contributed to this work, but most have been taken from the Inglenook Doctor Book.)

INFANTILE DISEASES.

Rules for the Baby.—(1) Keep the baby sweet and clean. (2) Have a regular time for the bath. (3) Begin early putting baby into the water. An earthen wash-bowl will answer the purpose when you have not a bath tub, but by all means, have the body in direct contact with the water. It is so much more effective than the "smear" most babies get which is called a bath. (4) Whenever possible to give it, do not omit the daily outing. Baby needs fresh air as much as grown people. (5) Do not feed the baby every time it cries. Over-feeding may often be the cause of the cry. (6) Remember to give baby water to drink several times daily. (7) do not allow people to kiss baby in the mouth. (8) Do not allow your baby to be picked up by the arms. (9) Never allow any sort of unnecessary handling. The little body may become sore from careless or too frequent handling. (10) Never cover the baby's face to a smothering closeness. (11) Never resort to artificial or prepared feeding unless absolutely necessary. You may try six kinds without success. (12) In warm weather a bath in tepid soda water, at baby's bed time, may do more toward a night's sleep than hours of " walking the floor."

To Prevent Bowel Trouble in Small Children.—Never allow a child's stomach and abdomen to get cold but take care that that part of its body is always properly clothed and it will not have the usual bowel troubles of babyhood.—*Mrs. E. G. Thomas, Butler, Ind.*

Summer Complaint.—A child usually begins with vomiting, purging and fever. After each action, cleanse the bowels with enemas, using warm water and sweet milk. Feed warm boiled milk, thickened milk, toast and the like, avoiding all green foods. For fever bathe the body, especially the spinal column, with tepid water. The spine should be sponged often, from fifteen to twenty minutes at a time, until the fever is reduced. Put a cool, wet compress of several folds of linen across the stomach and bowels and cover with flannel and a snug bandage to hold in place. Renew when warm. Keep the head cool and the feet and limbs warm. This treatment is good in any case of fever.—*Amanda Witmore, McPherson, Kans.*

Croup.—Give equal parts of butter and honey melted together, or lard and sugar, or onion juice and sugar, or equal parts of alum and sugar. If choking is bad give the white of an egg or something to cause vomiting, that the phlegm may be thrown up. Always grease the breast well with lard, and keep covered with flannel. Melt the lard and put it on as hot as can be borne. If nothing else helps, wrap the child in blankets and give hot drinks until sweating is induced, but after this treatment great care must be taken as the patient will take cold very easily.—*Sara Reese Eby, West Elkton, Ohio.*

—Slice raw onions very thin and sprinkle with sugar. Allow to dissolve and give the juice in teaspoonful doses frequently. This often relieves instantly.—*S. I. Bowman, Harrisonburg, Va.*

Give Onion Juice.—To extract the juice so as to give it in the most concentrated form remove the outer shells and roll the onion in dough made of flour and water, just as you would roll a dumpling, cover in hot ashes in your cook stove or any wood heater, place plenty of hot coals around it and roast one-half hour or more according to the size of the onion. Squeeze through a piece of coarse muslin. Sweeten if preferred. One large onion will make almost a half-teacupful of juice.—*Mrs. H. Kurtz, Hebron, Ill.*

Hives.—Rub the irritated skin or postules with castor oil, applied with the tip of the finger. Baby will pass from fretting to slumber while the process is going on, the relief will be so quick.—*S. Gnagey, Pasadena, Cal.*

THE THROAT—Colds.

—Drink hot lemonade, and soak the feet in hot water just before going to bed at night.—*Flora L. Moore Dougherty, Eldora, Iowa.*

—For a sudden cold on the lungs, and hoarseness, a cold compress applied at night and carefully covered with heavy woolen cloth will often relieve in one night. When a severe cold refuses to yield to all ordinary remedies, a Turkish bath taken within forty-eight hours after cold is contracted is certain relief. Persons suffering from cold should keep the bowels in good condition, and drink much water, hot water if troubled with chilly sensations.—*Lydia E. Taylor, Trained Nurse, 1014 Randolph St., Waterloo, Iowa.*

—For hoarseness, whip the white of a fresh egg to a stiff froth, add the juice of one lemon and sugar to taste. Take frequently in small doses.—*Barbara Mohler Culley, Elgin, Ill.*

Pneumonia.—Wring flannel out of hot strong salt water to which a little vinegar has been added, and lay on the lungs or affected part. Be very careful not to chill while using this, and have the flannel wrung so dry as not to wet the clothes badly. Cover with a dry cloth. This is good in lung fever, or rheumatism.—*Grandma Johnson, Redfield, Kans.*

Sore Throat.—Slice a thin piece of old smoked bacon, the older the better. Stitch this to a piece of flannel and make it black with pepper. Warm it and fasten closely around the throat. Do not remove until the inflammation has been drawn to the outside. When the meat is taken off anoint the throat with a good vaseline and bind up in flannel which must be left on until the throat is entirely well. —*Mrs. Lulu Goshorn, Ladoga, Ind.*

—Take vinegar and make it strong with salt and red pepper (black may be used), and gargle often.—*Mary Reddick, Sheridan, Mo.*

—Gargle with diluted listerine. Swallow a little occasionally.— *Flora L. Moore Dougherty, Eldora, Iowa.*

Tonsilitis.—Apply kerosene freely on the outside of the neck. Also apply it inside with a small syringe, or a swab made by tying a soft bit of cloth on the end of a stick. A piece of smoked bacon tied on the neck when retiring for the night is a good remedy when applied in time.—*Emma C. Newcomer, Lanark, Ill.*

Remedy for Consumption.—One tablespoonful of tar and the yolks of 3 hen's eggs beaten well together. Dose, 1 tablespoonful morning, noon and night.—*Sister Mary Gibson, Des Moines, Iowa.*

Pneumonia.—Some time ago the health board of Washington, N. J., published the following remedy and some other health boards are looking into the matter with a view of having the same thing published for the good of the general public: " Take six or ten onions, according to the size, and chop fine, put in a large spider over a hot fire, then add the same quantity of rye meal, and vinegar enough to thicken to a paste. Stir it thoroughly, letting it simmer ten minutes. Then put it in a cotton bag large enough to cover the lungs and apply to the chest as hot as the patient can bear. In about ten minutes apply another; and thus continue, by reheating the poultices, and in a few hours the patient will be out of danger. Continue always till the perspiration starts freely from the chest. This remedy was formulated years ago by one of New England's best physicians, who never lost a patient by the disease, and won his renown by simple remedies."—*Ezra Flory, Sterling, Ill.*

ERUPTIVE DISEASES.

Measles.—Give the patient all the cold lemonade he can drink. This will drive out the measles, check the fever and loosen the cough.—*Mary Netzley, Batavia, Ill.*

—In an eruptive disease, as measles or scarlet fever, where the eruption fails to come to the surface give a heaping teaspoonful of sulphur and a cup of warm tea.—*Mrs. L. N. Moomaw, Roanoke, Va.*

Hives.—Epsom salts will check bold hives. Dose, two table-spoonfuls. Continue taking one teaspoonful a day until no more hives appear.—*Flora L. Moore Dougherty, Eldora, Iowa.*

—Take a teaspoonful of flour in a glass of water. This is one dose. Repeat several times a day until relief is obtained. Hives are caused by too much acid in the blood and the flour counteracts this. —*Sara Reese Eby, West Elkton, Ohio.*

Mumps.—Eat sparingly, drink freely, use a gentle laxative if necessary to keep the bowels in order, carefully avoid drafts, cold and dampness. Hot flannels or other warm applications to the swollen glands add to the comfort of the patient.

FELONS, BOILS.

Felon.—When the finger begins to pain, dip it in and out of scalding water quite frequently till the water gets cool. The second application may be necessary.—*Annie Highbarger, Lydia, Md.*

—Poultice felons and other swellings with stewed pumpkin, cold.—*Elizabeth Calvert, Russellville, Ill.*

Boils.—To draw any gathering, as a boil or carbuncle, apply scraped raw beets as a poultice. Change as often as necessary until the swelling opens.—*Eliza Englar, New Windsor, Md.*

STOMACH AND BOWEL TROUBLES.

—For a heavy, distressed feeling in the stomach before going to bed, caused by eating something that is hard to digest, drink a pint of hot water as hot as you can take it.—*A. C. Goetze, Saratoga, Wyo.*

Indigestion.—Drink a cup of hot water, not too hot, an hour before each meal.—*Emma Katherine Spickler, Polo, Ill.*

Vomiting.—Put a teaspoonful of salt in a glass of water and drink. Repeat this even if it requires six doses, as it is safe.—*N. J. Roop, Warrensburg, Mo.*

Constipation.—Take a cup of hot water, with a teaspoonful of salt added, before going to bed at night and before breakfast.—*Emma Katherine Spickler, Polo, Ill.*

—Chop fine one-half pound of the best prunes and one-half pound of figs. Add one-half ounce of pure senna and enough molasses to make a thick paste. Simmer on the stove about twenty minutes. Take a piece of this paste about the size of a hickorynut. Repeat in four hours if necessary.—*Mary Lininger, Inman, Nebr.*

Cramp Colic.—For severe pain, as in cramp colic or rheumatism, wring towels out of hot water and apply to the seat of pain as hot as can be borne, covering with dry flannel. Take a hot lid from the stove, wrap well in paper and place over the towel. This will start sweating and ease the pain immediately.—*H. J. Mumah, Union City, Ind.*

—Take one quart of warm water with two tablespoonfuls of sweet oil and use as an enema.—*Fannie E. Light, Nurse, Pasadena, Cal.*

Bowel Complaints.—Boiled sweet oil is serviceable in all sorts of bowel complaints and colics and internal injury, as from falls, as it allays pain, scatters coagulated blood, prevents inflammation and heals gently.—*Sarah A. Crowl, Goshen, Ind.*

Summer Complaint.—Stir together one teaspoonful of ginger, one heaping teaspoonful of flour and two tablespoonfuls of water. Repeat as a dose as often as necessary.—*Mrs. E. F. Jones, Carrollton, Mo.*

Diarrhœa or Dysentery.—Take several blackberry or raspberry roots, wash clean, cut fine with a knife, cover with water and boil till a strong tea is made, drain off and strain. Now, add sugar to make a syrup. When finished, bottle, cork and seal to keep sweet. Dose, one teaspoonful one to three hours.—*Mrs. H. A. Whisler, Laton, Cal.*

—For violent pain in the stomach with diarrhœa, take one teaspoonful of black pepper in a glass of water. Don't try the " spice mill " pepper as that is half adulterants.—*N. J. Roop, Warrensburg, Mo.*

—For an adult give one heaping teaspoonful of flour mixed with pure cold water to the consistency of cream, every few hours. For children give less.—*Amanda Witmore, McPherson, Kans.; Annie E. Evans, Lancaster, Pa.*

HEADACHE.

—Put a cold cloth to the head and a bottle of hot water to the feet.—*Mrs. L. N. Moomaw, Roanoke, Va.*

Sick Headache.—Put one tablespoonful of ground mustard in a teacup, fill the cup with hot water and drink. This either settles the stomach or causes vomiting, either of which gives relief.—*Lena B. Fleshman, Lindside, W. Va.*

Biliousness.—Take the juice of one, two or three lemons, according to appetite, in as much ice water as is pleasant to drink, without sugar, before going to bed at night. In the morning, on rising, or at least one-half hour before breakfast, take the juice of one lemon in a glass of water without sugar. The stomach should not be irritated by eating lemons clear, but they should be properly diluted so as not to burn or draw the throat.—*Alice C. Garman, Lancaster, Pa.*

BLEEDING AT THE NOSE.

—Bathe the face and neck with cold water.—*Gertrude Rowland, Reid, Md.*

—Squeeze the juice of half a lemon into one-half cup of water, pour a small quantity of this at a time into the hollow of the hand and draw up, by sniffs into the nostrils.—*Lydia E. Taylor, Trained Nurse, Waterloo, Iowa.*

—Press your thumb or finger down along the edge of your jawbone on the same side the nostril is bleeding till you feel the beating of the artery, then press on it firmly for about five minutes and even the worst cases will stop.—*J. H. Crofford, Martinsburg, Pa.*

TOOTHACHE.

—Equal parts of oil of cloves and chloroform applied on a piece of cotton will relieve quickly and applied a few times will destroy the nerve.—*Clifford Ellis, Dixie, Wash.*

EARACHE.

—Dip cotton in molasses and put in the ear and the pain will cease.—*E. B. Lefever, Ephrata, Pa.*

—Put a few drops of melted butter in the ear.—*Hannah M. Felthouse, Elkhart, Ind.*

POULTICES, SALVES, LINIMENTS.

Mustard Poultice.—To make a mustard draft, beat up the white of an egg, add a tablespoonful of flour and enough vinegar to make a paste. Spread on a cloth and sprinkle with ground mustard. Cover with mosquito bar or a thin cloth. Warm before applying.—*Laura M. Shuey.*

Bread and Butter Poultice.—For bruises and sores, take equal quantities of butter and bread crumbs, mix thoroughly, adding a little water, and apply as a poultice. This reduces pain and swelling and prevents discoloration.—*Ada L. Early, Elgin, Ill.*

Drawing Salve.—Take one tablespoonful each of rosin, sheep's tallow, hard soap and brown sugar, and mix thoroughly with a knife till they form a salve.—*Sarah A. Sell, Newry, Pa.*

White Liniment.—Good for sprains, bruises, sores, sore throat, etc. Take one quart of sharp apple vinegar, one-half pint of turpentine, and three eggs, and shake well together. This is equally good for man or beast.—*Leona Shively, Newville, N. Dak.*

ACCIDENTS.

Cuts and Bleeding.—If an artery is severed, tie a small cord or handkerchief tightly above it, and inserting a round stick, improvise a tourniquet to hold the flow in check until the surgeon arrives.

—Bind plenty of dry flour on the cut.—*Mrs. H. A. Swab, Chelan, Wash.*

—Apply dry ashes immediately to stop bleeding and prevent soreness.—*Fannie L. Mason, Baker's Mill, Va.*

—A good remedy for painful scratches and small cuts is one ounce of rainwater with one teaspoonful of spirits of camphor and four drops of carbolic acid added.—*Ida Wampler Mohler, Leeton, Mo.*

—Nothing is better than turpentine if immediately applied, as it is painless and will heal without inflammation.—*Annie Pitzer, Cordell, Okla.; Sarah A. Sell, Newry, Pa.; Clifford Ellis, Dixie, Wash.; Mrs. J. H. Kimmel, Morrill, Kans.*

—To remove old scars, rub them every day with pure olive oil. To prevent the forming of scars keep the parts wet with pure olive oil.—*M. E. Rothrock, Hartland, Wash.*

Sprains.—A sprain or an unbroken bruise should be treated at once to an application of water as hot as can be borne. This may be done by showering hot water upon it, or by hot cloths applied frequently.—*Dora M. Ellis, Dixie, Wash.; B. F. Kintner, Ney, Ohio.*

—Cut several mullein stalks into small pieces and boil in one quart of cider vinegar. Apply to the sprain while warm.—*Maud A. Kline, Ginghamsburg, Ohio.*

Burns.—To draw the fire out, apply cider applebutter immediately.—*Sophia Voorhis, Waverly, Ind.*

—Scrape a raw potato and bind on with a white cloth.—*Lucinda Bailey, Mt. Etna, Iowa.*

—If the burn is not so dangerous as to require the services of a physician, apply kerosene to it and wrap with a cloth saturated with kerosene.—*Nora Brown, Navarre, Kans.*

—Apply the white of an egg mixed with a teaspoonful of lard. —*Vina E. Rench, Harrison, Okla.*

—Take one part carbolic acid and ten parts linseed oil and bind on with cotton.—*Elizabeth H. Calvert, Russellville, Ill.*

Lye Burns.—For burns from lye, wash with strong vinegar. Drink vinegar in case lye has been swallowed.—*Pearl Weimert, Larned, Kans.*

Excellent for Burns.—Take white of egg, beat until stiff, then add scant tablespoonful of lard (to white of each egg). Mix well, spread on white cloth ¼ inch thick and put on burns with egg and lard next to burns. Change whenever it begins to dry, or burn begins to smart. This will ease burns immediately and draw all fire out.—*Sister W. J. Haynes, Moorefield, Nebr.*

Rusty Nail and Similar Wounds.—For a wound caused by stepping on glass or a nail, bathe the part at once in baking soda in very hot water. Then grease the part with vaseline or lard.— *Lizzie A. Bitzer, Ephrata, Pa.*

—Apply grated or scraped raw beets as poultice. Renew as fast as it becomes dry.—*Anna Sniteman, Keota, Iowa; D. C. Summy, Mt. Pleasant, Pa.; Porter Kimmel; Morrill, Kans.*

Ivy Poison.—The active principle in ivy is a vegetable acid, and to counteract its effect upon the human system we must treat it to a counter-irritant. A proper alkali will neutralize the acid if correctly applied. Dissolve soda in your hand and apply to the affected parts as soon as the first symptom is manifested, or as soon as possible. If once in the blood the best way to reach it is to apply a strong solution of epsom salts, externally and internally.— *D. A. Lichty, Morrill, Kans.*

Poisons and Antidotes.—First, get rid of as much of the poison as possible by vomiting. This should be produced by the simplest means, when they are sufficient, such as tickling the throat with a feather, drinking lukewarm water and salt, or mustard and water. If these fail, try a powerful emetic, such as tartar-emetic, sulphate of copper, or the white of an egg. If vomiting cannot be excited, the stomach pump must be used by skillful hands, especially in arsenical or narcotic poisons. After getting rid of as much of the poison as possible, use some of the following simple and reliable antidotes: Acids are neutralized by alkalies, such as a thick soap-suds of soap and milk, chalk, soda, lime water, magnesia, or salera-tus. In cases of poisoning from sulphuric acid, do not use soapsuds or limewater. For nitric or oxalic acid, use magnesia and lime, and for prussic acid use dilute ammonia, and electricity. Alkalies are neutralized by acids, the vegetable acids, vinegar, or oils in large quantities. Opiums and narcotics are neutralized by strong coffee and frequent doses of aqua ammonia. For arsenic—probably the most difficult of all poisons to antidote—give peroxide of iron in tablespoonful doses every ten minutes until relief is obtained. When poisoned by bismuth, copper and their compounds, mercury, tin, zinc, and their salts, and creosote, use albumen in some form; as the white of egg, sweet milk, strong coffee, and mucilaginous drinks. For lead and its salts, use epsom salts, glauber salts, dilute sulphuric acid, or even lemonade in mild cases. For iodine, use starch, wheat flour, or arrowroot, beaten up in warm water. For gases, use di-lute ammonia, electricity and friction. In poisoning from animals, but little or no benefit is derived from vomiting, but we should re-sort to antidotes at once, and often to the actual cautery. For the bite of a mad dog, apply the actual cautery to the wound instantly, and give large doses of zinc or muriate or iron for several days. For serpents' bites, apply the cautery and give sufficient whisky or brandy to produce intoxication. For insect poison, apply iodine, hartshorn and oil to the part and give stimulants for a day or two. —*Sara Reese Eby, West Elkton, Ohio.*

Poison Oak.—Apply spirits of camphor to poison from poison oak. Copperas dissolved in water is also a very good remedy.—*L. C. Klepper, Cliff, Tenn.*

Mad Dog Bite.—Wash the bitten part with vinegar and water two or three times a day. Give a teaspoonful of vinegar, in half a glass of water, every morning for three or four days. I have never had a fatal case in thirty years of jungle life.—*Missionary Haegert, Bethel Santhal Mission, Jamtara, Bengal, India.*

Rattlesnake Bite.—Beat the yolk of a fresh egg and mix with salt to the consistency of a good salve. Apply to the bite as a poultice and change frequently till the poison is all out.—*Susan Eckard, Martinville, Mo.*

—Take vinegar and stir in salt enough to dip up with the hand, lay the salt on the bite and keep it on until all the swelling or poison is drawn out. Do not give the patient anything in his stomach. This is good for man or beast.—*Lucinda Bailey, Mt. Etna, Iowa.*

—For a snake bite, or any poisonous bite or sting, pound a lot of onions till soft, salt liberally and bind on as a poultice. Renew often.—*Nannie E. Neher, Palestine, Ark.*

Stings and Bites of Insects.—For a bee sting, cover the affected part with dampened salt.—*Fannie L. Mason, Bakers Mill, Va.*

—Apply sweet oil, and give a tablespoonful of it internally.

—Mix baking soda with water to the consistency of molasses, apply and let it dry on the wound.—*D. C. Summy, Mt. Pleasant, Pa.*

Chigger Bites.—Rubbing carbolic acid water—fifteen drops of carbolic acid and one-half cup of water—on chigger bites, or hives as they are sometimes called, will stop the itching.—*Flora L. Moore Dougherty, Eldora, Iowa.*

Choking.—A piece of food lodged in the throat may sometimes be pushed down with the finger or by two or three blows on the back between the shoulders.—*Mrs. H. A. Swab, Chelan, Wash.*

—To dislodge a fishbone from the throat, swallow the white of a raw egg.—*Barbara Mohler Culley, Elgin, Ill.*

Sunstroke.—Give the patient a cup of coffee as hot as he can drink. Do not give anything cold. Get the sweat started and the patient is out of danger.—*E. P. L. Dow.*

Simplified Method for the Restoration of Drowning Persons. —The following simplified method for the restoration of drowning persons, and of those who have lost consciousness through asphyxia or any other cause, was developed by Dr. J. V. Laborde, of the School of Anthropology, in Paris. It has proved efficacious in many cases. In one cited, of a child who had been submerged for nearly fifteen minutes, the return of breathing was accomplished in ten minutes. The translation here given is from a leaflet which Dr. Laborde distributes among his pupils:

1. As soon as the drowning man has been taken from the water, force open his mouth. If the teeth are clinched, separate them with the fingers, or by means of any hard object—*e. g.,* a piece of wood, the end of a cane, the handle of a knife, of a spoon, of a fork.

2. Firmly seize between the thumb and the first finger of the right hand the end of the tongue, using your handkerchief, or any piece of linen, to prevent the tongue from slipping; then repeatedly, rhythmically, and with decision, pull it from the mouth, and relax it alternately—at the rate of at least twenty times a minute, imitating the cadenced movements of expiration and inspiration.

3. At the same time introduce, far back into the throat, the first finger of the left hand, pressing upon the base of the tongue, so as to induce vomiting, and thus free the stomach of the water or food which encumbers it.

4. This treatment, the most efficacious known method of bringing back the respiration, must be begun without the slightest delay, and persistently continued for a half hour, an hour, or more. At the same time all the usual remedies must be applied. Most

important are the removal of the clothing, friction over the whole body, pressure upon the anterior part of the chest, the restoration of the bodily heat, and, where it is possible, the application upon the region of the heart of compresses of very hot water.

The same method may and should be applied, in the same manner, in all cases of asphyxia and of syncope (loss of consciousness), from whatever cause.

When a person has been taken from the water in an unconscious condition, the old Howard system of resuscitation should be used. It consists of kneeling over the lower part of the chest and relaxing the pressure. This simple operation should be repeated nine or ten times during a minute. The treatment should not be applied in a harsh manner. The Howard system is in vogue in most of the navies of the world. The Sylvester system is another good method. To get the water from the stomach and chest the patient is stripped to the waist and placed face downward with the pit of the stomach raised above the level of the mouth by a roll of clothing or other material placed transversely beneath the trunk. The tongue must be held out, the larynx kept open, and the mouth and throat cleared of mucus. Efforts to resuscitate should be continued an hour, for apparently inanimate individuals have been brought to life at the end of that time, after having been in the water half an hour or longer. Attempts to restore respiration should be accompanied by friction, such as the administration of stimulants and the application of heat to the abdomen and lower extremities.

THE FEET.

Frosted Feet.—Dissolve alum in water till very strong, dip the frosted part in the alum water, then hold by the fire. Repeat until relieved.—*Mrs. S. J. Kester, Chanute, Kans.*

—When the feet begin to pain and itch, remove shoes or boots and pour a little coal oil on the stocking over the frosted place, just enough to dampen the stocking, then put on the shoes again and that is the last of the frost. It is very seldom that a second application is necessary.—*M. W. Royer, Cordova, Md.*

Corns.—Add enough fine bread crumbs to one-fourth cup of cider vinegar to make a good poultice after standing about one-half hour. Apply this poultice when retiring at night. In the morning the soreness will be gone and the corn can be picked out. If a very obstinate corn two or more applications may be required to effect a cure.—*Laura B. Reiff, Idaville, Ind.; D. M. Weybright, New Paris, Ind.*

MISCELLANEOUS

To Use Stale Bread.—Take scraps of bread, biscuit, and graham bread, too, put them in the oven and dry thoroughly; if they brown a little, it makes no difference; then roll fine with rolling pin and put in a dry place for future use. In making batter cakes in the morning use half flour and half bread crumbs. Also nice to use in making scalloped tomatoes or potatoes or to roll veal cutlets in.—*Sister Prudence Miller, New Rockford, N. Dak.*

Corn Bread for Young Poultry.—Take 3 pints of sour milk or buttermilk, 2 large teaspoonfuls of soda dissolved in ½ cup of hot water and 1 tablespoonful of salt. Stir well, then add 1½ pints of wheat bran, 3 pints of fine corn meal and 4 tablespoonfuls of melted lard. Mix and pour into a dripping pan, bake 1 hour in a moderate oven. When fed, moisten with hot sweet milk or water and sprinkle with black pepper.—*Sister M. Jane Stauffer, Polo, Ill.*

Buttermilk Delda.—Let 2 quarts of buttermilk come to a boil, sweeten, add 4 tablespoonfuls of flour moistened with sweet milk, and stir till thick. To be eaten warm or cold.—*Sister Sarah A. Crowl, Nappanee, Ind.*

Mulled Buttermilk.—Take 2 quarts of fresh buttermilk, 1 scant teacupful of flour, 1 egg, 1 pint of new milk and 1 teacupful of sugar. Beat the egg, add the flour and milk, mixing it into a smooth batter, then put the buttermilk into a kettle over a hot fire, and stir constantly till it almost boils. Add the batter and continue to stir till it boils, add the sugar and serve warm. Some think a little nutmeg improves it.—*Sister Nannie H. Strayer, Johnstown, Pa.*

Cheese.—Take 2 gallons of thick milk and 1 gallon of sweet milk, and put into a vessel. Beat 6 eggs light, pour in the milk, salt; place on the stove, stirring it until it curdles, then pour it into a cloth or sack and place between two lids with a heavy weight, press 24 hours. Then take it out, and slice ready for the table.— *Sister C. J. Senseman, Covington, Ohio.*

Cottage Cheese.—Take good thick milk, place it on the stove. When it begins to draw whey around the outer edge pour it into a colander or thin sack made of cheese cloth. Care should be taken not to allow the cheese to scald too hard, as it will not then work up smooth. When well drained, put it into a vessel, work it smooth with a spoon or a cheese mixer. Salt to taste and stir in sweet cream to make as thin as desired.—*Sister C. J. Senseman, Covington, Ohio.*

Egg Cheese.—Put 4 quarts of fresh milk into a copper kettle and heat to the boiling point. While the milk is being heated beat 10 eggs thoroughly, and into the eggs stir 1 quart of thick milk; now stir this slowly into the hot milk, boil and stir it constantly until it curdles just enough to separate the cheese from the whey. Line a tin straining dish with a thin white cloth, strain off the whey and allow the cheese to cool. The straining dish will give shape to the cheese. Eat by cutting off in slices about ⅕ inch thick, lay it on a piece of bread and spread with molasses.—*Sister Sadie A. Bomberger, Palmyra, Pa.*

German Cheese.—Put 2 gallons of clabber in an iron pot over a moderate fire and bring to 180 degrees Fahrenheit in ¾ hour; now skim it out of the pot and put in the colander to drain. As soon as cool enough to work with the hands, press out most of the whey by handfuls and lay in another vessel, the warmer you work it the better, as the soda will have more effect. Now add 2 small teaspoonfuls of soda and 1 of salt, mix well and press down lightly in the vessel. It will be ready for use in an hour, although it can be kept several days. If properly made, it will rise and be light and when cut in slices and laid on a plate looks well on the table. If it is dry and crummy, it may have been scalded too hard or have been pressed too hard. If soft and sticky, not enough scalding and too much whey.—*Sister Catharine Wampler, Dayton, Va.*

Homemade Cheese.—Put 1 gallon of sweet milk on the stove; while it comes to a boil stir 6 well-beaten eggs in 1 pint of thick milk, salt to taste, add to the hot milk and let it all come to a boil till the milk and eggs separate, then pour into a clean flour sack and hang up to drain. Make in the morning and it will be ready to be used by suppertime.—*Sister Lizzie E. Smith, Morrill, Kans.*

Good Homemade Cheese.—Heat 4 gallons of fresh milk to eighty degrees, remove from the stove and stir in ⅕ of a rennet tablet, which has been dissolved in ¼ cup of water. Let sit until it is a thick clabber. Then stir and dip off the whey. Return to the stove and stir until warm; then remove and salt. Now spread a cheese cloth in a ring, which can be made by taking the bottom out of a syrup bucket. Place the ring on a board and put the cheese in and spread corners of cloth as smoothly as possible over the top of the cheese. Then put on a board which fits into a ring, and put weight enough on to press out the whey. In twelve hours turn the cheese and lift corners of cloth out and press again twelve hours. Then remove from the press and wash every day in salt water for two weeks, when it is ready to use.—*Sister Kate Moomaw, Versailles, Mo.*

To Keep Fresh Fish.—Take fresh fish, cut in slices for frying, salt and roll in flour and fry brown. Lay carefully in an open jar or granite pan and cover with melted lard. Will be like fresh fish when opened. Use as other fried-down meat.—*Sister Jennie Sheeler, Kingsley, Iowa.*

Quick Way to Hull Corn for Hominy.—Take 1 quart of shelled corn, 1 quart of strong lye, made of wood ashes, the stronger the better; let the lye come to a boil, put in the corn, let it boil 20 or 30 minutes, according to the strength of the lye; stir ⅓ of the time quite hard, with a knife; turn the corn into a colander; put it back in the kettle and boil and stir, draining off the water 3 times; then fill the kettle with water and let it cook all day. If done properly, you will have some very nice hulled sweet corn with a little labor.—*Sister Nancy Babcock, Nora Springs, Iowa.*

To Make Graham Flour.—Weigh 20 pounds of wheat flour, 5 pounds of bran, and 2½ pounds of shorts. Mix well together.—*Sister Clare Wells, Ellison, N. Dak.*

Dried Beef.—For 100 pounds of beef take the following ingredients: 6 gallons of water, 3 ounces of saltpetre, 3 pounds of sugar and 9 pounds of salt; mix well, then boil for a few minutes, and skim when boiling. After the mixture has been allowed to cool, put the beef in and leave 10 days, after which hang the beef up, and smoke it if preferred.—*Sister I. B. Trout, Lanark, Ill.*

To Corn Beef.—For 100 pounds of beef take 6 gallons of water, 7 pounds of salt, fine and coarse mixed, 2 pounds of brown sugar, 2 ounces of saltpetre and 1 ounce of soda; boil all together, and skim. Then pour the brine on the meat boiling hot. Keep the meat under the brine with a weight. After the blood is all drawn out, say in 3 or 4 weeks, take the meat out piece by piece and wash the blood off in pure, cold water. Wash out the jar, put the meat back; then boil the brine, adding a little soda to bring up all the blood. Skim carefully and let the brine get cold, then pour it on the meat again; add enough cold water to cover the meat. Be sure to keep the meat all under the brine.—*Sister Minnie Miller, Kidder, Mo.*

Keeping Meats.—Take fresh tenderloin or any lean pieces of pork or beef, cut in slices for frying. Salt and pepper, roll in flour and fry brown. Lay carefully in an open jar, put weight on meat and cover with melted lard. When cold remove weight and put on more lard. The larger the bulk the better.—*Sister Kate Howard, Cambridge City, Ind.*

Sausage, to Make.—Take 20 pounds of pork (¾ lean and ¼ fat), 6 ounces of salt, 1 ounce of pepper, 1½ ounces of sage or 1 ounce of ground cloves. Put the meat through a meat grinder, and mix all together well.—*Sister J. W. Trostle, Glendora, Cal.*

To Keep Sausage.—Fill a gallon jar within 2 inches of the top with fresh sausage meat, press, set in the oven and roast till there is no more water boiling out. Remove from the oven, put on a small weight, and after it is cold cover with lard and set in a cool place.—*Sister Carrie Walker, Glade, Pa.*

To Keep Sausage.—Take fresh sausage, put in frying pan and pour over it a little water. Fry slowly until thoroughly done and the water is all fried out. While hot put in 2 or 3 gallon jars, pour on the grease that fries out, cover with a plate, and press. Melt fresh lard, cover about 3 inches thick. When cold, remove plate and fill jar even full with fresh lard.—*Sister Sarah A. Crowl, Nappanee, Ind.*

To Keep Sausage for Summer Use.—Make sausage into cakes and bake in the oven until nicely browned. Pack in jars and cover with lard.—*Sister J. W. Trostle, Glendora, Cal.*

Canned Sausage.—After the sausage has been put into casings place in a dripping pan, pour over a little water and put in the oven. Let roast till the water is all out, then put in cans, cover with lard, and seal.—*Sister Carrie Walker, Glade, Pa.*

To Season Sausage.—Take ¼ of a pound of pepper and ¾ of a pound of salt to 40 pounds of meat.—*Sister Annie R. Stoner, Union Bridge, Md.*

Sugar Cure for Meat.—Take ½ pound of best saltpetre, ½ pound of ground black pepper, 1½ pounds of brown sugar, 5 quarts of salt and hot water enough to dissolve saltpeter. Mix all together, and rub in the meat well on all sides with the hands. Keep the meat where it will not freeze for 10 days or 2 weeks, and then smoke. These directions were intended for 500 pounds of meat, but we use the mixture some stronger.—*Sister Katie Moore Strickler, Eldora, Iowa.*

Sugar Cure for Pork.—Take ¾ of a pound of salpeter, ¾ of a pound of black pepper, 2 pounds of brown sugar, 5 quarts of ground rock salt, and 5 quarts of dairy salt. Dissolve the saltpeter in a quart of hot water, pour over the other ingredients and mix well. After the animal heat is well out of the meat, rub the mixture in well with the hands and repeat in a day. Two applications are required for hams and shoulders; only one for bacon. This preparation will be sufficient for five good-sized hogs. Let the meat lie on the table with the flesh side up, in a very cool place, just so it does not freeze, for ten days or two weeks, then hang up and smoke, not allowing the meat to become heated while smoking.—*Sister Emma Newcomer, Mount Carroll, Ill.*

To Cure Hams, Shoulders or Side Meat.—For 100 pounds of pork take 5 pounds of salt, 2 ounces of black pepper, 1 ounce of saltpetre and 1 quart of good molasses. All the ingredients should be well mixed except the molasses, which is applied first and only once. Smear well all over the meat, then rub on the balance of the preparation. A second or third application may be necessary to get it all on. Let lie on the bacon side, in the cellar or some place where it will not freeze, until salt is taken up, generally about 10 days or 2 weeks. Then it is ready for smoking. It does not matter if it freezes after it is ready for smoking.—*Sister Wm. C. Wolf, Plattsburg, Mo.*

To Cure Hams and Shoulders.—Take 3 quarts of fine salt, 4 pounds of sugar or 1 quart of molasses and 1 ounce of saltpetre. Pulverize and mix the above, reserving 2 quarts of the salt. Rub the meat *well* all over with the mixture and lay on boards in the cellar for 24 hours. Then place clean stones in the bottom of a barrel or tub and lay sticks across them so the meat will not soak in the liquor that drains from it. Pack the meat in layers sprinkling between them the remaining 2 quarts of salt. Let it lie in the cask 15 or 16 days, every day during this time tipping the cask to drain off the liquor, or draw it through a bunghole near the bottom. Pour this back in cups full over the meat. This amount will cure

80 pounds. Use the same proportion for larger quantity. The above directions are for meat that is to be smoked. If you do not care to smoke the meat, you can pack it down with dry salt, using 3 quarts to 100 pounds.—*Sister Amanda C. Houff, Fort Defiance, Va.*

To Keep Hams and Shoulders for Summer Use.—Cut the pork in slices large enough for a small roast, 3 to 4 pounds in size. Season and bake till water is all absorbed; then pack in jars and cover with lard.—*Sister J. W. Trostle, Glendora, Cal.*

Pawn Haas.—Take 1 quart of strong broth from fresh pork and beef, add to it ½ cup of lard, and season with salt and pepper. Set it on the stove and let it come to the boiling point, then stir in buckwheat flour till it is real stiff. Remove from the fire and knead till it comes off the ladle. Put it in a mold, let it get cold, and it is ready for use. Cut it in slices about ¼ inch thick and fry the same as corn meal mush.—*Sister Jos. Amick, Elgin, Ill.*

Mince Meat.—Take 5 or 6 pounds of a good boiling beef, cook till very tender, salting when getting partly done, and let boil as near dry as possible. Mince 3 pounds of beef suet; seed and cut 4 pounds of raisins; wash and dry 4 pounds of currants; cut 1 pound of citron into small thin pieces; chop very fine 4 quarts of good cooking apples. (This can be most conveniently done if a food chopper is at hand.) Put all into a large saucepan and add two ounces of cinnamon, one of cloves, one of ginger, 4 grated nutmegs, the juice and grated rinds of two lemons, 1 tablespoonful salt, 1 teaspoonful pepper, and 2 pounds sugar; put into a saucepan 1 quart of boiled cider or 1 quart of currant or grape juice, 1 quart of molasses and a large lump of butter. Let come to boiling point, and pour over the other ingredients. Then put in vinegar to make as sharp as you like. Put all on stove, and thoroughly heat through. It is ready to can to be used when you wish it.—*Sister Esther M. H. Brown, Omaja, Cuba.*

Mince Meat.—Take 5 pounds of steak, 1 pound of suet, 2 pounds of currants, 1 pound of raisins, 1 pound of butter, 1 table-spoonful each of salt, allspice, cinnamon and 1 teaspoonful cloves, 1 cup of vinegar, 1 gallon of apples and 1 lemon. Boil steak and suet together; when done, let it cool, then chop fine. Also chop apples, mix all together, sweeten to taste and boil ten minutes. Then put in cans like any other fruit.—*Sister L. Clanin, Hicksville, Wash.*

Mustard.—Take 1 tablespoonful of mustard, 2½ tablespoon-fuls of flour, 1 teaspoonful of sugar, ½ teaspoonful of salt and ½ teaspoonful of pepper. Add enough vinegar to make a paste and let stand ten or twelve hours before using.—*Sister Elva Deal, Brum-baugh, N. Dak.*

Prepared Mustard for Table Use.—Mix 4 tablespoonfuls of sugar with 4 tablespoonfuls of ground mustard; beat in 1 egg until perfectly smooth and then stir in 1 cup of vinegar very slowly to prevent curdling. Cook in a double boiler, stirring constantly. After removing from fire add 1 tablespoonful butter or olive oil and stir until thoroughly mixed.—*Sister Lucinda Bailey, Mt. Ida, Kans.*

A Recipe for Mustard as a Condiment, Using Home-Grown Seed.—Take a heaping tablespoonful of ground mustard, a pinch of salt, a teaspoonful of sugar, and sufficient vinegar to make a thin mustard, allowing it to stand a time for the absorption of the vinegar, adding more vinegar, if needed. Now take a heaping table-spoonful of finely-grated, fresh horseradish, and with a fork beat this into the mustard until thoroughly incorporated. This is one of the best and most expensive condiments, when you buy it. It should be made in small quantities, as it loses its horseradish flavor in time. This is an improvement on the horseradish or the mustard taken separately, and a little of it, freshly prepared, goes a long way. Useful on smoked meats in early spring.—*Sister Barbara Culley, Elgin, Ill.*

For the Laundry.—A teaspoonful of turpentine put into the boiler with white clothes will aid the whitening.—Clear boiling water poured through tea stains will remove them.—*Sister Charles H. Brown, Omaja, Cuba.*

Laundry Hints.—Two tablespoonfuls of sweet milk added to the bluing water in which white clothes are rinsed will prevent any particles of blue from adhering to the clothes and causing a streak or spot of blue.—To prevent colors from fading, put an ounce of sugar of lead into a pail of water. Soak the material in the solution for two hours and let dry before washing and ironing.—*Sister Edith Riley, Highland, Ohio.*

To Remove grass stains wash in cold water before putting in the wash.—*Sister Mollie Zarger, Franklin Grove, Ill.*

Home-Made Soap.—To 2 boxes of Lewis lye take 1 pound of resin, ½ pound of borax, 15 quarts of rain water, and 8 pounds of grease. Boil until thick.—*Sister Mary C. Beard Eshelman, Elgin, Ill.*

To Make Hard Soap.—Empty the contents of a can of Lewis lye, " patent perfumed, '98 " (any good concentrated lye will do), into a stone jar or iron vessel with 2½ pints of cold water, stir until lye dissolves and set aside until temperature by your thermometer is not over 80 degrees. Melt 5½ pounds of strained grease, tallow or lard in a pan over the fire until all dissolves. Then set aside until temperature is 120 degrees. Now slowly pour dissolved lye into the grease, stirring until lye and grease are thoroughly mixed and thick like honey; but do not stir too fast or too long, or it will separate. Then set in a warm place and cover up with a piece of old carpet for two days, when it may be cut into cakes. It is as fine as any white hard soap.—*Sister Jennie Sheeler, Kingsley, Iowa.*

When Boiling Apple Butter a small piece of butter put into the kettle when it is rising fast, will prevent it boiling over. Also a small piece of bread put into the kettle when rendering lard will prevent it boiling over.—*Sister Mary H. Hoerner, Auburn, Ill.*

In Mixing Flour Paste for starch or gravies, just take enough water or milk at first to make a thick batter and rub or beat till smooth, then add more water or milk, a little at a time, and you will avoid all lumps.—*Sister L. Clanin, Hicksville, Wash.*

Kerosene will soften boots and shoes that have become hardened by water.—*Sister Charles H. Brown, Omaja, Cuba.*

To Preserve smoked meat from the flies, thoroughly dust it with powdered borax.—*Sister Annie R. Stoner, Union Bridge, Md.*

The Best Way to keep nickel on steel range bright, wipe with a cloth wrung out of clean soapsuds, then rub with a soft dry cloth and it will shine as new, but must be repeated once or twice a month at least. Do not scour nickel.—*Sister L. Clanin, Hicksville, Wash.*

A TABLE OF MEASURES.

Sixty drops make a tablespoon.
Three teaspoons equal one tablespoon.
Eight rounded tablespoons of dry material equal one cupful.
Sixteen tablespoonfuls of liquid equal one cupful.
One cup of liquid is half a pint.
One heaping tablespoon sugar is one ounce.
One heaping tablespoon butter is two ounces.
One cup butter or sugar is half a pound.
Two cups of flour is a pound.
One cup of rice is half a pound.
One cup of Indian meal is six ounces.
One cup bread crumbs is two ounces.
One pint of ordinary liquid is one pound.